Reading STREET

Program Authors

Peter Afflerbach

Camille Blachowicz

Candy Dawson Boyd

Elena Izquierdo

Connie Juel

Edward Kame'enui

Donald Leu

Jeanne R. Paratore

P. David Pearson

Sam Sebesta

Deborah Simmons

Alfred Tatum

Sharon Vaughn

Susan Watts Taffe

Karen Kring Wixson

PEARSON

Glenview, Illinois • Boston, Massachusetts
Chandler, Arizona • Upper Saddle River, New Jersey

We dedicate Reading Street to
Peter Jovanovich.

His wisdom, courage,
and passion for education
are an inspiration to us all.

This work is protected by the United States copyright laws and is provided *solely for the use of teachers and administrators* in teaching courses and assessing student learning in their classes and schools. Dissemination or sale of any part of this work (including the World Wide Web) will destroy the integrity of the work and is *not* permitted.

Copyright © 2011 Pearson Education, Inc. or its affiliate(s). All Rights Reserved. Printed in the United States of America. This publication is protected by copyright, and permission should be obtained from the publisher prior to any prohibited reproduction, storage in a retrieval system, or transmission in any form or by any means, electronic, mechanical, photocopying, recording, or likewise. For information regarding permissions, write to Pearson Curriculum Group Rights & Permissions, One Lake Street, Upper Saddle River, New Jersey 07458.

Pearson, Scott Foresman, and Pearson Scott Foresman are trademarks, in the U.S. and/or other countries, of Pearson Education, Inc., or its affiliates.

ISBN-13: 978-0-328-47013-6
ISBN-10:   0-328-47013-9
2 3 4 5 6 7 8 9 10 V064 14 13 12 11 10
CC1

Any Path, Any Pace

"Welcome to
Reading Street!
Bienvenidos too."

PEARSON

Who said so?

The Leading Researchers,

Program Authors

Peter Afflerbach, Ph.D.
Professor
Department of Curriculum
and Instruction
University of Maryland
at College Park

Camille L. Z. Blachowicz, Ph.D.
Professor of Education
National-Louis University

Candy Dawson Boyd, Ph.D.
Professor
School of Education
Saint Mary's College of California

Elena Izquierdo, Ph.D.
Associate Professor
University of Texas at El Paso

Connie Juel, Ph.D.
Professor of Education
School of Education
Stanford University

Edward J. Kame'enui, Ph.D.
*Dean-Knight Professor of
Education and Director*
Institute for the Development of
Educational Achievement and
the Center on Teaching and Learning
College of Education
University of Oregon

Donald J. Leu, Ph.D.
*John and Maria Neag Endowed
Chair in Literacy and Technology
Director, The New Literacies
Research Lab*
University of Connecticut

Jeanne R. Paratore, Ed.D.
Associate Professor of Education
Department of Literacy and
Language Development
Boston University

P. David Pearson, Ph.D.
Professor and Dean
Graduate School of Education
University of California, Berkeley

Sam L. Sebesta, Ed.D.
Professor Emeritus
College of Education
University of Washington, Seattle

Deborah Simmons, Ph.D.
Professor
College of Education and
Human Development
Texas A&M University

Alfred W. Tatum, Ph.D.
*Associate Professor and Director
of the UIC Reading Clinic*
University of Illinois at Chicago

Sharon Vaughn, Ph.D.
*H. E. Hartfelder/Southland
Corporation Regents Professor
Director, Meadows Center for
Preventing Educational Risk*
University of Texas

Susan Watts Taffe, Ph.D.
Associate Professor in Literacy
Division of Teacher Education
University of Cincinnati

Karen Kring Wixson, Ph.D.
Professor of Education
University of Michigan

Consulting Authors

Jeff Anderson, M.Ed.
Author and Consultant
San Antonio, Texas

Jim Cummins, Ph.D.
Professor
Department of Curriculum,
Teaching and Learning
University of Toronto

Lily Wong Fillmore, Ph.D.
Professor Emerita
Graduate School of Education
University of California, Berkeley

Georgia Earnest García, Ph.D.
Professor
Language and Literacy Division
Department of Curriculum
and Instruction
University of Illinois at
Urbana-Champaign

George A. González, Ph.D.
Professor (Retired)
School of Education
University of Texas-Pan American,
Edinburg

Valerie Ooka Pang, Ph.D.
Professor
School of Teacher Education
San Diego State University

Sally M. Reis, Ph.D.
*Board of Trustees Distinguished
Professor*
Department of Educational
Psychology
University of Connecticut

Jon Scieszka, M.F.A.
*Children's Book Author
Founder of GUYS READ
Named First National Ambassador
for Young People's Literature 2008*

Grant Wiggins, Ed.D.
Educational Consultant
Authentic Education
Concept Development

Lee Wright, M.Ed.
Pearland, Texas

Practitioners, and Authors.

Consultant

Sharroky Hollie, Ph.D.
Assistant Professor
California State University
Dominguez Hills, CA

Teacher Reviewers

Dr. Bettyann Brugger
Educational Support Coordinator–Reading Office
Milwaukee Public Schools
Milwaukee, WI

Kathleen Burke
K–12 Reading Coordinator
Peoria Public Schools, Peoria, IL

Darci Burns, M.S.Ed.
University of Oregon

Bridget Cantrell
District Intervention Specialist
Blackburn Elementary School
Independence, MO

Tahira DuPree Chase, M.A., M.S.Ed.
Administrator of Elementary English Language Arts
Mount Vernon City School District
Mount Vernon, NY

Michele Conner
Director, Elementary Education
Aiken County School District
Aiken, SC

Georgia Coulombe
K–6 Regional Trainer/Literacy Specialist
Regional Center for Training and Learning (RCTL), Reno, NV

Kelly Dalmas
Third Grade Teacher
Avery's Creek Elementary, Arden, NC

Seely Dillard
First Grade Teacher
Laurel Hill Primary School
Mt. Pleasant, SC

Jodi Dodds-Kinner
Director of Elementary Reading
Chicago Public Schools, Chicago, IL

Dr. Ann Wild Evenson
District Instructional Coach
Osseo Area Schools, Maple Grove, MN

Stephanie Fascitelli
Principal
Apache Elementary, Albuquerque
Public Schools, Albuquerque, NM

Alice Franklin
Elementary Coordinator, Language Arts & Reading
Spokane Public Schools, Spokane, WA

Laureen Fromberg
Assistant Principal
PS 100 Queens, NY

Kimberly Gibson
First Grade Teacher
Edgar B. Davis Community School
Brockton, MA

Kristen Gray
Lead Teacher
A.T. Allen Elementary School
Concord, NC

Mary Ellen Hazen
State Pre-K Teacher
Rockford Public Schools #205
Rockford, IL

Patrick M. Johnson
Elementary Instructional Director
Seattle Public Schools, Seattle, WA

Theresa Jaramillo Jones
Principal
Highland Elementary School
Las Cruces, NM

Sophie Kowzun
Program Supervisor, Reading/Language Arts, PreK–5
Montgomery County Public Schools
Rockville, MD

David W. Matthews
Sixth Grade Teacher
Easton Area Middle School
Easton, PA

Ana Nuncio
Editor and Independent Publisher
Salem, MA

Joseph Peila
Principal
Chappell Elementary School
Chicago, IL

Ivana Reimer
Literacy Coordinator
PS 100 Queens, NY

Sally Riley
Curriculum Coordinator
Rochester Public Schools
Rochester, NH

Dyan M. Smiley
Independent Educational Consultant

Michael J. Swiatowiec
Lead Literacy Teacher
Graham Elementary School
Chicago, IL

Dr. Helen Taylor
Director of English Education
Portsmouth City Public Schools
Portsmouth, VA

Carol Thompson
Teaching and Learning Coach
Independence School District
Independence, MO

Erinn Zeitlin
Kindergarten Teacher
Carderock Springs Elementary School
Bethesda, MD

Any Path, Any Pace

v

UNIT 4

Our Changing World

In this Teacher's Edition Unit 4, Volume 2

Key

SI Strategic Intervention
OL On-Level
A Advanced
ELL ELL

WEEK 4 · The Night the Moon Fell

A New House 21st Century Skills

WEEK 5 · The First Tortilla

Wind Expository Text

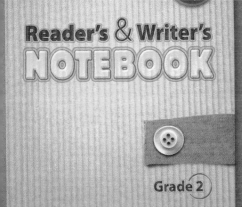

Reader's & Writer's NOTEBOOK

Grade 2

WEEK 6 · Interactive Review

How do things change? How do they stay the same?

Unit Wrap Up

In the **First Stop** on Reading Street

- **Dear Second Grade Teacher**

- **Research into Practice on Reading Street**

- **Guide to Reading Street**

- **Assessment on Reading Street**

- **Customize Writing on Reading Street**

- **Differentiated Instruction on Reading Street**

- **ELL on Reading Street**

- **Customize Literacy on Reading Street**

- **Digital Products on Reading Street**

- **Teacher Resources for Grade 2**

- **Index**

GO Digital!

See It!

- Big Question Video

- Concept Talk Video

- Interactive Sound-Spelling Cards

- Envision It! Animations

- Sing with Me Animations

Hear It!

- Sing with Me Animations

- eSelections

- Grammar Jammer

- eReaders

- Leveled Reader Database

Do It!

- Vocabulary Activities

- Story Sort

- 21st Century Skills Activities

- Online Assessment

- Letter Tile Drag and Drop

UNIT **1**

Exploration

Key
SI Strategic Intervention
OL On-Level
A Advanced
ELL ELL

Volume 1

Volume 2

UNIT 2
Working Together

Key
SI Strategic Intervention
OL On-Level
A Advanced
ELL ELL

Volume 1

Volume 2

UNIT 3

Creative Ideas

Key

SI Strategic Intervention
OL On-Level
A Advanced
ELL ELL

Volume 1

Volume 2

Key
SI Strategic Intervention
OL On-Level
A Advanced
ELL ELL

UNIT 4

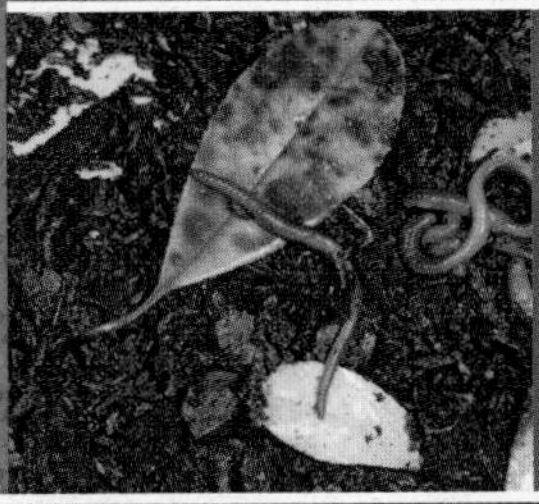

Our Changing World

Volume 1

Volume 2

Reader's & Writer's NOTEBOOK
Grade 2

UNIT 5

Responsibility

Key

SI Strategic Intervention
OL On-Level
A Advanced
ELL ELL

Volume 1

Volume 2

What does it mean to be responsible?

Unit Wrap Up

Reader's & Writer's NOTEBOOK

Grade 2

UNIT 6

Traditions

Key

SI Strategic Intervention
OL On-Level
A Advanced
ELL ELL

Volume 1

WEEK 1 • Just Like Josh Gibson
Realistic Fiction 360a–391l
How Baseball Began Expository Text
Differentiated Instruction **SI OL A ELL** .... DI•1–DI•21

WEEK 2 • Red, White, and Blue: The Story of the American Flag
Informational Text 392a–425l
"You're a Grand Old Flag" Poetry
Differentiated Instruction **SI OL A ELL** .... DI•22–DI•42

WEEK 3 • A Birthday Basket for Tía
Realistic Fiction 426a–457l
Family Traditions: Birthdays 21st Century Skills
Differentiated Instruction **SI OL A ELL** .... DI•43–DI•63

Volume 2

WEEK 4 • Cowboys
Informational Text 458a–495l
Cowboy Gear Informational Text
Differentiated Instruction **SI OL A ELL** .... DI•64–DI•84

WEEK 5 • Grace for President
Realistic Fiction.... 496a–529l
Home Sweet Home Informational Text
Differentiated Instruction **SI OL A ELL** .... DI•85–DI•105

WEEK 6 • Interactive Review
.... IR•1–IR•60

Are traditions and celebrations important in our lives?

Unit Wrap Up

UNIT 4

Skills Overview

Key

T Tested Skill

Target Skill

WEEK 1

A Froggy Fable
Fable pp. 28–41

Ben the Bullfrog
Tall Tale pp. 46–51

WEEK 2

Life Cycle of a Pumpkin
Expository Text pp. 62–75

"How Do Seeds Know Which Way Is Up?"
Poetry pp. 80–81

Get Ready to Read

	WEEK 1	WEEK 2
Question of the Week	How can familiar things help us with changes?	How do plants change over time?
Amazing Words	*preserve, represent, valuable, tough, concentration, frown, homeland, patient*	*adapt, annual, nutrients, blazing, drought, ancient, massive, sprout*
Phonics	T Final Syllable *le* Review Comparative Endings	T Vowel Patterns *oo, u* Review Final Syllable *le*
Spelling	Final Syllable *le*	Vowel Patterns *oo, u*

Read and Comprehend

	WEEK 1	WEEK 2
Comprehension	T **Skill** Draw Conclusions **Strategy** Background Knowledge Review **Skill** Character and Setting	T **Skill** Sequence **Strategy** Important Ideas Review **Skill** Fact and Opinion
Lesson Vocabulary	T *clearing, perfect, traveled, splashing, pond, crashed, spilling*	T *fruit, soil, root, harvest, vine, bumpy, smooth*
Vocabulary	Multiple-Meaning Words	Antonyms
Fluency	Accuracy and Appropriate Rate	Accuracy

Language Arts

	WEEK 1	WEEK 2
Writing	Friendly Letter Trait: Organization	Writing for Tests Trait: Word Choice
Conventions	T Adjectives and Our Senses	T Adjectives for Number, Size, and Shape
Speaking/Listening	Describe Media Techniques	Make an Announcement
Research Skills	Thesaurus	Personal Sources

How do things change? How do they stay the same?

WEEK 3	WEEK 4	WEEK 5	WEEK 6
Soil Expository Text pp. 92–109 **"Burrowing Animals"** Expository Text pp. 114–117	**The Night the Moon Fell** Myth pp. 128–143 **"A New House"** 21st Century Skills pp. 148–151	**The First Tortilla** Legend pp. 162–177 **"Wind"** Expository Text pp. 182–185	**Interactive Review**
What changes occur under the ground?	Why are some changes difficult?	How do changes in the weather affect us?	How do things change? How do they stay the same?
discovery, transform, underneath, blizzard, fine, incredible, land-scape, molten	*adjust, landmark, unexpected, quiver, tease, foreign, accent, forlorn*	*condition, predict, terrifying, breeze, whip, sparkle, funnel, swirl*	Review Unit 4 Amazing Words
T Diphthongs *ou, ow, oi, oy* Review Vowel Patterns *oo, u*	T Syllable Patterns Review Diphthongs	T Vowel Digraphs *oo, ue, ew, ui* Review Syllable Patterns	Review Final Syllable *le;* Vowel Patterns *oo, u;* Diphthongs *ou, ow, oi, oy;* Syllable Patterns; Vowel Digraphs *oo, ue, ew, ui*
Diphthongs *ou, ow, oi, oy*	Syllable Patterns	Vowel Digraphs *oo, ue, ew, ui*	Review Unit 4 Spelling Words
T **Skill** Fact and Opinion **Strategy** Questioning Review **Skill** Facts and Details	T **Skill** Plot and Theme **Strategy** Visualize Review **Skill** Draw Conclusions	T **Skill** Plot and Theme **Strategy** Monitor and Clarify Review **Skill** Main Idea and Details	Review Draw Conclusions, Sequence, Fact and Opinion, Plot and Theme
T *grains, materials, particles, seeps, substances, texture*	T *balance, canyons, coral, rattle, slivers, sway, whisper*	T *awaken, volcano, mountain, cliffs, suffer, rainbow, prize*	T Review Unit 4 Lesson Vocabulary
Suffixes	Multiple-Meaning Words	Prefixes	Review Multiple-Meaning Words, Antonyms, Suffixes, Prefixes
Appropriate Phrasing	Expression	Expression and Intonation	Read for Fluency
Short Expository Report Trait: Sentences	Narrative Poem Trait: Voice	Thank-You Note Trait: Focus/Ideas	Writing Process: Description
T Comparative and Superlative Adjectives	T Adverbs that Tell When and Where	T Adverbs That Tell How	Review Unit 4 Conventions
Speak Well	Describe Media Techniques	Give an Oral Summary	
Diagram	E-Mail	Natural and Personal Sources	

UNIT 4

Monitor Progress
Make Data-Driven Decisions

Data Management
- Assess
- Diagnose
- Prescribe
- Disaggregate

Classroom Management
- Monitor Progress
- Group
- Differentiate Instruction
- Inform Parents

Don't Wait Until Friday

SUCCESS PREDICTORS	WEEK 1	WEEK 2	WEEK 3	WEEK 4
Word Reading — Phonics	T Final Syllable *le*	T Vowel Patterns *oo, u*	T Diphthongs *ou, ow, oi, oy*	T Syllable Patterns
WCPM — Fluency	Read with Accuracy and Appropriate Rate 62–72 WCPM	Read with Accuracy 62–72 WCPM	Read with Appropriate Phrasing 62–72 WCPM	Read with Expression 62–72 WCPM
Vocabulary — Lesson Vocabulary	T clearing T perfect T traveled T splashing T pond T crashed T spilling	T fruit T soil T root T harvest T vine T bumpy T smooth	T grains T materials T particles T seeps T substances T texture	T balance T canyons T coral T rattle T slivers T sway T whisper
Vocabulary — Oral Vocabulary/ Concept Development (assessed informally)	preserve represent valuable tough concentration frown homeland patient	adapt annual nutrients blazing drought ancient massive sprout	discovery transform underneath blizzard fine incredible landscape molten	adjust landmark unexpected quiver tease foreign accent forlorn
Retelling — Text Comprehension	T **Skill** Draw Conclusions **Strategy** Background Knowledge	T **Skill** Sequence **Strategy** Important Ideas	T **Skill** Fact and Opinion **Strategy** Questioning	T **Skill** Plot and Theme **Strategy** Visualize

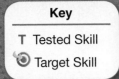

Key	
T	Tested Skill
◎	Target Skill

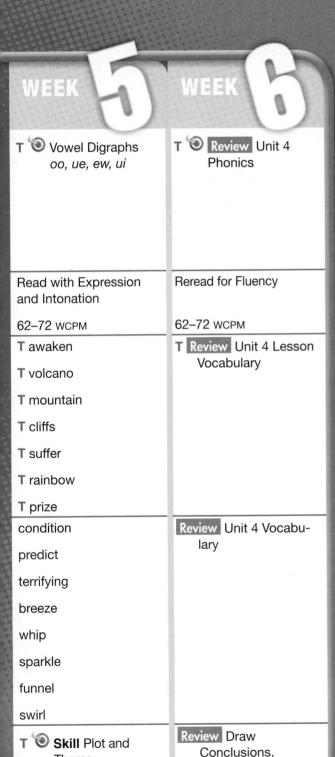

WEEK 5

T ◎ Vowel Digraphs
oo, ue, ew, ui

Read with Expression and Intonation

62–72 WCPM

T awaken

T volcano

T mountain

T cliffs

T suffer

T rainbow

T prize

condition

predict

terrifying

breeze

whip

sparkle

funnel

swirl

T ◎ **Skill** Plot and Theme

◎ **Strategy** Monitor and Clarify

WEEK 6

T ◎ Review Unit 4 Phonics

Reread for Fluency

62–72 WCPM

T Review Unit 4 Lesson Vocabulary

Review Unit 4 Vocabulary

Review Draw Conclusions, Sequence, Fact and Opinion, Plot and Theme

Online Classroom

Manage Data

- Assign the Unit 4 Benchmark Test for students to take online.

- Online Assessment records results and generates reports by school, grade, classroom, or student.

- Use reports to disaggregate and aggregate Unit 4 skills and standards data to monitor progress.

- Based on class lists created to support the categories important for AYP (gender, ethnicity, migrant education, English proficiency, disabilities, economic status), reports let you track adequate yearly progress every six weeks.

Group

- Use results from Unit 4 Benchmark Tests taken online through Online Assessment to measure whether students have mastered the English-Language Arts Content Standards taught in this unit.

- Reports in Online Assessment suggest whether students need Extra Support or Intervention.

Individualized Instruction

- Tests are correlated to Unit 4 tested skills and standards so that prescriptions for individual teaching and learning plans can be created.

- Individualized prescriptions target instruction and accelerate student progress toward learning outcome goals.

- Prescriptions include remediation activities and resources to reteach Unit 4 skills and standards.

UNIT 4

Assessment and Grouping
for Data-Driven Instruction

4-Step Plan for Assessment
1 Diagnose and Differentiate
2 Monitor Progress
3 Assess and Regroup
4 Summative Assessment

Baseline Group Tests

STEP 1 Diagnose and Differentiate

Diagnose

To make initial grouping decisions, use the Baseline Group Test, the Texas Primary Reading Inventory (TPRI), or another initial placement test. Depending on children's ability levels, you may have more than one of each group.

Differentiate

If... student performance is **SI** then... use the regular instruction and the daily **Strategic Intervention** small group lessons.

If... student performance is **OL** then... use the regular instruction and the daily **On-Level** small group lessons.

If... student performance is **A** then... use the regular instruction and the daily **Advanced** small group lessons.

Small Group Time

SI Strategic Intervention	**OL** On-Level	**A** Advanced
• Daily small group lessons provide more intensive instruction, more scaffolding, more practice, and more opportunities to respond. • Reteach lessons in the *First Stop on Reading Street* provide additional instructional opportunities with target skills. • Leveled readers build background and provide practice for target skills and vocabulary.	• Explicit instructional routines teach core skills and strategies. • Daily On-Level lessons provide more practice and more opportunities to respond. • Independent activities provide practice for core skills and extension and enrichment options. • Leveled reader provides additional reading and practice for core skills and vocabulary.	• Daily Advanced lessons provide instruction for accelerated learning. • Leveled reader provides additional reading tied to lesson concepts.

Additional Differentiated Learning Options

Reading Street Response to Intervention Kit
• Focused intervention lessons on the five critical areas of reading: phonemic awareness, phonics, vocabulary, comprehension, and fluency

My Sidewalks on Reading Street
• Intensive intervention for struggling readers

STEP 2 Monitor Progress

Don't Wait Until Friday

Use these tools during lesson teaching to **monitor student progress.**

- **Skill and Strategy** instruction during reading

- **Don't Wait Until Friday** boxes to check word reading, retelling, fluency, and oral vocabulary

- **Weekly Assessment** on Day 5 to check phonics and fluency

- **Reader's and Writer's Notebook** pages at point of use

- **Weekly Tests** to assess target skills for the week

- **Fresh Reads for Fluency and Comprehension**

Weekly Tests

Fresh Reads for Fluency and Comprehension

STEP 3 Assess and Regroup

Use these tools during lesson teaching to assess and regroup.

- **Weekly Assessments** Record results of weekly assessments in retelling, phonics, and fluency to track student progress.

- **Unit Benchmark Test** Administer this test to check mastery of unit skills.

- **Regroup** We recommend the first regrouping to be at the end of Unit 2. Use weekly assessment information and Unit Benchmark Test performance to inform regrouping decisions. Then regroup at the end of each subsequent unit.

First Stop on Reading Street Assessment Chart

Group					
Baseline →	Regroup →	Regroup →	Regroup →	Regroup →	End of Year
Group Test	Units 1 and 2	Unit 3	Unit 4	Unit 5	

Unit 1 Weeks 1–6	Unit 2 Weeks 7–12	Unit 3 Weeks 13–18	Unit 4 Weeks 19–24	Unit 5 Weeks 25–30	Unit 6 Weeks 31–36

Outside assessments, such as DRA, TPRI, and DIBELS, may recommend regrouping at other times during the year.

STEP 4 Summative Assessment

Use these tools after lesson teaching to assess students.

- **Unit Benchmark Tests** Use to measure a student's mastery of unit skills.

- **End-of-Year Benchmark Test** Use to measure a student's mastery of program skill covered in all six units.

Unit and End-of-Year Benchmark Tests

UNIT 4

Concept Launch

Understanding By Design

Grant Wiggins, Ed. D.
Reading Street Author

"Big ideas are the building material of understandings. They can be thought of as the meaningful patterns that enable one to connect the dots of otherwise fragmented knowledge."

Our Changing World

Reading Street Online

www.ReadingStreet.com
• Big Question Video
• eSelections
• Envision It! Animations
• Story Sort

THE BIG ?

How do things change? How do they stay the same?

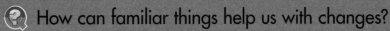

UNIT 4

Small Group Time
Flexible Pacing Plans

Small Group Time

Sometime you have holidays, programs, assemblies, or other interruptions to the school week. This plan can help you make Small Group Time decisions if you have less time during the week.

Key

SI Strategic Intervention
OL On-Level
A Advanced
ELL ELL

5 Day Plan

DAY 1	• Phonics • Reading Practice
DAY 2	• High-Frequency Words • Leveled Reader
DAY 3	• Phonics • Leveled Reader
DAY 4	• Selection Vocabulary • Reading Practice
DAY 5	• Phonics • Comprehension

4 Day Plan

DAY 1	• Phonics • Reading Practice
DAY 2	• Selection Vocabulary • Leveled Reader
DAY 3	• Phonics • Leveled Reader
DAY 4	• Selection Vocabulary • Reading Practice

3 Day Plan

DAY 1	• Phonics • Reading Practice
DAY 2	• Phonics • Leveled Reader
DAY 3	• Selection Vocabulary • Reading Practice

ELL

5 Day Plan

DAY 1	• Frontload Concept • Preteach Skills • Conventions and Writing
DAY 2	• Review Concept and Skills • Frontload and Read Main Selection • Conventions and Writing
DAY 3	• Review Concept and Skills • Reread Main Selection • Conventions and Writing
DAY 4	• Review Concept and Skills • Read ELL or ELD Reader • Conventions and Writing
DAY 5	• Review Concept and Skills • Reread ELL or ELD Reader • Conventions and Writing

4 Day Plan

DAY 1	• Frontload Concept • Preteach Skills • Conventions and Writing
DAY 2	• Review Concept and Skills • Frontload and Read Main Selection • Conventions and Writing
DAY 3	• Review Concept and Skills • Reread Main Selection • Conventions and Writing
DAY 4	• Review Concept and Skills • Read ELL or ELD Reader • Conventions and Writing

3 Day Plan

DAY 1	• Frontload Concept • Preteach Skills • Conventions and Writing
DAY 2	• Review Concept and Skills • Frontload and Read Main Selection • Conventions and Writing
DAY 3	• Review Concept and Skills • Read ELL or ELD Reader • Conventions and Writing

This Week's ELL Overview

ELL Handbook

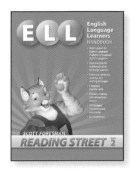

- Maximize Literacy and Cognitive Engagement
- Research Into Practice
- Full Weekly Support for Every Selection

The Night the Moon Fell
- Multi-Lingual Summaries in Five Languages
- Selection-Specific Vocabulary Word Cards
- Frontloading/Reteaching for Comprehension Skill Lessons
- ELD and ELL Reader Study Guides

- Transfer Activities
- Professional Development

Daily Leveled ELL Notes

ELL notes appear throughout this week's instruction and ELL Support is on the DI pages of your Teacher's Edition. The following is a sample of an ELL note from this week.

English Language Learners

Beginning After children decide on a topic, provide them with a framework for their events. Write the events that children dictate, but leave out words. Have children fill them in to complete the chart.

Intermediate After discussing topics, provide children with possible story events. Let them choose appropriate events for their topic.

Advanced Before children do the Quick Write, have them do a "think aloud" with a partner to discuss possible ideas for their poems.

Advanced High Have children share their completed sequence charts with a partner. Encourage partners to share their ideas about how to write a poem based on the sequence chart. Monitor children's discussions.

ELL by Strand

The ELL lessons on this week's Support for English Language Learners pages are organized by strand. They offer additional scaffolding for the core curriculum. Leveled support notes on these pages address the different proficiency levels in your class. See pages DI•75–DI•84.

ELL Guy
Dr. Jim Cummins

The Three Pillars of ELL Instruction

ELL Strands	Activate Prior Knowledge	Access Content	Extend Language
Vocabulary pp. DI•76–DI•77	Preteach	Reteach	Leveled Writing Activities
Reading Comprehension p. DI•80	Preteach	Reteach	Leveled Practice Activities
Phonics, Spelling, and Word Analysis p. DI•79	Preteach	Teach/Model	Leveled Practice Activities
Listening Comprehension p. DI•78	Prepare for the Read Aloud	First Listening	Second Listening
Conventions and Writing pp. DI•83–DI•84	Preteach	Leveled Practice Activities	Leveled Practice Activities/ Leveled Writing Activities
Concept Development p. DI•75	Prior Knowledge	Discuss Concept	Daily Concept and Vocabulary Development

This Week's Practice Stations Overview

Six Weekly Practice Stations with Leveled Activities can be found at the beginning of each week of instruction. For this week's Practice Stations, see pp. 120h–120i.

Small Group

Teacher-led

Classroom Management Handbook for Differentiated Instruction Practice Stations

Practice Stations

Daily Leveled Center Activities

 Below   Advanced

 On-Level   **E L L**

Practice Stations Flip Charts

	Word Wise	Word Work	Words to Know	Let's Write	Read for Meaning	Get Fluent
Objectives	• Spell words with *ou* and *ow* and *oi* and *oy*, and recognize the diphthongs that produce the /ou/ and /oi/ sounds.	• Identify /ou/ in words spelled *ou* and *ow* and /oi/ in words spelled *oi* and *oy*.	• Identify and use common suffixes to determine a word's meaning.	• Write a short expository report. • Connect sentences with transitional terms.	• Identify fact and opinion in expository text.	• Read aloud with appropriate phrasing.
Materials	• *Word Wise* Flip Chart • Teacher-made word cards: *around, royal, cow, flower, pound, clown, boil, enjoy, mountain, drowsy, brownie, soundproof* • Letter Tiles • paper, pencils	• *Word Work* Flip Chart • Sound-Spelling Cards: 15, 88, 94, 98, 100 • Teacher-made word cards: *out, cow, mountain, coil, clown, boy, boil, enjoy* • paper, pencils	• *Words to Know* Flip Chart • Teacher-made word cards: *cheer, market, kind, dull, peace, thin* • dictionaries • paper, pencils	• *Let's Write* Flip Chart • paper • pencils	• *Read for Meaning* Flip Chart • 2.4.3 Leveled Readers • paper, pencils	• *Get Fluent* Flip Chart • 2.4.3 Leveled Readers

This Week on Reading Street!

Question of the Week
Why are some changes difficult?

Daily Plan

Whole Group
- ◉ Syllable Patterns
- ◉ Plot and Theme
- • Fluency
- • Vocabulary

MONITOR PROGRESS | **Success Predictor**

Day 1	Day 2	Day 3	Day 4	Day 5
Check Word Reading	Check Lesson Vocabulary/High-Frequency Words	Check Retelling	Check Fluency	Check Oral Vocabulary

Small Group

Teacher-Led
- • Reading Support
- • Skill Support
- • Fluency Practice

Practice Stations

Independent Activities

Customize Literacy More support for a Balanced Literacy approach, see pp. CL•1–CL•45.

Customize Writing More support for a customized writing approach, see pp. CW•11–CW•20.

Whole Group
- • Writing: Narrative Poem
- • Conventions: Adverbs That Tell When and Where
- • New Literacies

Assessment
- • Weekly Tests
- • Day 5 Assessment
- • Fresh Reads

 You Are Here! Unit 4 Week 4

This Week's Reading Selections

Main Selection
Genre: **Myth**

Paired Selection

Decodable Practice Readers

Leveled Readers

ELL and ELD Readers

Resources on Reading Street!

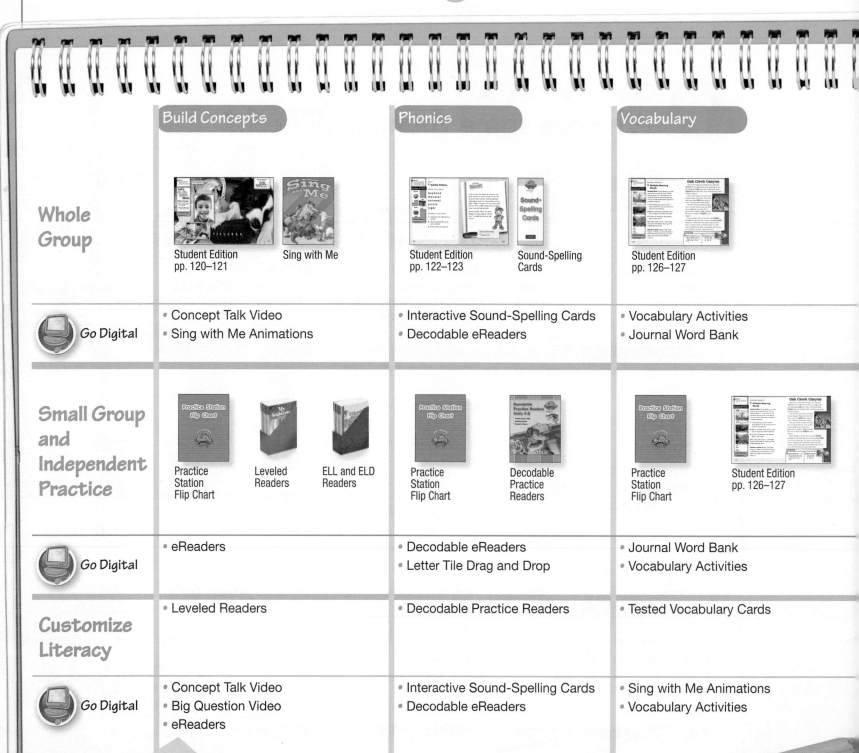

	Build Concepts	Phonics	Vocabulary
Whole Group	Student Edition pp. 120–121 / Sing with Me	Student Edition pp. 122–123 / Sound-Spelling Cards	Student Edition pp. 126–127
Go Digital	• Concept Talk Video • Sing with Me Animations	• Interactive Sound-Spelling Cards • Decodable eReaders	• Vocabulary Activities • Journal Word Bank
Small Group and Independent Practice	Practice Station Flip Chart / Leveled Readers / ELL and ELD Readers	Practice Station Flip Chart / Decodable Practice Readers	Practice Station Flip Chart / Student Edition pp. 126–127
Go Digital	• eReaders	• Decodable eReaders • Letter Tile Drag and Drop	• Journal Word Bank • Vocabulary Activities
Customize Literacy	• Leveled Readers	• Decodable Practice Readers	• Tested Vocabulary Cards
Go Digital	• Concept Talk Video • Big Question Video • eReaders	• Interactive Sound-Spelling Cards • Decodable eReaders	• Sing with Me Animations • Vocabulary Activities

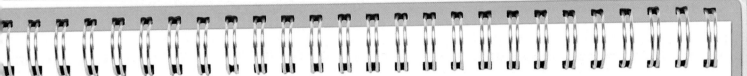

 Question of the Week
Why are some changes difficult?

Comprehension	Fluency	Conventions and Writing

Comprehension	Fluency	Conventions and Writing
Student Edition pp. 128–143	Decodable Practice Readers	Student Edition pp. 146–147
• Envision It! Animations • eSelections	• eSelections • eReaders	• Grammar Jammer

Comprehension			Fluency		Conventions and Writing	
Practice Station Flip Chart	Leveled Readers	ELL and ELD Readers	Practice Station Flip Chart	Decodable Practice Readers	Practice Station Flip Chart	Reader's and Writer's Notebook
• eReaders • Story Sort			• Decodable eReaders		• Grammar Jammer	
• Envision It! Skills and Strategies Handbooks • Leveled Readers			• Leveled Readers		*Reader's and Writer's Notebook*	
• Envision It! Animations • eReaders			• eReaders		• Grammar Jammer	

Week 4

You Are Here!
Unit 4
Week 4

My 5-Day Planner for Reading Street!

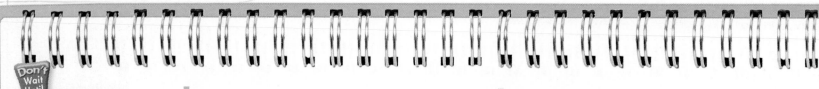

Don't Wait Until Friday SUCCESS PREDICTOR

	Check Word Reading **Day 1** pages 120j–125f	Check Lesson Vocabulary/ High-Frequency Words **Day 2** pages 126a–143f

Get Ready to Read	**Concept Talk,** 120j–121
	Oral Vocabulary, 121a–121b
	  adjust, landmark, unexpected
	Phonics, 122a–123a
	  ◉ Syllable Patterns
	Spelling, 123b Pretest
	READ Decodable Practice Reader 19A, 123c–123d
		Concept Talk, 126a–126b
		Oral Vocabulary, 126b
		  quiver, tease
		Review **Phonics,** 126c
		  Final Syllable *-le*
		  ◉ Syllable Patterns
		Spelling, 126d Practice

Read and Comprehend	**Build Comprehension,** 124a–125
	  ◉ Plot and Theme
	  ◉ Visualize
	Lesson Vocabulary, 125a Introduce
	balance, canyons, coral, rattle, slivers, sway, whisper
		Lesson Vocabulary, 126e–126f
		balance, canyons, coral, rattle, slivers, sway, whisper
		Vocabulary, 126g–127
		  ◉ Multiple-Meaning Words
		Fluency, 126–127 Paired Reading
		Build Background, 127a
		READ Main Selection—First Read, 128a–143a
		  The Night the Moon Fell
		Literary Text, 143a Sensory Words

Language Arts	**Conventions,** 125b Adverbs That Tell When and Where
	Writing, 125c–125d
	  Narrative Poem
	Research and Inquiry, 125e
	  Identify and Focus Topic
		Conventions, 143b Adverbs That Tell When and Where
		Writing, 143c–143d Narrative Poem
		  Writer's Craft: Selecting a Story to Tell
		Handwriting, 143e
		  Cursive *a, d, c*: Word Spacing
		Research and Inquiry, 143f
		  Research Skill: E-mail

You Are Here! Unit 4 Week 4

Question of the Week
Why are some changes difficult?

Check Retelling	Check Fluency	Check Oral Vocabulary
Day 3 pages 144a–147b	**Day 4** pages 148a–151f	**Day 5** pages 152a–153k
Concept Talk, 144a–144b **Oral Vocabulary**, 144b *foreign* **Phonics**, 144c ◉ Syllable Patterns **READ Decodable Practice Passage 19B**, 144d **Spelling**, 144e Dictation	**Concept Talk**, 148a–148b **Oral Vocabulary**, 148b *accent, forlorn* Review **Phonics**, 148c Diphthongs *ou, ow, oi, oy* Review **Fluent Word Reading**, 148d **READ Decodable Practice Reader 19C**, 148e–148f **Spelling**, 148g Partner Review	**Concept Wrap Up**, 152a Review **Oral Vocabulary**, 152b Review **Phonics**, 152c Syllable Patterns **Spelling**, 152d Test
Fluency, 144f Expression Review **Lesson Vocabulary**, 144g *balance, canyons, coral, rattle, slivers, sway, whisper* **Vocabulary**, 144g ◉ Multiple-Meaning Words **READ Main Selection—Second Read**, 128–143, 144h–145a	**21st Century Skills**, 148h **READ Paired Selection**, 148–151 "A New House" **Fluency**, 151a Expression	**Media Literacy**, 152–153 **Vocabulary**, 153a Multiple-Meaning Words **Fluency**, 153a Expression Review **Comprehension**, 153b Plot and Theme Review **Vocabulary**, 153b Lesson Vocabulary **Literary Text**, 153c Moral Lessons as Themes **Assessment**, 153d–153f Monitor Progress
Conventions, 146a Adverbs That Tell When and Where **Writing**, 146–147a Narrative Poem Writer's Trait: Voice **Research and Inquiry**, 147b Gather and Record Information	**Conventions**, 151b Adverbs That Tell When and Where **Writing**, 151c–151d Narrative Poem Revising Strategy **Media Literacy**, 151e Describe Media Techniques **Research and Inquiry**, 151f Review and Revise Topic	Review **Conventions**, 153g Adverbs That Tell When and Where **Writing**, 153h–153i Narrative Poem Writer's Craft: Rhyming Words **Research and Inquiry**, 153j Communicate **Wrap Up Your Week**, 153k Why are some changes difficult?

Week 4

Grouping Options for Differentiated Instruction
Turn the page for the small group time lesson plan.

Planning Small Group Time on Reading Street!

SMALL GROUP TIME RESOURCES

Look for this Small Group Time box each day to help meet the individual needs of all your children. Differentiated Instruction lessons appear on the DI pages at the end of each week.

DAY 1

Teacher-Led

SI Strategic Intervention

Teacher-Led
• Phonemic Awareness and Phonics
• **Read** *Decodable Practice Reader*

OL On-Level

Teacher-Led
• Phonics and Spelling
• **Read** *Decodable Practice Reader*

A Advanced

Teacher-Led
• Phonics and Comprehension
• **Read** *Advanced Selection*

ELL Place English language learners in the groups that correspond to their reading abilities in English.

Practice Stations
• Listen Up
• Word Work

Independent Activities
• *Reader's and Writer's Notebook*
• Concept Talk Video

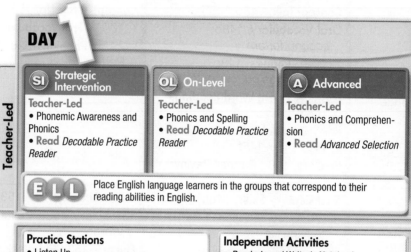

ELL Reader
Advanced
Advanced-High

Adam's New Soccer Team
by Will Lee
Illustrated by Gary Torrisi

ELD Reader
Beginning
Intermediate

Adam's New Soccer Team
by Will Lee
Illustrated by Gary Torrisi

ELL Poster

You Are Here!
Unit 4
Week 4

Day 1

SI Strategic Intervention	**Phonics**, DI•64 **Read** *Decodable Practice Reader 19A*, DI•64
OL On-Level	**Phonics and Spelling**, DI•69 **Read** *Decodable Practice Reader 19A*, DI•69
A Advanced	**Phonics and Comprehension**, DI•72 **Read** *Advanced Selection*, DI•72
ELL English Language Learners	DI•75–DI•84 **Concepts and Oral Vocabulary** **Listening (Read Aloud)**

Question of the Week
Why are some changes difficult?

SI Strategic Intervention

OL On-Level

A Advanced

Below-Level Reader

Decodable Practice Readers

On-Level Reader

Advanced Reader

Advanced Selection

Concept Literacy Reader

Small Group Weekly Plan

Day 2	Day 3	Day 4	Day 5
Lesson Vocabulary, DI•65 **Read Concept Literacy Leveled Reader,** DI•65	**Phonics,** DI•66 **Read Below-Level Leveled Reader,** DI•66	**Lesson Vocabulary,** DI•67 **Read Decodable Practice Reader 19C,** DI•67	**Phonics and Comprehension,** DI•68 **Reread Main Selection,** DI•68
Lesson Vocabulary, DI•69 **Reread Decodable Practice Reader 19A,** DI•69	**Read On-Level Leveled Reader,** DI•70	**Conventions,** DI•71 **Read Leveled Reader,** DI•71	**Phonics Review,** DI•71 **Reread On-Level Leveled Reader,** DI•71
Comprehension, DI•72 **Read Main Selection,** DI•72	**Read Advanced Leveled Reader,** DI•73	**Comprehension,** DI•74 **Read Paired Selection,** DI•74	**Fluency and Comprehension,** DI•74 **Reread Advanced Selection,** DI•74
DI•75–DI•84 Concepts Vocabulary Phonics and Spelling Conventions	DI•75–DI•84 Concepts Vocabulary Comprehension Skill Main Selection	DI•75–DI•84 Concepts Vocabulary ELL/ELD Readers ELL Workshop	DI•75–DI•84 Concepts Vocabulary

week 4

Practice Stations for Everyone on Reading Street!

Word Wise

Spell words with *ou* and *ow* sounded /ou/, and *oi* and *oy* sounded /oi/.

Objectives
- Spell words with *ou* and *ow* sounded /ou/ *(loud)* and *oi* and *oy* sounded /oi/ *(oil)*.
- Recognize the two diphthongs that produce the /ou/ and /oi/ sounds.

Materials
- *Word Wise* Flip Chart
- Teacher-made word cards: *around, royal, cow, flower, pound, clown, boil, enjoy, mountain, drowsy, brownie, soundproof*
- Letter Tiles • paper • pencils

Differentiated Activities
- A **diphthong** is a pair of different vowels that make a phoneme.

- Spell *out, gown, coil,* and *toy* using the Letter Tiles. Note the /ou/ sound in *out* and *gown*. Note the /oi/ in *coil* and *toy*. Now find one card with the same diphthong and sound of each word.

- Find two cards for each diphthong *ou, ow, oi,* and *oy*. Make a two-column chart headed /ou/ and /oi/. Write each word in the correct column. Then write a new word for each diphthong.

- Make a two-column chart for /ou/ and /oi/. Find two cards for each diphthong. Write each word in its correct column. Write a story using all the /ou/ and /oi/ words you can. Underline each word.

Technology
- Interactive Sound-Spelling Cards

Word Work

Recognize and say words with the /ou/ and /oi/ diphthongs.

Objectives
- Identify the /ou/ phoneme in words spelled *ou* and *ow* and the /oi/ phoneme in words spelled *oi* and *oy*.
- Pronounce the /ou/ and /oi/ phonemes in words spelled with *ou, ow, oi,* and *oy*.

Materials
- *Word Work* Flip Chart
- Sound-Spelling Cards: 15, 94, 98, 100, 88
- Teacher-made word cards: *out, cow, mountain, coil, clown, boy, boil, enjoy*
- paper • pencils

Differentiated Activities

- Find one card for each vowel pattern *ou, ow, oi,* and *oy*. Quietly say each word. Draw a picture for each word and label it. Underline the vowel sound.

- Find two cards for each diphthong *ou, ow, oi,* and *oy*. Say each word quietly. Write the eight words. Think of one new word for each diphthong, and write them down, underlining the diphthong.

- Write this sentence. "We toiled for toys; we counted the cows." Circle the /ou/ diphthongs and underline the /oi/ diphthongs. Write as many new words as you can with the /ou/ and the /oi/ phonemes.

Technology
- Interactive Sound-Spelling Cards

Words To Know

Use suffixes to determine meaning.

Objectives
- Identify and use common suffixes to determine a word's meaning.

Materials
- *Words to Know* Flip Chart
- Teacher-made word cards: *cheer, market, kind, dull, peace, thin*
- dictionaries
- paper • pencils

Differentiated Activities

- A **suffix** is a letter or letters added to the end of a word. Suffixes change a word's meaning.

- Write *watchful*. Use the suffix to guess at its meaning. Check it in a dictionary. Add *-able* to *read,* and *bend*. Guess and check the words' meanings.

- Write *sorrowful, readiness,* and *reachable*. Use each word's suffix to define it. Check a dictionary. Now find a word card to join with each suffix. Write three sentences, using each new word.

- Find two word cards to join with suffixes *-ful, -ness,* and *-able*. Make two new words with each suffix. Use each in a sentence. Now try defining *soulful, livable,* and *droopiness*. Check your work in a dictionary.

Technology
- Online Tested Vocabulary Activities

You Are Here!
Unit 4
Week 4

Use this week's materials from the
*Reading Street Leveled Practice Stations
Kit* to organize this week's stations.

Key

● Below-Level Activities

▲ On-Level Activities

■ Advanced Activities

Practice Station
Flip Chart

Let's Write!
Write a short expository report.

Objectives
• Write a short expository report.
• Connect short, related sentences with transitional terms such as *also, usually, as an example, especially, instead of.*

Materials
• *Let's Write!* Flip Chart
• paper
• pencils

Differentiated Activities
• An **expository report** offers information found in a source, such as a book. It includes the title and author of the source text.

● Write a short expository report on the soil near your school. Draw a picture. Write two sentences.

▲ Write an expository report on the soil near your school. Use transition words to combine short, choppy sentences. Draw a diagram.

■ Write an expository report on the soil near your school. Use transition words to combine short, related sentences. Compare it to the soil near your home.

Read For Meaning
Identify fact and opinion in expository text.

Objectives
• Identify fact and opinion in expository text.

Materials
• *Read for Meaning* Flip Chart
• 2.4.3 Leveled Readers
• paper
• pencils

Differentiated Activities
• A **fact** is something that can be proved.
• An **opinion** tells feelings or thoughts.

● Read *How a Seed Grows.* Find an opinion in the text. Write the opinion. Then find two facts.

▲ Read *A Slice of Mud Pie,* and look for facts and opinions. Write a sentence identifying an opinion you found in the text. Then write a sentence naming a fact.

■ As you read *Compost: Recycled Waste,* look for facts and opinions. Write a paragraph identifying one opinion and three facts. Use words such as *first* and *next* to link ideas.

Technology
• Online Student Edition
• Leveled eReaders

Get Fluent
Practice fluent reading.

Objectives
• Read aloud with appropriate phasing.

Materials
• *Get Fluent* Flip Chart
• 2.4.3 Leveled Readers

Differentiated Activities
● Work with a partner. Take turns reading pages from *How a Seed Grows.* As you read, look at how words are grouped and read with appropriate phrasing. Punctuation can help you read with appropriate phrasing. Give your partner feedback.

▲ Work with a partner. Take turns reading pages from *A Slice of Mud Pie.* As you read, look at how words are grouped and read with appropriate phrasing. Punctuation can help you read with appropriate phrasing. Give your partner feedback.

■ Work with a partner. Take turns reading pages from *Compost: Recycled Waste.* As you read, look at how words are grouped and read with appropriate phrasing. Punctuation can help you read with appropriate phrasing. Give your partner feedback.

Technology
• Reading Street Readers CD-ROM

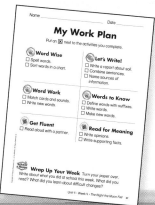

My Weekly Work Plan

Week 4

Objectives

- Introduce concept: some changes are difficult.
- Share information and ideas about the concept.

Today at a Glance

Oral Vocabulary
adjust, landmark, unexpected

Phonics and Spelling
◉ Syllable Patterns

Fluency
Oral Rereading

Comprehension
◉ Plot and Theme
◉ Visualize

Lesson Vocabulary
balance, canyons, coral, rattle, slivers, sway, whisper

Conventions
Adverbs That Tell When and Where

Writing
Narrative Poem: Introduce

Research and Inquiry
Identify and Focus Topic

Concept Talk

 Question of the Week

Why are some changes difficult?

Introduce the concept

To build concepts and to focus children's attention, tell them that this week they will talk, sing, read, and write about why some changes are difficult. Write the Question of the Week and track the print as you read it.

ROUTINE **Activate Prior Knowledge** **Team Talk**

① **Think** Have children think for a minute about why a change such as making new friends can be difficult.

② **Pair** Have pairs of children discuss the question.

③ **Share** Have children share their ideas with the group. Guide discussion and encourage elaboration with prompts such as: Why wasn't the change easy to make? What made it difficult?

Routines Flip Chart

Anchored Talk

Develop oral language

Have children turn to pages 120–121 in their Student Editions. Read the title and look at the photos. Use these questions to guide discussion and create a "Why are some changes difficult?" concept map (shown on the next page).

- Look at the photo of the people with boxes. What is happening? (The family is moving.) This family will have to *adjust*, or get used to a new situation. Moving to a new place is a difficult change. We'll add this information to our map.

- Now look at the photo of the boy. How do you think his smile changed as he grew older? (Possible response: He lost his baby teeth. Now he is waiting for his permanent teeth to grow in.) Why might this be a difficult change for the boy? (Possible response: He has a hard time chewing. He can only eat certain things.) Everyone grows older. Sometimes this can bring a difficult change. Let's add this information to our map.

 Objectives
• Listen closely to speakers and ask questions to help you better understand the topic. • Share information and ideas about the topic. Speak clearly and at a correct pace.

Oral Vocabulary

Let's Talk About

Difficult Changes
• Share information about why it is difficult to live in a new place.
• Share ideas about why it is difficult to grow older.

READING STREET ONLINE
CONCEPT TALK VIDEO
www.ReadingStreet.com

You've learned
1 4 5
Amazing Words ★
so far this year!

Student Edition pp. 120–121

Amazing Words

You've learned **1 4 5** words so far.

You'll learn **0 0 8** words this week!

adjust	foreign
landmark	tease
unexpected	accent
quiver	forlorn

 Writing on Demand

Develop Writing Fluency
Ask children to write about a time when they lost a tooth and why the change was difficult. Have them write for two to three minutes. Children should write as much as they can. Tell them to try to do their best writing. You may want to discuss what children wrote during writing conferences.

Connect to reading

Explain that this week, children will read an old story about a time when the moon felt sad and lost when she moved to a new place. *Let's add* You may feel sad and lost *to our map.*

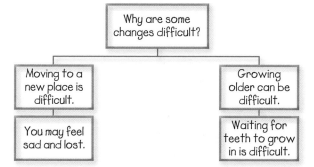

Why are some changes difficult?

Moving to a new place is difficult.

Growing older can be difficult.

You may feel sad and lost.

Waiting for teeth to grow in is difficult.

ELL Preteach Concepts Use the Day 1 instruction on ELL Poster 19 to assess and build background knowledge, develop concepts, and build oral vocabulary.

ELL

English Language Learners
Listening Comprehension
English learners will benefit from additional visual support to understand the key terms in the concept map. Use the picture on ELL Poster 19 to scaffold understanding.

Extra Support for ELL
Additional ELL support and modified instruction is provided in the *ELL Handbook* and in the ELL Support lessons on pp. DI•75–DI•84.

ELL Poster 19

The Night the Moon Fell • **120–121**

Objectives
- Build oral vocabulary.
- Discuss the concept to develop oral language.
- Share information and ideas about the concept.

Oral Vocabulary
Amazing Words

Introduce Amazing Words

Display page 19 of the *Sing with Me* Big Book. Tell children they are going to sing about moving to a new place. Ask children to listen for the Amazing Words *adjust*, *landmark*, and *unexpected* as you sing. Sing the song again and have children join you.

 Sing with Me Big Book Audio

Sing with Me Big Book p. 19

Teach Amazing Words

Amazing Words Oral Vocabulary Routine

1) **Introduce the Word** Relate the word *adjust* to the song: The song says the family will have to *adjust* to many new things. Supply a child-friendly definition: When you *adjust* to something new, you get used to it. Have children say the word.

2) **Demonstrate** Provide examples to show meaning: The children will soon *adjust* to their new school. The crossing guards will *adjust* to the freezing weather. Some animals must *adjust* to living in an animal shelter.

3) **Apply** Have children demonstrate their understanding: Would you prefer to *adjust* to living in a desert or living in a rain forest? Why?

See p. OV•1 to teach *landmark* and *unexpected*.

Routines Flip Chart

Check understanding of Amazing Words

Have children look at the picture on page 19. It looks like the family is moving out of their home. What will the little girl take with her? (a teddy bear) How will her toy help the girl *adjust* to her new home? Use *adjust* in your answer. (Possible response: The teddy bear will help her adjust because it will be something familiar and not new.)

The song says the move was *unexpected.* Explain what this means. Use *unexpected* in your answer. (Possible response: The move was unexpected because it was a surprise to the family.)

Why is the boy looking at a map? (Possible response: He wants to learn his way around the new neighborhood.) What *landmark* might the boy see on the map to guide him? Use *landmark* in your answer. (Possible response: He may see a landmark like a building or a park.)

Apply Amazing Words

Have children demonstrate their understanding of the Amazing Words by completing these sentences orally.

> We need to **adjust** to the new _____.
>
> A **landmark** is a feature like _____.
>
> The _____ was **unexpected**.

Corrective feedback

If... children have difficulty using the Amazing Words, then... remind them of the definitions. Then provide opportunities for children to use the words in sentences.

Preteach Academic Vocabulary

Write the following on the board:

- myth
- plot
- theme
- adverbs

Have children share what they know about this week's Academic Vocabulary. Use children's responses to assess their prior knowledge. Preteach the Academic Vocabulary by providing a child-friendly description, explanation, or example that clarifies the meaning of each term. Then ask children to restate the meaning of the Academic Vocabulary in their own words.

Amazing Words

adjust	tease
landmark	foreign
unexpected	accent
quiver	forlorn

Differentiated Instruction

(A) Advanced

Amazing Words Have children draw a map of their neighborhood, creating a key of landmarks that would be a useful guide for newcomers.

English Language Learners
Pronunciation Speakers of mostly monosyllabic languages such as Cantonese, Hmong, Khmer, Korean, and Vietnamese may have difficulty understanding that multisyllabic words are single words. Model first and then have children practice pronouncing *unexpected* as a single word.

Objectives

- ⦿ Read words with closed syllable patterns (VCCV) and open syllable patterns (VCV).
- ⦿ Read multisyllabic words containing vowel digraphs and diphthongs.
- • Decode words in context and independent of context.

Skills Trace

⦿ **Syllable Patterns**
Introduce U4W4D1
Practice U4W4D2; U4W4D3; U4W4D4
Reteach/Review U4W4D5; U4W5D4
Assess/Test Weekly Test U4W4
Benchmark Test U4
Key:
U=Unit   W=Week   D=Day

Phonics—Teach/Model
🔄 Syllable Patterns

VC/CV
bas/ket

Sound-Spelling
Card 147

V/CV
ti/ger

Sound-Spelling
Card 149

ROUTINE — Word Parts Strategy

1. **Connect** Write *donate*. Point out to children that they have already studied two-syllable words like this. Ask them to read the word. Explain that today they will divide words into syllables by looking at different vowel and consonant syllable patterns.

2. **Use Sound-Spelling Cards** Display Card 147. Point to the word *basket*. This word has two consonants in the middle with a vowel on each side. We divide it between the two consonants and read the first syllable with a short vowel sound. Display Card 149. Point to the word *tiger*. This word has one consonant in the middle with a vowel on each side. When we divide it after the first vowel, we read that vowel with its long sound.

3. **Model** Write *basket*. Divide the word between the two consonants. I say the first syllable with a short vowel: /b/ /a/ /s/. Then I say the second syllable: /k/ /e/ /t/. Read the two syllables together: *basket*.

   Write *tiger*. Divide the word after the first vowel. I say the first syllable with a long vowel: /t/ /ī/. Then I say the second syllable: /g/ /ėr/. Read the two syllables together: *tiger*.

   Write *playground*. Divide the word after *ay*. In this word two vowels stand for one sound in the first syllable, and two vowels spell the sound /ou/ in the second. Each vowel pair stays together in its own syllable. Read the two syllables together: *playground*.

4. **Guide Practice** Have children read *basket, tiger,* and *playground* with you. Write the words below. Have the group tell how to divide each word into syllables and then read the word.

| paper | picnic | chapter | boyhood | frozen | downtown |
| sailboat | window | robot | pencil | oatmeal | soybean |

5. **Review** What do you know about reading words with more than one syllable? (If a word has two consonants in the middle, divide between them; the first vowel is usually short. If a word has a consonant between two vowels and you divide after the first vowel, it is usually long. Vowel pairs that spell sounds form their own syllables.)

Routines Flip Chart

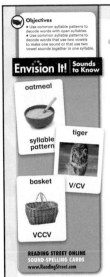

Objectives
- Use common syllable patterns to decode words with open syllables.
- Use common syllable patterns to decode words that use two vowels to make one sound or that use two vowel sounds together in one syllable.

Envision It! | Sounds to Know

oatmeal

syllable pattern | tiger

basket | V/CV

VCCV

READING STREET ONLINE
SOUND-SPELLING CARDS
www.ReadingStreet.com

Phonics

Syllable Patterns

Words I Can Blend

b o y h o o d

m o n s t e r

o a t m e a l

p i c n i c

t i g e r

Sentences I Can Read

1. In boyhood, kids might believe in monsters.

2. We ate oatmeal muffins at my picnic yesterday.

3. Did he see that new tiger yet?

I Can Read!

I think up super plans about how things can work better outdoors. It's kind of a hobby with me. I tell my plans to Mom and Dad. Once they believed I might explain my plan for saving raindrops with an expert. "Super!" I thought, until it was time to speak with him. All of a sudden I forgot what I was going to say. I was confused and upset.

Mom said quietly, "Relax, don't panic. Pretend we are just speaking with each other." It worked! And that man liked my plan.

You've learned
Syllable Patterns

122 | 123

Student Edition pp. 122–123

Model

Envision It!

Have children turn to page 122 in their Student Editions. Look at the pictures on this page. I see a picture of *oatmeal*. The word *oatmeal* is a compound word. It has two syllables and two vowel digraphs, *oa* and *ea*. You would divide the word between the two smaller words. I also see a picture of a *tiger*. The word *tiger* has one consonant between two vowels. Since the first vowel is long, you would divide the word after the first vowel.

Guide practice

For each word in "Words I Can Blend," ask for the sounds of each syllable. Make sure children can identify the two syllables in each word. Then have children read the whole word.

Corrective feedback

If... children have difficulty reading words with different syllable patterns,
then... model breaking a word into syllables and saying the parts together to read the word, and then ask children to read it with you.

Differentiated Instruction

A **Advanced**

Syllables Tell students to write the words in "Words I Can Blend." Then have them divide the words into syllables. Discuss why they divided the words where they did. Read the words together.

Vocabulary Support

You may wish to explain the meaning of these words.

boyhood the time in a male's life when he is a boy

soybean a bean that is an important source of food

ELL

English Language Learners

Pronunciation Divide the words from the "Words I Can Blend" list into syllables. Have children read each syllable of a word and then put them together to read the whole word aloud.

Language Transfer Some languages such as Cantonese, Hmong, and Vietnamese are comprised of one-syllable words. You may need to give extra explanation for multisyllabic and compound words.

Objectives

◎ Read words with closed syllable patterns (VCCV) and open syllable patterns (VCV).

◎ Read multisyllabic words containing diphthongs and vowel digraphs.

• Decode words in context and independent of context.

• Spell words with closed syllable patterns (VCCV), open syllable patterns (VCV), and diphthongs and digraphs.

Check Word Reading

SUCCESS PREDICTOR

Phonics
Word Analysis

Decode words independent of context

After children can successfully combine word parts to read the words on page 122 in their Student Editions, point to words in random order and ask children to read them naturally.

Decode words in context

Have children read each of the sentences on page 122. Have them identify the vowel sounds in multisyllabic words.

Team Talk Pair children and have them take turns reading each of the sentences aloud.

Chorally read the **I Can Read!** passage on page 123 along with the children. Then have them read the passage aloud to themselves.

On their own

Use *Reader's and Writer's Notebook*, p. 325.

Reader's and Writer's Notebook p. 325

Don't Wait Until Friday

MONITOR PROGRESS Check Word Reading ↻ Syllable Patterns

Write the following words and have the class read them. Notice which words children miss during the group reading. Call on individuals to read some of the words.

bonus	problem	pilgrim	music	velvet	Spiral Review
freeway	raincoat	bailout	cookout	cowboy	**Row 2** reviews digraphs.
joyful	flower	oily	powder	thousand	**Row 3** reviews diphthongs.

If... children cannot read words with different syllable patterns,

then... use the Small Group Time Strategic Intervention lessons, p. DI•64, to reteach syllable patterns. Continue to monitor children's progress using other instructional opportunities during the week. See the Skills Trace on p. 122a.

Day 1	Day 2	Day 3	Day 4	Day 5
Check Word Reading	Check Lesson Vocabulary/ High-Frequency Words	Check Retelling	Check Fluency	Check Oral Vocabulary

Success Predictor

Spelling Pretest
Syllable Patterns

Dictate spelling words

Dictate the spelling words. Have children write the words. If needed, break words into meaningful parts, clarify the pronunciations, and give meanings of words. Have children check their pretests and correct misspelled words.

1.	**downstairs**	I always leave my backpack **downstairs.**
2.	**football**	We watched the **football** game on Sunday.
3.	**cowboy**	The **cowboy** rounded up the cattle.
4.	**houseboat**	My aunt lives in a **houseboat** on a lake.
5.	**railroad**	The **railroad** tracks go through the town.
6.	**rainbow***	After the storm we saw a **rainbow.**
7.	**boyhood**	He spent his **boyhood** living on a farm.
8.	**oatmeal**	Mom made us **oatmeal** for breakfast.
9.	**soybean**	My uncle owns a **soybean** farm.
10.	**roadway**	The **roadway** had four lanes.
11.	**outplay**	Our team can **outplay** the visiting team.
12.	**daydream**	Jean tries not to **daydream** while working.

*Words marked with asterisks come from the selection *The Night the Moon Fell.*

On their own Use Let's Practice It! p. 209 on the *Teacher Resource DVD-ROM.*

Let's Practice It!
TR DVD•209

Small Group Time

DAY 1

Break into small groups after spelling and before the comprehension lesson.

Teacher-Led

(SI) Strategic Intervention
Teacher-Led Page DI•64
• Phonics
Read *Decodable Practice Reader 19A*

(OL) On-Level
Teacher-Led Page DI•69
• Phonics and Spelling
Read *Decodable Practice Reader 19A*

(A) Advanced
Teacher-Led Page DI•72
• Phonics and Comprehension
Read *Advanced Selection 19*

(ELL) Place English language learners in the groups that correspond to their reading abilities in English.

Practice Stations
• Word Work
• Read for Meaning

Independent Activities
• Read independently/Reading Log on *Reader's and Writer's Notebook*, p. RR4
• Concept Talk Video

Differentiated Instruction

 Strategic Intervention
Check Spelling Write the spelling words for children, leaving blanks for the vowels. Have children fill in the missing letters.

 Advanced
Extend Spelling Allow children who spell words correctly to spell more challenging words such as: *needlepoint, downspout, coattail, counterpoint, mainstay,* and *steamboat.*

Phonics/Spelling

Generalization Each spelling word is a compound word with a diphthong or digraph syllable pattern.

Spelling Patterns

VCCCV If a word has three consonants together in the middle and two form a blend, divide between the blend and the other consonant (e.g., *monster*).

CV When a syllable ends with a single vowel, the vowel is usually long.

English Language Learners
Identify Syllable Patterns Write the spelling words, dividing them so children can identify the two smaller words.

123b

Success Predictor

Objectives
- Apply knowledge of sound-spellings and word parts to decode unknown words when reading.
- Decode and read words in context and independent of context.
- Practice fluency with oral rereading.

Decodable Practice Reader 19A
Syllable Patterns

Decode words independent of context

Have children turn to the first page and decode each word.

Read high-frequency words

Have children identify and read the high-frequency words *young, travel, direction,* and *clear* on the first page.

Preview Decodable Reader

Have children read the title and preview the story. Tell them they will use syllable patterns to decode two-syllable words containing vowel digraphs and diphthongs.

Decode words in context

Pair children for reading, and listen as they decode. One child begins. Children read the entire story, switching readers after each page. Partners reread the story. This time the other child begins.

Decodable Practice Reader 19A

Gramps told Gina about his boyhood dreams.
"When I was young, I dreamt about being a cowboy," he told her.

56

"I always saw myself riding an old horse named Seaweed," Gramps explained.
"Seaweed?" asked Gina.
"Yep," replied Gramps smiling.

57

"In my daydreams, I fed Seaweed oats.
I ate oatmeal.
Then we rode out on cattle roundups," added Gramps.

58

"We rode hard in daytime.
At night, we would enjoy cowboy cookouts," said Gramps.

59

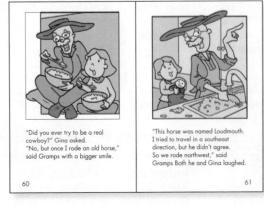

"Did you ever try to be a real cowboy?" Gina asked.
"No, but once I rode an old horse," said Gramps with a bigger smile.

60

"This horse was named Loudmouth.
I tried to travel in a southeast direction, but he didn't agree.
So we rode northwest," said Gramps Both he and Gina laughed.

61

"It was clear I would not be a good cowboy!" Gramps said to Gina
Gina hugged Gramps.
"But you are a great granddad," she said.

62

Corrective feedback

If... children have difficulty decoding a word,

then... refer them to the Sound-Spelling Cards to identify the sounds in a decodable word; prompt them to blend the word. If the word is a compound word, tell children to chunk the word and say the parts of the word, first separately and then together.

- What is the new word?
- Is the new word a word you know?
- Does it make sense in the story?

Check decoding and comprehension

Have children retell the story to include characters, setting, and events. Then have children find two-syllable words containing at least one vowel digraph or diphthong. Children should supply *boyhood, cowboy, Seaweed, daydreams, oatmeal, roundups, daytime, cookouts, Loudmouth,* and *southeast.*

Reread for Fluency

Have children reread Decodable Practice Reader 19A to develop automaticity decoding words with syllable patterns containing vowel digraph or diphthong combinations.

ROUTINE **Oral Rereading**

1. **Read** Have children read the entire book orally.

2. **Reread** To achieve optimal fluency, children should reread the text three or four times.

3. **Corrective Feedback** Listen as children read. Provide corrective feedback regarding their fluency and decoding.

Routines Flip Chart

ELL

English Language Learners
Syllable Patterns
Beginning Ask questions about any of the words from the list on page 55 and give one sample answer. Then have children supply other answers that use the word. For example, *What do you know about a* cowboy? (A cowboy wears boots.) *What do you eat at a* cookout? (I eat hamburgers at a cookout.)

Intermediate Have pairs of children read the parts of Gramps and Gina. Then have them identify the two-syllable words with vowel digraphs and diphthongs.

Advanced/Advanced-High Tell pairs of children to go through the story and ask each other questions. Tell them to ask questions that have answers using two-syllable words with vowel digraphs and diphthongs. For example: *What did Gramps dream about?* (He dreamt about being a cowboy.) *What was the name of the horse he saw himself riding?* (The horse was named Seaweed.)

Objectives

◎ Analyze the plot and theme of a myth.
◎ Create sensory images to adjust comprehension.

Skills Trace

◉ **Plot and Theme**
Introduce U4W4D1; U4W5D1; U5W3D1
Practice U4W4D2; U4W4D3; U4W4D4; U4W5D2; U4W5D3; U4W5D4; U5W3D2; U5W3D3; U5W3D4
Reteach/Review U1W1D3; U3W1D3; U4W4D5; U4W5D5; U5W3D5; U5W4D3
Assess/Test Weekly Tests U4W4; U4W5; U5W3
Benchmark Tests U1

Key:
U=Unit   W=Week   D=Day

Skill ↔ Strategy
↻ Plot and Theme
↻ Visualize

Introduce plot and theme

Many things happen to characters in a story. These events make up the story plot. Where do good readers look in a story to figure out the story **plot**? (They look at events that happen at the beginning, middle, and end of the story.) Once good readers identify the story plot, they use this information to help them figure out the story theme.

Student Edition pp. EI•14–EI•15

A story **theme** is the "big idea" that the author wants the reader to learn from reading a story. What kind of theme do some stories have? (Some stories have a moral lesson as their theme.) Have children turn to pp. EI•14–EI•15 in the Student Edition to review identifying a story plot and theme. Then read "The Space Flight" with children.

Model the skill

Think Aloud Today we're going to read about a space flight. Have children follow along as you read aloud the first four paragraphs of "The Space Flight." In the beginning of the story, we learn that Maria cuts a hole in a big box, and she and Pedro decorate it to look like a space ship. These two events make up the plot in the beginning of the story.

Guide practice

Have children finish reading "The Space Flight" on their own. After they read, have them use a graphic organizer like the one on page 124 to record story events in the beginning, middle, and end of the story that make up the plot. Then have them use these events to identify the theme or "big idea" of the story and record it in the chart.

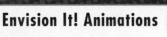
Objectives
- Identify themes in well-known fables, legends, myths, or stories.
- Check your understanding and make corrections when you do not understand what you are reading.

Envision It! Skill/Strategy

Skill

Strategy

READING STREET ONLINE
ENVISION IT! ANIMATIONS
www.ReadingStreet.com

124

Comprehension Skill
Plot and Theme
- The plot is what happens at the beginning, middle, and end of a story.
- A story's theme is "the big idea" that the author wants the reader to learn from the story. This can be a moral lesson.
- Use what you learned about identifying plot and theme and fill out a chart like the one below as you read "The Space Flight."

Beginning → Middle → End → The Big Idea

Comprehension Strategy
Visualize
Good readers picture how something looks, sounds, feels, tastes, or smells when they read. This is called visualizing. Picturing these details can help you monitor and adjust as you read. It also makes reading more fun.

The Space Flight

Maria brought a huge box in from the garage. She cut a square hole on one side.
"What's that?" Pedro asked.
"It's a window on our spaceship."
Maria and Pedro added buttons for the controls. Then they colored the side of the ship. Soon both kids were inside the box.
"Ready for take-off, Astronaut Pedro?"
"Ready!"
Maria counted down. Both kids shook the box back and forth as the ship took off. "Look over there, Pedro. Look how big the moon is!"
Pedro looked out the window. He did not see the sofa or the curtains. He saw outer space. "You're right. It's amazing!"
"See? With your imagination, you can go anywhere."

Strategy What do you see? How does this help you monitor and adjust your understanding?

Skill What is the theme of this story? What lesson could be learned?

Your Turn!

Need a Review? See the *Envision It! Handbook* for additional help with plot and theme and visualizing.

Ready to Try It? As you read *The Night the Moon Fell*, use what you've learned to understand the text.

125

Student Edition pp. 124–125

Strategy Possible response: I see two children peering out from a box, I feel the box moving back and forth, and I hear the loud roar of rockets. Seeing, hearing, and feeling these things help me understand what the characters are experiencing as they blast off on a pretend space flight.

Skill Possible answer: The story theme is that your imagination allows you to experience many things that may not be possible in real life.

Academic Vocabulary
plot a series of related events at the beginning, middle, and end of a story; the action of a story

theme the big idea or author's message in a story

visualize picture in one's mind what is happening in the text. Visualizing helps readers imagine the things they read about.

Strategy check

Visualize Remind children that they can visualize to help them understand the plot and theme of "The Space Flight." Model the strategy to monitor and adjust understanding of the plot.

Model the strategy

Think Aloud After reading the first paragraph, I pictured in my mind a girl cutting a square in the side of a huge packing box. When I read the fourth paragraph, I could see the control buttons and the bright colors and designs the children drew on the sides of the box to make it look like a spaceship. When I read about the countdown and lift off, I could feel the vibration of the ship, and I could hear the sound of powerful rockets lifting the ship into space. Creating these images in my mind helps me better understand these events. Have children review the strategy of visualization on p. EI•27 of the Student Edition.

Envision It!

On their own Use p. 327 in the *Reader's and Writer's Notebook* for additional practice with plot and theme.

Student Edition p. EI•27

Reader's and Writer's Notebook p. 327

ELL

English Language Learners
Visualize Tell children to close their eyes and listen carefully as you retell the beginning of "The Space Flight" using simpler language. Have children share the pictures they see in their minds as Maria and Pablo build their spaceship from a cardboard box. Repeat this activity with the middle and the end of the story. As children share their visualizations, encourage them to use words from the story in their descriptions.

Objectives

- Activate prior knowledge of words.
- Identify and use adverbs.

Vocabulary
Lesson Vocabulary

Lesson vocabulary Display the lesson vocabulary words. Have children check their glossary for the meanings of unknown words.

Activate prior knowledge Read aloud each list below. Ask children to name the vocabulary word that fits in the same category. Discuss reasons.

- steadiness, upright, footing (*balance*—all have to do with standing up)
- clatter, clink, jangle (*rattle*—all are noises)
- mumble, shout, babble (*whisper*—all are ways of talking)
- slices, chunks, chips *(slivers—all are pieces of something)*
- valleys, mountains, cliffs (*canyons*—all are land formations)
- swing, jump, glide (*sway*—all are movements)
- seaweed, sand, shells (*coral*—all are things found in the ocean)

By the end of the week, children should know the lesson vocabulary words. Have them demonstrate their understanding by adding a new word to each of the above categories.

On their own Use *Reader's and Writer's Notebook,* p. 326.

Name ____________ The Night the Moon Fell

Pick a word from the box to complete each sentence. **Write** the word on the line.

balance canyons coral rattle slivers sway whisper

1. When school is out, my friend and I hike in the deep canyons near our home.
2. When hiking, we do not move if we hear the rattle of a snake.
3. We love to hear the wind whisper through the trees.
4. Yesterday we saw a baby bird try to balance on a twig.
5. The bird was lucky that the tree did not sway too much in the wind.
6. My friend had to pull some slivers of wood out of her socks.
7. Tomorrow, we will hike to a beach with pretty coral in the water.

326 Vocabulary

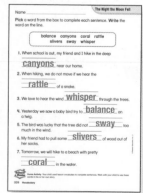

Reader's and Writer's Notebook p. 326

Conventions
Adverbs That Tell When and Where

Model

Remind children that a **verb** tells what someone or something does. Explain that an **adverb** is a word that tells more about a verb. *Today* and *upstairs* are adverbs that tell when and where something happens. Adverbs such as *first, next,* and *last* tell the order in which things happen.

Display Grammar Transparency 19. Read the definition aloud. Model identifying the adverb in each example. Then read the directions and model number 1.

- *Yesterday* is an adverb that tells about the verb *fell. Yesterday* tells when the moon fell.

- I will underline the adverb *yesterday* and write the word *when* on the line.

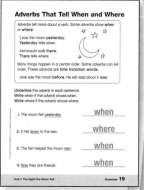

Grammar Transparency 19
TR DVD

Guide practice

Continue with items 2–4, having children underline the adverb in each sentence and identify whether the adverb tells when or where.

Connect to oral language

Have the class complete these sentence frames orally using adverbs that tell when or where or signal time order.

> 1. We will have a test _____.
> 2. When it rains, I play _____.
> 3. Seth will play the piano first and I will play _____.

On their own

Team Talk Pair children and have them talk about where and when they might play during different kinds of weather. Then have them identify the adverbs they used during their discussion.

Differentiated Instruction

SI Strategic Intervention

Adverbs That Tell When and Where Say the following adverbs: *now, later, inside, there, here, tomorrow, daily, outside,* and *next.* Have children repeat each adverb and raise one hand if it tells when and two hands if it tells where. Then call on volunteers to use each adverb in an oral sentence.

Academic Vocabulary

adverb a word that tells how, when, or where something happens. Adverbs also tell how much or how little is meant. Adverbs often end in *-ly.*

verb a word that tells what something or someone does or is

Daily Fix-It

1. I wipd my hands on the cloh.
   I <u>wiped</u> my hands on the <u>cloth</u>.

2. the childrin yelled with joy.
   <u>The</u> <u>children</u> yelled with joy.

Discuss the Daily Fix-It corrections with children. Review sentence capitalization, the *th* digraph, and rules for adding *-ed.*

English Language Learners

Options for Conventions Support To provide children with practice with adverbs, use the modified conventions lessons on p. 376 in the *ELL Handbook.*

Objectives

• Recognize features of a narrative poem.

MINI-LESSON

5 Day Planner
Guide to Mini-Lessons

DAY 1	Read Like a Writer
DAY 2	Story Sequence in a Poem
DAY 3	Use Voice and Sensory Details
DAY 4	Revising Strategy: Adding Sentences
DAY 5	Proofread for Rhyming Words and Adverbs

Writing—Narrative Poem
Introduce

MINI-LESSON

Read Like a Writer

■ **Introduce** This week you will write a narrative poem. A **narrative poem** is a poem that tells a story. Poems often have words that rhyme.

Prompt	Think about a change that has happened in your life. Now write a poem about it.
Trait	Voice
Mode	Narrative

Reader's and Writer's Notebook p. 328

■ **Examine Model Text** Let's listen to a narrative poem. Track the print as you read aloud "Time to Move" on *Reader's and Writer's Notebook* p. 328. Have children follow along.

■ **Key Features** Help children find the key features of the narrative poem. Does the poem tell a story? What's it about? (It tells a story about a person who's moving away.) How does the author use repetition? (The first and third lines of each stanza repeat.) How does the author use rhyme? (The ends of the second and fourth lines of each stanza rhyme.) Underline the two different words that rhyme in each stanza. (date/late; sad/mad; good-bye/cry; school/cool) Circle the words that tell how the author feels about moving. (happy, sad, mad, cry) Which words describe how things might be in the new place? (good, cool)

Academic Vocabulary

adverb a word that tells how, when, or where something happens

narrative a story, made up or true, that someone tells or writes

poem an expressive, imaginative piece of writing often arranged in lines having rhythm and rhyme. In a poem, the patterns made by the sounds of the words have special importance.

Review key features

Review key features of a narrative poem with children. You may want to post these key features in the classroom to allow children to refer to them as they work on their poems.

Key Features of a Narrative Poem

- tells a story
- may have rhyming words
- can describe something or can express feelings

Connect to familiar texts

Connect the poem to other poems the children have read or heard. You may want to connect it to the poem "How do seeds know which way is up?" from pages 80–81 of the Student Edition. Point out how narrative poems tell a story and have rhyming words, but each poem is describing something different and tells how the author feels.

Look ahead

Tell children that tomorrow they will plan their own narrative poem.

 ROUTINE **Quick Write for Fluency** **Team Talk**

1. **Talk** Read these questions about "Time to Move" aloud, and have children respond with adverbs that tell where or when.

   Which adverb tells where the author is moving? (away)

   Which adverb tells when the author is leaving friends? (today)

2. **Write** Have children write short sentences to answer the questions. Make sure their sentences include an adverb that tells where or when.

3. **Share** Partners can read their answers to one another.

Routines Flip Chart

Objectives
- Identify a topic connected to this week's concept.
- Narrow the focus of the topic by formulating inquiry questions related to the topic.
- Explore change.

Research and Inquiry
Identify and Focus Topic

Teach

Display and review the graphic organizer that explores this week's question: *Why are some changes difficult?* What ideas about difficult changes would you like to know more about? Ask children to share their interests. Help them identify some difficult changes.

Model

Think Aloud To learn why some changes are difficult, let's ask ourselves questions about the topic and then look for the answers. One thing I think would be helpful to know is what kinds of changes we think are difficult. I'll make a list of such questions.

Guide practice

Give children time to think about questions that, when answered, would help them find out why some changes are difficult. Record children's questions in a chart.

Topic: Why Some Changes Are Difficult	
Question	**Answer**
What kinds of changes are difficult?	

Wrap Up Your Day

✔ **Phonics: Syllable Patterns** Write *basket, paper,* and *down-town*. Ask children how many syllables are in each word and have them show how to divide the word into syllables. (bas ket, pa per, down town)

✔ **Spelling** Say *oatmeal*. Have students write the word and spell it orally. Continue with *houseboat, football,* and *soybean*.

✔ **Build Concepts** Ask children to recall what happened in the song "We Are Moving." Why might it be difficult for the person in this song to make the change to a new house? (Possible response: The move was unexpected and that was a sudden change.)

✔ **Homework** Send home this week's Family Times Newsletter from Let's Practice It! pp. 205–206 on the *Teacher Resource DVD-ROM*.

Let's Practice It!
TR DVD•205–206

Preview DAY 2

Tell children that tomorrow they will read a myth about a change that happened when the moon fell from the sky.

Objectives
- Discuss the concept to develop oral language.
- Build oral vocabulary.

Today at a Glance

Oral Vocabulary
quiver, tease

Phonics and Spelling
◉ Syllable Patterns

Lesson Vocabulary
balance, canyons, coral, rattle, slivers, sway, whisper

Vocabulary
◉ Multiple-Meaning Words

Fluency
Paired Reading

Comprehension
◉ Plot and Theme
◉ Visualize

Conventions
Adverbs That Tell When and Where

Writing
Narrative Poem

Handwriting
Cursive *a, d, c*/Word Spacing

Research and Inquiry
Research Skill: E-mail

Concept Talk

Question of the Week

 Why are some changes difficult?

Build concepts

To reinforce concepts and to focus children's attention, have children sing "We Are Moving" from the *Sing with Me* Big Book. In the song we hear that the move was unexpected. What might be the cause of an unexpected move? (Possible responses: A parent may get a job in a different town.)

Sing with Me Big Book Audio

Introduce Amazing Words

Explain that today you will read about a boy named Emilio who has a problem at school in "All the Same, Only Different" by Uma Krishnaswami. In the story, the author uses the word *tease* to describe what happens to Emilio. Have children listen to "All the Same, Only Different" to find out what school is like for Emilio.

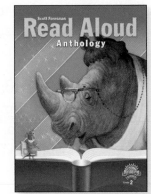

Read Aloud Anthology
"All the Same, Only Different"

ELL **Reinforce Vocabulary** Use the Day 2 instruction on ELL Poster 19 to teach lesson vocabulary and discuss the lesson concept.

ELL Poster 19

Go Digital!   Sing with Me Animations   Concept Talk Video

Whole Group

Oral Vocabulary
Amazing Words

Teach Amazing Words

 **Amazing Words** Oral Vocabulary Routine

1. **Introduce the Word** Relate the word *tease* to the story. Emilio is upset because the children at school *tease* him. Supply a child-friendly definition. One meaning for *tease* is "to make fun of another person in an unkind way." Have children say the word.

2. **Demonstrate** Provide examples to show meaning. That mean boy will *tease* me about my hair cut. We shouldn't *tease* my mom about her singing. I tripped and the kids started to *tease* me.

3. **Apply** Have children demonstrate their understanding. Is *tease* something a bully might do or a leader might do? Why?

   See p. OV•1 to teach *quiver.*

Routines Flip Chart

Anchored Talk

Add to the concept map

Discuss why some changes can be difficult as you add to the concept map.

- In the song "We Are Moving," why does the boy look at a map for a landmark? (Possible response: He wants to learn his way around his new neighborhood.) It can be difficult to move to a new place because you don't know your way around. Let's add this information to our map.

- In "All the Same, Only Different," Emilio doesn't like school. Why does he feel this way? (Possible response: He wants to play with the other children, but they won't let him. He wants to make friends, but the other children tease Emilio.) Sometimes it is difficult to make new friends, especially when the other children tease. Let's add these ideas to our map.

Amazing Words

adjust	tease
landmark	foreign
unexpected	accent
quiver	forlorn

Differentiated Instruction

A Advanced

Amazing Words Have children note that people can tease in a playful way or a hurtful way. Organize children into small groups. Have each group create and present a brief skit in which the characters tease in a playful way. Have them discuss how this kind of teasing would affect Emilio.

 ELL

English Language Learners
Amazing Words: Physical Response Teach the word *quiver* by acting it out and having children join you. Have children demonstrate *quiver* using their hands, legs, and voice.

Objectives

• Apply knowledge of letter-sound correspondences and syllable patterns to decode words in context and independent of context.

• Spell words using syllable patterns for compound words that include digraphs and diphthongs.

Phonics
Final Syllable -*le*; Syllable Patterns

Review

Review words with final syllable -*le* and other common syllable patterns using Sound-Spelling Cards 134, 147, and 149.

Decode words independent of context

Display these words. Have the class combine word parts to read the words. Then point to the words in random order and ask children to decode them quickly.

outlook	picnic	silent
payload	open	griddle
fable	tender	boyhood

Corrective feedback

Model combining word parts to read the words and then ask children to read them with you.

Read words in context

Display these sentences. Have the class read the sentences.

Team Talk Then have pairs take turns reading the sentences naturally.

Yellow tulips and **purple lilacs** lined the **roadway.**

The **cowboy** has a **cozy cabin** with **plenty** of **windows.**

A **number** of **outbound railroad** trains were not **able** to leave.

Spelling
Syllable Patterns

Guide practice

Tell children that you will break the spelling words into meaningful word parts. They should say the parts of each word aloud as they write them. Check the spelling of each word before saying the next word.

1. down stairs **downstairs**
2. foot ball **football**
3. cow boy **cowboy**
4. house boat **houseboat**
5. rail road **railroad**
6. rain bow **rainbow**
7. boy hood **boyhood**
8. oat meal **oatmeal**
9. soy bean **soybean**
10. road way **roadway**
11. out play **outplay**
12. day dream **daydream**

On their own

Use *Reader's and Writer's Notebook,* p. 329.

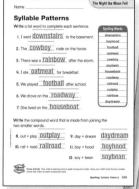

Reader's and Writer's
Notebook p. 329

Small Group Time

DAY 2

Break into small groups after spelling and before the comprehension lesson.

Teacher-Led

SI **Strategic Intervention**	OL **On-Level**	A **Advanced**
Teacher-Led Page DI•65	Teacher-Led Page DI•69	Teacher-Led Page DI•72
• Lesson Vocabulary	• Selection Vocabulary	• Comprehension
• **Read** *New Faces and Places*	• **Reread** *Decodable Practice Reader 19A*	• **Read** *The Night the Moon Fell*

 **ELL** Place English language learners in the groups that correspond to their reading abilities in English.

Practice Stations
• Words to Know
• Get Fluent

Independent Activities
• Read independently/Reading Log on *Reader's and Writer's Notebook* p. RR4
• Audio Text of Main Selection

ELL

English Language Learners
Spell Syllable Patterns Post the spelling list, and have children practice writing and reading each word part by itself. Then have them write the word parts together to make the complete words.

Objectives

- Learn lesson vocabulary:
  *balance, canyons, coral, rattle,
  slivers, sway, whisper.*
- Use new vocabulary words
  correctly.

**Check Lesson
Vocabulary/
High-Frequency Words**

SUCCESS PREDICTOR

Lesson Vocabulary

Review
Lesson
vocabulary

Display the lesson vocabulary words. Read them aloud and review their meanings. Divide the words into syllables to help children decode the words. Have children say each word after you.

bal • ance footing; even placement of weight that lets someone stand upright

can • yons deep valleys with steep sides

cor • al an underwater stony substance made by marine life

rat • tle make sharp knocking sounds as a result of being shaken

sliv • ers a small, thin piece of something that has been split off

sway move back and forth or side to side

whis • per make a soft sound

Tell children that being able to read these words and knowing their meanings will help them as they read this week's selection, *The Night the Moon Fell.*

 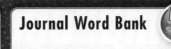

Differentiated Instruction

 Strategic Intervention

Words in Common Give children three words that have a connection to one of the vocabulary words. Ask children which vocabulary word best fits in with the following groups of words: *deep, valleys, high sides (canyons); move, swing, back-and-forth (sway); quiet, murmur, breathe (whisper); underwater, stony, sea life (coral); steadiness, footing, standing (balance); shaking, clatter, noise (rattle); chips, pieces, splinters (slivers).*

 Don't Wait Until Friday

MONITOR PROGRESS | Check Lesson Vocabulary/High-Frequency Words

Write the following words and have the class read them. Listen for children who miss words during the reading. Call on those children to read some of the words individually.

rattle	balance	slivers	sway
whisper	coral	canyons	
friend	move	love	pretty ←
school			←

Spiral Review
Rows 3 and 4 review previously taught high-frequency words.

If... children cannot read these words,

then... use the Small Group Time Strategic Intervention lesson, p. DI•65, to reteach the words. Monitor children's fluency with these words during reading and provide additional practice.

Day 1	Day 2	Day 3	Day 4	Day 5
Check Word Reading	**Check Lesson Vocabulary/ High-Frequency Words**	Check Retelling	Check Fluency	Check Oral Vocabulary

Success Predictor

 **ELL**

English Language Learners
Visual Support Show children pictures of *canyons* and *coral* reefs. Next, show *slivers* of crayons, paper, and/or wood. Then demonstrate the following words and have children participate in the actions to experience the words: *balance, sway, rattle* (objects), and *whisper.*

Multilingual Vocabulary Lists
Children can apply knowledge of their home languages to acquire new English vocabulary by using the Multilingual Vocabulary Lists (*ELL Handbook*, pages 429–440).

Objectives
- Use context clues to determine the relevant meaning of multiple-meaning words.
- Read grade-level text with fluency.

Vocabulary Strategy for
Multiple-Meaning Words

Teach multiple-meaning words

Tell children that some words have more than one meaning. Explain how using context clues can help them figure out which is the relevant meaning of the multiple-meaning word in the sentence they are reading. Refer children to *Words!* on p. W•10 in the Student Edition for additional practice. Then read "Oak Creek Canyon" on page 127 with children.

Envision It!

Student Edition p. W•10

Model the strategy

Think Aloud

Write on the board: *The branches began to rattle in the high wind.* I am having difficulty figuring out the meaning of *rattle* in this sentence. I know a *rattle* can be a baby's toy. *Rattle* can also mean "to make sharp knocking sounds as a result of being shaken." The other words in this sentence help me figure out that this second meaning is what *rattle* means in this sentence.

Guide practice

Write this sentence: *The girl tried to keep her balance on the slippery rocks.* Have children identify several meanings for *balance*. Have them use context clues to determine the relevant meaning of *balance* in the sentence.

On their own

Read "Oak Creek Canyon" on page 127. Have children use context clues to help them determine and then list the relevant meaning of lesson vocabulary words. For additional practice, use *Reader's and Writer's Notebook* p. 330.

Reader's and Writer's Notebook p. 330

Objectives
• Use context clues to figure out the meanings of words you don't know or words that have more than one meaning.

Envision It! Words to Know

balance

canyons

coral

rattle
slivers
sway
whisper

READING STREET ONLINE
VOCABULARY ACTIVITIES
www.ReadingStreet.com

Vocabulary Strategy for

🔘 Multiple-Meaning Words

Context Clues During reading, you may come across a word you know, but the meaning doesn't fit in the sentence. The word may have more than one meaning. You can use the context clues to figure out its relevant meaning.

1. Try the meaning you know. Does it make sense? If not, the word may have more than one meaning.

2. Read on and look at the nearby words. Can you figure out another meaning?

3. Try the new meaning in the sentence. Does it make sense?

Read "Oak Creek Canyon." Use context clues to find the relevant meaning of the multiple-meaning words.

Words to Write Reread "Oak Creek Canyon." Where is your favorite place to walk? What do you see when you walk there? Use words from the *Words to Know* list.

126

Oak Creek Canyon

Nature has many great things to see. Fish and coral fill the sea. Mountains stretch up high to the sky. Tall grasses sway over miles of flat land. Deep canyons dig into the land. Oak Creek Canyon is one of these canyons.

Oak Creek Canyon has rocks with strange shapes. Over time, wind and water wore away slivers and chips of rocks. This gave them their shapes.

Visit the canyon in early morning. You can watch the sun come up. You can see light hit the rocks. It is a good time to explore! Walk carefully. You want to keep your balance as you explore.

Stop and listen. Do you hear the wind whisper through the tall trees? Do you hear something rattle? It may be a rattlesnake. You want to stay far away from it. Look around. Lizards live here too. The canyon is filled with sights and sounds, and it is not very cold. You will have a good time here.

Your Turn!

⏸ **Need a Review?** For more help with context clues and multiple-meaning words, see *Words!* on pp. W·7 and W·10.

▶ **Ready to Try It?** Read *The Night the Moon Fell* on pp. 128–143.

127

Student Edition pp. 126–127

Reread for Fluency

Have children reread the last paragraph of "Oak Creek Canyon."

ROUTINE Paired Reading

1 **Reread** To achieve optimal fluency, have partners reread the text three or four times.

2 **Corrective Feedback** Listen as children read. Provide corrective feedback regarding their fluency and decoding.

Routines Flip Chart

Lesson Vocabulary

balance footing; even placement of weight that lets someone stand upright
canyons deep valleys with steep sides
coral an underwater stony substance made by marine life
rattle make sharp knocking sounds as a result of being shaken
sliver a small thin piece of something that has been split off
sway move back and forth from side to side
whisper make a soft sound

Differentiated Instruction

SI Strategic Intervention
Multiple-Meaning Words
Discuss with children the additional meanings of *balance* (instrument for weighing things, remainder, condition in which things are equal) *coral* (a reddish-orange color), *sway* (influence), and *whisper* (rumor).

English Language Learners
Cognates Point out the Spanish cognates in this week's lesson vocabulary: *canyon/cañán* and *coral/coral*. Explain that the English word *canyon* comes directly from the Spanish language as do other words that name landforms found in the Southwest, such as *mesa* and *arroyo*.

Objectives

- Build background on different explanations of a natural event.
- Preview and predict.
- Use key features of a myth to improve understanding of text.
- Set a purpose for reading text.

Build Background
The Night the Moon Fell

Background Building Audio

Have children listen to the CD. Tell them to listen to how a scientist and a storyteller explain what happens when the moon covers the sun during an eclipse.

 Background Building Audio

Discuss explanations of an eclipse

Team Talk Have children turn to a partner and use these questions for discussion:

- What is an eclipse of the sun?
- How does the scientist explain what really happens during an eclipse?
- How does the storyteller explain what the ancient Chinese thought happened during an eclipse?

Organize information in a T-chart

Draw a T-chart or display Graphic Organizer 25. Have children recall the scientific explanation of an eclipse and what happens in the ancient Chinese story about an eclipse. Record their responses.

Scientist's Explanation of an Eclipse	Storyteller's Explanation of an Eclipse
The moon passes between Earth and the sun.	A dragon attacks the sun.
	The dragon swallows the sun.
The moon covers the sun.	
The moon blocks the sun's light for a short time.	People make noise to make the dragon cough up the sun.

Graphic Organizer 25

Connect to selection

We learned how a scientist and a storyteller have different explanations for an eclipse, which is a natural event. In the story we are about to read, *The Night the Moon Fell,* we'll learn how the Maya people made up a myth long ago to try to explain another natural event that happens in the sky.

Student Edition pp. 128–129

Main Selection—First Read
The Night the Moon Fell

Practice the skill

 **Plot and Theme** Remind children that the story plot consists of the events in the beginning, middle, and end of the story. The story theme tells the story's "big idea."

Introduce the strategy

Visualize Explain that good readers stop as they read and picture in their minds what is happening in the text. Forming these mental pictures helps readers understand what they are reading. Have children turn to page EI•27 in their Student Edition.

Envision It!

Think Aloud Look at the picture. Visualizing is picturing in your mind what you are reading. What is the boy visualizing from the story the teacher is reading? (a knight) As I read *The Night the Moon Fell,* I will use details in the text and what I already know to help me visualize what is happening in the story.

Student Edition p. EI•27

Introduce genre

Let's Read A **myth** is a made-up story that attempts to explain something that happens in nature, such as why leaves change color or why a rainbow appears in the sky. As they read *The Night The Moon Fell,* ask children to think about events in nature this story tries to explain.

Preview and predict

Have children identify the title of the story, the author, and the illustrator. Have children describe the roles of the author and illustrator. Help children look through the selection and use the title and illustrations to predict events that might happen in the story.

Set a purpose

Good readers read for a purpose. Setting a purpose helps us to think and understand more as we read. Guide children to set a purpose for reading the story.

Tell children that today they will read *The Night the Moon Fell* for the first time. Use the Day 2 Guide Comprehension notes to help children develop their comprehension.

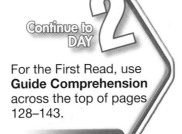

Continue to DAY 2

For the First Read, use **Guide Comprehension** across the top of pages 128–143.

First Read

Strategy Response Log

Genre Have children use p. RR25 in their *Reader's* and *Writer's Notebook* to identify the characteristics of myth. Have children look for these characteristics as they read *The Night the Moon Fell.*

Academic Vocabulary

visualize picture in one's mind what is happening in the text

myth a story that attempts to explain something in nature

ELL

English Language Learners
Build Background Before children listen to the CD, build background and elicit prior knowledge. On the CD, you will listen to a scientist and to a storyteller give two explanations for an eclipse when the sun is covered by the moon. Thinking about these explanations can help you understand how people long ago made up stories to explain things they did not understand. Have children provide explanations of another natural event in the sky such as sunrise or sunset.

Frontload Main Selection Show children pictures of a full moon. Point out its features and explain that shadows on the moon's surface make it look like a face. Explain that in this story, the author imagines that the moon is someone named Luna. Ask children how Luna might feel if she suddenly fell out of her home in the night sky. How could she get home again?

Objectives
◎ Visualize events described in the story text.
◎ Identify the plot and theme of a myth.
• Determine word meaning and use newly acquired vocabulary.
• Discuss ideas related to, but not expressed in the literature.

DAY 2

Guide Comprehension
Skills and Strategies

Connect to Concept

Our Changing World Look at the pictures on pages 128 and 129. How might things on Earth change if the moon fell from the sky? (The sky would be dark at night; creatures that depend on the moon's light might have difficulty adjusting to the dark.)

Amazing Words
Have children continue discussing the concept using the Amazing Words *adjust, landmark, unexpected, quiver,* and *tease* as they read.

The Night the Moon Fell

Question of the Week
Why are some changes difficult?

Genre A **myth** is an old story that often explains something about nature.

A Mayan myth retold by
Pat Mora

illustrated by
Domi

128   129

Student Edition pp. 128–129

DAY 3

Extend Thinking
Think Critically

Higher-Order Thinking Skills
Evaluation How does the illustrator portray the moon? Do you think the illustrations fit the story?

If... children cannot decide whether showing the moon as a character fits the story,
then... point out the moon's features and ask children what the moon's name is in the story and how she is described.

Strategies

 Visualize Remind children that good readers try to picture in their minds the events described by the author in the text. Have them describe the mental images they see in their minds when they read pages 130 and 131.

If... children had difficulty visualizing,

then... model a mental image: *As I read page 130, I picture in my mind a large, round moon rolling like a ball through the sky and dropping into the sea where it shatters into a million shining pieces—just like a broken mirror.*

One night long ago, Luna the moon hummed high in the night sky. Stars twinkled, and Luna's friend the wind dozed nearby. The night was hushed and peaceful.

Suddenly, the sky shook. A loud *WHOOSH!* rattled the stars and startled the moon. Luna's grandfather had shot his blowgun, and Luna jumped in surprise. She lost her balance and started to roll and roll.

Luna rolled through stars, and she rolled through clouds. She rolled, rolled down to the earth and splashed into the ocean's cold, dark waves. She broke into shimmering slivers and bits on the sandy bottom of the sea.

130

The huge sky became black and still as the deepest ocean. Stars shut their eyes. Flowers bowed their heads, and all the birds in the world rose looking for the moon. They flew into loud storms. They soared down black canyons. They darted into huge caves calling.

"Luna, come back, bring us your light. Shine your white light for us tonight." Silence. Luna's amigo, the wind, raced up mountains whispering and then roaring. "Luna, come back, bring us your light. Shine your white light for us tonight." All the world waited. All the world listened. Silence.

131

Student Edition pp. 130–131

Review Draw Conclusions/Analysis Why doesn't Luna answer the calls of the birds and the wind? (The text says that Luna is far beneath the water at the bottom of the sea, where she probably doesn't hear the calls of the birds and the wind.)

Higher-Order Thinking Skills

Synthesis Describe the appearance of the night sky before and after Luna falls. If you were an illustrator, how would you make these two scenes look?

Skills and Strategies, continued

DAY 2

Skills

⦿ **Plot and Theme** What happens to Luna in this part of the story? (She makes friends with the tiny fish who make her laugh and smile.) What does this tell you about friendship? (You can make new friends in a new place; friends can cheer you up.)

Word Reading

Decoding Have children check their reading of new words using these questions:

• Did I blend the sounds?

• Did the new word make sense?

• Did I look for word parts?

Where was the moon?
The tiny fish at the bottom of the sea knew. They saw Luna's white glow, and they heard her lonely song.
"Where am I? Where's the sky? Broken, sad, lost am I."
The fish swam around and around the broken moon. "What can we do? What can we do?" they whispered.
"We'll be your friends," said the tiniest fish. "What's your name?"
"Luna," the moon sniffled.
"Are you the shining light that hums high in the sky?" asked the roundest fish.
Luna sniffed,
"I was the light high in the sky, Now broken, sad, lost am I."

132

The tiny fish and Luna looked up together. They looked up through all that deep, dark water. The little fish missed seeing the moonlight high in the night sky. They missed playing in Luna's white light.
In a sad voice, Luna sighed,
"Oh, sweet fish, how sad am I. I miss my home high in the sky."
The little fish felt sorry for Luna. "Watch this," said the tiniest fish, and he and the other little fish began blowing bubbles in wonderful and funny shapes to make her laugh and smile.
"New friends, you are good for me. You make me laugh in this cold, dark sea."
The tiny fish began to hum, and in time Luna hummed too. She hummed herself to sleep.

133

Student Edition pp. 132–133

Think Critically, continued

DAY 3

Higher-Order Thinking Skills

Analysis How does Luna feel as she lies on the bottom of the sea? Why does she feel this way? (She is feeling confused, lost, and sad. She feels this way because she no longer looks like herself, and she is alone in an unfamiliar place.)

If... children have trouble explaining Luna's feelings,
then... relate Luna's feelings about her situation to how children might feel if they fell out of a tree and woke up in the hospital with a broken arm.

Vocabulary

Lesson Vocabulary Have children locate the lesson vocabulary word *coral* on page 134. What does it mean when the author says Luna saw forests of coral? (Since coral is an underwater stony substance, it means that Luna saw many large pieces of coral close together that looked like trees in a forest.)

Strategies

Visualize What picture comes to your mind when you read the first paragraph on page 135?

If... children have trouble visualizing,
then... have them close their eyes as you read the paragraph aloud emphasizing the descriptive phrase *large, dark shape with eyes cold as stones*, and have them describe the sea creature they picture.

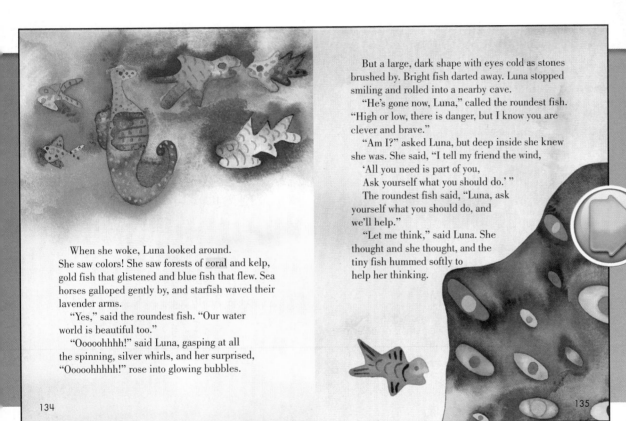

When she woke, Luna looked around. She saw colors! She saw forests of coral and kelp, gold fish that glistened and blue fish that flew. Sea horses galloped gently by, and starfish waved their lavender arms.

"Yes," said the roundest fish. "Our water world is beautiful too."

"Ooooohhhh!" said Luna, gasping at all the spinning, silver whirls, and her surprised, "Ooooohhhh!" rose into glowing bubbles.

134

But a large, dark shape with eyes cold as stones brushed by. Bright fish darted away. Luna stopped smiling and rolled into a nearby cave.

"He's gone now, Luna," called the roundest fish. "High or low, there is danger, but I know you are clever and brave."

"Am I?" asked Luna, but deep inside she knew she was. She said, "I tell my friend the wind,

'All you need is part of you,
Ask yourself what you should do.'"

The roundest fish said, "Luna, ask yourself what you should do, and we'll help."

"Let me think," said Luna. She thought and she thought, and the tiny fish hummed softly to help her thinking.

135

Student Edition pp. 134–135

Higher-Order Thinking Skills

Analysis Why does the underwater scene appear so different to Luna when she wakes up? (The night before, the sea seemed cold and dark because there was no moonlight shining through the water. In the morning, the sunlight makes it possible to see the colorful sea plants and animals.)

Synthesis What does the roundest fish mean when it says, "High or low, there is danger?" (There is danger in the sky from storms, and danger under the sea from the shark or whatever the dark shape was.)

If... children do not understand this reference,
then... point out that danger up high means danger in the sky while danger down low means danger in the sea.

Skills and Strategies, continued

DAY 2

Vocabulary

Lesson Vocabulary Have children locate the lesson vocabulary word *swaying* on page 136. Use your body to show what Luna does as she starts swaying to the fishes' humming. (Children should gently move their bodies back and forth.)

Strategies

Visualize What picture comes to mind as you read the last paragraph on page 136? (Possible response: I see the fish using their fins and tails like little brooms in order to gather up glowing bits of moon.)

Luna started swaying to their music, and the fish swayed with her. Then Luna began to hum and to roll to her music, and as she rolled in the strange new land, she began to collect herself.

"How can we help?" asked the tiniest fish.
Luna sang,
"All you need is part of you.
Ask yourself what you should do."
The tiny fish thought and thought. They whispered, "*Pppzzz, pppzzz. Pppzzz, pppzzz.*" And then they knew what to do. The little fish looked inside shells and deep in cold sea caves for bits of glowing moon. With their silvery fins, they began to sweep together the slivers and bits, and on the strange sand, the moon rolled and rolled into herself.

She said,
"Pezecitos,
little fish,
Smooth me
whole. Please
grant my wish."
The fish swam
round-round
Luna, patching and
smoothing.
With their silvery fins,
they smoothed her roundness.
Luna laughed at the tickly fins. When she studied herself, Luna knew she needed just a bit of her friends to stay together, so she said,
"Now what I need is part of you.
Will you be my silvery glue?"

136

137

Student Edition pp. 136–137

Think Critically, continued

DAY 3

Higher-Order Thinking Skills

Evaluation In your opinion, do Luna and the fish come up with a good solution for Luna's problem?

If... children have trouble evaluating the solution,
then... ask them how they would mend a broken plate that had fallen on the floor.

Analysis Why do you think the author has Luna and the fish sing to each other in rhymes? (The singing rhymes make the text more musical and dreamlike, which is appropriate for the retelling of a myth from long ago.)

Skills

Plot and Theme What happens on page 138? (With the help of the fish, Luna finds a way to put herself together again.) What is the last remaining problem that Luna and her friends must solve? (She must find a way to get back up to her home in the sky.)

Vocabulary

Multiple-Meaning Words Some words, like *patch* on page 138, have more than one meaning. To determine this word's relevant meaning, I use context clues. Find the word *scales* on page 138. What two meanings can this word have? (machine for weighing; covering on a fish) What context clues help you figure out its relevant meaning? (the references to fish)

The little fish looked at themselves. The tiny fish thought and thought. They whispered, "*Pppzzz, pppzzz, pppzzz.*" Luna smiled and hummed. The fish began to wriggle and dance. And they knew what to do. They shook themselves to loosen a few of their silvery scales, and with their fins they patched the rolling moon. As Luna rolled into herself, the sea around her glistened. Luna began to hum and glow.

Oh, how beautiful she looked when she was round and whole again! The deep ocean was filled with her white light. Waves rolled rainbows. The little fish rested.

Luna then said,
"Gracias, mis amigos, thank you.
Thank you for your silvery glue."

138

139

Student Edition pp. 138–139

Higher-Order Thinking Skills

Analysis Why does Luna need the help of the fish?

If... children have trouble analyzing the situation, **then...** ask them to compare the pictures of the fish and the moon on page 139. How could the armless moon have gathered up tiny bits of herself and then patched, smoothed, and glued them together?

Connect to Science

Phases of the Moon The revolution of the moon around Earth makes the moon appear to change shape in the sky. The changing shape of the lighted part of the moon that we see is called its phase.

Team Talk Have children discuss with a partner the different shapes of the moon that they have noticed in the night sky. Have them comment on how much light a full moon provides on a clear night.

Skills and Strategies, continued

DAY 2

Strategies

⊙ Visualize What comparison do the fish use when describing how Luna looks and feels as she begins to float? (They compare her to a balloon.) How does this comparison help you visualize the scene? (I see a balloon slowly rising up in the air.)

Strategy Self-Check

Have children recall the pictures they visualized in their mind as they read the story. Then have them identify words in the text and prior knowledge and experiences that helped them create these mental pictures.

"You're so happy, you're like a balloon," said the littlest fish, watching the moon begin to float.
    Luna laughed,
    "Now round and whole am I,
    And can float home to my sky."
    The fish watched Luna float slowly up from the bottom of the sea. They whispered,
    "Pppzzz, pppzzz. Pppzzz, pppzzz."

140

And then they knew what to do. Holding on to one another's tails, the tiny fish wove themselves into a silvery net around Luna.
    "That tickles, friends, but I agree.
    Come swim the sky. Accompany me."
    Slowly, Luna and the tiny fish rose through the clouds and through the stars. When they were high in the night sky, Luna began to hum, and the night sky changed. Luna's white light opened the stars' eyes, and her friend the wind purred. Flowers lifted their heads, and birds flew high, sang one note, and then nestled in trees and on rooftops.

141

Student Edition pp. 140–141

Think Critically, continued

DAY 3

Higher-Order Thinking Skills

Analysis What reason might the fish have for accompanying Luna on her journey back to the sky? (Possible responses: They like Luna so much that they don't want their friendship to end, or they want to help and protect her.)

If... children have trouble identifying a reason the fish wanted to stay with Luna,

then... ask them to describe how they would feel if a good friend was going to a faraway place.

Skills

Plot and Theme What happens at the end this myth? (Luna returns to the sky with the fish who become the Milky Way. Things return to the way they were before Luna fell.) What is the theme, or big idea, of this myth? (Friends can comfort us in times of trouble and give us the help and confidence we need to find the inner strength to pull ourselves together.)

If... children have trouble identifying the story theme,
then... have them recall story events and use them to figure out what Luna learned about friendship and herself when everything in her life seemed to have fallen apart.

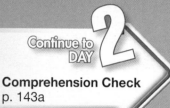
Continue to DAY 2
Comprehension Check
p. 143a

The moon was home, and she sang new songs of gold fish and starfish, of coral and kelp, of rolling <u>rainbow</u> waves.
Luna's friends, the tiny fish, started swimming in the huge night sky. They heard her voice, sweeter than the scent of a thousand flowers, softer than the *ssshhh, ssshhh, ssshhh* of waves at dawn.

142

Luna sang,
"Please, dear friends, stay here with me.
Swim my skies, my star bright sea."
And they did.
Look up. High in the sky, Luna's friend the wind dozes, and her amigos, the tiny fish, swim nearby. They twinkle through the night, and Luna smiles her white light.

143

Student Edition pp. 142–143

Higher-Order Thinking Skills

Synthesis A myth tries to explain an event that happens in nature. What event or events in nature does this story try to explain? (It explains why the moon seems to disappear and then reappear in the night sky. It also explains how the stars in the Milky Way came to be.)

If... children have difficulty linking the story events to events in nature,
then... ask children what they notice about the appearance of the moon over time as well as the huge number of tiny stars twinkling in the Milky Way.

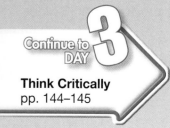
Continue to DAY 3
Think Critically
pp. 144–145

Objectives

- Use the title and illustrations to confirm predictions.
- Understand the use of sensory language to create images in a myth.
- Identify and use adverbs that tell time and manner in reading, writing, and speaking.
- Identify and use time-order transition words in reading, writing, and speaking.

Comprehension Check

Have children discuss each question with a partner and share responses.

☑ **Myth** What event in the natural world does this myth explain? (It explains why the moon disappears and reappears in the night sky.)

☑ **Confirm predictions** How did the title and the illustrations help you predict that this myth would be about an accidental event that happened to the moon? (Possible response: The title provides a clue that the story is about the moon falling; the illustrations show the moon broken into pieces.) Were your predictions correct?

☑ **Connect text to self** How can you apply the moral lesson of this story to your own life? (Children may give examples of how friends could help them when they are having difficulty dealing with an unexpected change in their lives.)

Literary Text
Sensory Words

Identify the purpose of sensory words

Use *The Night the Moon Fell* to review the use of sensory words in descriptions.

- **Sensory words** are words that appeal to the five sense of seeing, hearing, smelling, tasting, and feeling. Authors often use sensory words in descriptions to help readers visualize settings, characters, and events.

- Sometimes, authors use words that sound like the sounds they describe. These words are called **onomatopoeia**. Examples of onomatopoeia include *crash, bang,* and *ring*. What onomatopoetic word does Pat Mora use to describe the noise of Grandfather's blowgun? (the word *whoosh*)

Guide practice

Together, find and analyze examples of sensory words in *The Night the Moon Fell*. In the left column of a T-chart, summarize the example. In the right column, describe the purpose of the sensory words. For example:

Example of Sensory Words	Effect of Sensory Words
• On page 130, the author says that Luna rolled through stars and clouds.	• These words help us picture the moon rolling like a giant ball through the sky.

Graphic Organizer 25

On their own

Have partners work together to locate and describe the effect of other sensory words in *The Night the Moon Fell* and record this information in Graphic Organizer 25. Have partners share their charts with the class.

Conventions
Adverbs That Tell When and Where

Model adverbs that tell when and where

Write *Mae walked here.* Point to each word as you read it. Ask children to identify the adverb in the sentence. (*here*) Then ask them to name the verb it tells about. (*walked*) What can an adverb tell about a verb? (It can tell when or where something happens.)

Guide practice

Write the following sentences on the board. Have children read the sentences and identify the adverb in each sentence. Then have them tell whether the adverb tells when or where or signals time order.

1. **She will visit Tim later. (later, when)**
2. **My friend's house is there. (there, where)**
3. **I forgot my book bag yesterday. (yesterday, when)**
4. **We will read a story first. (first, time order)**

Connect to oral language

Have the class complete these sentence frames orally using adverbs that tell when or where or signal time order.

1. **The teacher's desk is _____.**
2. **I will read this book _____.**
3. **Our class eats lunch _____ the first grade class.**

On their own

Use *Reader's and Writer's Notebook* p. 331.

Reader's and Writer's Notebook p. 331

Differentiated Instruction

SI Strategic Intervention

Practice Adverbs If children have difficulty identifying adverbs, have them ask these questions about a sentence: *What is happening?* That's the verb. *When or where is it happening?* That's the adverb.

Daily Fix-It

3. The coboy ride his horse fast.
   The cowboy rode his horse fast.
4. Did jill enjoy the show.
   Did Jill enjoy the show?

Discuss the Daily Fix-It corrections with children. Review sentence punctuation, the capitalization of proper nouns, the diphthong *ow,* and verb tenses.

ELL

English Language Learners

Support Conventions To simplify the sentence completion exercise, list the following adverbs on the board: *here, there, today, tomorrow, before, after.* Have children use these words to complete the sentence frames.

Objectives
- Generate ideas for a narrative poem.
- Recognize features of a narrative poem.

Writing—Narrative Poem
Writer's Craft: Selecting a Story to Tell

Introduce the prompt

Review with children the key features of a narrative poem. Point out that "How do seeds know which way is up?" is a narrative poem. Assure them that they can write a narrative poem about a change that has happened in their life. Explain that today children will plan their own narrative poem. Read aloud the writing prompt.

Writing Prompt

> Think about a change that has happened in your life. Now write a poem about it.

Sharing the Writing

Help children generate narrative poem ideas

 Think Aloud To plan your narrative poem, think about some changes that people go through. That will be the topic of your poem. I'll start with *moving*.

Guide children in telling about changes people go through. Possible ideas are shown.

> **Moving**
>
> **New baby**
>
> **Changing schools**
>
> **New school year**
>
> **Getting a pet**

Record the responses and keep the chart displayed so that children can refer to it as they plan and draft their poems.

Have each child think about and decide what change in their life they would like to write a poem about. Circulate to guide them.

MINI-LESSON

Story Sequence in a Poem

- **Introduce** Use *Reader's and Writer's Notebook* p. 332 to model how to plan a narrative poem. To plan my poem, I will use a story sequence chart.

- **Model** First, I will write a title for my poem based on my topic. I will write *A New School* in the Title box. In the Characters box, I will write *me*. The setting, telling where and when, will be *in third grade, on the first day of school*. Now, I need to decide on the events I want in my poem and write them in sequence in the Events boxes. The first event is *I waited for the bus*. In the Next box, I will write *I saw students from my old school*. In the Then box, I will write *I met students from other schools*. Last, I *arrived at my new school*. Now you will complete your own story sequence chart about the change you experienced. Think about what you saw, heard, or felt during that experience.

Circulate to guide and assist children.

Reader's and Writer's Notebook p. 332

ROUTINE — Quick Write for Fluency — Team Talk

1. **Talk** Have children take two minutes to tell a partner about their topic and the events they will write about. Encourage them to think of sensory details.

2. **Write** Each child briefly fills in the story sequence chart with the title, characters, setting, and events.

3. **Share** Each child reads their plan to the partner.

Routines Flip Chart

Differentiated Instruction

SI Strategic Intervention

Topic Selection If children have trouble thinking of a change in their lives to write about or don't want to write about a change in their own lives, suggest that they write about a change in the life of a character from a favorite story.

ELL

English Language Learners
Support Prewriting
Beginning After children decide on a topic, provide them with a framework for their events. Write the events that children dictate, but leave out words. Have children fill them in to complete the chart.
Intermediate After discussing topics, provide children with possible story events. Let them choose appropriate events for their topic.

Advanced/Advanced-High Before children do the Quick Write, have them do a "think aloud" with a partner to discuss possible ideas for their poems.

Objectives

• Write legible letters with proper spacing between words.

• Understand how to read and compose an e-mail.

• Determine what sources of information are relevant for answering inquiry questions.

Handwriting
Cursive Letters *a, d, c*/Word Spacing

Model letter formation

Display lower-case letters: *a, d,* and *c.* Use the stroke instructions pictured below to model proper letter formation. Have children write each letter several times and circle the best one.

D'Nealian Cursive™

Model word spacing

Explain that when we write words, the words should be evenly spaced. Write the phrase *take the cake* using correct spacing between words. When I write words in a phrase, I need to pay attention to the spaces between the words. Write *take the cake* again, with the words too close to each other. The words should not be so close together that the words run together. Write *take the cake* a third time, with the words too far from each other. The words should not be so far apart that it's hard to tell that they are in the same phrase or sentence. By correctly spacing words, I make it easier for others to read what I write. Ask children which of the three writing examples is easiest to read and have them explain why.

Guide practice

Write the following phrase, using word spacing that is too crowded and too far apart: *call the duck.*

Team Talk Have children work in pairs to discuss what is wrong with the words in this phrase and how they would fix them. Have children write the phrase correctly. Have them share with the class.

Research and Inquiry
Research Skill: E-mail

Academic Vocabulary

e-mail a way to communicate through the Internet

source a person, place, or thing that provides information

Teach

Tell children that a **source** is a person, place, or thing that provides information. Review sources of information they have learned about. Tell children that one way to share information with people is to use e-mail. An **e-mail** is like a letter, but it is sent using a computer through the Internet. For example, if I wanted to ask a friend a question about something, I could send her an e-mail.

Model

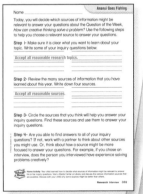

Think Aloud

Display Research Transparency 19. This is an example of an e-mail. I can see it was written by Anna Ruiz and sent to Mr. Chin. Their e-mail addresses are next to their names in the FROM and TO lines. In the SUBJECT line, I learn that this e-mail is about a question that Anna has about an animal report. The body of the e-mail is the message and is below the SUBJECT line.

Guide practice

Using Research Transparency 19, guide children in preparing an e-mail response from Mr. Chin to Anna.

On their own

Use *Reader's and Writer's Notebook* p. 333 to help children understand e-mails.

Research Transparency 19
TR DVD

Reader's and Writer's
Notebook p. 333

Wrap Up Your Day

✔ **Build Concepts** Monitor children's use of oral vocabulary as they respond. Recall the main selection, *The Night the Moon Fell*. What happened unexpectedly to make Luna fall from the sky? (Luna heard a loud WHOOSH from the blowgun that belonged to her grandfather.) What did Luna have a difficult time adjusting to? (She had a difficult time adjusting to the ocean.)

Preview DAY 3

Tell children that tomorrow they will reread *The Night the Moon Fell*.

Objectives

- Build oral vocabulary.
- Identify details in text.
- Share information and ideas about the concept.

Today at a Glance

Oral Vocabulary
foreign

Phonics and Spelling
◉ Syllable Patterns

Fluency
Read with Expression

Lesson Vocabulary
balance, canyons, coral, rattle, slivers, sway, whisper

Vocabulary
◉ Multiple-Meaning Words

Comprehension
Draw Conclusions

Conventions
Adverbs That Tell When and Where

Writing
Narrative Poem

Research and Inquiry
Gather and Record Information

Concept Talk

 Question of the Week

Why are some changes difficult?

Build concepts

To reinforce concepts and to focus children's attention, have children sing "We Are Moving" from the *Sing with Me* Big Book. Revisit the picture on page 19. What can help you adjust when you move to a new place? (Possible response: Familiar things, your family, and a map that shows landmarks can help you adjust.)

Sing with Me Big Book Audio

Monitor listening comprehension

As children listen to "All the Same, Only Different," have them think about the big idea of the story.

- What was Nina trying to tell Emilio about the little piece of dough? (Possible response: The little piece of dough can be bread, a tortilla, or a roti—all the same, only different. It can be anything it wants to be.)

- What is the big idea behind this story? When you read this story what did you learn about people? (Possible response: People are all the same, only different, and they can be anything they want to be.)

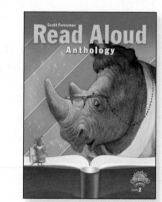

Read Aloud Anthology
"All the Same, Only Different"

ELL **Expand Vocabulary** Use the Day 3 instruction on ELL Poster 19 to expand children's use of English vocabulary to communicate about lesson concepts.

ELL Poster 19

Oral Vocabulary
Amazing Words

Teach Amazing Words

Amazing Words — Oral Vocabulary Routine

1. **Introduce the Word** Relate the word *foreign* to the story. Papi looked *foreign* with a turban on his head. Supply a child-friendly definition. Someone or something from outside your own country is *foreign.* Have children say the word.

2. **Demonstrate** Provide examples to show meaning. Miguel is a *foreign* exchange student from Spain. A ship with a *foreign* flag entered the harbor. The bank teller handed Dad some *foreign* money by mistake.

3. **Apply** Have children demonstrate their understanding. If a *foreign* student came to your school, how would you help him or her? What things might be most difficult to adjust to for a foreign student?

Routines Flip Chart

Anchored Talk

Add to the concept map

Use these questions to discuss why some changes are difficult as you add to the concept map.

- In *The Night the Moon Fell,* Luna has an unexpected change. What difficult change does Luna have to adjust to? (Possible response: Luna fell from the sky to the bottom of the sea. She moved to a new place.) Why is Luna sad? (Possible response: She misses her old home in the sky.) Let's add *You miss your old home* to our map.

- Who was Luna's friend in the sky? (The wind was Luna's friend.) How can you tell that Luna misses her friend, the wind? (Possible response: She remembers her old friend. She tells her new friends, the fish, what she told her old friend about helping.)

Amazing Words

adjust	tease
landmark	foreign
unexpected	accent
quiver	forlorn

Differentiated Instruction

SI Strategic Intervention

Amazing Words Help children list things that can be foreign, such as people, countries, ships, airplanes, money, flags and languages. Have children use the word *foreign* in an oral sentence that includes a word from the list.

English Language Learners
Amazing Words: Pronunciation
Discuss children's awareness of silent letters in their home languages before pointing out the silent letters in *foreign.*

Objectives

◎ Read multisyllabic words with closed syllable patterns (CVC), and open syllable patterns (CV), including compound words containing diphthongs and vowel digraphs.

• Break words with closed syllable patterns (CVC) and open syllable patterns (CV) into syllables.

• Decode words in context and independent of context.

Phonics
Build Words

Model word building

Now we are going to build words from syllables. Write the two syllables *mu* and *sic*. I am going to combine syllables to make words. I put these two syllables together to make the word *music*. Read the word with me. Model building the words *cir-cus* and *rain-drop*.

Guide practice

Have children copy the syllables from the first two columns and write the words. Then have children decode each word as you point to it. Monitor children's work.

First Syllable	Second Syllable	Word
pen	cil	pencil
ro	bot	robot
house	boat	houseboat
tu	lip	tulip
sil	ver	silver
down	spout	downspout

Corrective feedback

For corrective feedback, have children read each word and the two syllables that make up the word. Model the correct pronunciation and syllable breaks for each word as needed.

Fluent Word Reading

Model

Write *picnic.* I know that when a two-syllable word has two consonants in the middle, I divide the syllables between them. I know that the vowel sound in each syllable is short because the syllables are closed, that is, they end with a consonant. I read the word parts *pic* and *nic.* I put the parts together and read the word *picnic.*

Guide practice

Write the words below. Look for word parts you know. When I point to the word, we'll read it together. Allow one second per sound previewing time for the first reading.

| tiger | basket | soymilk | frozen | window | boyhood |

On their own

Have children read the list above three or four times until they can read one word per second.

Blend and Read

Decode words independent of context

Have children turn to page 63 in Decodable Practice Readers 2.2 and find the first list of words. Each word in this list has two syllables. Let's read these words.

Next, have children read the high-frequency words.

Decodable Practice Readers 2.2, pp. 63–64

Decode words in context

Chorally read the story along with children. Have children identify words in the story that have two syllables.

Team Talk Pair children and have them take turns reading the story aloud to each other. Monitor children as they read to check for proper pronunciation and appropriate pacing.

Differentiated Instruction

 Strategic Intervention

Identifying Syllables If children have difficulty seeing two syllables in words, remind them that each syllable will have at least one vowel sound. Tell them that after they identify the vowels, they should look for the word parts. Provide extra practice with the words *carton, lilac, driver, bacon, beanbag,* and *seaweed.*

A **Advanced**

Combining Syllables If children can easily read words with two syllables, challenge them to read words with three or more syllables. Have them break the following words into syllables, put the parts together in their head, and read each word: *sensible, incorrect, dinnertime, community.*

ELL

English Language Learners

Identifying Syllables Write these words on the board: *silver, doghouse, spider, sailboat, number, and paper.* Read the words slowly, pausing slightly between syllables. Have volunteers draw a line between the two syllables as you pause. Then have children repeat the words and pause at the syllable break. Provide visual support as needed.

Objectives
- Spell compound words with vowel digraphs and diphthongs.
- Spell high-frequency words.
- Read aloud fluently with expression.

Spelling
Syllable Patterns

Spell high-frequency words

Write *none* and *hour*. Have children say and spell the words with you and then without you.

Dictation

Have children write these sentences. Say each sentence. Then repeat it slowly, one word at a time.

> 1. One cowboy spent his boyhood on a ranch.
> 2. None of the football teams can outplay the home team.
> 3. In one hour we will go downstairs to eat oatmeal cookies.

Proofread and correct

Write each sentence. Have children circle and rewrite any misspelled words.

On their own

Use *Reader's and Writer's Notebook* p. 334.

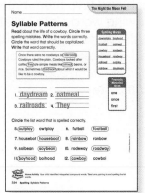

Reader's and Writer's Notebook p. 334

Small Group Time

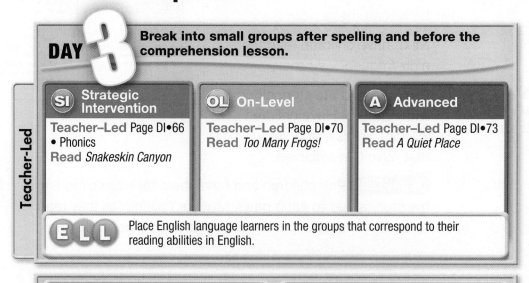

DAY 3 Break into small groups after spelling and before the comprehension lesson.

Teacher-Led

SI Strategic Intervention	**OL** On-Level	**A** Advanced
Teacher–Led Page DI•66 • Phonics **Read** *Snakeskin Canyon*	Teacher–Led Page DI•70 **Read** *Too Many Frogs!*	Teacher–Led Page DI•73 **Read** *A Quiet Place*

ELL Place English language learners in the groups that correspond to their reading abilities in English.

Practice Stations
- Read for Meaning
- Let's Write

Independent Activities
- Read independently/Reading Log on *Reader's and Writer's Notebook* p. RR4
- Audio Text of Main Selection

Model Fluency
Read with Expression

Model fluent reading

Have children turn to Student Edition p. 132. Follow along as I read this page. When I read the words a character says, I want to read as if the character is speaking. To do this, I think about how the character feels when saying these words.

Guide practice

Have children read the page with you. Then have them reread the page as a group without you until they read with appropriate expression that reflects characterization. Continue in the same way with p. 133.

Corrective feedback

If... children have difficulty reading while expressing characterization,

then... prompt:

- Did you think about the characters' feelings before reading the words they spoke?
- Did you read the words as the characters would say them?

Reread for Fluency

 Choral Reading

1. **Select a Passage** For *The Night the Moon Fell,* use p. 134.
2. **Model** First, have children track the print as you read.
3. **Guide Practice** Then have children read along with you.
4. **Corrective Feedback** Have the class read aloud without you. Monitor progress and provide feedback. For optimal fluency, children should reread three to four times.

Routines Flip Chart

Check comprehension

Why do you think Luna gradually becomes more cheerful as she spends time with the fish? (Their cheerful, upbeat attitude helps her feel better about her situation; they give her confidence that she can find a solution to her problem.)

Differentiated Instruction

 Strategic Intervention

Fluency Distribute sticky notes and have children annotate the text on pp. 133–134 with drawings and words that show and tell how Luna and the fish feel. Encourage children to refer to their annotations to help them capture the characters' emotions as they read expressively.

 Advanced

Fluency Provide additional practice by assigning children to groups of three and having children take the parts of Luna, the fish, and a narrator. Have them take these roles as they practice and then present a fluent reading of p. 134.

Spelling Words

Syllable Patterns

1. downstairs
2. football
3. cowboy
4. houseboat
5. railroad
6. rainbow
7. boyhood
8. oatmeal
9. soybean
10. roadway
11. outplay
12. daydream

High-Frequency Words

13. none
14. hour

Academic Vocabulary

(read with) expression use intonation and various pitches in voice when reading

Options for Oral Rereading

Use *The Night the Moon Fell* or the Day 1 Decodable Reader.

Objectives
- Review lesson vocabulary.
- Review multiple-meaning words.
- Establish purpose for reading text.
- Review key features of a myth.

Vocabulary
Lesson Vocabulary

Review
Lesson vocabulary

Display and review the lesson vocabulary words *balance, canyons, coral, rattle, slivers, sway,* and *whisper.* Have children read the words aloud.

Team Talk Have children work in pairs to write clues about the lesson vocabulary words. Then have them exchange clues with another pair of children to choose the vocabulary word that matches each clue. Here are some examples: *These small pieces of wood may be found under a workbench. (slivers). If you trip and fall, what did you lose? (balance)*

Multiple-Meaning Words

Review
Multiple-meaning words

Remind children that sometimes a word has two or more different meanings. For example, the word *fall* can mean "to drop to a lower place or come down" or "the time of year between summer and winter." When reading, children can use the other words around the word, or the context, to figure out the word's relevant meaning. Sometimes, children may need to use a dictionary. A dictionary lists all the different meanings that a word has. Each meaning has a number in front of it.

Guide practice

Write *roll.* Let's look up this word in the dictionary. *Roll* can mean "to move or cause to move by turning over and over." It can also mean "a small-sized loaf of bread usually round in shape."

Write the following words and have children use a dictionary to find two different meanings:

> **light:** 1. a lamp. 2. not heavy
>
> **fly:** 1. move through the air by wings. 2. an insect with one pair of wings
>
> **waves:** 1. moves up and down. 2. curving ridges of water along the surface of a lake or ocean
>
> **rattle:** 1. to make sharp knocking sounds. 2. a baby's toy that makes noise when shaken

Discuss the meanings. Have children use the words in sentences that show the word's relevant meaning.

On their own

Team Talk Have partners use a dictionary to find multiple meanings for the following words and use the words in sentences: *chip, stand, track, file.*

Main Selection— Second Read
The Night the Moon Fell

Review
Draw conclusions

Recall this week's main selection, *The Night the Moon Fell.* Tell children that today they will read the story again. Remind children that good readers **draw conclusions** as they read. Explain that to draw a conclusion, you must think about facts and details in the story and decide something about them using prior knowledge and experiences. Explain that drawing conclusions about the characters and story events can help readers better understand the story. For more practice on drawing conclusions, see Let's Practice It! p. 208 on the *Teacher Resource DVD-ROM.*

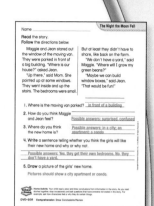

Let's Practice It!
TR DVD • 208

Review
Genre: myth

Let's Read Remind children that a myth is a made-up story that tries to explain something that happens in nature. Have children identify what events in nature are explained in the story. (why the moon disappears sometimes; how the Milky Way came to be)

Set a purpose

Remind children that good readers read for a purpose. Guide children to set a new purpose for reading *The Night the Moon Fell* today, perhaps to consider how Luna and her new friends work together to solve Luna's problem.

Extend thinking

Tell children they will now read *The Night the Moon Fell* for the seond time. Use the Day 3 Extend Thinking notes to encourage children to use higher-order thinking skills to go beyond the details of the selection.

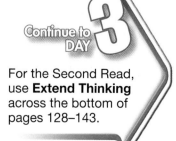

Second Read

For the Second Read, use **Extend Thinking** across the bottom of pages 128–143.

Differentiated Instruction

SI Strategic Intervention

Review Genre If children have difficulty identifying events in nature that this myth attempts to explain, ask them how and why Luna's shape changes during the story and have them compare that to what they see in the night sky. Then display a picture of the Milky Way in the night sky. Have them compare this band of stars to a school of tiny fish swimming in the sea.

Lesson Vocabulary

balance footing; even placement of weight that lets someone stand upright

canyons deep valleys with steep sides

coral an underwater stony substance made by marine life

rattle make sharp knocking sounds as a result of being shaken

slivers small thin pieces of something that have been split off

sway to swing slowly from one side to the other

whisper make a soft sound

Academic Vocabulary

draw conclusions arrive at decisions or opinions after thinking about facts and details and using prior knowledge

Objectives

- Retell a narrative.
- Identify plot events of a myth.
- Visualize story events.
- Identify the lesson of a myth.
- Write clear, coherent sentences.

Check Retelling
SUCCESS PREDICTOR

Objectives
- Identify themes in well-known fables, legends, myths, or stories.
- Read by yourself for a period of time and paraphrase what you read.
- Check your understanding and make corrections when you do not understand what you are reading.

Envision It! Retell

READING STREET ONLINE
STORY SORT
www.ReadingStreet.com

144

Think Critically

1. What does the moon look like in the sky? How does it change? Text to World

2. Why do you think the author retells this myth? What lesson does the author want to teach? Think Like an Author

3. What happens when Luna returns to the sky at the end of the myth? Plot and Theme

4. Tell what you see when you read about Luna falling from the sky to the sea. Visualize

5. **Look Back and Write** Look back at pages 136–138. What do the little fish do to help Luna return to the sky? Provide evidence to support your answer.

TEST PRACTICE Extended Response

Meet the Illustrator
Domi

Domi is a Mazatec Indian from Mexico. She uses many native traditions in her art.

At a young age, she watched her aunts weave native clothing. At night, she practiced on her own, creating brightly colored patterns. When she was 20, she first tried painting. She painted colorful figures on a wall in her living room.

Domi feels that art is extremely important in our day-to-day lives. "You must paint, dance, do something creative so that you can stay healthy."

Read two more books illustrated by Domi.

Napi Goes to the Mountain

The Race of Toad and Deer

Use the Reader's and Writer's Notebook to record your independent reading.

145

Student Edition pp. 144–145

Retelling

Envision It! Have children work in pairs, retelling the story to one another. Remind children to include the characters, setting, and events from the beginning, middle, and end of the story. Children should use the retelling strip in the Student Edition as they retell. Monitor children's retelling.

Scoring rubric

Top-Score Response A top-score response makes connections beyond the text, elaborates on the author's purpose, and describes in detail the characters, setting, and plot.

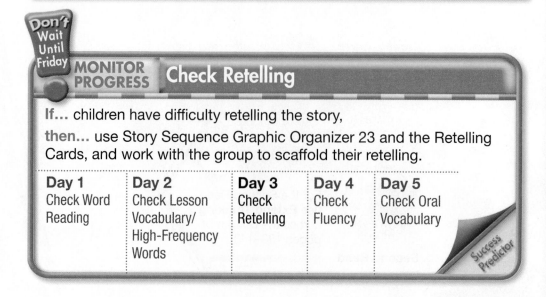

Don't Wait Until Friday

MONITOR PROGRESS Check Retelling

If... children have difficulty retelling the story,

then... use Story Sequence Graphic Organizer 23 and the Retelling Cards, and work with the group to scaffold their retelling.

Day 1	Day 2	Day 3	Day 4	Day 5
Check Word Reading	Check Lesson Vocabulary/ High-Frequency Words	Check Retelling	Check Fluency	Check Oral Vocabulary

Success Predictor

Think Critically

Text to World

1. Possible response: The moon sometimes looks like a large, white sphere in the sky. Its shape appears to change during the month from no moon, to a crescent moon, to a half moon, to a full moon, and then back again.

Think Like an Author

2. Possible response: The author retells this myth because it is a beautiful story that tells how to deal with change. The author teaches us that friends can comfort us when we face change and give us the help and confidence needed to deal with it.

Plot and Theme

3. When Luna returns to the sky, the tiny fish come with her. Her white light changes the night sky. The stars begin to shine, the wind blows, flowers lift their heads, and birds fly and then fall asleep.

Visualize

4. Possible response: I see Luna rolling like a large, white ball past stars and through clouds and then crashing down into the sea where she smashes into hundreds of silvery pieces just like a broken mirror.

 Writing on Demand

5. **Look Back and Write** For writing fluency, assign a five-minute time limit. As children finish, encourage them to reread their response and proofread for errors.

Scoring rubric

> **Top-Score Response** A top-score response uses details from the text to describe what the fish do to help Luna return to the sky. For example:
>
> The fish help Luna return to the night sky. First, they use their fins to gather up bits of the moon. After Luna rolls herself into a ball again, the fish patch and smooth her with their fins. Then they use their scales as glue to hold the pieces together.

Meet the illustrator

Read aloud page 145 as children follow along. Ask children why Domi feels that art is important.

On their own

Use p. 335 in the *Reader's and Writer's Notebook* for additional practice with plot and theme.

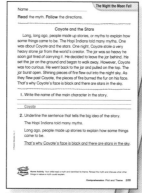

Reader's and Writer's Notebook p. 335

Differentiated Instruction

A Advanced

Look Back and Write Ask children who show proficiency with the writing prompt to explain how they believe Luna's experience may have changed her.

 INTERACT with TEXT

Strategy Response Log

Genre Have children revisit p. RR25 in their *Reader's and Writer's Notebook* where they identified characteristics of a myth. After reading the story, have them add examples of these characteristics that they found in *The Night the Moon Fell*.

Plan to Assess Retelling

☐ Week 1: Strategic Intervention

☐ Week 2: Advanced

☐ Week 3: Strategic Intervention

☑ This week assess On-Level children.

☐ Week 5: Strategic Intervention

☐ Week 6: Assess any children you have not yet checked during this unit.

145a

Retelling

Success Predictor

Objectives
- Understand and use adverbs that tell when and where in writing and speaking.
- Understand and use time-order adverbs in writing and speaking.
- Write a draft of a narrative poem.

Conventions
Adverbs That Tell When and Where

Review
Adverbs that tell when and where

Remind children that an adverb is a word that tells more about a verb. Adverbs can tell when or where something happens. Adverbs can also signal time order. _Before_ school, we wait _here_ for the bus.

Guide practice

Write this sentence on the board, have children read it aloud, and identify the adverbs that tell when or where something happens or signal time order. (inside, then, outside)

We will eat inside and then go outside to play.

What other adverbs could we use in place of _inside_, _then_, and _outside_?

Team Talk Have children say the sentence using their adverbs. Then have children write two sentences using adverbs.

Connect to oral language

Have children complete these sentence frames orally using adverbs that tell when or where or signal time order.

1. The meeting will be held _____.

2. Please put your books _____.

3. _____ put on your socks and then put on your shoes.

On their own

Use Let's Practice It! p. 211 on the _Teacher Resource DVD-ROM_.

Let's Practice It!
TR DVD•211

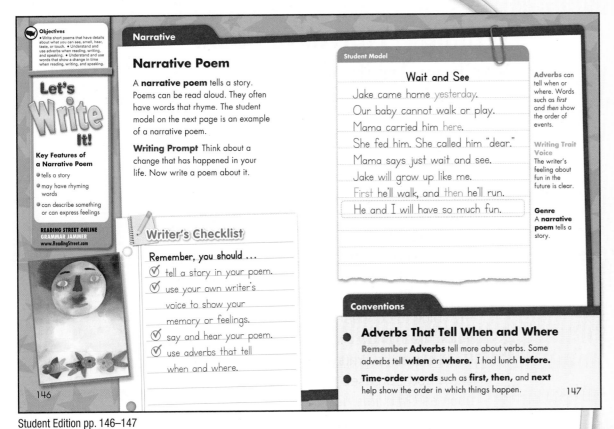

Student Edition pp. 146–147

5. Did you here that noise.
   Did you <u>hear</u> that noise<u>?</u>

6. A wave destroy my
   sandcastle
   A wave destroy<u>ed</u> my
   sandcastle<u>.</u>

Discuss the Daily Fix-It corrections with children. Review the spelling of homophones *here* and *hear,* sentence punctuation, and verbs ending in *-ed.*

Let's Write It!

Teach

Use pp. 146–147 in the Student Edition. Read aloud the Key Features of a Narrative Poem and the definition of a narrative poem. Help children better understand the Writing Prompt by reading it aloud and by discussing the Writer's Checklist.

Review the student model

Then read "Wait and See" on page 147 to children. Point out one set of rhyming words: *yesterday* and *play.* Ask children to identify other rhyming words in the poem. Read aloud and briefly discuss the side notes about Genre, the Writing Trait, adverbs that tell when and where, and time-order words.

Scoring rubric

Top-Score Response Help children understand that a top-score response is an interesting story about change. It follows a logical sequence and clearly shows the author's feelings about the topic. The lines are smooth and may contain rhyming words. For a complete rubric see Writing Rubric 19 from the *Teacher Resource DVD-ROM.*

Connect to conventions

Read to children the Conventions note about Adverbs That Tell When and Where and Time-order words.

Objectives
• Write a draft of a narrative poem.
• Recognize and use voice in writing.
• Gather information.

Writing—Narrative Poem
Writing Trait: Voice

MINI-LESSON

Use Voice and Sensory Details

■ **Introduce** Use your story sequence chart from yesterday and Writing Transparency 19A to model how writers use voice. When I wrote my poem, I used my story sequence chart to help me organize my poem. I also tried to use my voice to connect with readers. In writing, **voice** means how a writer feels about a subject. Read aloud the draft on the Transparency to show how you used voice. Point out examples such as *I'm a little nervous,* and *I want to be cool.* Point out details that appeal to the sense of sight: *Now I see. It's [the bus] almost half full.* Then talk about how you used rhyme.

A New School

Thrid grade. First day of skool.
I'm a little nervous i want to be cool.
Here comes the bus. Now I see.
It's almost half full. Will the other kids like me.
I see some kids I know, and others I do'nt.
I smile and say "Hi." I won't be shy. I won't.
a new school is scary, exciting fun!
And I'll be finished with day number won.

Writing Transparency 19A
TR DVD

■ Explain how children can use their story sequence charts to draft their poem. Discuss how they can improve voice.
• Use details that appeal to the senses.
• Use words that clearly show your feelings about the topic.
• Use punctuation marks to show how you feel.
Today's goal is to write the poem but not to rewrite each word perfectly. They can edit later to correct the words.

Guide poem writing   Now it is time to write your poem about a change in your life. Have children use their story sequence chart. Help them organize their ideas. Guide children as they draft the narrative poems.

ROUTINE Quick Write for Fluency   Team Talk

1) **Talk** Have partners talk about how they can use voice in their poems.
2) **Write** Each child writes a line of their poem that shows their feelings.
3) **Share** Partners point out how the line could show feelings clearly by adding or changing words or punctuation marks.

Routines Flip Chart

Research and Inquiry
Gather and Record Information

Teach

Tell children that today they will answer the questions from Day 1. Their goal is to find out why some changes are difficult.

Model

Think Aloud Display the list of questions that the class created on Day 1. We asked questions about difficult changes. Now let's answer the questions. I'm interested in what kinds of changes are difficult. We can use what we know and what we've read to help answer that question. Ask the question, and have children give answers. Record the answers next to the question.

Guide practice

Have pairs ask or answer one of the inquiry questions. Explain that tomorrow they will review their topic and make sure all of their questions have been answered.

Topic: Why Some Changes Are Difficult	
Question	**Answer**
What kinds of changes are difficult?	moving to a new home, getting a baby brother

Wrap Up Your Day

✔ **Plot and Theme** What is the "big idea" of *The Night the Moon Fell?* (Some changes are difficult.) *Plot* is what happens in the beginning, middle, and end of the story. Who helped Luna feel better in the middle of the story while she was in the ocean? (The fish helped her.)

✔ **Visualizing** As you read, you can visualize, or picture things in your mind. Visualizing can help you understand what you read. What did you visualize as you read *The Night the Moon Fell?*

Differentiated Instruction

SI **Strategic Intervention**

Alternate Answers If children do not want to share difficult changes in their lives, have them think of characters they have read about that went through difficult times. Have the children ask and answer the questions with that character in mind.

Academic Vocabulary

voice how a writer feels about a subject

Preview DAY 4

Tell children that tomorrow they will read another story about changes.

Objectives
- Discuss the concept to develop oral language.
- Build oral vocabulary.
- Identify details in text.

Today at a Glance

Oral Vocabulary
accent, forlorn

Phonics and Spelling
Review Diphthongs *ou, ow, oi, oy*

High-Frequency Words
Review

Comprehension
◉ Summarize

Fluency
Read with Expression

Conventions
Adverbs That Tell When and Where

Writing
Narrative Poem

Listening and Speaking
Describe Media Techniques

Research and Inquiry
Review and Revise Topic

Concept Talk

Question of the Week
Why are some changes difficult?

Build concepts

To reinforce concepts and to focus children's attention, have children sing "We Are Moving" from the *Sing with Me* Big Book. What is a landmark in your neighborhood that would serve as a guide to newcomers? (Possible response: The post office and the library are landmarks. The park and the playground are landmarks.)

 Sing with Me Big Book Audio

Review
Genre: narrative poem

Discuss the key features of a **narrative poem:** It can be humorous or dramatic. It usually has a regular rhyme and rhythm. It has carefully chosen words arranged in lines. It includes the story elements of character, setting, plot and theme. Explain that today children will hear about a boy named Lazlo who must adjust to a difficult change in "The Brand New Kid" by Katie Couric.

Read Aloud Anthology
"The Brand New Kid"

Monitor listening comprehension

Recall how Luna experienced a difficult change when she found herself in a new place in *The Night the Moon Fell.* Have children listen to "The Brand New Kid" to find out what happens when Lazlo moves to a new place. Read the narrative poem.

ELL Produce Oral Language Use the Day 4 instruction on ELL Poster 19 to extend and enrich language.

Oral Vocabulary
Amazing Words

Teach Amazing Words

> **Amazing Words** **Oral Vocabulary Routine**
>
> **1) Introduce the Word** Relate the word *forlorn* to the narrative poem. Lazlo's mother had tears in her eyes and she seemed *forlorn*. Supply a child-friendly definition. If someone is *forlorn*, the person is lonely and sad. Have children say the word.
>
> **2) Demonstrate** Provide examples to show meaning. Some campers were *forlorn* on their first day away from home. The lost puppy looked *forlorn*. Grandma looked *forlorn* as she waved good-bye to us.
>
> **3) Apply** Have children demonstrate their understanding. Describe a time when you felt *forlorn*.
>
> See p. OV•1 to teach *accent*.

Routines Flip Chart

Anchored Talk

Add to the concept map

Discuss why some changes are difficult.

- In "The Brand New Kid," Lazlo's family has moved to a new place. What difficult change does Lazlo have to adjust to? (He must adjust to a new school.) Changing schools is difficult. We can add this idea to our map.

- Why do you think it's difficult to change schools? (Possible response: No one knows what you are like. You don't know anyone.) These are important ideas to add to our map.

- Why was it difficult for Lazlo to make friends at his new school? (Possible response: Lazlo looked different and he spoke with an accent.) Sometimes children make fun of new kids if they look or speak differently. Then it's hard to make friends. We'll add this to our map.

Amazing Words

adjust	tease
landmark	foreign
unexpected	accent
quiver	forlorn

Differentiated Instruction

SI Strategic Intervention
Amazing Words Have children draw pictures to show the meaning of the word *forlorn*. Have children share the pictures and discuss how they might help to change the situation pictured.

English Language Learners
Frontload Comprehension
Use a concept web to help children discover or recall what it is like to change schools. Write "Changing Schools is Difficult" in the center oval. Add spokes as children discuss how they made new friends, found their way around the building, learned the language, and gained understanding of school customs.

DAY 4 Get Ready to Read

Objectives

- Read and identify words with vowel sound /ou/ spelled *ou, ow* and /oi/ spelled *oi, oy.*
- Read words fluently in context and independent of context.

Phonics Review
Diphthongs *ou, ow, oi, oy*

Review Sound-spellings

To review last week's phonics skill, write *found, cow, soil,* and *toy.* You studied words like these last week. What do you know about the vowel sounds in these words? (The vowels in *found* and *cow* have the sound /ou/ spelled with *ou* and *ow,* and the vowels in *soil* and *toy* have the sound /oi/ spelled *oi* and *oy.*)

Corrective feedback

If children are unable to answer the question about diphthongs *ou, ow, oi,* and *oy,* refer them to Sound-Spelling Cards 94, 98, 88, and 100.

Guide practice

Write the *ou, ow, oi,* and *oy* words from the chart below on cards. Then write *ou, ow, oi,* and *oy* as headings in a four-column chart. Tell children they will be sorting words. Show *enjoy.* How many syllables are in this word? (2) What are they? (en joy) What's the word? (enjoy). What is the spelling for /oi/? (oy). Write the word in the appropriate column.

Distribute the remaining word cards to children. Have them blend and combine meaningful word parts to read their words before they place their cards under the appropriate heading. Monitor children's work and provide feedback. Have children copy the completed chart and circle the sound-spellings that stand for the sounds /ou/ and /oi/.

ou	ow	oi	oy
crouch	crowd	choices	enjoy
outfit	towel	oily	annoy
count	plow	checkpoint	oyster
surround	powder	rejoice	soybean
flour	tower	spoil	boyhood

On their own

Use Let's Practice It! p. 207 on the *Teacher Resource DVD–ROM.*

Let's Practice It!
TR DVD•207

Fluent Word Reading
Spiral Review

Read words independent of context

Display these words. Tell children they can blend or chunk some words on this list, and others are Word Wall words.

Have children read the list three or four times until they can read at the rate of two to three seconds per word.

school	summer	booklet	Shannon	raincoat
closer	put	move	David	bulldog
friend	oatmeal	pretty	good	downstream
rowboat	pilot	lookout	love	pull

Word Reading

Corrective feedback

If...children have difficulty reading whole words,
then...have them blend or combine word parts for decodable words or have them say and spell high-frequency words.
If...children cannot read fluently at a rate of two to three seconds per word,
then...have pairs practice the list until they can read it fluently.

Read words in context

Display these sentences. Call on individuals to read a sentence. Then randomly point to review words and have children read them. To help you monitor word reading, high-frequency words are underlined and decodable words are italicized.

My <u>friend</u> read a *booklet* on how to become a *good pilot*.

<u>Move</u> the *rowboat closer* to the *lookout* point *downstream*.

The *bulldogs* <u>love</u> to *pull* on their leashes.

David had *oatmeal* and a *mug* of milk before <u>school</u>.

In the *summer* storm *Shannon put* on a <u>pretty</u> *raincoat*.

Sentence Reading

Corrective feedback

If...children are unable to read an underlined high-frequency word,
then...read the word for them and spell it, having them echo you.
If...children have difficulty reading an italicized decodable word,
then...guide them in blending or combining word parts.

Differentiated Instruction

SI Strategic Intervention

Similar Sounds Write the words from the list that have the /u̇/ sound as in *pull* and the short *u* sound as in *mug*. Have students echo read those words until they can hear the difference in vowel sounds.

Spiral Review

These activities review
- previously taught high-frequency words *friend, love, move, pretty, school.*
- syllable patterns.
- vowels *oo, u /u̇/.*
- short *u.*

ELL

English Language Learners
Fluent Word Reading Have children listen to a more fluent reader model the words or have pairs read the words together.

Objectives

- Apply knowledge of sound-spellings and word parts to decode unknown words when reading.
- Decode and read words in context and independent of context.
- Practice fluency with oral rereading.

Decodable Practice Reader 19C
Syllable Patterns

Decode words independent of context

Have children turn to the first page and decode each word.

Read high-frequency words

Have children identify and read the high-frequency words *clear, several, wide, street,* and *music* on the first page.

Preview Decodable Reader

Have children read the title and preview the story. Tell them they will use syllable patterns to decode two-syllable words containing vowel digraphs and diphthongs.

Decode words in context

Pair children for reading, and listen as they decode. One child begins. Children read the entire story, switching readers after each page. Partners reread the story. This time the other child begins.

Decodable Practice Reader 19C

Corrective feedback

If... children have difficulty decoding a word, **then...** refer them to the Sound-Spelling Cards to identify the sounds in a decodable word; prompt them to blend the word. If the word is a compound word, tell children to chunk the word and say the parts of the word, first separately and then together.

- What is the new word?
- Is the new word a word you know?
- Does it make sense in the story?

Check decoding and comprehension

Have children retell the story to include characters, setting, and events. Then have children find two-syllable words containing at least one vowel digraph or diphthong. Children should supply *oatmeal, raincoat, townhouse, downtown, soybeans, seaweed,* and *rainbows*.

Reread for Fluency

Have children reread Decodable Practice Reader 19C to develop automaticity decoding words with syllable patterns containing vowel digraph/diphthong combinations.

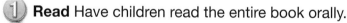

ROUTINE **Oral Rereading**

① **Read** Have children read the entire book orally.

② **Reread** To achieve optimal fluency, children should reread the text three or four times.

③ **Corrective Feedback** Listen as children read. Provide corrective feedback regarding their fluency and decoding.

Routines Flip Chart

English Language Learners
Syllable Patterns
Beginning Preview the story through a picture walk. Point out items in the pictures and say their names. If the name appears on the page, point to the word, say it again, and have children repeat it.

Intermediate Write these words on the board: *downtown, rainbows, townhouse, raincoat, seaweed, oatmeal, soybeans.* Go through the words one at a time and have children locate the words in the story. Then have them read the sentence that contains each word.

Advanced/Advanced-High
Write these words on cards: *downtown, rainbows, townhouse, raincoat, seaweed, oatmeal, soybeans.* Cut them in half between the two smaller words that make up the compound word. Have children put the words together to make words that were used in the story. Then ask them to identify the vowel digraphs and diphthongs in the words.

Objectives
- Spell words with syllable patterns.
- Spell high-frequency words.
- Recognize the elements and purposes of an e-mail.
- Relate prior knowledge to new text.
- Set purpose for reading.

Spelling
Syllable Patterns

Partner Review

Supply pairs of children with index cards on which the spelling words have been written. Have one child read a word while the other writes it. Then have children switch roles. Have them use the cards to check their spelling and correct any misspelled words.

On their own

Use Let's Practice It! p. 210 on the *Teacher Resource DVD-ROM*.

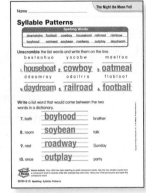

Let's Practice It!
TR DVD•210

Small Group Time

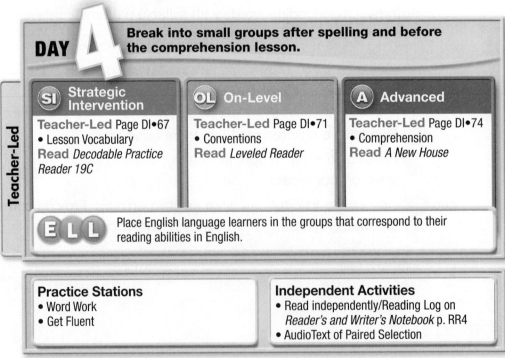

DAY 4 Break into small groups after spelling and before the comprehension lesson.

SI Strategic Intervention
Teacher-Led Page DI•67
- Lesson Vocabulary
Read Decodable Practice Reader 19C

OL On-Level
Teacher-Led Page DI•71
- Conventions
Read Leveled Reader

A Advanced
Teacher-Led Page DI•74
- Comprehension
Read A New House

ELL Place English language learners in the groups that correspond to their reading abilities in English.

Practice Stations
- Word Work
- Get Fluent

Independent Activities
- Read independently/Reading Log on Reader's and Writer's Notebook p. RR4
- AudioText of Paired Selection

E-Mail

Academic Vocabulary

e-mail an electronic message sent from one computer to another over the Internet

21st Century Skill: e-mail

Explain that **e-mail** is short for "electronic mail." An e-mail message is sent from one computer to another over the Internet. An e-mail is like a letter, but it is addressed and sent in a different way.

Strategy: Summarize

Point out that good readers summarize an e-mail message by telling the most important information in the e-mail in a logical sequence, or order.

Preview and predict

Read the title and the first paragraph of the selection on pages 148–151 of the Student Edition. Have children look through the selection and predict what they might learn. (Possible response: They might learn how to write and send an e-mail.) Ask them what clues helped them make that prediction. (Possible response: Key words in the last sentence of the first paragraph tell the topic; the diagram identifies e-mail options, the heading tells that the text will describe how to send an e-mail.)

Genre

E-mail Review the key features of an e-mail: an e-mail is an electronic mail message. Rather than sending the message by the postal service, an e-mail is instantly sent from one computer to another over the Internet. To send an e-mail, you must have the recipient's e-mail address and a computer with Internet access. As they read this selection, children will learn to identify various written conventions used when sending and receiving e-mails.

Activate prior knowledge

Ask children if they have ever sent or received an e-mail and have them describe the experience. Explain that in this selection, they will learn more about how to write and send their own e-mail.

Set a purpose

As children read, have them pay attention to the different parts of an e-mail message and how to write each part.

Objectives

- Summarize important ideas in an e-mail message.
- Identify the parts of an e-mail message.

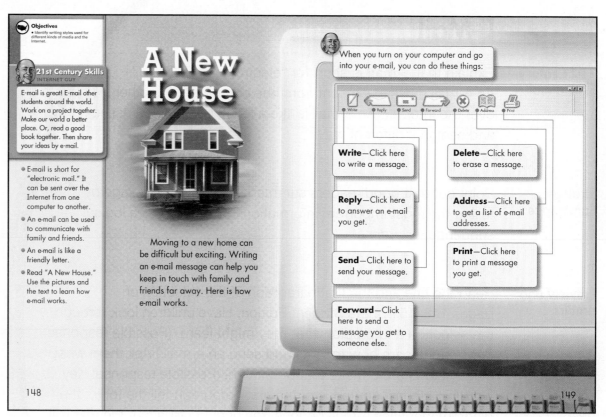

Student Edition pp. 148–149

Guide Comprehension
Summarize

Guide practice

Think Aloud Good readers look for important ideas as they read so they can summarize a story or a selection. When I finished reading *The Night the Moon Fell*, I recalled that the fish in the sea helped the moon by finding her pieces and patching her together. I will pay attention to the important ideas found in the explanatory text and the e-mail message as I read "A New House."

E-mail messages

Think Aloud I think about the title of this selection—"A New House." I wonder what an e-mail has to do with moving to a new house. I read that e-mail messages are a good way to stay in touch with family and friends when you move to a new home. That makes sense because I know that an e-mail is like a friendly letter than you can send anyplace in the world. This makes e-mail a great way to keep in touch with faraway friends and family members.

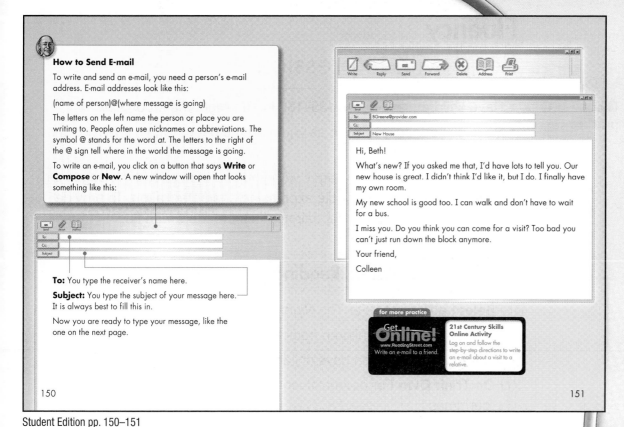

Social Studies Vocabulary

e-mail an electronic message sent from one computer to another over the Internet

Internet a worldwide system of interconnected computer networks

e-mail address a location to which e-mail messages can be delivered. It consists of the user's name followed by the @ symbol and the domain name.

Guide Comprehension, continued

Author's Purpose What is the purpose of this selection? (The author's purpose is to teach readers what an e-mail is and provide instructions on how to write and send an e-mail message.)

E-mail Conventions Review the written conventions for using e-mail described on page 150. Where is Beth's e-mail address in this sample e-mail? (in the "To" area) How is this a typical e-mail address? (It has "@" and ".com" in it.) What is the subject of the message? (New House)

Sequence What do you do after you type the recipient's e-mail address? (You type the topic of your message in the Subject line.)

Summarize How would you summarize the important ideas in Colleen's e-mail message? (Colleen likes her new house and her new school, but she misses Beth, a friend from her old neighborhood, and wants her to visit.)

Get Online! Begin the activity by logging on to the site listed in the Student Edition. Have children follow the directions to search for Internet sites in a protected environment.

Objectives
• Read aloud fluently with expression.
• Understand and use adverbs that tell when and where.
• Understand and use time-order transition words.

Check Fluency WCPM
SUCCESS PREDICTOR

Fluency
Read with Expression

Guide practice

• Have children turn to pp. 135–136 in *The Night the Moon Fell*.

• Have children follow along as you read the pages with expression that captures characterization.

• Have the class read the pages with you and then reread the pages as a group until they read while expressing characterization. To provide additional fluency practice, pair nonfluent readers with fluent readers.

ROUTINE **Paired Reading**

1️⃣ **Select a Passage** For *The Night the Moon Fell*, use pp. 140-141.

2️⃣ **Model** First, have children track the print as you read.

3️⃣ **Guide Practice** Then have children read along with you.

4️⃣ **On Their Own** For optimal fluency, have partners reread three or four times.

Routines Flip Chart

 Don't Wait Until Friday

MONITOR PROGRESS **Check Fluency WCPM**

As children reread, monitor their progress toward their individual fluency goals. Current Goal: 62–72 words correct per minute. End-of-Year-Goal: 90 words correct per minute.

If... children cannot read fluently at a rate of 62–72 words correct per minute,
then... have children practice with text at their independent level.

Day 1	Day 2	Day 3	Day 4	Day 5
Check Word Reading	Check Lesson Vocabulary/ High-Frequency Words	Check Retelling	Check Fluency	Check Oral Vocabulary

 Success Predictor

Conventions
Adverbs That Tell When and Where

Test practice
Use *Reader's and Writer's Notebook* p. 336 to help children recognize and use adverbs that tell when or where or signal time order. Model recognizing adverbs by writing this sentence on the board, reading it aloud, and underlining the adverbs.

We <u>always</u> go <u>inside</u> before dark.

Then read the *Reader's and Writer's Notebook* p. 336 directions. Guide children as they mark the answer for number 1.

On their own
Use *Reader's and Writer's Notebook* p. 336.

Connect to oral language
After children mark the answers to numbers 1–6, review the correct choices aloud, and have children read each sentence aloud. Have them identify each adverb and if it tells when or where or signals time order.

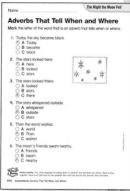

Reader's and Writer's Notebook p. 336

Differentiated Instruction

 Advanced

WCPM If children already read at 90 words correct per minute, allow them to read independently.

Fluency Assessment Plan

Do a formal fluency assessment with 8 to 10 children every week. Assess 4 to 5 children on Day 4, and 4 to 5 children on Day 5. Use the fluency passage, Teacher's Edition, p. 153f.

Options for Oral Rereading

Use *The Night the Moon Fell* or one of the week's Decodable Practice Readers.

Daily Fix-It

7. a good friend is loial.
<u>A</u> good friend is <u>loyal</u>.

8. Did dee make that sound.
Did <u>Dee</u> make that sound<u>?</u>

Discuss the Daily Fix-It corrections with children. Review the capitalization of sentences and proper nouns, sentence punctuation, and the vowel diphthong *oy*.

Success Predictor

Objectives

- Evaluate graphics to identify facts and opinions.
- Follow rules for discussion, including listening and making appropriate contributions.
- Review answers to inquiry questions.
- Revise topics.

Media Literacy
Describe Media Techniques

Teach media techniques

Tell children that good users of media know how to identify, describe, and evaluate graphics used in different types of media.

- A **graphic** is a visual presentation, such as a picture, an illustration, a photo, a map, or a graphic organizer. A graphic could be a mural on a wall. It could also be a photo or diagram in a book, magazine, or newspaper, or a video on a TV, movie screen, or the Internet.

- Graphics convey information. Sometimes this information is factual and can be proven. Sometimes this information expresses opinions, which are a person's thoughts or beliefs about something. Sometimes graphics can present misleading information.

- Good users of media think carefully about the type of information presented in a graphic. They are on the lookout for misleading information, and they are careful to separate facts from opinions.

Model

Use the passage below to model identifying and evaluating graphics.

Think Aloud When I read magazines and newspapers, I see many graphics in the articles. As I look at the pictures and photos, I ask myself what information is being presented in these graphics. In thinking about these images, I also ask myself what has been left out. If the same story is being covered on television or on the Internet, I compare the different images that the creators of those stories used when presenting the information.

Guide practice

Divide children into groups. Have children within the group gather diverse media resources, such as newspapers, magazines, books, Internet downloads, and DVDs on the same topic, such as an event in nature. Have children examine the graphics used to communicate information in each media format. Then have them work together to identify facts, opinions, or misleading information conveyed by the graphics.

On their own

Pair small groups and have each group explain to the other what they learned about how graphics communicate a message to viewers. Remind them to focus on specific examples of facts, opinions, and misleading information they found in their examination of graphics and to speak clearly at an understandable pace using the conventions of language.

Research and Inquiry
Review and Revise Topic

Teach

Tell children that the next step in their inquiry project is to review the topic to see if they have the information they set out to find. Or, did their answers lead to a different topic?

Model

We planned to find out about why some changes are difficult changes. Display the list of inquiry questions and the answers recorded. First, I asked, "What kinds of changes are difficult?" Some answers are moving to a new neighborhood and getting a new brother. These give me good examples and ideas about why a change might be difficult. So we have answered our original topic, and it does not need to change.

Guide practice

Read the other inquiry question and answers. After each answer is read, have children turn to a partner to discuss whether or not the answer gives information about difficult changes. Note any new questions the children have and revise the original topic if necessary. Finally, tell children that tomorrow they will organize all the information in order to share it with others.

Wrap Up Your Day

✔ **Phonics** Write these words: *tiger, pencil, frozen,* and *cowboy*. Have children read the words and show how to divide the word into syllables. (*ti ger, pen cil, fro zen, cow boy*)

✔ **Fluency** Display *Roy and his boyhood friend from school rowed downstream to a local park for a picnic.* Have children read the sentence three or four times until they can do so fluently.

Differentiated Instruction

 Strategic Intervention

Adjusting the Topic If children have a difficult time with the concept of change, rephrase the inquiry by asking, "What might happen that is new or different?"

 Advanced

Time for Discussion If new questions arise after children report their answers, allow them time to discuss.

Preview DAY 5

Tell children that tomorrow they will hear more about a girl who changes her attitude toward the new kid.

Objectives
- Review the concept: some changes are difficult.
- Build oral vocabulary.
- Identify details in text.

Today at a Glance

Oral Vocabulary
Review

Phonics
◉ Review Syllable Patterns

Lesson Vocabulary
Review

Comprehension
Plot and Theme

Conventions
Adverbs That Tell When and Where

Writing
Narrative Poem

Research and Inquiry
Communicate

Check Oral Vocabulary
SUCCESS PREDICTOR

Concept Wrap Up

Question of the Week
Why are some changes difficult?

Review
Concept

This week we have read and listened to selections about why some changes are difficult. Today you will listen to find out what makes Lazlo's difficult change to a new school easier. Read the story.

- What makes Lazlo's change easier? (Possible response: Ellie makes friends with Lazlo and then Carrie does too.)

Review
Amazing Words

Orally review the meaning of this week's Amazing Words. Then display this week's concept map. Have children use Amazing Words such as *adjust, unexpected, tease,* and *foreign,* as well as the map, to answer the question, "Why are some changes difficult?"

Read Aloud Anthology
"The Brand New Kid"

Why are some changes difficult?

| Moving to a new place is difficult. | Growing older can be difficult. | Making new friends can be difficult. | Changing schools is difficult. |

You may feel sad and lost.

Waiting for new teeth to grow in is difficult.

Children sometimes tease.

No one knows what you are like.

You don't know your way around.

Children may make fun if you look or speak differently.

You don't know anyone.

You miss your old home.

ELL **Check Concepts and Language** Use the Day 5 instruction on ELL Poster 19 to monitor children's understanding of the lesson concept.

ELL Poster 19

Oral Vocabulary
Amazing Ideas

Connect to the Big Question

Team Talk Pair children and have them discuss how the Question of the Week connects to this unit's Big Question, "How do things change? How do they stay the same?" Tell children to use the concept map and what they've learned from this week's Anchored Talks and reading selections to form an Amazing Idea—a realization or "big idea" about **change.** Then ask each pair to share their Amazing Idea with the class. Amazing Ideas might include these key concepts:

- Changes like moving to a new place, growing older, making new friends, and changing schools are difficult.

- You can adjust to feeling lonely and missing your old home.

It's Friday

MONITOR PROGRESS | **Check Oral Vocabulary**

Call on individuals to use this week's Amazing Words to talk about why some changes are difficult. Prompt discussion with the questions below. Monitor children's ability to use Amazing Words and note which words children are unable to use.

- **How can *teasing* new kids make them feel *forlorn*?**
- **What would be difficult to *adjust* to in a *foreign* country?**
- **How can a *landmark* help us when we are lost in a new place?**
- **When someone speaks with an *accent,* what does it tell you about that person?**
- **What is something *unexpected* you might see at a new school?**
- **What might make your voice *quiver*?**

If... children have difficulty using the Amazing Words, **then...** reteach the unknown words using the Oral Vocabulary Routines, pp. 121a, 126b, 144b, 148b.

Day 1	Day 2	Day 3	Day 4	Day 5
Check Word Reading	Check Lesson Vocabulary/ High-Frequency Words	Check Retelling	Check Fluency	Check Oral Vocabulary

Success Predictor

Amazing Words

adjust	tease
landmark	foreign
unexpected	accent
quiver	forlorn

ELL

English Language Learners

Amazing Words Rephrase the questions and use facial expressions to help children understand the words. For example: Someone teases you. Show me how you feel. Have children show how they feel when they are teased. You feel forlorn. Have children repeat.

Objectives

◎ Review words with closed syllable patterns (VCCV) and open syllable patterns (VCV).

◎ Review multisyllabic words containing diphthongs and vowel digraphs.

Assess

• Spell multisyllabic words containing diphthongs and vowel digraphs.

• Spell high-frequency words.

Phonics
 Syllable Patterns

Review
Target phonics skill

Write the following sentences on the board. Have children read each one, first quietly to themselves and then aloud as you track the print.

> 1. Dad made meatloaf with gravy for dinner.
>
> 2. After the sudden thunderstorm, there was a pretty rainbow.
>
> 3. We can see a hundred miles from the lookout on the seacoast.
>
> 4. The hikers had a good outlook even though they were snowbound in a cabin.

Team Talk Have children discuss with a partner how they divided each multisyllabic word and what vowel sound each syllable has. Then call on individuals to share with the class.

Spelling Test
Syllable Patterns

Dictate spelling words

Say each word, read the sentence, repeat the word, and allow time for children to write the word.

1.	downstairs	We play **downstairs** in the family room.
2.	football	He ran 50 yards during the **football** game.
3.	cowboy	The **cowboy** always rode a gentle horse.
4.	houseboat	The view from the **houseboat** is beautiful.
5.	railroad	There are lights at the **railroad** crossing.
6.	rainbow	A **rainbow** is an arch of colors in the sky.
7.	boyhood	He had a happy **boyhood** living in the city.
8.	oatmeal	Mom makes **oatmeal** treats for snacks.
9.	soybean	People eat foods made from **soybeans**.
10.	roadway	The ice made the **roadway** slippery.
11.	outplay	No one could **outplay** our soccer team.
12.	daydream	She likes to **daydream** about getting a dog.

High-Frequency Words

13.	none	**None** of my friends can come now.
14.	hour	Can you meet me in an **hour?**

Differentiated Instruction

SI Strategic Intervention

Check Spelling Write each word on the board with the letters scrambled. Have children unscramble the letters to spell each word correctly.

A Advanced

Extend Spelling Have children arrange the list of spelling words in alphabetical order. Suggest that children compare their list with lists of others to check for accuracy.

Small Group Time

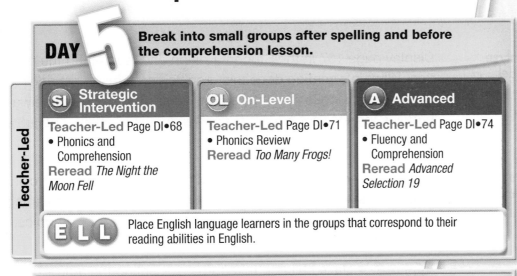

DAY 5 **Break into small groups after spelling and before the comprehension lesson.**

Teacher-Led

SI Strategic Intervention
Teacher-Led Page DI•68
• Phonics and Comprehension
Reread *The Night the Moon Fell*

OL On-Level
Teacher-Led Page DI•71
• Phonics Review
Reread *Too Many Frogs!*

A Advanced
Teacher-Led Page DI•74
• Fluency and Comprehension
Reread *Advanced Selection 19*

ELL Place English language learners in the groups that correspond to their reading abilities in English.

Practice Stations
• Words to Know
• Let's Write

Independent Activities
• Read independently/Reading Log on *Reader's and Writer's Notebook* p. RR4
• Concept Talk Video

English Language Learners
Match Syllable Patterns
Provide children with flashcards on which a part of each spelling compound word has been written. Have partners construct the compound words by matching word parts.

Objectives

- Describe media techniques.
- Identify the meaning of multiple-meaning words.
- Speak clearly at an appropriate rate.
- Listen attentively.
- Read aloud fluently with expression.

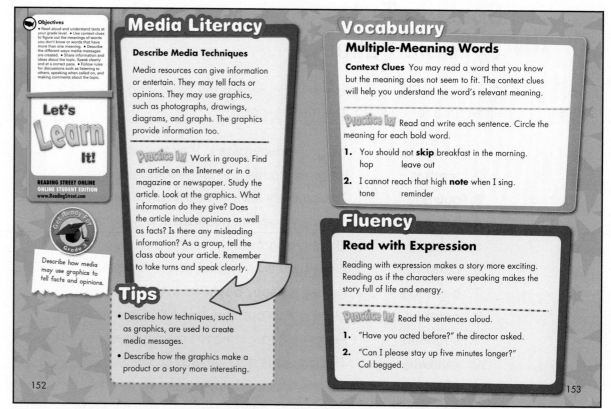

Student Edition pp. 152–153

Media Literacy
Describe Media Techniques

Teach

Read and discuss the Media Literacy lesson on page 152 of the Student Edition. Remind children that graphics provide facts or opinions about the topic of the media. Point out that the captions or labels of these graphics may contain adverbs that tell when or where.

Analyze model

Display page 107 in the Student Edition and read aloud the picture caption. What information does this graphic and caption provide? (It shows what clay soil looks like. It tells how water drains through clay and why puddles form.) What adverb tells when in this caption? (the adverb *often*)

Introduce prompt

Read the Media Literacy Practice It! prompt and the tips. Provide magazines, newspapers, or Internet access so children can find articles to analyze. Have them focus on information provided by graphics. Remind them to look for adverbs that tell when or where.

Team Talk Have children take turns presenting the article they analyzed to the whole class. Tell children that good speakers wait to speak until recognized and good listeners are able to tell several important ideas that the speaker presented.

Vocabulary
Multiple-Meaning Words

Teach

Have children turn to page 153 of the Student Edition. Read and discuss the Vocabulary lesson together. Explain how to use context clues to determine the relevant meaning of a multiple-meaning word.

Model

The word *play* can mean "to take part in a game" or "a story acted out on a stage." Write the sentence *We watched the actors in the play.* What is the meaning of *play* in this sentence? (a story acted out on a stage) What context clues helped you figure out the meaning? (the word *actors*)

Guide practice

Read the instructions for the Vocabulary Practice It! Activity. Read the first sentence and the meanings that follow. I will use context clues to figure out which meaning of *skip* is being used. This sentence is about a meal, so I think *skip* in this sentence means "leave out." After testing it in the sentence to see if it makes sense, I will circle the phrase *leave out*.

On their own

Have pairs identify the meaning of the word *note* in the second sentence.

Corrective feedback

Circulate around the room and listen as children use context clues to identify the relevant meaning. Provide assistance as needed.

Fluency
Expression

Teach

Read and discuss the Fluency instructions.

Read words in context

Give children a moment to look at the sentences. Then have them read each sentence three or four times until they can read each sentence with expression.

Differentiated Instruction

 SI Strategic Intervention

Analyze Articles To minimize problems with unfamiliar concepts and vocabulary, have children focus on one section of *Soil*, for example pp. 104–107. Have them tell how graphics affect their understanding of different types of soil and how the photos make the selection more interesting.

Describe Media Techniques

In addition to describing how media uses sound and graphics to tell facts and opinions, children at Grade 3 should also be able to explain how various design techniques used in media—for example, shape, color, or sound—influence the message.

ELL

English Language Learners
Fluency Provide alternative sentences that use familiar basic vocabulary for fluency practice, for example: "I don't want to go to bed," said Juan. "Look at that big bug!" said Inez. "Do you have your book?" Mom asked. Before children practice, discuss how the speaker probably feels in each sentence.

Objectives
- ◉ Identify the plot and theme of a story.
- • Read lesson vocabulary.
- • Identify moral lessons as themes.
- • Compare and contrast themes in literature across cultures.

Comprehension
🔄 Plot and Theme

Review
Plot and theme

Remember that all stories contain a plot and a theme. Good readers look for both to help them understand and remember what is happening in a story. What is the plot of a story? (a series of events put together to tell a story) What is the big idea of a story? (the theme) How can you figure out the story theme? (by thinking about the big idea that the plot suggests)

To check children's understanding of the story plot and theme, read aloud the following story and have children answer the questions that follow.

> Kathleen bit her lip and tried not to cry. Her mom promised that their new neighborhood had lots of kids, but she was sure they wouldn't compare to the friends she'd left behind. "We're here," said her mom as she brought the car to a halt in their new driveway. "Just look at the welcoming committee!" Kathleen peered out the window and saw a group of kids holding a big welcome sign. Maybe moving wouldn't be so bad after all.

1. What important events make up the story plot? (Kathleen feels sad because she's moving. Kathleen worries that the new kids she'll meet won't be as nice as her old friends. When they reach their new home, kids are waiting in the driveway to welcome her. Kathleen thinks that maybe moving to a new place won't be as bad as she thought.)

2. What is the theme, or big idea, of this story? (While moving brings many changes, it's possible to find good friends almost anyplace.)

Vocabulary
Lesson Vocabulary

Review
Lesson vocabulary

Write the words *balance, canyons, coral, rattle, slivers, sway,* and *whisper.* Have children answer these questions: *Could you get slivers from canyons? Would coral in the sea rattle? If you lost your balance would you sway back and forth? Would you whisper if you wanted to rattle the china?*

Corrective feedback

If... children cannot identify what the lesson vocabulary words mean, **then...** review the definitions on p. 144h.

Literary Text
Moral Lessons as Themes

Review
Moral lessons as themes

Review with children that the **theme** or "big idea" of a myth may be a moral lesson shared by the author with readers.

Teach

In addition to explaining an event in the natural world, a myth also has a moral lesson that teaches the difference between right and wrong or teaches an important value or behavior. Sometimes this moral lesson is stated directly at the end of the myth. Other times, good readers must analyze plot events to figure out the moral.

Model

 Think Aloud The selection *The Night the Moon Fell* is an example of a myth that contains a moral lesson. Plot events that help us figure out the moral include Luna plunging into the sea and breaking apart, the fish comforting her and giving her confidence, the fish helping her gather up her pieces, and the fish helping Luna patch herself together and return to her home in the sky.

Guide practice

Ask the following questions to guide children in identifying examples of moral lesson in this and other selections.

- What moral lesson do these plot events suggest about how friends can help in times of change? (Friends can comfort us and give us confidence to pull ourselves together.)

- Folk tales also contain moral lessons as themes. Think back to the Native American folk tale "Coyote and the Mice." How did the mice in this folk tale behave towards Coyote? (They were mean to him.) Why did they act this way? (They wanted to get back at him for all the tricks he had played.)

- How does this moral lesson differ from that in *The Night the Moon Fell*? (In "Coyote and the Mice" the moral is that others may hurt you if you hurt them. In *The Night the Moon Fell,* friends help each other.)

On their own

Have children work with a partner. Tell them to think about another folk tale or fable they have heard or read, identify the moral lesson, and compare it to the moral in *The Night the Moon Fell.* Possible choices for analysis and comparison include: *The Crow and the Pitcher, Anansi Goes Fishing,* and *One Good Turn Deserves Another.*

Differentiated Instruction

 **Strategic Intervention**

Moral Lessons To assist children in identifying the moral lesson found in another fable or folk tale, work with them to identify story elements in the selection using Graphic Organizer 10. Then have them use the completed chart to help them compare the theme or moral lesson with that found in *The Night the Moon Fell.*

Academic Vocabulary

moral the lesson or teaching of a fable or story

myth a story that attempts to explain something in nature

ELL

English Language Learners

Moral Lesson as Themes As you discuss plot events in *The Night the Moon Fell* that lead to the moral lesson, display illustrations in the myth that illustrate each of these events. Point out details in the art that show Luna breaking into parts on page 132, the fish helping Luna by gathering up bits of broken moon on page 136, the fish patching Luna on page 137, and the fish helping Luna return to her home on page 140. Have children use these examples to explain how the fish helped Luna deal with a big change in her life.

Assess

- ● Words with Closed Syllable Patterns (CVC) and Open Syllable Patterns (CV)
- ● Multisyllabic Words with Diphthongs and Vowel Digraphs
  - • Fluency: WCPM
- ● Plot and Theme

Fluency Goals

Set individual fluency goals for children to enable them to reach the end-of-the-year goal.

- • **Current Goal:** 62–72 WCPM
- • **End-of-Year Goal:** 90 WCPM

Assessment
Monitor Progress

For a written assessment of syllable patterns and plot and theme, use Weekly Test 19, pp. 109–114.

Assess words in context

Sentence reading Use the following reproducible page to assess children's ability to read words in context. Call on children to read two sentences aloud. Start over with sentence one if necessary.

> **MONITOR PROGRESS** — **Sentence Reading**
>
> **If...** children have trouble reading syllable patterns,
> **then...** use the Reteach Lesson in *First Stop*.
>
>

Assess

Fluency Take a one-minute sample of children's oral reading. Have children read the fluency passage on p. 153f.

Comprehension Have the child read the entire passage. (If the child had difficulty with the passage, you may read it aloud.) Then have the child identify the theme of the passage.

> **MONITOR PROGRESS** — **Fluency and Comprehension**
>
> **If...** a child does not achieve the fluency goal on the timed reading,
> **then...** copy the passage and send it home with the child for additional fluency practice, or have the child practice with a fluent reader.
>
> **If...** a child cannot identify the theme,
> **then...** use the Reteach Lesson in *First Stop*.
>
>

Monitor accuracy

Record scores Have children monitor their accuracy by recording their scores using the Sentence Reading Chart and by recording the number of words read correctly per minute on their Fluency Progress Chart in *First Stop*.

Read the Sentences

1. His boyhood was filled with daydreams of cowboys and horses.

2. Grace will bring baskets of oatmeal muffins for our bake sale.

3. The snowplow cleaned our playground when the winter storm ended.

4. We need plenty of space to download music we like.

5. The flavors and odors at the cookout made me lick my lips.

6. The baby held her stuffed rabbit made of pink velvet.

Reproducible Page. See also Assessment Handbook. © Pearson Education, Inc.

Name _____

Read the Story

Roy the Cowboy

Roy was a cowboy. He had one problem. He   9
could not eat much of the food that the other cowboys   20
ate. So, he ate soybeans.   25

In the morning, Roy ate fried soybeans. He had   34
boiled soybeans for lunch and mashed soybeans for   42
dinner. For snacks, he ate dry roasted soybeans.   50

One cowboy asked, "Roy, why do you eat so many   60
soybeans?"   61

"Well, I do not eat meat. I enjoy eating soybeans.   71
They are good for you, and they don't spoil in my   82
saddlebag."   83

But one day Roy did get tired of eating soybeans.   93
He wanted something else. So he tried oatmeal.   101

At first Roy liked the oatmeal. Then all Roy ate   111
was oatmeal, until he couldn't eat another bite.   119

Now Roy eats soybeans one day. The next day,   128
he eats oatmeal—just for something different.   135

Reproducible Page. See also Assessment Handbook. © Pearson Education, Inc.

MONITOR
PROGRESS
• Check Fluency
• Plot and Theme

Objectives
- Identify adverbs.
- Understand and use adverbs that tell when and where in writing and speaking.
- Understand and use time-order adverbs in writing and speaking.

Conventions
Adverbs That Tell When and Where

Review

Remind children that adverbs are words that tell about a verb. Adverbs can tell when or where something happens. Adverbs can also signal time order. Have children give examples of each type of adverb.

Guide practice

Write the following sentences. Have children complete each sentence by writing an adverb in the blank that tells when or where or signals time order.

> 1. The car is parked _____.
>
> 2. On rainy days we have recess _____.
>
> 3. First choose a book and _____ read it!

Connect to oral language

Display and read the following sentence frame. Have children work in pairs to name as many adverbs as they can to tell when and where the action takes place. Then have children share their responses with the class.

> _____, the family moved _____.

On their own

Use Let's Practice It! p. 212 on the *Teacher Resource DVD-ROM.*

Daily Fix-It

9. Sam collect baseball cards
   Sam <u>collects</u> baseball cards<u>.</u>
10. Did your team win the gam.
    Did your team win the <u>game?</u>

Discuss the Daily Fix-It corrections with children. Review sentence punctuation, subject-verb agreement, and long vowels VC*e.*

Let's Practice It!
TR DVD • 212

The Night the Moon Fell • **153g**

Objectives
- Edit a draft for spelling, punctuation, and capitalization.
- Create a final draft and present.

Writing—Narrative Poem
Writer's Craft: Rhyming Words

Review Revising Remind children that yesterday they revised their poems. They may have added sentences to show the writer's voice or sensory details. Today they will proofread their poems.

MINI-LESSON

Proofread for Rhyming Words and Adverbs

■ **Teach** When we proofread, we check to make sure the rhyming words and other words are spelled correctly. I can use a dictionary to check them. We also check for capital letters and punctuation. It's a good idea to check for just one thing at a time.

■ **Model** Let us look at my poem "A New School." Display Writing Transparency 19C. Explain that you will look at the correct spelling for rhyming words, adverbs, and other words. *Are my rhyming words spelled correctly?* Show how you would change misspellings. *Skool* and *cool* rhyme, but I see that *skool* is misspelled. *Fun* and *won* rhyme, but I see that *won* should be the number word *one.* Show how you would change those (*skool* to *school; won* to *one*) and other misspellings (*thrid* to *third; do'nt* to *don't*). I also see that I would like to add an adverb. I will add the word *soon* in the last line. Show how to insert *soon* between *And* and *I'll.* Model how you would change a letter at the beginning of a sentence if it were not capitalized or add an ending punctuation mark. Add a period after *nervous* and capitalize the *i* in the second line. Make other corrections as noted on the transparency.

Writing Transparency 19C
TR DVD

Teacher Note

Self-Evaluation Make copies of the Self-Evaluation form from the *Teacher Resource DVD-ROM,* and hand them out to children.

Proofread

Display the Proofreading Tips. Have children proofread their poems to correct any misspellings, missing capital letters, or errors with end punctuation. Remind children that their poems must be understandable to the reader. Circulate to assist children.

Proofreading Tips

✔ Are my rhyming words and other words spelled correctly? Check a dictionary.

✔ Did I use capital letters and punctuation correctly?

✔ Is my poem understandable to the reader?

Present

Have children make a final draft of their poem, with their revisions and proofreading corrections. Help as appropriate. Choose an option for children to present their poems.

Have children write their poems on lined paper and then tape the poem to a larger piece of construction paper. Have them decorate the border. Display the poem posters.	Have children practice reading their poems. Schedule a poetry reading where children take turns in "the poet's chair" and read their poems. If possible, record their readings for future listening.

When they have finished, help them complete a Self-Evaluation form.

ROUTINE **Quick Write for Fluency**  **Team Talk**

1) **Talk** Have children talk about some smaller changes that occur in their daily lives, such as sports activities, shopping, visiting people, etc.

2) **Write** Each child writes a two- or four-line poem about this everyday change. Encourage children to use adverbs that tell when and where.

3) **Share** Partners trade poems and read them aloud.

Routines Flip Chart

E L L

English Language Learners

Support Editing Make a correct copy of each child's poem. Tell them to compare the two to find where their mistakes were. Then have them make the proofreading marks on their original copy.

Objectives
- Review concepts: why some changes are difficult.
- Organize information.
- Create a visual display.
- Present results of an inquiry project.

Research and Inquiry
Communicate

Teach

Tell children that today they will organize the information from the questions and answers about difficult changes. They will use the answers to compose a pretend e-mail to communicate what they have learned.

Model

Think Aloud Display the list of inquiry questions and the answers recorded. I will review the questions and answers and circle the information I would like to include. For instance, my first question was "What kinds of changes are difficult?" One of the answers is moving to a new home. I will include that example in an e-mail to a friend of mine who recently moved.

Guide practice

Review the questions and answers with children, and have them prompt you to circle what else you might include in an e-mail about the difficulty of moving.

On their own

Have children select the information they would like to include in their own e-mails about why some changes are difficult. Then tell them to choose a friend or family member to whom they would like to send a mock e-mail. Give them the format of the e-mail they saw on Transparency 12. When they are finished, have them share their mock e-mails with the class. Point out that they will not really be sending the e-mails. Remind them how to be good speakers and listeners:

- Good speakers share ideas and speak clearly at a good pace. They show expression as they read.

- Good listeners are quiet and do not talk while the speaker is reading. They raise their hand to ask questions only when the speaker is finished.

Topic: Why Some Changes Are Difficult	
Question	**Answer—Does it address the topic?**
What kinds of changes are difficult?	moving to a new home, getting a baby brother—**YES**

Wrap Up Your Week!

Question of the Week

Why are some changes difficult?

Think Aloud This week we discovered why some changes are difficult. In the myth *The Night the Moon Fell,* we read how the moon had to adjust to a difficult change. In the e-mail "A New House," we learned how a girl used e-mail to help adjust to a move. Have children recall their Amazing Ideas about change. Then have children use these ideas to help them demonstrate their understanding of the Question of the Week.

ELL

English Language Learners

Poster Preview Prepare children for next week by using Week 5, ELL Poster 20. Read the Poster Talk-Through to introduce the concept and vocabulary. Ask children to identify and describe objects and actions in the art.

Selection Summary Send home the summary of *The First Tortilla,* in English and the child's home language if available. Children can read the summary with family members.

Preview NEXT WEEK

Tell children that next week they will read how rain brings a change to people's lives.

Weekly Assessment

Use pp. 109–114 of *Weekly Tests* to check:

✔ **Phonics** Syllable Patterns

✔  **Comprehension Skill** Plot and Theme

✔ **Lesson Vocabulary**

balance	slivers
canyons	sway
coral	whisper
rattle	

Weekly Tests

A
Advanced

OL
On-Level

SI
Strategic
Intervention

Differentiated Assessment

Use pp. 109–114 of *Fresh Reads for Fluency and Comprehension* to check:

✔ 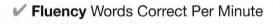 **Comprehension Skill** Plot and Theme

✔ Review **Comprehension Skill** Draw Conclusions

✔ **Fluency** Words Correct Per Minute

Fresh Reads for Fluency and Comprehension

Managing Assessment

Use *Assessment Handbook* for:

✔ **Weekly Assessment Blackline Masters for Monitoring Progress**

✔ **Observation Checklists**

✔ **Record-Keeping Forms**

✔ **Portfolio Assessment**

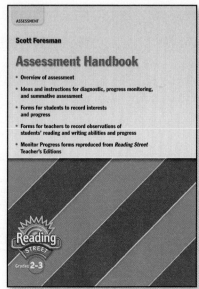

Assessment Handbook

Eve's First Night at Camp

It was Eve's first night at camp, and she could not fall asleep. It was too dark. Her camp pillow was too hard. Her camp blanket was too rough. However, the dark room, the pillow, and the blanket were not the real problem. Eve was homesick. She missed her parents. She missed her dog. She missed her playhouse and her bedroom with the streetlight shining in her window. She liked camp, but it was very different from home. "Is camp a big mistake?" Eve thought.

For over an hour, Eve lay in bed listening to the noises outside the cabin. She thought she heard an owl. It sounded like some squirrels were scampering around on the roof. These were not like the downtown noises of the city she was used to. She began to daydream about home.

Then Eve remembered that her mother put a box in her camp bag and told her not to open it until later that night. Eve got out of bed quietly and opened the box with the silver ribbon. Inside was a CD player with headphones. Printed on a small piece of paper were the words "Sweet dreams. I love you."

Eve put on the headphones and pressed Play. She heard her mother's voice reading her favorite book. She closed her eyes and thought, "This is a difficult change, but my mom is helping me." Then Eve fell asleep as the story ended.

Reproducible Page. © Pearson Education, Inc.

Advanced Selection 19   **Vocabulary:** headphones, favorite

Small Group Time

5 Day Plan	
DAY 1	• Phonics • Decodable Reader
DAY 2	• Lesson Vocabulary • Leveled Reader
DAY 3	• Phonics • Leveled Reader
DAY 4	• Lesson Vocabulary • Decodable Reader
DAY 5	• Phonics Review • Comprehension Review

3 or 4 Day Plan	
DAY 1	• Phonics • Decodable Reader
DAY 2	• Lesson Vocabulary • Leveled Reader
DAY 3	• Phonics • Leveled Reader
DAY 4	• Lesson Vocabulary • Decodable Reader

3 Day Plan: Eliminate the shaded box

SI *Strategic Intervention*   **DAY 1**

Phonics

■ 🔊 **Syllable Patterns** Reteach p. 122a of the Teacher's Edition. Have children combine word parts to read the words. Then have them divide the words into syllables. Monitor their work.

basket	(bas ket)
frozen	(fro zen)
download	(down load)
soybean	(soy bean)
silver	(sil ver)
oatmeal	(oat meal)

Decodable Practice Reader 19A

■ **Review** Review words with syllable patterns and the high-frequency words *young, travel, direction,* and *clear.* Then have children blend and read these words from the story: *dreamt, explained, direction, agree,* and *clear.*

> **If...** children have difficulty with any of these words,
> **then...** reteach the word by modeling. Have children practice the words, with feedback from you, until they can read them independently.

Have children reread the text orally. To achieve optimal fluency, children should reread the text three or four times.

Decodable Practice Reader 19A

Objectives
• Use common syllabication patterns to decode words including closed syllable (CVC).
• Use common syllabication patterns to decode words including vowel digraphs.

 **DAY 2**

Lesson Vocabulary

■ **Review** Using Tested Vocabulary Cards, have the group practice reading *balance, canyons, coral, rattle, slivers, sway,* and *whisper.* Then read "Oak Creek Canyon" on Student Edition p. 127 and discuss the meanings of the words.

For a complete literacy instructional plan and additional practice with this week's target skills and strategies, see the **Leveled Reader Teaching Guide.**

Concept Literacy Leveled Reader

■ **Preview and Predict** Read the title and the author's name. Have children look at the cover and ask them to describe what they see. Help children activate their prior knowledge by asking them to look through the book and to use the photos to predict things that might take place.

■ **Set a Purpose** Remind children that setting a purpose for reading can help them better understand what they read. Guide children to pay attention to how some things change and how some things stay the same.

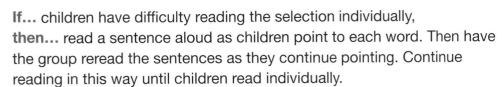
Concept Literacy

■ **Read** Provide corrective feedback as children read the selection orally. During reading, ask them if they were able to confirm any of the predictions they made prior to reading.

> **If...** children have difficulty reading the selection individually, **then...** read a sentence aloud as children point to each word. Then have the group reread the sentences as they continue pointing. Continue reading in this way until children read individually.

■ **Retell** Have children take turns retelling the selection. Help them identify what the children in the selection like and what they miss. What are some things the children like in the new places they live? What are some things they miss? How did things change? How did they stay the same?

More Reading

Use Leveled Readers or other text at children's instructional level.

Objectives
• Use context to determine the relevant meaning of unfamiliar words.
• Paraphrase what the reading was about, maintaining meaning.

Small Group Time

Phonics

■ 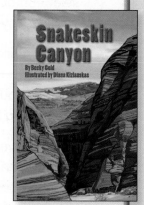 **Syllable Patterns** Reteach p. 144d of the Teacher's Edition. First, have children combine word parts to read the words. Then have them divide the words below into syllables to help them practice the target phonics skill.

tiger	pencil	houseboat	static	soybean	picnic
(ti ger)	(pen cil)	(house boat)	(stat ic)	(soy bean)	(pic nic)

For a complete literacy instructional plan and additional practice with this week's target skills and strategies, see the **Leveled Reader Teaching Guide.**

Below-Level Leveled Reader

■ **Preview and Predict** Read the title, the author's name, and the illustrator's name. Have children look at the cover and ask them to describe what they see. Help children activate their prior knowledge by asking them to look through the story and to use the illustrations to predict things that might take place.

■ **Set a Purpose** Remind children that setting a purpose for reading can help them better understand what they read. Guide children to pay attention to what happens at the beginning, in the middle, and at the end of the story and what they think is the message, or big idea, of the story.

■ **Read** Provide corrective feedback as children read the story orally. During reading, ask them if they were able to confirm any of the predictions they made prior to the story.

If... children have difficulty reading the story individually,
then... read a sentence aloud as children point to each word. Then have the group reread the sentences as they continue pointing.

■ **Visualize** Have children tell what was described in the story that helped them visualize, or picture it, in their mind. Lead children to see how this helped them to better understand the story.

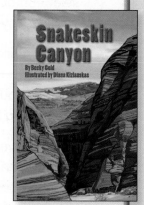

Objectives
• Use common syllabication patterns to decode words including closed syllable (CVC).
• Use ideas to make predictions.

DAY **4**

Lesson Vocabulary

■ **Review** Use pp. 126e–126f in the Teacher's Edition to review the vocabulary words. Ask questions to check children's understanding of the words. For example:

Is it possible for thunder to make the windows <u>rattle</u>?

Where are some places you might <u>whisper</u> instead of talk out loud?

Describe a time when you lost your <u>balance</u>.

When the wind makes trees <u>sway</u>, what happens to them?

Where would you find <u>coral</u>?

Which of these cannot produce <u>slivers</u>—glass, water, or wood?

If you walk through <u>canyons</u>, what do you see around you?

Decodable Practice Reader 19C

■ **Review** Use the word lists to review syllable patterns. Be sure children understand that words can have a digraph/diphthong combination. Have children combine word parts to read the words. Then have children reread the text orally.

> **If...** children have difficulty reading the story individually, **then...** read a sentence aloud as children point to each word. Then have the group reread the sentences as they continue pointing. Continue reading in this way until children read individually.

Check comprehension by having children retell the story including the characters, plot, and setting. Have children locate words in the story that have syllable patterns with digraph/diphthong combinations. List the words children identify. Then have children divide the words into syllables.

Decodable Practice Reader 19C

oatmeal	raincoat	townhouse	downtown
soybeans	seaweed	rainbows	

More Reading
Use Leveled Readers or other text at children's instructional level.

Objectives
• Use context to determine the relevant meaning of unfamiliar words.
• Use common syllabication patterns to decode words including vowel digraphs.

Small Group Time

More Reading

Use Leveled Readers or other text at children's instructional level.

Phonics Review

■ 🔊 **Syllable Patterns** Write these sentences on the board. Have children read them aloud as you track the print. Then call on individuals to combine word parts to read the underlined words.

> The <u>local</u> <u>playground</u> was close to <u>downtown</u>.
>
> <u>David</u> and his <u>sister</u> cooked <u>tender</u> <u>sirloin</u> and <u>seafood</u> <u>chowder</u>.
>
> A <u>number</u> of <u>houseboats</u> were built on the <u>cozy</u> <u>seacoast</u>.
>
> <u>Tyler</u> saw a brown <u>spider</u> on the <u>silver</u> <u>downspout</u>.

Comprehension Review

■ 🔊 **Plot and Theme** Review that the plot of a story is what happens at the beginning, in the middle, and at the end. The theme is the message, or the big idea, of the story. Recall the plot and theme for the comprehension passage on Student Edition p. 125.

The Night the Moon Fell

■ **Read** Have children reread this week's main selection, *The Night the Moon Fell*.

• As you read, think about what happens in each part of the story—the beginning, the middle, and the end.

• Ask yourself what the message, or the big idea, of the story is.

After reading, have children recap what happened in the beginning, middle, and end of the story. Then ask them what the message, or big idea, of the story is.

Objectives
• Use common syllabication patterns to decode words including vowel digraphs.
• Analyze theme.

 **On-Level** **DAY 1**

Phonics • Spelling

- ■ ◉ **Syllable Patterns** Write the following words on the board and have children combine word parts to practice reading words with syllable patterns.

cowboy	oatmeal	outplay	rainbow

Then have children divide the words into syllables.

- ■ **Syllable Patterns** Remind children that each spelling word has two syllables. Children must combine the word parts to read and spell the words. Together, work on reading and spelling these words: *daydream, railroad,* and *football.*

Objective
- Use common syllabication patterns to decode words including vowel digraphs.

5 Day Plan

DAY 1	• Phonics • Spelling • Decodable Reader
DAY 2	• Lesson Vocabulary • Decodable Reader
DAY 3	• Leveled Reader
DAY 4	• Conventions • Leveled Reader
DAY 5	• Phonics Review • Leveled Reader

3 or 4 Day Plan

DAY 1	• Phonics • Spelling • Decodable Reader
DAY 2	• Lesson Vocabulary • Decodable Reader
DAY 3	• Leveled Reader
DAY 4	• Conventions • Leveled Reader

3 Day Plan: Eliminate the shaded box

 **On-Level** **DAY 2**

Lesson Vocabulary

- ■ **Review Word Meaning** Hold up the Tested Vocabulary Cards for *balance, canyons, coral, rattle, slivers, sway,* and *whisper* and review meanings and pronunciation. Continue holding the cards and have children chorally read each word. To help children demonstrate their understanding of the words, provide them with oral sentence frames such as:

A gymnast who works on a beam must have good ___. (balance)

High-Frequency/ Tested Word Cards for Grade 2

High-Frequency/Tested Word Cards

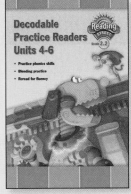

Decodable Practice Readers Units 4–6
- Practice phonics skills
- Blending practice
- Reread for fluency

Decodable Practice Readers

Objective
- Use context to determine the relevant meaning of unfamiliar words.

Small Group Time

For a complete literacy instructional plan and additional practice with this week's target skills and strategies, see the **Leveled Reader Teaching Guide.**

On-Level Leveled Reader

■ **Preview and Predict** Read the title, the author's name, and the illustrator's name. Have children look at the cover, and ask them to describe in detail what they see. Help children preview the story by asking them to look through the story and to use the pictures to predict things that might take place.

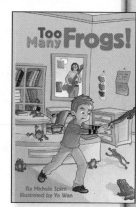

On-Level

■ ◎ **Plot and Theme** Before reading, remind children that setting a purpose for reading can help them better understand what they read. Guide children to pay attention to the beginning, the middle, and the end of the story. Tell them to be alert to the message, or big idea, of the story.

■ **Read** During reading, monitor children's comprehension by providing higher-order thinking questions. Ask:

- What problem did the boy in the story have?

- What advice would you have given the character to help him solve the problem?

- Was the problem solved at the end? Do you think the characters made a good decision? Why or why not?

To help children gain a better understanding of the text, build upon their responses with a group discussion.

■ ◎ **Visualizing** Remind children that good readers visualize as they read. They visualize, or picture something in their mind. Ask:

- What did you picture in your mind as you read the story?

- How did this help you better understand the story?

■ **Text to Text** Help children make connections to other stories they've read. Ask:

- Did this story remind you of any other story you've read? In what ways are they similar?

Objectives
- Monitor comprehension.
- Analyze theme.

OL *On-Level*

DAY 4

Conventions

■ **Adverbs That Tell When and Where** Remind children that adverbs are words that tell about verbs. Tell them that adverbs can tell when or where something happens and can also signal time order.

- The word *yesterday* is an adverb that tells when something happened. Write *yesterday* and use it in an oral sentence. I visited my grandmother *yesterday*.

- The word *outdoors* is an adverb that tells where something happened. Write *outdoors* and use it in an oral sentence. Ned likes to play *outdoors*.

- The words *first, next, then,* and *last* tell the order in which things happen. Write *first* and *then*. Use them in an oral sentence. *First* read the story, and *then* answer the questions.

Continue modeling with other adverbs that tell when and where such as *again, sometimes, down, inside, today,* and *finally*. Ask children to think of other adverbs that tell where and when and use them in sentences.

Objectives
- Understand and use adverbs about time in the context of reading, writing, and speaking.
- Understand and use time-order transition words in the context of reading, writing, and speaking.

More Reading

Use Leveled Readers or other text at children's instructional level.

OL *On-Level*

DAY 5

Phonics Review

■  **Syllable Patterns** Have children practice combining word parts to read words with syllable patterns that contain this week's target phonics skills. Write the following words on the board, and read each word with the children.

rowboat	panic	magic	velvet	pilgrim
label	soymilk	music	downstream	enjoy

Then have children divide the words into syllables.

Objectives
- Use common syllabication patterns to decode words including closed syllable (CVC).
- Use common syllabication patterns to decode words including vowel digraphs.

Small Group Time

5 Day Plan

DAY 1	• Phonics • Comprehension
DAY 2	• Comprehension • Main Selection
DAY 3	• Leveled Reader
DAY 4	• Comprehension • Paired Selection
DAY 5	• Fluency • Comprehension

3 or 4 Day Plan

DAY 1	• Phonics • Comprehension
DAY 2	• Comprehension • Main Selection
DAY 3	• Leveled Reader
DAY 4	• Comprehension • Paired Selection

3 Day Plan: Eliminate the shaded box

A — Advanced — DAY 1

Phonics • Comprehension

■ **Syllable Patterns** Have children practice with longer words containing syllable patterns. Have them choose several words to use in sentences.

decide	underground	overpower	countdown
gymnast	greenhouse	rotate	urgent
needlepoint	climate		

■ **Advanced Selection 19** Before reading, have children identify these words from the story: *headphones* and *favorite.* If they do not know the words, provide oral sentences with the words in context. After reading, have children recall the two most important ideas of the story.

Advanced Selection 19

Objectives
• Use common syllabication patterns to decode words including closed syllable (CVC).
• Use common syllabication patterns to decode words including vowel digraphs.

A — Advanced — DAY 2

Comprehension

■ **Comprehension** Have children silently read this week's main selection, *The Night the Moon Fell.* Discuss the plot—what happened in the beginning, the middle, and the end. Ask what the message, or big idea, of the story is. (You can rely on friends to help you through difficult times.) Talk about what makes *The Night the Moon Fell* a myth. (It attempts to explain something in nature.)

■ **Text to Self** Have children discuss whether they have ever had friends help them out as Luna's new friends did.

The Night the Moon Fell

Objectives
• Identify moral lessons as themes in well-known fables, legends, myths, or stories.

A Advanced DAY **3**

For a complete literacy instructional plan and additional practice with this week's target skills and strategies, see the **Leveled Reader Teaching Guide.**

Advanced Leveled Reader

■ **Activate Prior Knowledge** Read the title, the author's name, and the illustrator's name. Have children look at the cover and ask them to describe in detail what they see. Then activate children's prior knowledge by asking them to identify and describe both noisy and quiet places in their community.

■ **Plot and Theme** Before reading, remind children that setting a purpose for reading can help them better understand what they read. Guide children to pay attention to the plot of the story—what happens at the beginning, in the middle, and at the end.

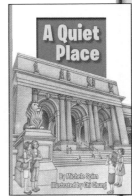

Advanced Leveled Reader

■ **Read** During reading, monitor children's comprehension by providing higher-order thinking questions. Ask:

• How would you describe the way Cindy felt about the move to New York City?

• What did she miss?

• Do you think meeting Lola was important to Cindy? In what ways was she important?

Build on children's answers to help them gain a better understanding of the text.

■ **Visualize** Remind children that when they visualize something, they picture it in their mind. Ask:

• How did you visualize New York City as you read the story?

• What did you visualize about Cindy's life in Arizona?

■ **Text to World** Help children make connections to the story. Ask:

• What other places in the world that you know about are similar to New York City? In what ways are they similar?

More Reading
Use Leveled Readers or other text at children's instructional level.

Objectives
• Monitor comprehension.
• Analyze theme.

Small Group Time

More Reading

Use Leveled Readers or other text at children's instructional level.

A Advanced

DAY 4

Comprehension

- **Comprehension** Have children silently read this week's paired selection, *A New House*. Discuss what e-mail is and why people use it. Then ask children questions about various conventions of e-mail, such as *What word do you click on to answer an e-mail you get?* (Reply) Then have children summarize what they have learned about e-mail.

  Talk about what makes *A New House* a 21st Century Skill. (E-mail is a necessary skill to use in present-day life. You use it to communicate with friends and family members, and you use it in business correspondence.)

- **Text to Self** Have children compare and contrast what they read about e-mail and their own personal experiences with e-mail.

A New House

Objectives
- Identify various written conventions for using digital media.

A Advanced

DAY 5

Fluency • Comprehension

- **Fluency** Using the first few sentences of Advanced Selection 19, model reading with expression. Then have children read the selection to a partner as you listen to their reading. Provide corrective feedback as needed.

- **Comprehension** After they have finished reading the selection, have children tell what happens at the beginning, in the middle, and at the end of the story. Then, on the back of the selection page, have them draw a picture of how they visualized the camp and write one or two sentences to describe it.

Advanced Selection 19

Objectives
- Read aloud grade-level appropriate text with fluency.
- Read aloud grade-level appropriate text with comprehension.

The ELL lessons are organized by strands. Use them to scaffold the weekly curriculum of lessons or during small group time instruction.

Academic Language

Children will hear or read the following academic language in this week's core instruction. As children encounter the vocabulary, provide a simple definition or concrete example. Then ask children to suggest an example or synonym of the word and identify available cognates.

Skill Words	syllable *(sílaba)*	voice *(voz)*
	pattern *(pauta)*	feelings *(sentimientos)*
	plot *(parcela)*	author *(autor)*
	theme *(tema)*	
Concept Words	moon *(luna)*	color *(color)*
	changes	difficult *(difícil)*

Spanish cognates in parentheses

Concept Development

 Why are some changes difficult?

■ **Preteach Concept**

• **Prior Knowledge** Have children turn to pages 84–85 in the Student Edition. Call attention to the picture of the boy's teeth and tap into children's knowledge of losing baby teeth. Have you lost any teeth? How many have you lost? What was it like to lose your teeth? Did it hurt? Did it make you look or feel different?

• **Discuss Concept** Elicit children's knowledge and experience of changes that can be difficult. Do you think that having a new puppy could be hard? Why? Do you think that moving to a new home could be hard? Supply background information as needed.

• **Poster Talk-Through** Read the Poster Talk-Through on ELL Poster 19 aloud and work through the Day 1 activities.

■ **Daily Concept and Vocabulary Development** Use the daily activities on ELL Poster 19 to build concept and vocabulary knowledge.

Objectives
• Internalize new basic language by using and reusing it in meaningful ways in speaking activities that build concept and language attainment.
• Listen to and derive meaning from a variety of media such as audiotape, video, DVD, and CD ROM to build and reinforce concept and language attainment.

Content Objectives
• Use concept vocabulary related to change.

Language Objectives
• Express ideas in response to art and discussion.
• Reinforce concept through media.

Daily Planner

DAY 1	• **Frontload** Concepts • **Preteach** Comprehension Skill, Vocabulary, Phonics/Spelling, Conventions • **Writing**
DAY 2	• **Review** Concepts, Vocabulary, Comprehension Skill • **Frontload Main Selection** • **Practice** Phonics/Spelling, Conventions/Writing
DAY 3	• **Review** Concepts, Comprehension Skill, Vocabulary, Conventions/Writing • **Reread Main Selection** • **Practice** Phonics/Spelling
DAY 4	• **Review Concepts** • **Read ELL/ELD Readers** • **Practice** Phonics/Spelling Conventions/Writing
DAY 5	• **Review** Concepts, Vocabulary, Comprehension Skill, Phonics/Spelling, Conventions • **Reread ELL/ELD Readers** • **Writing**

See the ELL Handbook for ELL Workshops with targeted instruction.

Concept Talk Video

Use Concept Talk Video Routine (*ELL Handbook*, page 464) to build background knowledge about bringing diverse people together. Have students respond orally to information presented in the video to build and reinforce concept attainment.

Support for English Language Learners

Language Objectives

- Understand and use basic vocabulary.
- Learn meanings of grade-level vocabulary.

English Opportunity

Understand Main Points
Use the reading on p. 127 in the Student Edition as a listening opportunity for children. Read the story aloud. Have children listen to identify the main points about Oak Creek Canyon, then retell in pairs.

Basic Vocabulary

■ **High-Frequency Words** Use the ELL Vocabulary Routines on p. 456 of the *ELL Handbook* to systematically teach the high-frequency words from this week's core lesson. The *ELL Handbook* (page 491) contains a bank of strategies that you can use to ensure children's mastery of the high-frequency words.

Lesson Vocabulary

■ **Preteach** Introduce this routine to preteach the Lesson Vocabulary:

1. Distribute copies of this week's Word Cards (*ELL Handbook*, page 137).

2. Display ELL Poster 19 and reread the Poster Talk-Through.

3. Using the poster illustrations, model how a word's meaning can be expressed with other similar words: The *canyon,* or deep valley, looks beautiful at sunset.

4. Use these sentences to reveal the meaning of the other words.

   - I can *balance* on a log. (keep your body steady and not fall over)
   - Some kinds of *coral* move with the sea current. (a sea animal with an exoskeleton, or skeleton on the outside of its body)
   - Do you hear the *rattle?* (a short sequence of sharp sounds)
   - *Slivers* of glass were all over the floor. (small pieces)
   - The trees *sway* in the breeze. (rock back and forth)
   - Can you *whisper* your answer to me? (speak in a soft, hushed voice)

Objectives

- Use strategic learning techniques such as concept mapping, drawing, memorizing, comparing, contrasting, and reviewing to acquire basic and grade-level vocabulary.
- Internalize new basic language by using and reusing it in meaningful ways in speaking activities that build concept and language attainment.
- Understand the general meaning, main points, and important details of spoken language ranging from situations in which topics, language, and contexts are familiar to familiar.

 English Language Learners

 Leveled Support

■ **Reteach** Give pairs of children copies of the Word Cards. Have them cut the Word Cards into puzzle pieces of various sizes and shapes. Tell children to mix up the puzzle pieces and lay them on the table in front of them, face up. Have partners take turns putting words back together.

Beginning/Intermediate After children put a word together, have them say the word and tell or show what it means.

Advanced/Advanced-High Have children use the Lesson Vocabulary aloud in a sentence each time they reassemble a word.

■ **Writing** Give each pair of children a set of Word Cards. Provide clues for each vocabulary word's meaning, such as standing on one foot to show *balance*. Have pairs hold up the appropriate Word Card as you present the clues.

Beginning Model the correct pronunciation of each word. Have children say the Lesson Vocabulary word as you present each clue.

Intermediate Have children read and repeat the words aloud. Have each pair of children create a clue for one of the words.

Advanced/Advanced-High Monitor children as they take turns reading the words to a partner. Then have them make a clue for each word.

Language Objectives

• Produce drawings, phrases, and short sentences to understand vocabulary.

ELL Teacher Tip

According to Dr. Jim Cummins, "A systematic exploration of language is essential if children are to develop a curiosity about language and deepen their understanding of how words work. Children should become language detectives who investigate the mysteries of language and how it has been used throughout history to shape and change society."

Objectives
• Use accessible language and learn new and essential language in the process.

Support for English Language Learners

Content Objectives

- Monitor and adjust oral comprehension.

Language Objectives

- Discuss oral passages.
- Use a graphic organizer to take notes.
- Use contextual support to confirm understanding.

ELL Workshop

As you give directions for using the graphic organizer, you might use *Follow Directions (ELL Handbook,* pages 396–397) to support children in comprehending increasingly complex spoken directions.

Listening Comprehension

Someone New

Ellie McSnelly and Carrie O'Toole were running and laughing—their first day of school. As they took their seats they saw someone new. His name was Lazlo S. Gasky. He came from the town of Delasky.

The class sat and stared and some of them glared. They weren't used to a new kid in class.

In gym class, they picked teams to play a game. But no one mentioned Lazlo's name. At lunch someone tripped him and his food spilled all over.

Some kids even called Lazlo names. This went on for weeks. Ellie began to feel really sorry for him.

So one day, Ellie went to Lazlo's locker. She said, "Want to come over and play soccer?" Ellie and Lazlo hung out and had lots of fun. And Ellie told Carrie that Lazlo was just like you and me.

Prepare for the Read Aloud The modified Read Aloud above prepares children for listening to the oral reading "The Brand New Kid" on page 99 of the Read Aloud Anthology.

- **First Listening: Listen to Understand** Write the title of the Read Aloud on the board. This is about a boy who is new at school. Listen to find out what happens to him at the new school. What happens to him? How do other children treat him? Afterward, ask the questions again and have children share their answers.

- **Second Listening: Listen to Check Understanding** Using Story Map B (*ELL Handbook*, page 471), work with children to record the characters, setting, and events of the story. Reread the story. Have children double-check what they have recorded in their story map.

Objectives

- Use visual, contextual, and linguistic support to enhance and confirm understanding of increasingly complex and elaborated spoken language.
- Demonstrate English comprehension and expand reading skills by employing basic reading skills such as demonstrating understanding of supporting ideas and details in text and graphic sources, summarizing text and distinguishing main ideas from details commensurate with content area needs.

Phonics and Spelling

■ **Syllable Patterns**

- **Preteach** Write the word *lemon* on the board and draw a small picture of a lemon. This is a lemon, /l/ /e/ /m/ /o/ /n/. How many vowel sounds do you hear in the word *lemon*? Say it with me /l/ /e/ /m/ /o/ /n/, *lemon*.

- **Teach/Model** Draw a line between the two syllables. When you hear a word with more than one vowel sound, divide it into parts. When there is one consonant between two vowels, you must figure out where to divide the word. Point out that the first syllable in *lemon* has a short vowel sound. Explain that this means the *m* is part of the first syllable. The first vowel sound in *lemon* is short. This means the first syllable ends with a consonant. Say it with me: *lemon, lem/on*.

- **Assess** Write the following words on the board: *water, frozen, silent, tiger, seven*. Challenge children to divide the words into syllables in the proper place. Have them say the words aloud, identify the vowel sound as long or short, then divide the word.

Vocabulary Skill: Multiple-Meaning Words

■ **Teach/Model** Write *light* on the board. Then write these two sentence frames: *The feather is light. The teacher turned on the light.* Read the sentences aloud. Some words have multiple-meanings. In the first sentence, *light* means "easy to lift." In the second sentence, *light* means "electric lamp."

■ **Practice** Write the following sentences on the board: *The bat hit the ball. The bat flew out of the cave.* Have children figure out the meaning of bat in each sentence.

 Leveled Support

Beginning/Intermediate Give children these two definitions: *wooden stick* and *animal that flies*. Help students match the definition to its proper sentence.

Advanced/Advanced-High Have partners work together to create two definitions for *bat*. Have them write their definitions down. Then have the partners share their definitions with other groups of children.

Content Objectives

- Identify and define multiple-meaning words.
- Identify syllable patterns in words.
- Distinguish syllable patterns.

Language Objectives

- Apply phonics and decoding skills to vocabulary.
- Discuss the meanings of multiple-meaning words.

 Transfer Skills

Speakers of monosyllabic languages such as Cantonese, Hmong, Khmer, Korean, and Vietnamese may pronounce a two-syllable word as two separate words. Have students practice saying each two-syllable word.

Objectives
- Use prior knowledge and experiences to understand meanings in English.
- Practice producing sounds of newly acquired vocabulary such as long and short vowels, silent letters, and consonant clusters to pronounce English words in a manner that is increasingly comprehensible.

Content Objectives

- Identify the plot and theme of a text.

Language Objectives

- Write the plot and theme of a text as you identify them.

ELL Workshop

Encourage children to ask questions to monitor their understanding of instruction of comprehension skills. Use *Ask Clarifying Questions* (*ELL Handbook*, pages 402–403) for practice.

ELL *English Language Learners*

Comprehension
Plot and Theme

■ **Preteach** The plot of a story is what happens. A plot must have a clear beginning, middle, and end. The theme of a story is the main, or big, idea. Have children turn to Envision It! on page EI•14 in the Student Edition. Read the text aloud together. Have children talk about the literary elements that are drawn on the page. Ask them to point out the plot and theme. Ask them what happens in the beginning, middle, and end of the "story" and what the main idea was.

■ **Reteach** Distribute copies of the Picture It! (*ELL Handbook*, p 138). Have children look at the pictures and sentences to find out what happens in the story. Read the directions and the story aloud to your children. As they listen, tell children to remember what happens and to think about the main idea of the story. Have children re-read the story in pairs. Then have them answer the questions on the bottom of the page. (**Answers** 1. It's Miguel's first day and he is sad. 2. The teacher smiles at him. 3. New things can be as good as old things.)

 Beginning/Intermediate Read the questions aloud to children. Have them dictate their answers to the questions. Write their answers on the lines for them.

Advanced/Advanced-High Have children work with their partners to complete this activity independently.

MINI-LESSON

Social Language

Tell children that people often share stories about things that happen to them, using informal English. They tell their friends about the things they did over the weekend and what they did when they came back to school on Monday. These stories, like the stories they read in school, must have a plot, (beginning, middle, and end), in order to make sense. Have children write a short paragraph about what they did over the weekend. Provide the following sentence frames: *On Friday after school I ___. Then, on Saturday, I ___. Finally, on Sunday I ___.*

Objectives

- Monitor oral and written language production and employ self-corrective techniques or other resources.
- Demonstrate an increasing ability to distinguish between formal and informal English and an increasing knowledge of when to use each one commensurate with grade-level learning expectations.

 English Language Learners

Student Edition pp. 128–129

Reading Comprehension
The Night the Moon Fell

■ **Frontloading** Have children look through pages 128–143 of *The Night the Moon Fell* in the Student Edition and tell what they think makes it look like fiction, a kind of writing that has been made up. Why do you think this selection is fiction? Distribute copies of the English summary of *The Night the Moon Fell* (*ELL Handbook*, page 139). Have children read the summary aloud with you. Encourage them to ask questions about any ideas or unfamiliar words. If you have sent copies of the summary home, have children read it again with family members. Preview the selection by having children look at the pictures. Have children work to fill in the Story Map graphic organizer as they read.

Sheltered Reading Ask questions such as the following to guide children's comprehension:

- p. 130: Why did Luna fall? (She was startled by a loud noise.)

- p. 132: Where did Luna fall? (into the sea)

- p. 133: How did the fish try to cheer her up? (They hummed and blew bubbles.)

- p. 136: How did the fish help Luna? (They used their fins to sweep her pieces together.)

■ **Fluency: Expression** Remind children that reading with expression means to read the words like you are speaking to a friend. Read the first paragraph on page 133, modeling expressive reading. Have pairs choose a paragraph on page 137. Have children read with expression as their partner listens and then offers feedback. For more practice, use the Fluency: Oral Rereading Routine (*ELL Handbook*, page 461).

After Reading Help children recall parts of the story using the Retelling Cards. Have pairs or small groups sequence the cards to show how Luna got back into the sky.

Content Objectives
- Monitor and adjust comprehension.
- Make and adjust predictions.

Language Objectives
- Read grade-level text with expression.
- Summarize text using visual support.
- Use peer support to read.

Graphic Organizer

Title _____
Beginning
↓
Middle
↓
End

Audio Support

Prepare children for reading *The Night the Moon Fell* by using the eSelection or the AudioText CD. See the AudioText CD Routine (*ELL Handbook*, page 464) for suggestions on using these learning tools.

ELL Workshop

Children can act out or draw meanings of words and concepts in a shared reading. Use *Act Out or Draw Meaning* (*ELL Handbook*, pages 418–419) for extra child support.

Objectives
- Distinguish sounds and intonation patterns of English with increasing ease.
- Use visual and contextual support from peers and teachers to read grade-appropriate content area text, enhance and confirm understanding, and develop vocabulary, grasp of language structures, and background knowledge needed to comprehend increasingly challenging language.

Support for English Language Learners

ELL Reader

ELD Reader

For additional leveled instruction, see the **ELL/ELD Reader Teaching Guide.**

Comprehension:
Adam's New Soccer Team

■ **Before Reading** Distribute copies of the ELL and ELD Readers, *Adam's New Soccer Team*, to children at their reading level.

• **Preview** Read the title aloud with children. This is a story about a boy named Adam. He is on a new soccer team and doesn't know anybody. Invite children to look through the pictures and name what they see. Have them predict what will happen in the story based on the picture clues.

• **Set a Purpose for Reading** Let's read to find out how Adam does on his new soccer team.

■ **During Reading** Follow the Reading Routine for both reading groups.

1. Read the entire Reader aloud slowly.

2. Read pages 1–5, pausing to build background or model comprehension. Have Beginning children finger-point as you read. Use the questions in the chart to check children' comprehension.

3. Have children silently reread pages 1–5 independently.

4. Repeat steps 2–3 above for pages 6–8 of the Reader.

■ **After Reading** Use the exercises on the inside back cover of each Reader and invite children to share their writing. In a whole-group discussion, ask children, How do you think Adam feels about his new soccer team now? Record their answers on the board and invite them to point to pictures in the book to support their answers.

ELD Reader Beginning/Intermediate

■ **pp. 4–5:** Who was Adam's first game against? (*his former team*) Read aloud the sentence that gives you the answer. (*The first game was against the Comets.*)

■ **pp. 6–7:** Who wins the game? (*Adam's team*) Read aloud the sentence that gives you the answer. (*The game is over. "We Win!"*)

Writing Find a sentence in the story that shows one thing Adam did to be a good teammate on his new team. Copy the sentence. Then read it aloud to your partner.

ELL Reader Advanced/Advanced-High

■ **pp. 2–3:** What team did Adam play on last year? (*Comets*) Read aloud the sentence that gives you the answer. (*Last year, Adam was on the Comets.*)

■ **pp. 6–7:** Which team won the game? What was the score? (*The Strikers, 4–3*) Read aloud the sentence that gives you the answer. (*The Strikers won, four goals to three!*)

Study Guide Distribute copies of the ELL Reader Study Guide (*ELL Handbook*, page 142). Scaffold comprehension by helping children identify the beginning, middle, and end of the story. Have them write what they think the theme of the story is. (**Answers:** See *ELL Handbook*, pp. 209–212.)

Objectives
• Understand the general meaning, main points, and important details of spoken language ranging from situations in which topics, language, and contexts are familiar to unfamiliar.
• Read silently and with increasing ease and comprehension for longer periods.

Conventions
Adverbs that Tell When or Where

■ **Preteach** Explain that an *adverb* is a word that can tell when or where something happens. Write the following words in a T-chart on the board: *WHEN? early, late, again, sometimes, usually, now, never, recently; WHERE? above, away, down, outdoors, inside, here, forward, below.* Use gestures or pictures to ensure comprehension of the words.

■ **Practice** Use the adverbs above in sentences. Point out that they tell when or where something happens.

 Beginning/Intermediate Think of a sentence with an adverb and say it aloud for children. Ask them to identify whether the adverb tells *where* or *when*.

Advanced/Advanced-High Have children write their own sentences using any of the above adverbs. Next to each sentence, have children identify whether the adverb tells *when* or *where*.

■ **Reteach** Use school activities to demonstrate how to use adverbs that tell when and where. For example, look at the clock and say, We will eat lunch *soon.* We *usually* eat in the cafeteria. At recess, we will go *outdoors*. After that, you will come *inside.* Repeat this task several times using different adverbs that tell *when* and *where.*

■ **Practice** Have children use adverbs in sentences.

 Beginning/Intermediate Have children work in pairs to use one of the adverbs in a sentence about school. Monitor spelling and pronunciation.

Advanced/Advanced-High Have children write sentences with adverbs telling *when* and *where.* Invite children to share their sentences with the class.

For more practice with irregular plural nouns, see page 369 of the *ELL Handbook.*

Content Objectives
• Decode and use adverbs that tell *when* or *where.*

Language Objectives
• Speak using adverbs that tell *when* or *where.*
• Ask and give information.
• Write phrases or sentences using adverbs that tell *when* or *where.*

Transfer Skills
The languages of Chinese, Hmong, and Vietnamese rely on adverbs or expressions of time to indicate when an action has taken place. Verbs in these languages do not change to show tense.

Grammar Jammer
For more practice with adverbs, use the Grammar Jammer for this target skill. See the Grammar Jammer Routine (*ELL Handbook*, page 465) for suggestions on using this learning tool.

Objectives
• Ask and give information ranging from using a very limited bank of high-frequency, high-need, concrete vocabulary, including key words and expressions needed for basic communication in academic and social contexts, to using abstract and content-based vocabulary during extended speaking assignments.

Support for English Language Learners

ELL English Language Learners

Combining Sentences

■ **Introduce** Display the paragraph model and read it aloud. Review that authors use their *voice* to share their feelings about a topic. What is the author writing about? (*the moon*) How does he feel about his topic? (*He thinks it is pretty.*) What are some of the words the author uses that help you understand his feelings? (*beautiful; shines its light; illuminates; brings a glow*) Have children underline the words in the paragraph that describe the topic and show the author's feelings.

Writing Model
The moon is a beautiful globe. It shines its light in the dark. It illuminates the night and brings a glow to the Earth. Luna is a night goddess.

■ **Practice** Write this incomplete paragraph on the board. Work together to choose words to show that the author loves dogs. (Possible responses: *best; fun; play; run; lick; happy*)

Dogs are the ___ pets. I love my dog. Dogs are ___. They can ___ with you and ___ with you. They greet you with a ___ at the end of the day. They are always ___ to see you.

■ **Write** Have children write a paragraph about something they feel strongly about. They should write with the goal of having their readers know what they feel.

 Leveled Support

Beginning Have children write their topic at the top of their paper. Have them draw details about their feelings toward that topic and then dictate to you one sentence for each drawing. Write out their sentences and have children copy them.

Intermediate Supply children with the following sentence starter: *I___ [my topic]*. Have them fill in their topic and a word to show how they feel about it. Have children use this as their topic sentence. They can use it to start their paragraph.

Advanced/Advanced-High Have children develop their paragraph independently. Then have pairs exchange papers and provide feedback for revising and editing. Encourage partners to state how the author feels about his or her subject.

Objectives
• Narrate, describe, and explain with increasing specificity and detail as more English is acquired.

Content Objectives
• Identify words that show what an author is feeling.

Language Objectives
• Write a paragraph, showing the feelings that you (as the author) have toward the subject.
• Share feedback for editing and revising.

ELL Teaching Routine
For practice spelling words related to change, use the Spelling Routine (*ELL Handbook*, page 463).

ELL Workshop
Children may use classroom resources to respond to questions they have about their writing. *Use Classroom Resources (ELL Handbook, pages 404–405) provides extra support.*

This Week's ELL Overview

ELL Handbook

- Maximize Literacy and Cognitive Engagement
- Research Into Practice
- Full Weekly Support for Every Selection

The First Tortilla
  - Multi-Lingual Summaries in Five Languages
  - Selection-Specific Vocabulary Word Cards
  - Frontloading/Reteaching for Comprehension Skill Lessons
  - ELD and ELL Reader Study Guides

- Transfer Activities
- Professional Development

Daily Leveled ELL Notes

ELL notes appear throughout this week's instruction and ELL Support is on the DI pages of your Teacher's Edition. The following is a sample of an ELL note from this week.

English Language Learners

Beginning To help children focus their thoughts, have them draw a food they like to eat. Next, make a list of the names of the foods. Then ask them who prepares the foods. Write names on the board.

Intermediate Discuss ingredients in foods they like to eat. Ask them what preparations have to be done to the food before eating, such as chopping, boiling, baking, and so on. Then have them tell who does the preparing.

Advanced Lead a small-group discussion to focus on holiday meals. Discuss foods children eat on these special days and who prepares the food.

Advanced High Have children who speak other languages tell about holiday meals and foods that are family favorites. Write the food and holiday names on the board and have other children use them to write sentences.

ELL by Strand

The ELL lessons on this week's Support for English Language Learners pages are organized by strand. They offer additional scaffolding for the core curriculum. Leveled support notes on these pages address the different proficiency levels in your class. See pages DI•96–DI•105.

ELL Guy
Dr. Jim Cummins

——— The Three Pillars of ELL Instruction ———

ELL Strands	Activate Prior Knowledge	Access Content	Extend Language
Vocabulary pp. DI•97–DI•98	Preteach	Reteach	Leveled Writing Activities
Reading Comprehension p. DI•101	Preteach	Reteach	Leveled Practice Activities
Phonics, Spelling, and Word Analysis p. DI•100	Teach/Model	Practice	Leveled Practice Activities
Listening Comprehension p. DI•99	Prepare for the Read Aloud	First Listening	Second Listening
Conventions and Writing pp. DI•104–DI•105	Preteach	Leveled Practice Activities	Leveled Practice Activities/ Leveled Writing Activities
Concept Development p. DI•96	Prior Knowledge	Discuss Concept	Daily Concept and Vocabulary Development

This Week's Practice Stations Overview

Six Weekly Practice Stations with Leveled Activities can be found at the beginning of each week of instruction. For this week's Practice Stations, see pp. 154h–154i.

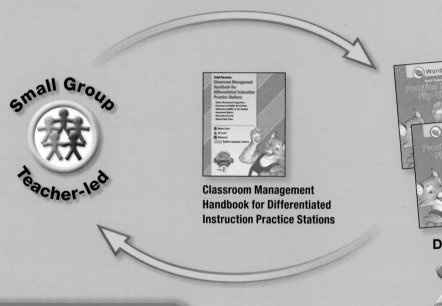

Practice Stations

Small Group Teacher-led

Classroom Management Handbook for Differentiated Instruction Practice Stations

Daily Leveled Center Activities

Below   Advanced

On-Level   E L L

Practice Stations Flip Charts

	Word Wise	**Word Work**	**Words to Know**	**Let's Write**	**Read for Meaning**	**Get Fluent**
Objectives	• Spell words with "vowel-team" syllable patterns. • Spell compound words.	• Identify the "vowel team" syllable pattern.	• Use context clues to identify and determine meaning of words with multiple meanings.	• Write a narrative poem. • Use words and voice to show feelings.	• Identify a story's plot. • Determine a story's theme.	• Real aloud with expression (characterization).
Materials	• *Word Wise* Flip Chart • Teacher-made word cards for compound words • Letter Tiles • paper • pencils	• *Word Work* Flip Chart • Teacher-made word cards for compound words • paper • pencils	• *Words to Know* Flip Chart • Teacher-made word cards: *band, cart, light, yard, plate, pit, bowl, mean, box* • dictionaries • paper • pencils	• *Let's Write* Flip Chart • paper • pencils	• *Read for Meaning* Flip Chart • 2.4.4 Leveled Readers • paper • pencils	• *Get Fluent* Flip Chart • 2.4.4 Leveled Readers

This Week on Reading Street!

 Question of the Week

How do changes in the weather affect us?

Daily Plan

Don't Wait Until Friday

Whole Group

- ◉ Vowel Digraphs *oo, ue, ew, ui*
- ◉ Plot and Theme
- • Fluency
- • Vocabulary

MONITOR PROGRESS	Success Predictor			
Day 1 Check Word Reading	Day 2 Check Lesson Vocabulary/High-Frequency Words	Day 3 Check Retelling	Day 4 Check Fluency	Day 5 Check Oral Vocabulary

Small Group

Teacher-Led

- • Reading Support
- • Skill Support
- • Fluency Practice

Practice Stations

Independent Activities

Customize Literacy More support for a Balanced Literacy approach, see pp. CL•1–CL•45.

Customize Writing More support for a customized writing approach, see pp. CW•11–CW•20.

Whole Group

- • Writing: Thank-You Note
- • Conventions: Adverbs That Tell How
- • New Literacies

Assessment

- • Weekly Tests
- • Day 5 Assessment
- • Fresh Reads

You Are Here! Unit 4 Week 5

This Week's Reading Selections

Main Selection
Genre: **Legend**

Paired Selection

Decodable Practice Readers

Leveled Readers

ELL and ELD Readers

Resources on Reading Street!

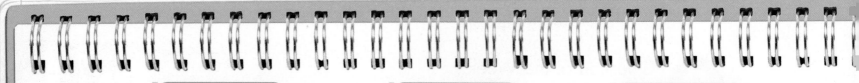

	Build Concepts	**Phonics**	**Vocabulary**
Whole Group	 Student Edition pp. 154–155 — Sing with Me	Student Edition pp. 156–157 — Sound-Spelling Cards	 Student Edition pp. 160–161
Go Digital	• Concept Talk Video • Sing with Me Animations	• Interactive Sound-Spelling Cards • Decodable eReaders	• Vocabulary Activities • Journal Word Bank
Small Group and Independent Practice	Practice Station Flip Chart — Leveled Readers — ELL and ELD Readers	Practice Station Flip Chart — Decodable Practice Readers	 Practice Station Flip Chart — Student Edition pp. 160–161
Go Digital	• eReaders	• Decodable eReaders • Letter Tile Drag and Drop	• Journal Word Bank • Vocabulary Activities
Customize Literacy	• Leveled Readers	• Decodable Practice Readers	• Tested Vocabulary Cards
Go Digital	• Concept Talk Video • Big Question Video • eReaders	• Interactive Sound-Spelling Cards • Decodable eReaders	• Sing with Me Animations • Vocabulary Activities

Question of the Week

How do changes in the weather affect us?

Week 5

Comprehension

Student Edition
pp. 162–163

- Envision It! Animations
- eSelections

Fluency

Decodable
Practice
Readers

- eSelections
- eReaders

Conventions and Writing

Student Edition
pp. 180–181

- Grammar Jammer

Practice
Station
Flip Chart

Leveled
Readers

ELL and ELD
Readers

Practice
Station
Flip Chart

Decodable
Practice
Readers

Practice
Station
Flip Chart

Reader's and
Writer's Notebook

- eReaders
- Story Sort

- Decodable eReaders

- Grammar Jammer

- Envision It! Skills and Strategies Handbooks
- Leveled Readers

- Leveled Readers

- *Reader's and Writer's Notebook*

- Envision It! Animations
- eReaders

- eReaders

- Grammar Jammer

You Are Here!
Unit 4
Week 5

My 5-Day Planner for Reading Street!

Don't Wait Until Friday
SUCCESS PREDICTOR

	Check Word Reading **Day 1** pages 154j–159f	Check Lesson Vocabulary/ High-Frequency Words **Day 2** pages 160a–177f

Get Ready to Read	**Concept Talk,** 154j–155
	Oral Vocabulary, 155a–155b
	  condition, predict, terrifying
	Phonics, 156a–157a
	  ◉ Vowel Digraphs *oo, ue, ew, ui*
	Spelling, 157b Pretest
	READ Decodable Practice Reader 20A, 157c–157d
		Concept Talk, 160a–160b
		Oral Vocabulary, 160b
		  breeze, whip
		Review **Phonics,** 160c
		  Vowel Pattern *oo,* /u̇/
		  ◉ Vowel Digraphs *oo, ue, ew, ui*
		Spelling, 160d Practice

Read and Comprehend	**Build Comprehension,** 158a–159
	  ◉ Plot and Theme
	  ◉ Monitor and Clarify
	Lesson Vocabulary, 159a Introduce
	  awaken, cliffs, mountain, prize, rainbow, suffer, volcano
		Lesson Vocabulary, 160e–160f
		  awaken, cliffs, mountain, prize, rainbow, suffer, volcano
		Vocabulary, 160g–161
		  ◉ Prefixes
		Fluency, 160–161 Paired Reading
		Build Background, 161a
		READ Main Selection—First Read, 162a–177a
		  The First Tortilla
		Literary Text, 177a Moral Lessons as Themes

Language Arts	**Conventions,** 159b Adverbs That Tell How
	Writing, 159c–159d
	  Thank-You Note
	Research and Inquiry, 159e
	  Identify and Focus Topic
		Conventions, 177b Adverbs That Tell How
		Writing, 177c–177d Thank-You Note
		  Writing Trait: Focus/Ideas
		Handwriting, 177e
		  Cursive *n, m, x:* Letter Size
		Research and Inquiry, 177f
		  Research Skill: Natural and Personal Sources

You Are Here!
Unit 4
Week 5

Question of the Week
How do changes in the weather affect us?

Check Retelling	Check Fluency	Check Oral Vocabulary
Day 3 pages 178a–181b	**Day 4** pages 182a–185f	**Day 5** pages 186a–187k
Concept Talk, 178a–178b **Oral Vocabulary,** 178b *sparkle* **Phonics,** 178c ◉ Vowel Digraphs *oo, ue, ew, ui* **READ Decodable Practice Passage 20B,** 178d **Spelling,** 178e Dictation	**Concept Talk,** 182a–182b **Oral Vocabulary,** 182b *funnel, swirl* Review **Phonics,** 182c Syllable Patterns Review **Fluent Word Reading,** 182d **READ Decodable Practice Reader 20C,** 182e–182f **Spelling,** 182g Partner Review	**Concept Wrap Up,** 186a Review **Oral Vocabulary,** 186b Review **Phonics,** 186c Vowel Digraphs *oo, ue, ew, ui* **Spelling,** 186d Test
Fluency, 178f Expression and Intonation Review **Lesson Vocabulary,** 178g *awaken, cliffs, mountain, prize, rainbow, suffer, volcano* **Vocabulary,** 178g ◉ Prefixes **READ Main Selection—Second Read,** 162–177, 178h–179a	**Science in Reading,** 182h **READ Paired Selection,** 182–185 "Wind" **Fluency,** 185a Expression and Intonation	**Vocabulary,** 186–187 Prefixes **Fluency,** 187a Expression/Intonation **Listening and Speaking,** 187a Give an Oral Summary Review **Comprehension,** 187b Plot and Theme Review **Vocabulary,** 187b Lesson Vocabulary **Literary Text,** 187c Author's Craft **Assessment,** 187d–187f Monitor Progress
Conventions, 180a Adverbs That Tell How **Writing,** 180–181a Thank-You Note Writer's Craft: Sequence **Research and Inquiry,** 181b Gather and Record Information	**Conventions,** 185b Adverbs That Tell How **Writing,** 185c–185d Thank-You Note Revising Strategy **Listening and Speaking,** 185e Give an Oral Summary **Research and Inquiry,** 185f Review and Revise Topic	**Conventions,** 187g Review Adverbs That Tell How **Writing,** 187h–187i Thank-You Note Writer's Craft: Adverbs **Research and Inquiry,** 187j Communicate **Wrap Up Your Week,** 187k How do changes in the weather affect us?

Week 5

Grouping Options for Differentiated Instruction
Turn the page for the small group time lesson plan.

Planning Small Group Time on Reading Street!

SMALL GROUP TIME RESOURCES

Look for this Small Group Time box each day to help meet the individual needs of all your children. Differentiated Instruction lessons appear on the DI pages at the end of each week.

DAY 1

Teacher-Led

SI Strategic Intervention

Teacher-Led
- Phonemic Awareness and Phonics
- **Read** *Decodable Practice Reader*

OL On-Level

Teacher-Led
- Phonics and Spelling
- **Read** *Decodable Practice Reader*

A Advanced

Teacher-Led
- Phonics and Comprehension
- **Read** *Advanced Selection*

ELL Place English language learners in the groups that correspond to their reading abilities in English.

Practice Stations
- Listen Up
- Word Work

Independent Activities
- *Reader's and Writer's Notebook*
- Concept Talk Video

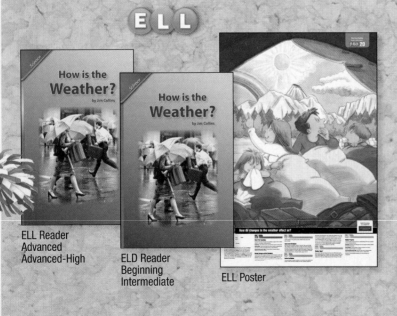

ELL

ELL Reader
Advanced
Advanced-High

ELD Reader
Beginning
Intermediate

ELL Poster

You Are Here!
Unit 4
Week 5

Day 1

SI Strategic Intervention	Phonics, DI•85 **Read** Decodable Practice Reader 20A, DI•85
OL On-Level	Phonics and Spelling, DI•90 **Read** Decodable Practice Reader 20A, DI•90
A Advanced	Phonics and Comprehension, DI•93 **Read** Advanced Selection, DI•93
ELL English Language Learners	DI•96–DI•105 **Concepts and Oral Vocabulary** **Listening (Read Aloud)**

Reading Street
Response to
Intervention Kit

Reading Street Leveled
Practice Stations Kit

SI Strategic Intervention

Below-Level Reader

Decodable Practice Readers

Concept Literacy Reader

OL On-Level

On-Level Reader

A Advanced

Advanced
Reader

Advanced Selection

Small Group Weekly Plan

Day 2	Day 3	Day 4	Day 5
Lesson Vocabulary, DI•86 **Read Concept Literacy Leveled Reader,** DI•86	**Phonics,** DI•87 **Read Below-Level Leveled Reader,** DI•87	**Lesson Vocabulary,** DI•88 **Read Decodable Practice Reader 20C,** DI•88	**Phonics and Comprehension,** DI•89 **Reread Main Selection,** DI•89
Lesson Vocabulary, DI•90 **Reread Decodable Practice Reader 20A,** DI•90	**Read On-Level Leveled Reader,** DI•91	**Conventions,** DI•92 **Read Leveled Reader,** DI•92	**Phonics Review,** DI•92 **Reread On-Level Leveled Reader,** DI•92
Comprehension, DI•93 **Read Main Selection,** DI•93	**Read Advanced Leveled Reader,** DI•94	**Comprehension,** DI•95 **Read Paired Selection,** DI•95	**Fluency and Comprehension,** DI•95 **Reread Advanced Selection,** DI•95
DI•96–DI•105 **Concepts** **Vocabulary** **Phonics and Spelling** **Conventions**	DI•96–DI•105 **Concepts** **Vocabulary** **Comprehension Skill** **Main Selection**	DI•96–DI•105 **Concepts** **Vocabulary** **ELL/ELD Readers** **ELL Workshop**	DI•96–DI•105 **Concepts** **Vocabulary**

Week 5

Practice Stations for Everyone on Reading Street!

Word Wise

Identify and use syllable patterns to help spell common words.

Objectives
• Spell words with two syllables.
• Spell compound words.

Materials
• *Word Work* Flip Chart
• Letter Tiles • paper • pencils

Differentiated Activities
• A **digraph** is two vowels, like *oa*, with one sound.
• A **compound word** is a word made up of two or more words.

⬤ Spell *rainbow* and *hotel* using the Letter Tiles. Say the words, counting their syllables. Now write the words. Draw a picture.

▲ Spell *comic* and *oatmeal* using the Letter Tiles. Count the syllables. Split each word into syllables. Write a sentence with the words.

■ Spell the words *cowboy, salad, motor, ripen, panic,* and *soybean.* Divide and count the syllables in each word. Sort them by diphthong/short vowel/long vowel in the first syllable.

Technology
• Interactive Sound-Spelling Cards

Word Work

Identify syllable patterns.

Objectives
• Identify the "vowel team" syllable pattern.

Materials
• *Word Work Flip* Chart
• Teacher-made word cards: *downstairs, downspout, football, cowboy, houseboat, railroad, rainbow, oatmeal, soybean, outplay, daydream*
• paper
• pencils

Differentiated Activities

⬤ Find the word cards *railroad* and *oatmeal*. Quietly say each word as you write it. Find each vowel team and circle it. Now pronounce its sound. Do this process again with two more cards.

▲ Choose six word cards and quietly say each word. Write the words. Circle the vowel teams, and say each sound. For each different vowel team, write a new word with that team and sound.

■ Scan the word cards. Write any words that have vowel teams, and circle the vowel teams in each. For each different vowel team, write two new words with that vowel pattern and sound.

Technology
• Interactive Sound-Spelling Cards

Words To Know

Use context clues to define words with multiple meanings.

Objectives
• Use context clues to identify words with multiple meanings.
• Use context clues to determine the relative meaning of multiple-meaning words.

Materials
• *Words to Know* Flip Chart
• Teacher-made word cards: *band, cart, light, yard, plate, pit, bowl, mean, box*
• dictionaries • paper •pencils

Differentiated Activities

⬤ Write the word *season*. Now write these sentences: Frida <u>seasons</u> her food with pepper. Of the four <u>seasons</u>, spring is best. Write the meaning of season in each sense. Check definitions in a dictionary.

▲ Choose three word cards. Write two meanings for each word. If you are unsure, look up each word in a dictionary. Then write two sentences for each, one for each meaning.

■ Choose five word cards, and write two meanings for each. Check meanings in a dictionary. Now write five sentences, each using the word in two senses.

Technology
• Online Tested Vocabulary Activities

You Are Here!
Unit 4
Week 5

Use this week's materials from the
*Reading Street Leveled Practice Stations
Kit* to organize this week's stations.

Key

 Below-Level Activities

△ On-Level Activities

■ Advanced Activities

Practice Station
Flip Chart

Let's Write!
Write a narrative poem.

Objectives
• Write a narrative poem.
• Use words and voice to show feelings.

Materials
• *Let's Write!* Flip Chart
• paper
• pencils

Differentiated Activities
• A **narrative poem** tells a story with emotion and style. It may or may not rhyme.
• **Voice** is a writer's style of using language.

 Write a narrative poem about a change in your life. Use words and a picture to show how you feel about it. Use sensory details.

△ Write a narrative poem about an important change in your life. Let your voice and words show how you feel about the change. Illustrate your poem.

■ Write a narrative poem about an important change in your life. Let your voice and words express your feelings about the change. Use sensory details, and frame your experience as a poetic story.

Read For Meaning
Identify the plot and theme of a story.

Objectives
• Identify a story's plot by recognizing its narrative series of events.
• Determine a story's theme by considering the narrative as a whole.

Materials
• *Read for Meaning* Flip Chart
• 2.4.4 Leveled Readers
• paper
• pencils

Differentiated Activities
• The **plot** is what happens in the story.
• The **theme** is a story or poem's message about life. In myths and folk tales, theme is often a moral lesson about behavior.

 Read *Snakeskin Canyon*. What are the main things that happen in it? Write one or two key plot events. Write a sentence telling what the theme is.

△ Read *Too Many Frogs!*. What is it mostly about? What message does the story suggest? Write a paragraph telling several key plot events. Then write one sentence explaining the story's theme.

■ Read *A Quiet Place*. Explain the plot in a paragraph or two. Then write a sentence identifying the theme of the story. Finally, explain in a few sentences how you identified the story's theme.

Technology
• Online Student Edition
• Leveled eReaders

Get Fluent
Read with expression.

Objectives
• Read aloud with expression (characterization).

Materials
• *Get Fluent* Flip Chart
• 2.4.4 Leveled Readers

Differentiated Activities
• **Expression** is how the voice shows emotion or sets a **mood**.
• **Characterization** is how a writer or speaker shows a character.

 Work with a partner. Take turns reading pages from *Snakeskin Canyon.* Read with expression. Pay attention to punctuation. Give your partner feedback.

△ Work with a partner. Take turns reading pages from *Too Many Frogs!*. Read with expression. Pay attention to punctuation. Give your partner feedback.

■ Work with a partner. Take turns reading pages from *A Quiet Place.* Read with expression. Pay attention to punctuation. Give your partner feedback.

Technology
• Reading Street Readers CD-ROM

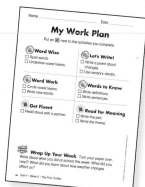

My Weekly Work Plan

Week 5

Objectives

- Introduce concept: effects of changing weather.
- Share information and ideas about the concept.

Today at a Glance

Oral Vocabulary
condition, predict, terrifying

Phonics and Spelling
◉ Vowel Digraphs *oo, ue, ew, ui*

Fluency
Oral Rereading

Comprehension
◉ Plot and Theme
◉ Monitor and Clarify

Lesson Vocabulary
awaken, cliffs, mountain, prize, rainbow, suffer, volcano

Conventions
Adverbs That Tell How

Writing
Thank-You Note: Introduce

Research and Inquiry
Identify and Focus Topic

Concept Talk

Question of the Week
? How do changes in the weather affect us?

Introduce the concept

To build concepts and to focus children's attention, tell them that this week they will talk, sing, read, and write about how changes in the weather affect us. Write the Question of the Week and track the print as you read it.

ROUTINE **Activate Prior Knowledge** **Team Talk**

1. **Think** Have children think for a minute about the weather and how it affected what they wore to school this morning.

2. **Pair** Have pairs of children discuss the question.

3. **Share** Have children share their ideas with the group. Guide discussion and encourage elaboration with prompts such as: How can a change in the weather affect our choices of clothing and activities?

Routines Flip Chart

Anchored Talk

Develop oral language

Have children turn to pages 154–155 in their Student Editions. Read the title and look at the photos. Use these questions to guide discussion and create a "How do changes in the weather affect us?" concept map.

- Look at the picture of the children wearing boots. What is the weather? (It is rainy.) How does this weather affect us? (It affects what we wear.) Let's add *Weather affects what we wear* to our chart.

- Which picture shows hot, dry weather? (the girl with the goats.) What are the effects of this weather? (The girl must make sure the goats have enough water.) Yes, weather affects what we do. Let's add this information to our chart.

- What does the last picture show? (It shows a tornado destroying houses.) A tornado is another kind of weather. This terrifying storm can affect property. We will add this to our chart.

Oral Vocabulary

Let's Talk About

Changes in the Weather

- Share information about how weather can cause damage.
- Share ideas about how weather affects food supply.

READING STREET ONLINE
CONCEPT TALK VIDEO
www.ReadingStreet.com

Objectives
• Listen closely to speakers and ask questions to help you better understand the topic. • Share information and ideas about the topic. Speak clearly and at a correct pace.

You've learned **1 5 3** Amazing Words so far this year!

154   155

Student Edition pp. 154–155

Amazing Words

You've learned **1 5 3** words so far.

You'll learn **0 0 8** words this week!

condition	whip
predict	sparkle
terrifying	funnel
breeze	swirl

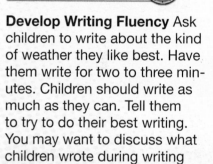

Writing on Demand

Develop Writing Fluency Ask children to write about the kind of weather they like best. Have them write for two to three minutes. Children should write as much as they can. Tell them to try to do their best writing. You may want to discuss what children wrote during writing conferences.

Connect to reading
Explain that this week, children will read about a girl whose bravery changes the weather so crops can grow. *Let's add Weather affects what we grow to our map.*

How do changes in the weather affect us?

| Weather affects what we wear. | Weather affects what we do. | Weather affects property. | Weather affects what we grow. |

ELL **Preteach Concepts** Use the Day 1 instruction on ELL Poster 20 to assess and build background knowledge, develop concepts, and build oral vocabulary.

ELL Poster 20

ELL

English Language Learners

Listening Comprehension
English learners will benefit from additional visual support to understand the key terms in the concept map. Use the picture on pp. 154–155 to scaffold understanding. For example, when talking about how weather affects what we wear, point to the puddles of water in the photo and explain that when it rains a lot, we wear boots to protect our feet from this water.

ELL Support
Additional ELL support and modified instruction is provided in the *ELL Handbook* and in the ELL Support lessons on pp. DI•96–DI•105.

Objectives
- Build oral vocabulary.
- Discuss the concept to develop oral language.
- Share information and ideas about the concept.

Oral Vocabulary
Amazing Words

Introduce Amazing Words

Display page 20 of the *Sing with Me Big Book*. Tell children they are going to sing about changing weather. Ask children to listen for the Amazing Words *condition*, *predict*, and *terrifying* as you sing. Sing the song again and have children join you.

Sing with Me Big Book p. 20

 Sing with Me Big Book Audio

Amazing Words Oral Vocabulary Routine

1 **Introduce** Relate the word *condition* to the song: The song says that no weather *condition* stays the same for long. Supply a child-friendly definition: A *condition* is the way something or someone is. Have children say the word.

2 **Demonstrate** Provide examples to show meaning: The weather *condition* is snowy. Because Amy was sick, she was in no *condition* to play soccer. The bike is in rusty *condition* because it was left out in the rain.

3 **Apply** Have children demonstrate their understanding: Which would be in the best *condition*—a person who is healthy or sick, a house that is abandoned or lived in, a stuffed animal that is old or new?

See p. OV•2 to teach *predict* and *terrifying*.

Routines Flip Chart

Check understanding of Amazing Words

Have children look at the picture on page 20. It looks like the two children are enjoying their walk. How would you describe the weather *conditions*? Use *conditions* in your answer. (Possible response: The weather conditions look sunny and warm.)

Look at the weather forecaster's chart. What weather condition does she *predict*? Use *predicts* in your answer. (Possible response: The forecaster predicts stormy weather.)

When might a storm be *terrifying*? Use *terrifying* in your answer. (Possible response: A storm might be terrifying if there is thunder, lightning, and high winds.)

Apply Amazing Words

Have children demonstrate their understanding of the Amazing Words by completing these sentences orally.

The _____ was in good **condition**.

The forecaster **predicts** _____ for tomorrow.

The _____ was **terrifying** to the young child.

Corrective feedback

If... children have difficulty using the Amazing Words, **then...** remind them of the definitions and provide opportunities for children to use the words in sentences.

Preteach Academic Vocabulary

Write the following on the board:

- **legend**
- **plot**
- **theme**
- **adverbs**

Have children share what they know about this week's Academic Vocabulary. Use children's responses to assess their prior knowledge. Preteach the Academic Vocabulary by providing a child-friendly description, explanation, or example that clarifies the meaning of each term. Then ask children to restate the meaning of the Academic Vocabulary in their own words.

Amazing Words

condition	whip
predict	sparkle
terrifying	funnel
breeze	swirl

Differentiated Instruction

SI Strategic Intervention

Build Oral Vocabulary In the song, children learned that even forecasters get tricked when it comes to predicting the weather. Say: A forecaster is someone who tells us what the weather will be like at a later time. Have children tell about weather forecasters they have heard on the radio or seen on television.

Professional Development

Research shows that combining shared book reading activities with explicit, direct teaching of target vocabulary increases the amount of vocabulary that children with smaller initial vocabularies who are at risk for reading difficulties learn.

English Language Learners
Cognates Spanish speakers may recognize the cognates *condición* (condition) and *predecir* (to predict).

Objectives
- ⊚ Associate the sound /ü/ with the spelling patterns *oo, ue, ew,* and *ui.*
- ⊚ Blend and read words with /ü/ spelled *oo, ue, ew,* and *ui.*
- • Decode words in context and independent of context.

Skills Trace
⊚ **Vowel Digraphs *oo, ue, ew, ui***

Introduce U4W5D1

Practice U4W5D2; U4W5D3; U4W5D4

Reteach/Review U4W5D5; U5W1D4

Assess/Test Weekly Test U4W5 Benchmark Test U4

Key:
U=Unit   W=Week   D=Day

Sound-Spelling
Card 90

Sound-Spelling
Card 102

Sound-Spelling
Card 68

Sound-Spelling
Card 103

Phonics—Teach/Model
↻ Vowel Digraphs *oo, ue, ew, ui*

ROUTINE **Blending Strategy**

1. **Connect** Write *foot.* Ask children what they know about the vowel sound in this word. (The vowel sound /ū/ is spelled *oo.*) Explain that today they will learn to spell and read words in which *oo* stand for another vowel sound, /ü/. The vowel pair *oo* is one of four ways to spell this sound.

2. **Use Sound-Spelling Cards** Display Card 90. Point to *oo.* The sound /ü/ you hear in *moon* can be spelled *oo.* Have children say /ü/ several times as you point to *oo.* Repeat this procedure for the sound /ü/ spelled *ue, ew,* and *ui* using Cards 102, 68, and 103.

3. **Model** Write *food.* In this word, the letters *oo* stand for the sound /ü/. Segment and blend *food;* then have children blend with you: /f/ /ü/ /d/, *food.* Follow this procedure to model *blue, dew,* and *fruit.*

4. **Guide Practice** Continue the process in step 3. This time have children blend with you. Remind children that the sound /ü/ can be spelled *oo, ue, ew,* or *ui.*

zoo	flew	carpool	suitcase	clue	threw
due	news	bruise	Tuesday	jewel	shampoo

5. **Review** What do you know about reading these words? (The letters *oo, ui, ew,* or *ui* can stand for the sound /ü/.)

Routines Flip Chart

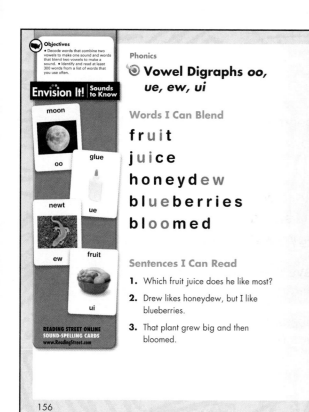

Objectives
- Decode words that combine two vowels to make one sound and words that blend two vowels to make a sound.
- Identify and read at least 300 words from a list of words that you use often.

Envision It! Sounds to Know

moon
oo

glue
ue

newt
ew

fruit
ui

READING STREET ONLINE
SOUND-SPELLING CARDS
www.ReadingStreet.com

Phonics

 Vowel Digraphs *oo*, *ue*, *ew*, *ui*

Words I Can Blend

f r u i t
j u i c e
h o n e y d e w
b l u e b e r r i e s
b l o o m e d

Sentences I Can Read

1. Which fruit juice does he like most?
2. Drew likes honeydew, but I like blueberries.
3. That plant grew big and then bloomed.

I Can Read!

Lewis has a new pool. Each day at noon he puts on his swimsuit, leaves his room, and jumps in the pool. Lewis believes it is true that working out in the pool is good for you. After his workout, Lewis drinks a cool glass of fruit juice. Last week, Lewis threw a pool party. There was gobs of good food, and Lewis made some new friends too. He's glad he has a pool.

You've learned

Vowel Digraphs *oo*, *ue*, *ew*, *ui*

156

157

Student Edition pp. 156–157

Model

Envision It!

Have children turn to page 156 in their Student Editions. Look at the pictures on this page. I see a *moon, glue,* a *newt,* and *fruit.* All the words have the /ü/ vowel sound, but the sound is spelled differently in each word. In *moon* the /ü/ sound is spelled *oo.* In *glue* the /ü/ sound is spelled *ue.* In *newt* the /ü/ sound is spelled *ew.* In *fruit* the /ü/ sound is spelled *ui.*

Guide practice

For each word in "Words I Can Blend," ask for the sound of each letter or group of letters. Then have children blend the words.

Corrective feedback

If... children have difficulty blending a word,
then... model blending the word, and then ask children to blend it with you.

Differentiated Instruction

 **Strategic Intervention**

Segment and Blend Segment a word slowly. Have children echo your sounds. Then blend the word. Have children echo the blending. Repeat for each word.

Vocabulary Support

You may wish to explain the meaning of these words.
due required, owed, or expected to arrive
bruise an injury on the skin that causes it to change colors

ELL

English Language Learners
Pronunciation Assist children with the articulation of phonemes. For multisyllabic words, take time to enunciate the phonemes for each syllable.

Language Transfer Show pictures of *fruit, juice, honeydew, blueberries,* and plants that have *bloomed.* Allow children to share the words from their native languages that mean the same as the English words.

Objectives

◉ Associate the sound /ü/ with the spelling patterns *oo, ue, ew,* and *ui.*

◉ Blend and read words with /ü/ spelled *oo, ue, ew,* and *ui.*

• Decode words in context and independent of context.

• Segment and spell words with /ü/ spelled *oo, ue, ew,* and *ui.*

Check Word Reading
SUCCESS PREDICTOR

Phonics
Blend and Read

Decode words independent of context

After children can successfully segment and blend the words on page 156 in their Student Editions, point to words in random order and ask children to read them naturally.

Decode words in context

Have children read each of the sentences on page 156. Have them identify words in the sentences that have /ü/ spelled *oo, ue, ew,* and *ui.*

Team Talk Pair children and have them take turns reading each of the sentences aloud.

Chorally read the **I Can Read!** passage on page 157 along with the children. Then have them read the passage aloud to themselves.

On their own Use *Reader's and Writer's Notebook* p. 337.

Reader's and Writer's
Notebook p. 337

MONITOR PROGRESS Check Word Reading 🔄 /ü/Spelled oo, ue, ew, ui

Write the following words and have the class read them. Notice which words children miss during the group reading. Call on individuals to read some of the words.

cool	due	brewing	juicy	raccoon	**Spiral Review**
stew	tooth	bloom	chewy	untrue ←	**Row 2** reviews blends and digraphs.
music	unit	huge	cube	pupil ←	**Row 3** reviews long *u.*

If... children cannot blend *oo, ue, ew,* and *ui* words at this point,

then... use the Small Group Time Strategic Intervention lessons, p. DI•85, to reteach the vowel digraphs *oo, ue, ew,* and *ui.* Continue to monitor children's progress using other instructional opportunities during the week. See the Skills Trace on p. 156a.

Day 1 Check Word Reading	**Day 2** Check Lesson Vocabulary/ High-Frequency Words	**Day 3** Check Retelling	**Day 4** Check Fluency	**Day 5** Check Oral Vocabulary

Success Predictor

Spelling Pretest
Vowel Digraphs *oo, ue, ew, ui*

Dictate spelling words

Dictate the spelling words. Have children write the words. If needed, segment the words, clarify the pronunciations, and give meanings of words. Have children check their pretests and correct misspelled words.

1.	**too**	Don't spend **too** much time playing games.
2.	**new**	Someone built a **new** house on our block.
3.	**fruit**	Pears and peaches were in the **fruit** bowl.
4.	**blue***	The sky was **blue** with no clouds at all.
5.	**true**	Is the answer **true** or false?
6.	**fool**	She tried to **fool** me by hiding.
7.	**suit**	I wore my green bathing **suit** to the beach.
8.	**spoon**	She uses a small **spoon** to eat her cereal.
9.	**clue**	Please give me a **clue** to solve the puzzle.
10.	**juice**	I had apple **juice** and crackers for a snack.
11.	**drew**	Mom hung a picture on the wall that I **drew**.
12.	**flew***	The door suddenly **flew** open.

*Words marked with asterisks come from the selection *The First Tortilla*.

On their own

Use Let's Practice It! p. 219 on the *Teacher Resource DVD-ROM*.

Let's Practice It!
TR DVD•219

Small Group Time

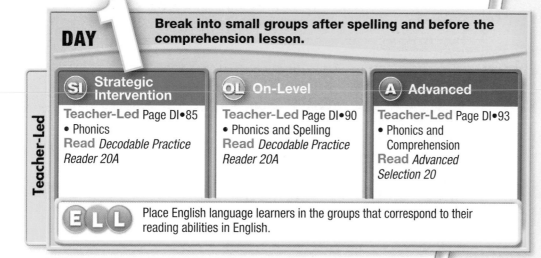

DAY 1

Break into small groups after spelling and before the comprehension lesson.

Teacher-Led

(SI) Strategic Intervention	(OL) On-Level	(A) Advanced
Teacher-Led Page DI•85 • Phonics **Read** *Decodable Practice Reader 20A*	**Teacher-Led** Page DI•90 • Phonics and Spelling **Read** *Decodable Practice Reader 20A*	**Teacher-Led** Page DI•93 • Phonics and Comprehension **Read** *Advanced Selection 20*

ELL Place English language learners in the groups that correspond to their reading abilities in English.

Practice Stations
• Word Work
• Read for Meaning

Independent Activities
• Read independently/Reading Log on *Reader's and Writer's Notebook*, p. RR4
• Concept Talk Video

A Advanced

Extend Provide children who can segment and blend all the words correctly with more challenging words, and allow children who spell words correctly to spell more challenging words such as: *cruise, shampoo, suitcase, nephew, igloo,* and *jewel.*

SI Strategic Intervention

Check Spelling Have children choose the correct spelling of each word from three random spellings.

Phonics/Spelling Generalization

Each spelling word has the /ü/ vowel sound spelled *oo, ue, ew,* or *ui.*

Spelling Patterns

/ü/ *oo, ue, e, ui* The sound /ü/, as in *blue,* may be spelled *oo, ue, ew, ui.* The letters *oo* can spell the short *oo* sound (*book*) or the long *oo* sound (*moon*). The context provides the clue to pronunciation.

English Language Learners
Spelling: Vowel Digraphs To clarify meanings, provide visual support by showing objects or pantomiming.

Word Reading

Success Predictor

Objectives

- Apply knowledge of sound-spellings to decode unknown words when reading.
- Decode and read words in context and independent of context.
- Practice fluency with oral rereading.

Decodable Practice Reader 20A
Vowel Digraphs *oo, ue, ew, ui*

Decodable Practice Reader 20A

Decode words independent of context	Have children turn to the first page and decode each word.
Read high-frequency words	Have children identify and read the high-frequency words *eyes, moon, another, picture, single, only,* and *thought* on the first page.
Preview Decodable Reader	Have children read the title and preview the story. Tell them they will decode words with vowel digraphs *oo, ue, ew,* and *ui.*
Decode words in context	Pair children for reading and listen carefully as they decode. One child begins. Children read the entire story, switching readers after each page. Partners reread the story. This time the other child begins.

Sue needed to see
if it is true that a
cow that went "moo"
flew over the moon.
74

Sue will read to find a clue.
This book is full of cow facts.
But not a single cow flew!
75

Sue read about moon facts too.
It did not give proof that cows
ever came near the moon!
76

Sue had another clue
about what to do.
She asked an old cow
if she had ever flown over the moon.
That cow only said, "Moo."
77

Sue drew a picture of this cow.
She thought that wings
would suit the cow she drew.
Her hope grew that
she might soon learn if cows flew.
78

Sue waited and waited for
this cow to fly by.
But she soon grew tired
and her eyes closed tight.
79

Just as Sue started sleeping,
what do you think went by,
flying and leaping?
That cow zoomed
right over the moon!
80

Corrective feedback

If... children have difficulty decoding a word,
then... refer them to the Sound-Spelling Cards to identify the sounds in the word. Then prompt them to blend the word.

- What is the new word?
- Is the new word a word you know?
- Does it make sense in the story?

Check decoding and comprehension

Have children retell the story to include characters, setting, and events. Then have children find words with the vowel digraphs *oo, ue, ew,* and *ui* in the story. Children should supply *Sue, true, moo, flew, moon, clue, too, proof, drew, suit, grew, soon,* and *zoomed.*

Reread for Fluency

Have children reread Decodable Practice Reader 20A to develop automaticity decoding words with vowel digraphs *oo, ue, ew,* and *ui.*

ROUTINE **Oral Rereading**

1. **Read** Have children read the entire book orally.

2. **Reread** To achieve optimal fluency, children should reread the text three or four times.

3. **Corrective Feedback** Listen as children read. Provide corrective feedback regarding their fluency and decoding.

Routines Flip Chart

English Language Learners
Vowel Digraphs *oo, ue, ew, ui*
Beginning Take a preview walk through *Is it True?* while pointing to and naming things in the pictures. Have children repeat words that contain the *oo, ue, ew,* and *ui* digraphs. Write each word on the board as you say it.

Intermediate Write *too,* read it aloud, and have children read it. Change the *t* to an *m* and have children read the word aloud. Add the letter *n* to the end. Read it and have children read it. Proceed in the same way, changing letters, for other words with vowel digraphs *oo, ue, ew,* and *ui* in the story.

Advanced/Advanced-High
Have children supply a word with the digraph *oo, ue, ew,* or *ui* to complete these rhymes:
Very soon.
We will see the _____. (moon)
I looked at Sue.
She gave me a _____. (clue)
As soon as it grew,
Away the bird _____. (flew)
He ate some fruit.
It dropped on his _____. (suit)

30–35 min.

Objectives
- Analyze the plot and theme of a fable.
- Monitor comprehension by asking questions and rereading text to locate the answers.

Skills Trace

◉ **Plot and Theme**
Introduce U4W4D1; U4W5D1; U5W3D1
Practice U4W4D2; U4W4D3; U4W4D4; U4W5D2; U4W5D3; U4W5D4; U5W3D2; U5W3D3; U5W3D4
Reteach/Review U1W1D3; U3W1D3; U4W4D5; U4W5D5; U5W3D5; U5W4D3
Assess/Test Weekly Tests U4W4; U4W5; U5W3
Benchmark Tests U1
Key:
U=Unit   W=Week   D=Day

Skill ↔ Strategy
🔁 Plot and Theme
🔁 Monitor and Clarify

Introduce plot and theme

Many things happen in the beginning, the middle, and the end of a story. What do we call what happens in these three story parts? (We call it the story plot.) Good readers use the story plot to help them identify the theme of the story. What is the story theme? (The story theme is the "big idea" that the author wants readers to learn

Student Edition EI•14–EI•15

Envision It!

from the story.) Remember that some stories, such as fables, myths, and legends, have a moral lesson as their theme. Have children turn to pages EI•14–EI•15 in the Student Edition to review identifying a story plot and theme. Then read "The Grasshopper and the Ant" with children.

Model the skill

Think Aloud

Today we're going to read a fable about two animal characters—the grasshopper and the ant. As in most fables, these animals behave like people. Have children follow along as you read aloud the first four paragraphs of "The Grasshopper and the Ant." In the beginning of the fable, we meet the characters. We learn the ant is hard working and thinks ahead. We also learn that the grasshopper likes to sing and doesn't think ahead. These events make up the plot in the beginning of the fable.

Guide practice

Have children finish reading "The Grasshopper and the Ant" on their own. After they read, have them use a graphic organizer like the one on page 158 to record story events that make up the plot in the beginning, middle, and end of the story. Then have them use these events to talk about the theme or moral lesson of the fable.

Objectives
- Identify themes in well-known fables, legends, myths, or stories.
- Ask questions, clear up anything you don't understand, look for facts and details in the stories you read, and support your answers with evidence.

Envision It! | Skill | Strategy

Skill

Strategy

Monitor and Clarify

READING STREET ONLINE
ENVISION IT! ANIMATIONS
www.ReadingStreet.com

Comprehension Skill

Plot and Theme

- A plot is what happens at the beginning, middle, and end of a story.
- A story's theme is the "big idea" that the author wants the reader to learn from the story. This can be a moral lesson.
- Use what you learned about identifying theme and plot and fill out an organizer like the one below as you read "The Grasshopper and the Ant."

Beginning	
Middle	
End	

Comprehension Strategy

Monitor and Clarify

Good readers make sure they understand what they read. Does something seem confusing to you as you read? Seek clarification. First, ask yourself a question. Then reread the paragraph. Think about what it says. Does it answer your question?

158

The Grasshopper and the Ant

Long ago, a grasshopper met an ant. The ant carried a piece of corn on her back.

The grasshopper said, "Hello! Would you like to sing with me?"

The ant said, "I have no time to sing. I have to get a lot of corn to my nest. I will need the food for winter."

"Why worry about winter?" asked the grasshopper. "Winter will not be here for a long time."

"You won't have any food in the winter if you do not work now," said the ant. The grasshopper laughed at the ant.

Many months passed. Winter came. All the leaves were gone. Snow was all around. The grasshopper could not find food and was very hungry.

The ant was not hungry. She had plenty of corn to eat. The ant was ready for winter because she had prepared for it.

Strategy Did you read something you did not understand? Ask a question. Reread the text to find the answer.

Skill What is the lesson to be learned? What is the theme of the story?

Your Turn!

⏸ **Need a Review?** See the *Envision It! Handbook* for additional help with plot and theme and monitor and clarify.

▶ **Ready to Try It?** As you read *The First Tortilla*, use what you've learned to understand the text.

159

Student Edition pp. 158–159

Strategy Possible response: As I read, I didn't understand why the ant turned down the grasshopper's invitation. So I asked myself that question and reread to find the answer. I discovered that the ant felt she needed to work because she wanted to store food for winter.

Skill Possible answer: The lesson is that it is important to plan ahead. The theme is that a wise person thinks about the future and not just about the present.

Academic Vocabulary

plot the events at the beginning, middle, and end of a story

theme the big idea or author's message in a story

monitor and clarify a comprehension strategy by which readers actively think about understanding their reading and know when they understand and when they do not. Readers use appropriate strategies to make sense of difficult words, ideas, or passages.

Strategy check

Monitor and Clarify Remind children that they can use the monitor and clarify strategy to help them understand "The Grasshopper and the Ant." Model the strategy by asking questions and rereading to adjust understanding.

Model the strategy

Think Aloud After reading about the hungry grasshopper, I wasn't sure why he wasn't hungry when he and the ant first met. I asked myself this and then I reread. One clue I found was when Grasshopper said, "Winter will not be here for a long time." I figured out that they first met in summer when food was plentiful. Have children review the strategy of Monitor and Clarify on p. EI•21 of the Student Edition.

Student Edition p. EI•21

On their own

Use p. 339 in the *Reader's and Writer's Notebook* for additional practice with plot and theme.

INTERACT with TEXT

Reader's and Writer's Notebook p. 339

Ⓔ Ⓛ Ⓛ

English Language Learners

Plot and Theme Have children draw pictures showing events in the beginning, middle, and end of the story. Then have them talk about these events and tell what lesson the grasshopper learned.

Objectives

• Use context clues to find meanings of unfamiliar words.

• Activate prior knowledge of words.

• Identify and use adverbs.

Vocabulary
Lesson Vocabulary

Activate prior knowledge

Display the vocabulary words and ask oral questions like those below.

• Would you expect lava to come out of a *volcano*?

• If you received a *prize*, would you be upset?

• Do you jump rope before you *awaken* in the morning?

• If you had the chicken pox, would you *suffer* from itching?

• Does the land drop down at the edge of high *cliffs*?

• Can you use a sailboat on a *mountain*?

• Is a *rainbow* colorful?

Children should respond *yes* or *no* and give reasons for their choices.

To broaden children's understanding of words, have them change the questions where they responded *no*, so the response is *yes*.

Review compound words

Use *rainbow* to review compound words. Have children identify the two words in *rainbow* (*rain* and *bow*).

On their own

Use *Reader's and Writer's Notebook,* p. 338.

Reader's and Writer's Notebook p. 338

Conventions
Adverbs That Tell How

Model

An **adverb** can tell about a verb by telling how something happens. This type of adverb often ends in *-ly. Carefully, beautifully,* and *loudly* are adverbs that tell how.

Display Grammar Transparency 20. Read the definition aloud. Model identifying the adverb in the example. Then read the directions and model number 1.

- The verb in this sentence is *listen*. I will read the adverbs in the box and look for one that tells how someone could listen.

- Someone could listen carefully, so I will write the adverb *carefully* on the line.

Adverbs That Tell How

An adverb can tell more about a verb by telling how an action is done. **Adverbs** that tell how usually end in -ly.

When she looked up, she saw the mountain **clearly.**

Clearly tells how she saw the mountain.

Write an adverb from the box to complete each sentence. Use each adverb once.

| quietly | loudly | wildly |
| quickly | carefully | suddenly |

1. "I must listen _____ **carefully** _____," she said.
2. She left her village _____ **quietly**
3. _____ **Suddenly** _____ the mountain shook.
4. "Why have you come?" it asked _____ **loudly**
5. The wind blew _____ **wildly** _____
6. She ran _____ **quickly** _____ down the path.

Unit 4 The First Tortilla   Grammar **20**

Grammar Transparency 20
TR DVD

Guide practice

Continue with items 2–6, having children choose the adverb that tells more about the verb in each sentence.

Connect to oral language

Have the class complete these sentence frames orally using adverbs that tell how.

> 1. **Please speak _____ in the library.**
>
> 2. **Pia plays the piano _____.**
>
> 3. **Karen brushed her teeth _____.**

On their own

Team Talk Pair children and have them talk about how they might speak if they were in a restaurant, on the soccer field, or in a movie theatre. Then have them identify the adverbs they used during their discussion.

Differentiated Instruction

 Strategic Intervention

Adverbs About Manner If children omit the *-ly* ending in their oral sentences, then say the sentences several times, emphasizing the adverb, and have children repeat the sentences with you.

Academic Vocabulary

adverb a word that tells how, when, or where something happens. It can modify a verb, an adjective, or another adverb.

Daily Fix-It

1. Dee wore a blew sweater
   Dee wore a <u>blue</u> sweater.
2. Who drue this picture.
   Who <u>drew</u> this picture?

Discuss the Daily Fix-It corrections with children. Review sentence punctuation and the vowel digraphs *ue* and *ew*.

ELL

English Language Learners

Options for Conventions Support To provide children with practice with adjectives, use the modified conventions lessons on p. 377 in the *ELL Handbook*.

Cognates Point out to Spanish speakers that the adverb ending *-ly* is like the ending *-mente* in Spanish. Give a few examples with cognates such as *rapidly/rápidamente; probably/probablemente; absolutely/absolutamente.*

Objectives
• Recognize features of a thank-you note.

MINI-LESSON

5 Day Planner
Guide to Mini-Lessons

DAY 1	Read Like a Writer
DAY 2	Important Ideas
DAY 3	Sequence
DAY 4	Revising Strategy: Deleting Phrases
DAY 5	Proofread for Adverbs and Format

Writing—Thank-You Note
Introduce

MINI-LESSON

Read Like a Writer

■ **Introduce** This week you will write a thank-you note. A thank-you note is a short friendly letter thanking someone for something they did.

Prompt	Think about how thankful people are for food during any season. Write a thank-you note to someone who has prepared food for you.
Trait	Focus
Mode	Thank-You Note

INTERACT with TEXT

Name _____

Writing • Thank-You Note

March 7, 2011

Dear Uncle Roy,

Thank you for making my favorite soup for lunch yesterday. I knew you made the soup as soon as I walked into the kitchen. The air was filled with the wonderful smell of simmering vegetables. The carrots tasted so sweet, and the broth had a tangy flavor from the onions and spices.

You must have put a lot of time into preparing the lunch. First, you carefully chose fresh vegetables. Next, you cut the vegetables evenly into little chunks. Then, you cooked the soup slowly for hours. It was so delicious that we ate it much too quickly. You are a great cook!

Love,
Mike

Key Features of a Thank-You Note
• a short message that thanks someone
• has a greeting and a closing, like a letter

340 Writing Thank-You Note

Reader's and Writer's Notebook p. 340

■ **Examine Model Text** Let's listen to a thank-you note. Track the print as you read aloud the thank-you note on *Reader's and Writer's Notebook* p. 340. Have children follow along.

■ **Key Features** Help children find the key features of the thank-you note. What does the thank-you note look like? (a letter) The thank-you note begins with the date. What follows the date? (the greeting) Where do you find the reason for writing? (in the body) What is the reason for the author to write this thank-you note? (to thank his uncle for making his favorite soup) What comes after the body? (the closing) What punctuation mark comes after the closing? (comma) What follows the closing? (the signature)

Review key features

Review key features of a thank-you note with children. You may want to post these key features in the classroom to allow children to refer to them as they work on their thank-you notes.

Key Features of a Thank-You Note

- a short message that thanks someone
- has a date, greeting, and a closing

Connect to familiar texts

Connect the thank-you to other thank-you notes children may have written or received. You may want to connect it to the Persuasive Letter they wrote during the first week of this unit. Ask what is similar and what is different between the two kinds of writing. Point out how all thank-you notes have a date, greeting, and a closing like letters do. Discuss how the purposes are different.

Look ahead

Tell children that tomorrow they will plan their own thank-you note.

Write Guy
Jeff Anderson

The Sunny Side

I like to look for what's *right* in children's writing rather than focusing on things I can edit or fix. Most students don't write flawlessly—who does? However, they will learn what they are doing well if we point it out.

Academic Vocabulary

thank-you note a short friendly letter thanking someone for something they did

---

ROUTINE **Quick Write for Fluency** **Team Talk**

1. **Talk** Read these questions aloud, and have children respond with adverbs that tell how.
   Which adverb tells how Uncle Roy cut the vegetables? (evenly)
   Which adverb tells how Uncle Roy cooked the soup? (slowly)

2. **Write** Have children write short sentences to answer the questions. Make sure their sentences include an adverb that tells how.

3. **Share** Partners can read their answers to one another.

Routines Flip Chart

Objectives
- Identify a topic connected to this week's concept.
- Narrow the focus of the topic by formulating inquiry questions related to the topic.
- Explore weather changes.

Research and Inquiry
Identify and Focus Topic

Teach

Display and review the concept web that explores this week's question: *How do changes in the weather affect us?* What ideas about weather changes and our lives would you like to learn more about? Ask children to share their ideas. Help them identify different weather conditions and their effects in people's daily lives. Together, generate a list of topics that children in the class are interested in exploring further.

Model

Think Aloud To learn how changes in the weather affect us, let's ask ourselves questions about the topics we've listed and then look for the answers. The first thing I think would be helpful to know is what we do when the weather is nice. I'll record that question.

Guide practice

Give children time to think about and develop some questions that, when answered, would help them learn more about how changes in weather affect us. Record children's questions in a chart.

Topic: How Weather Changes Affect Us	
Question	**Answer**
What do we do when the weather is nice?	

Wrap Up Your Day

✔ **Phonics: Vowel Digraphs *oo, ue, ew, ui*** Write *food, glue, threw,* and *bruise.* Ask children what vowel sound they hear in each word and which letters spell the sound. (*/ü/, oo, ue, ew, ui*)

✔ **Spelling** Say *true, spoon, juice,* and *drew.* Have children write each word and then spell the words orally.

✔ **Build Concepts** Ask children to recall "Changing Conditions." How did the weather change in the song? (Possible response: Yesterday there was a terrible storm, and today the weather was nice and warm.)

✔ **Homework** Send home this week's Family Times Newsletter from Let's Practice It! pp. 215–216 on the *Teacher Resource DVD-ROM.*

Let's Practice It!
TR DVD•215–216

Preview DAY 2

Tell children that tomorrow they will read a legend of how a young girl helped bring rain to her village to grow vegetables.

Objectives
- Discuss the concept to develop oral language.
- Build oral vocabulary.

Today at a Glance

Oral Vocabulary
breeze, whip

Phonics and Spelling
◉ Vowel Digraphs *oo, ue, ew, ui*

Lesson Vocabulary
awaken, cliffs, mountain, prize, rainbow, suffer, volcano

Vocabulary
◉ Prefixes

Fluency
Paired Reading

Comprehension
◉ Plot and Theme
◉ Monitor and Clarify

Conventions
Adverbs That Tell How

Writing
Thank-You Note

Handwriting
Cursive *n, m, x* / Letter Size

Research and Inquiry
Research Skill: Natural and Personal Sources

Concept Talk

Question of the Week

How do changes in the weather affect us?

Build concepts

To reinforce concepts and to focus children's attention, have children sing "Changing Conditions" from the *Sing with Me* Big Book. In the song, we hear that weather is so strange. What is strange about the weather? (Possible response: The weather is strange because it changes every day.)

💿 *Sing with Me* Big Book Audio

Introduce Amazing Words

Explain that today you will read about how a girl named Tessa and her friends plan a party in the story "Happy Birthday, Old Man Winter!" by Julie Brooks Hiller. In the story, the author uses the word *breeze* to describe the wind that blows during the party. Have children listen as you read the story to find out what weather has to do with the children's party.

Use the Oral Vocabulary routine on the next page to teach *breeze* and *whip*.

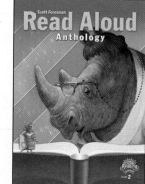

Read Aloud Anthology "Happy Birthday, Old Man Winter!"

ELL Reinforce Vocabulary Use the Day 2 instruction on ELL Poster 20 to teach Lesson Vocabulary and discuss the lesson concept.

ELL Poster 20

Oral Vocabulary
Amazing Words

Teach Amazing Words

Amazing Words Oral Vocabulary Routine

1. **Introduce the Word** Relate the word *breeze* to the story. During the party, a *breeze* sweeps across the playground. Supply a child-friendly definition. A *breeze* is a light, gentle wind. Have children say the word.

2. **Demonstrate** Provide examples to show meaning. The *breeze* blew through the windows and cooled the house. The *breeze* filled the sail, pushing the boat across the water.

3. **Apply** Have children demonstrate their understanding. Which of these things would a *breeze* do: make a flag flap, knock over a big tree, blow a paper off a desk, snap a power line, blow a leaf across the yard?

See p. OV•2 to teach *whip*.

Routines Flip Chart

Amazing Words

condition	whip
predict	sparkle
terrifying	funnel
breeze	swirl

Anchored Talk

Add to the concept map

Discuss the weather and its effects.

- How would you describe the weather conditions in "Happy Birthday, Old Man Winter!"? (The weather is cold and snowy.) How does cold, snowy weather affect what the characters wear? (They wear heavy clothes to keep warm.) Let's add *We wear heavy clothes to keep warm in cold weather* to our concept map.

- What are the effects of cold, snowy weather on what Tessa and her friends do? (Possible response: They make a pretend cake out of snow.) Yes, we can build things out of snow. Where can we add this information? (We can add it under the heading *Weather affects what we do*.)

 ELL

English Language Learners
Amazing Words Have children repeat the word *breeze* after you and then blow gently on their hand to see what a breeze feels like. Then give them classroom objects like a tissue, a heavy block, a plastic cube, and a dictionary, and have them experiment to see if a breeze could blow each object. Remind them to use the word *breeze* as they describe their findings.

Objectives

• Apply knowledge of letter-sound correspondences and syllable patterns to decode words in context and independent of context.

• Spell words with vowel sound /ü/ spelled *oo*, *ue*, *ew*, and *ui*.

Phonics
oo /u̇/; *oo, ue, ew, ui* /ü/

Review Review words with /u̇/ spelled *oo* as in *book* using Sound-Spelling Card 89 and /ü/ spelled *oo, ue, ew*, and *ui* using Sound-Spelling Cards 68, 90, 102, and 103.

Decode words independent of context

Display these words. Have the class blend the words. Then point to the words in random order and ask children to read them quickly.

tooth	screw	bruise
hood	clueless	shook
moonlight	dewdrop	suitcase

Corrective feedback | Model blending decodable words and then ask children to blend them with you.

Decode words in context

Display these sentences. Have the class read the sentences.

Team Talk Then have pairs take turns reading the sentences naturally.

Sue stood at the **foot** of the hill and set **loose** her **bluebird**.

Andrew took the **cookbook** to **look** up how to make **fruit** pies.

The **Tuesday afternoon cruise** was **too good** to be **true**.

Spelling
Vowel Digraphs *oo, ue, ew, ui*

Guide practice

Tell children that you will segment the sounds in each spelling word. They should repeat the sounds in each word as they write them. Check the spelling of each word before saying the next word.

1. /t/ /ü/ **too**
2. /n/ /ü/ **new**
3. /f/ /r/ /ü/ /t/ **fruit**
4. /b/ /l/ /ü/ **blue**
5. /t/ /r/ /ü/ **true**
6. /f/ /ü/ /l/ **fool**

7. /s/ /ü/ /t/ **suit**
8. /s/ /p/ /ü/ /n/ **spoon**
9. /k/ /l/ /ü/ **clue**
10. /j/ /ü/ /s/ **juice**
11. /d/ /r/ /ü/ **drew**
12. /f/ /l/ /ü/ **flew**

On their own Use *Reader's and Writer's Notebook*, p. 341.

Small Group Time

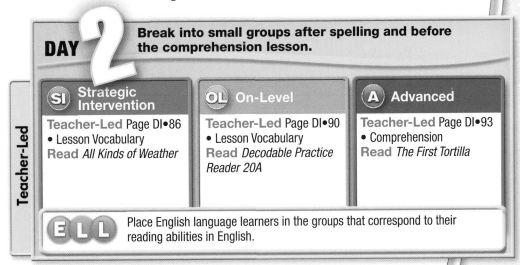

DAY 2 **Break into small groups after spelling and before the comprehension lesson.**

Teacher-Led

SI Strategic Intervention
Teacher-Led Page DI•86
• Lesson Vocabulary
Read *All Kinds of Weather*

OL On-Level
Teacher-Led Page DI•90
• Lesson Vocabulary
Read *Decodable Practice Reader 20A*

A Advanced
Teacher-Led Page DI•93
• Comprehension
Read *The First Tortilla*

ELL Place English language learners in the groups that correspond to their reading abilities in English.

Practice Stations
• Words to Know
• Get Fluent

Independent Activities
• Read independently/Reading Log on *Reader's and Writer's Notebook* p. RR4
• AudioText of Main Selection

Reader's and Writer's Notebook p. 341

 ELL

English Language Learners
Vowel Digraphs oo, ue, ew, ui
The many spellings for the sound /ü/ may be confusing for children. Sort the spelling words according to the digraph they contain. Have children practice reading the lists.

Objectives

• Learn lesson vocabulary: *awaken, cliffs, mountain, prize, rainbow, suffer, volcano.*

• Use new vocabulary words correctly.

Check Lesson Vocabulary/High-Frequency Words

SUCCESS PREDICTOR

Lesson Vocabulary

Review
Lesson vocabulary

Display the lesson vocabulary words. Read them aloud and review their meanings. Divide the words into syllables to help children decode the words. Have children say each word after you.

a • wak • en cause to stop sleeping

cliffs steep rock faces, like those at the edge of the sea

moun • tain a high, steep hill that is often rocky

prize something given to someone as a reward

rain • bow a display of many colors

suf • fer to experience something bad or unpleasant

vol • ca • no a cone-shaped mountain with a hole in the top that sends out melted rock and gases

Tell children that being able to read these words and knowing their meanings will help them as they read this week's selection, *The First Tortilla.*

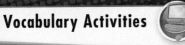
 **Strategic Intervention**

Ask Questions Ask these questions and have children supply the correct vocabulary words. *Which words name Earth formations that a person might climb? (cliffs, mountain, volcano) What makes colors in the sky? (rainbow) Which word means the opposite of "feel good"? (suffer) What happens when your alarm clock goes off? (I awaken) If you won a trophy, what would you have? (prize)*

Don't Wait Until Friday

MONITOR PROGRESS — Check Lesson Vocabulary/High-Frequency Words

Write the following words and have the class read them. Listen for children who miss words during the reading. Call on those children to read some of the words individually.

cliffs	suffer	mountain	volcano	
awaken	cliffs	prize		**Spiral Review**
enough	took	around	many ←	Rows 3 and 4 review previously taught high-frequency words.
thought			←	

If... children cannot read these words,
then... use the Small Group Time Strategic Intervention lesson, p. DI•86, to reteach the words. Monitor children's fluency with these words during reading and provide additional practice.

Day 1	Day 2	Day 3	Day 4	Day 5
Check Word Reading	Check Lesson Vocabulary/ High-Frequency Words	Check Retelling	Check Fluency	Check Oral Vocabulary

 Success Predictor

ELL

English Language Learners

Visual Support Use pictures from the story or others of a *mountain*, a *volcano*, and *cliffs* and point out the differences in meanings. Have children draw pictures of the words and label them. Then draw a picture of a blue ribbon to show *prize*. Demonstrate *awaken* by pretending to sleep and then waking up.

Multilingual Vocabulary Lists Children can apply knowledge of their home languages to acquire new English vocabulary by using the Multilingual Vocabulary Lists (*ELL Handbook*, pages 429–440).

Success Predictor

Vocabulary/High-Frequency Words

Objectives

- Use word structure to determine the meaning of words beginning with a prefix.
- Read grade-level text with fluency.

Vocabulary Strategy for
Prefixes

Teach prefixes

Tell children that some words begin with a prefix, which is a word part added to the beginning of a word to change its meaning or to make another word. Explain that using the meaning of a prefix can sometimes help them figure out the meaning of a word they don't know. Refer children to *Words!* on p. W•5 in the Student Edition for additional practice. Then read "Hector and the Scarecrow" on page 161 with children.

Envision It!

Student Edition p. W•5

Model the strategy

Think Aloud Write on the board: *The boy rewrote his paragraph about a rainbow.* I can use my knowledge of prefixes and how they change word meanings to help me figure out the meaning of *rewrote.* I know that when the prefix *re-* is added to a word, it makes the word mean *"___ again."* Knowing this helps me figure out that the word *rewrote* means "wrote again." To test this, I will try this meaning in the sentence to see if it makes sense: *The boy wrote* again *his paragraph about a rainbow.*

Guide practice

Write this sentence on the board: *The sign disallows children younger than ten from climbing the cliffs.* Have children locate the word with a prefix, identify the base word, and insert the base word in the phrase "not _____." Then have them try this meaning in the sentence to see if it makes sense.

On their own

Read "Hector and the Scarecrow" on page 161. Have children identify words with a prefix and use the meaning of each prefix to help them determine the meaning of the words. Then have them write what they think happens next to Hector and the scarecrow using words from the Words to Know list. For additional practice, use *Reader's and Writer's Notebook* p. 342.

Reader's and Writer's Notebook p. 342

Student Edition pp. 160–161

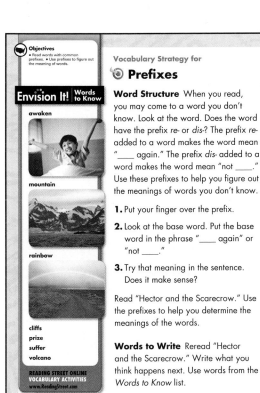

Objectives
• Read words with common prefixes. • Use prefixes to figure out the meaning of words.

Envision It! Words to Know
awaken
mountain
rainbow
cliffs
prize
suffer
volcano

READING STREET ONLINE
VOCABULARY ACTIVITIES
www.ReadingStreet.com

160

Vocabulary Strategy for

Prefixes

Word Structure When you read, you may come to a word you don't know. Look at the word. Does the word have the prefix re- or dis-? The prefix re- added to a word makes the word mean "____ again." The prefix dis- added to a word makes the word mean "not ____." Use these prefixes to help you figure out the meanings of words you don't know.

1. Put your finger over the prefix.

2. Look at the base word. Put the base word in the phrase "____ again" or "not ____."

3. Try that meaning in the sentence. Does it make sense?

Read "Hector and the Scarecrow." Use the prefixes to help you determine the meanings of the words.

Words to Write Reread "Hector and the Scarecrow." Write what you think happens next. Use words from the Words to Know list.

Hector and the Scarecrow

Hector heard people tell and retell stories about the volcano near his home. They said that it was a scary place. They said everything there could talk, even the trees and rocks. Hector disagreed. He did not think it could be that scary, so he quietly left his home one morning. He did not want to awaken the other people in town. They would try to stop him if they were awake.

Hector climbed the volcano. He reached some cliffs near the top. Tall, green cornstalks grew on the cliffs. A single scarecrow stood nearby. The scarecrow wore a red coat, blue pants, and a yellow hat. "He looks like a rainbow. What a prize!" thought Hector. Then the scarecrow said, "Oh. Hello there." Hector was amazed! The scarecrow spoke, but it sounded sad.

Hector asked, "Is something wrong?"

The scarecrow said, "I dislike this place. I want to visit a different mountain."

Hector did not want to see the scarecrow suffer. He said, "Come home with me. We will sleep tonight. Tomorrow, I will help you find another mountain."

Your Turn!

Need a Review? For more help with using prefixes to determine the meaning of a word, see Words! on p. W•5.

Ready to Try It? Read The First Tortilla on pp. 162–176.

161

Reread for Fluency

Have children reread paragraph 1 of "Hector and the Scarecrow."

ROUTINE **Paired Reading**

1. **Reread** To achieve optimal fluency, have partners reread the text three or four times.

2. **Corrective Feedback** Listen as children read. Provide corrective feedback regarding their fluency and decoding.

Routines Flip Chart

Lesson Vocabulary

awaken cause to stop sleeping

cliffs steep rock faces, like those at the edge of the sea

mountain a high, steep hill that is often rocky

prize something given to someone as a reward

rainbow a display of many colors

suffer to experience something bad or unpleasant

volcano a cone-shaped mountain with a hole in the top that sends out melted rock and gases

Differentiated Instruction

SI Strategic Intervention

Prefixes Write on large cards: redo, replace, respell, retie, regain, and return. Display each card and use the word in an oral sentence. Then have a child fold back the card to hide the prefix, put the base word in the phrase "___ again," and try the meaning in the sentence to see if it makes sense. Repeat this procedure with these words: displace, disallow, dislike, and distrust. Have children use the phrase "not ___" to determine the meaning of the prefixed word.

 ELL

English Language Learners
Cognates Point out the Spanish cognates in this week's selection vocabulary: mountain/montaña, suffer/sufrir, and volcano/volcán.

Objectives

- Build background on legends and heroes.
- Preview and predict.
- Use key features of a legend to improve understanding of text.
- Set a purpose for reading text.

Build Background
The First Tortilla

Background Building Audio

Have children listen to the CD. Explain that first they will hear a trailer for a movie based on the legend of a Swiss hero named William Tell. Then they will hear one family member try to convince others to see the movie.

Background Building Audio

Discuss legends and heroes

 Have children turn to a partner and use these questions for discussion:

- What is a legend?
- Why are legends passed down from generation to generation?
- What important characteristics do heroes of legends share?

Organize information in a chart

Draw a chart or display Graphic Organizer 25. Have children recall what they learned about the elements of a legend and the characteristics of a legendary hero. Record their responses.

Legend	Hero
a story from the past	brave and courageous
tells the great deeds of a hero	fights injustice
may be based on real people and events	a model for others
not historically true	
teaches values and lessons	

Graphic Organizer 25

Connect to selection

We learned about the elements of a legend and about some characteristics of a legendary hero. In the legend we are about to read, *The First Tortilla,* we'll read about a young hero who faces great risks to help save her people and preserve their way of life.

Student Edition pp. 162–163

 **Double Day Read!**

Main Selection—First Read
The First Tortilla

Practice the skill

 **Plot and Theme** Remind children that the story **plot** consists of events in the beginning, middle, and end of a story. The story **theme** tells the story's "big idea" or author's message.

Introduce the strategy

Monitor and Clarify Good readers monitor their understanding of the text. If the text is not making sense, good readers ask questions about anything they don't understand and reread to find answers to their questions. Have children turn to page EI•21 in their Student Edition.

Envision It!

Think Aloud Look at this picture. What is the girl doing to clarify what she doesn't understand? (She identifies what she doesn't understand and then rereads to help her figure it out.) As I read *The First Tortilla*, I will monitor my comprehension, ask myself questions if I don't understand, and then reread to answer my questions using information found in the text.

Student Edition p. EI•21

Introduce genre

Let's Read A **legend** is a short story that was told long ago about the deeds of a hero. As they read *The First Tortilla,* ask children to look for events that show the main character is a hero.

Discuss genre

Explain to children that legends often use mythical spirits to explain things in nature. In *The First Tortilla*, the villagers believe a Mountain Spirit lives in the volcano because they don't understand the natural reasons why the volcano erupts.

Tell children they will read *The First Tortilla* for the first time. Use the Day 2 Guide Comprehension notes to help children develop their comprehension of the story.

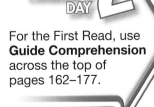 **Continue to DAY 2**

Double Day Read!

For the First Read, use **Guide Comprehension** across the top of pages 162–177.

First Read

 INTERACT with TEXT

Strategy Response Log

Monitor and Clarify
Have children use p. RR26 in their *Reader's and Writer's Notebook* to describe ways to monitor and clarify their understanding of what they read. Have children apply these techniques as they read *The First Tortilla.*

Academic Vocabulary

legend a story coming down from the past about the great deeds of a hero
plot a series of related events at the beginning, middle, and end of a story; the action of a story
theme the big idea or author's message in a story

 ELL

English Language Learners
Build Background Before children listen to the CD, build background and elicit prior knowledge. On the CD, you will hear a story about a brave person who helped others in danger. We call a person like this a hero. Think of heroes in our community. Who are they, and what do they do to help others? Use the picture on page 166 to give visual support for the vocabulary words *volcano* and *mountain*. Point out the volcano's smoke and explain that melted rock from the volcano formed a mountain.

Frontload Main Selection
Take a picture walk to frontload the selection, then review the selection summary (*ELL Handbook,* p. 145). Use the Retelling Cards to provide visual support for the summary.

DAYS 2&3 Read and Comprehend

Objectives

◎ Identify the plot and the theme of a legend.

◎ Monitor comprehension and clarify understanding by rereading relevant portions of a legend.

• Determine word meaning and use newly acquired vocabulary.

• Discuss ideas related to, but not expressed in the literature.

Guide Comprehension
Skills and Strategies

DAY 2

Connect to Concept

Our Changing World Look at the picture. What kinds of weather changes do crops need to grow? (Weather conditions need to include both sunny and rainy days for crops to grow.)

Amazing Words Have children continue discussing the concept using the Amazing Words *condition, predict, terrifying, breeze,* and *whip* as they read.

The First Tortilla

by Rudolfo Anaya
illustrated by Amy Córdova

Genre A **legend** is an old story that tells about the great deeds of a hero. Now read about how a young girl becomes a hero in her village.

162

Question of the Week
How do changes in the weather affect us?

Student Edition pp. 162–163

Extend Thinking
Think Critically

DAY 3

Higher-Order Thinking Skills

Analysis I see details in the picture that tell me where this legend takes place. Using these details, explain what you think the place is like and who lives there.

If... children cannot explain that this looks like a volcanic region where native people live as farmers, **then...** provide a model: I see a mountain range with a volcano pictured in the background; in the foreground, I see corn growing and a girl dressed in traditional clothing.

Strategies

Monitor and Clarify Remind children that good readers monitor their comprehension. When they do not understand, they ask themselves questions and then read to find answers. This selection has a glossary of Spanish words on page 177. Find an unfamiliar Spanish word on page 164. Then tell how you would clarify its meaning.

If... children have difficulty identifying the word *metate* and clarifying its meaning,
then... model how to monitor and clarify. *When I reached the word* metate, *I realized I'd never seen it before, so I asked myself if this could be a Spanish word. I looked in the glossary and found that a* metate *is a concave rock where corn is ground. Now I understand what Jade's mother is doing.*

Jade opened her eyes and yawned. She knew she had slept late because the sun had already risen.

"Time to awaken, precious Jade," her mother whispered. She was crushing dry chile pods in a metate.

"Time to greet the sun," her father said. He was weaving a basket. Each day Jade's parents went to the village market to sell their colorful baskets.

164

Jade jumped out of the hammock and greeted her parents. After breakfast she hurried outside to water the garden.

A huge volcano towered over Jade's village. On the peak of the mountain lived the Mountain Spirit. When the Mountain Spirit spoke, the earth rumbled and smoke filled the sky. Sometimes burning lava poured down the mountainside. Jade said a prayer. "Mountain Spirit, send us rain. Our bean and squash plants are dying."

165

Student Edition pp. 164–165

Higher-Order Thinking Skills

Analysis What can you infer about the character Jade from the way she begins her day? (Possible response: Jade is obedient to her parents, cheerful, and responsible about her chores.)

Connect to Science

Landforms Remind children that legends often use mythical spirits to explain natural occurrences. In this story, Jade's people create a spirit that inhabits the mountain and causes the volcano to erupt. Actually, a volcano erupts when pressure in an underground magma chamber increases. The resulting eruption blows out lava, smoke, ash, pumice, and rocks.

Skills and Strategies, continued

DAY 2

Skills

⦿ **Plot and Theme** Who visits Jade and what is the purpose of this visit? (A blue hummingbird visits Jade. The bird tells Jade that she must go to the Mountain Spirit to ask for rain, and she must take a gift.)

Strategies

Monitor and Clarify How could you clarify Jade's parents' reactions? (I could ask, "Why did they believe Jade?" By rereading, I learn that her father believed birds were messengers and her mother remembered a hummingbird visit when Jade was born.)

She picked up a clay pot and walked to the lake. Jade greeted the other village girls who were also collecting water. The once beautiful lake was almost dry. She filled the pot and returned to the garden. As she worked a lovely <u>blue</u> hummingbird <u>flew</u> in front of her.

"You must go to the Mountain Spirit and ask for rain," the hummingbird whispered. "And you must take a gift."

Her father had told her the small birds brought messages from the Mountain Spirit. Jade <u>knew</u> she must listen.

"The path is very dangerous," she said.

"I will guide you," the hummingbird replied.

166

Jade ran back into the hut.

"What is it, my daughter?" her mother asked.

Jade told her parents what had happened.

Her mother smiled and said, "A <u>blue</u> hummingbird <u>flew</u> over your crib when you were born. It was a special sign."

"Why don't the rains come?" Jade asked her father.

"Years ago we had rain and good harvests, but the people forgot to thank the Mountain Spirit. We did not take gifts to the mountain. Now it is angry, and there is no rain."

167

Student Edition pp. 166–167

Think Critically, continued

DAY 3

Review **Main Idea and Details**

Analysis Why is Jade's father's information about the Mountain Spirit's anger important? (When Jade learns there is no rain because people forgot to honor and thank the Mountain Spirit, it gives her a reason for why she must go to the Mountain Spirit.)

If... children have trouble explaining the importance of this information, **then...** ask them to reread the last paragraph of page 167 to find out what the people forgot to do and how the Mountain Spirit reacted.

Vocabulary

Lesson Vocabulary Using what you know about the meaning of *cliffs*, do you think Jade's father has good reason to be concerned when he fears that Jade may fall from the cliffs? (Yes, a cliff is a high area of land with one very steep side, so it would be easy to fall.)

Skills

Plot and Theme What important decision does Jade make on page 169? How might this decision affect the plot in the middle and end of the story? (Possible response: Jade decides she will visit the Mountain Spirit despite the dangers. Events in the middle of the story may tell about her journey and meeting with the spirit. Events at the end of the story may tell what happens when she returns home.)

"I can take a gift of food," Jade said.

Her father shook his head. "A girl cannot climb the mountain. You will fall from the cliffs like a bird without wings."

"Our gardens are dying," her mother said. "Soon we must leave our home in search of food. That will be the end of our way of life."

Jade grew sad. She knew the people did not want to leave their village. They had lived at the foot of the volcano for many generations. This had been the home of their ancestors.

When her parents were gone to market, Jade walked in the garden, wondering what she could do to help her village.

The blue hummingbird appeared again.

"The Mountain Spirit will listen to you," the hummingbird whispered.

168

"Can I do it?" Jade asked.

Her father had said that she might fall from the cliff like a bird without wings. But if she didn't go the entire village would suffer.

"Yes, I will go," she decided.

She warmed a bowl of beans and squash and sprinkled chile powder on the food.

"I hope this pleases the Mountain Spirit," she said.

She gathered a *rebozo* around her shoulders and followed the hummingbird up the narrow path. Suddenly the mountain shook and boulders came crashing down.

"This way!" the hummingbird cried.

169

Student Edition pp. 168–169

Higher-Order Thinking Skills

Evaluation Explain why Jade's mother believed their way of life would end without rain. Do you agree with her assessment?

Analysis What do you think would have happened to Jade if the hummingbird had not acted as her guide? (She probably would have been hit by the falling boulders.)

Skills and Strategies, continued

DAY 2

Word Reading

Decoding Have children check their reading of new words using these questions:

- Did I blend the sounds?
- Did it make sense?
- Did I look for word parts?

Vocabulary

Prefixes A prefix is a word part added to the beginning of a word to change its meaning. I know the word *uncovered* on page 171 begins with the prefix *un-*, which means "not." How can this information help you figure out the meaning of *uncovered*? (Uncovered means "not covered.")

Jade jumped aside, and the boulders missed her.

Finally they arrived at the home of the Mountain Spirit, where butterflies danced among a rainbow of flowers. A waterfall cascaded into a clear, blue lake.

"Why have you come?" the Mountain Spirit asked. Thunder and smoke filled the sky.

170

"I came to ask for rain," Jade replied. "Without rain our plants will die and we will starve."

"Your people no longer honor me!" the Mountain Spirit said.

"I have not forgotten you," Jade answered. "I brought you a gift."

She uncovered the bowl of beans and squash. A pleasant aroma filled the air,

The Mountain Spirit was pleased.

"You are a brave girl. I will send rain. And I will give you a gift. You may have the food the ants store in the cave."

Jade looked at the ants scurrying on the ground. "The ants carry pebbles," Jade said.

"Look closely," the Mountain Spirit whispered. Jade fell on her knees.

"What are you carrying?" she asked the ants. "This is corn," one ant replied.

"Taste it," another ant said, offering a kernel. Jade chewed the corn. "Oh, what a sweet flavor!" she cried. "Where does it come from?"

171

Student Edition pp. 170–171

Think Critically, continued

DAY 3

Higher-Order Thinking Skills

Synthesis Legends are told about a hero's brave deeds. What evidence can you find that this story fits the pattern of legends? (Possible response: Jade shows bravery when she climbs the mountain and speaks to the angry Mountain Spirit.)

If... children have trouble identifying Jade's heroic actions,

then... ask them to recall what happens when Jade climbs the steep mountain pathway and describe Jade's interview with the Mountain Spirit.

Skills

🔄 **Plot and Theme** What happens in this part of the story? (Possible response: After Jade is given the gift of corn by the Mountain Spirit, she returns safely home and introduces this new food to her family.)

Vocabulary

Lesson Vocabulary Have children locate the word *prize* on page 172. Why does the author describe the corn as a *prize*? (A prize is something valuable given to someone as a reward. In this story, Jade wins the respect of the Mountain Spirit and is given the valuable gift of corn in return.)

"It grows here on Corn Mountain. We gather the grains and store them in a cave. Come with us."

Jade followed the ants into the cavern. On the floor she found piles of corn.

"Corn is a gift from the Mountain Spirit," the ant said. "Take all you want."

Jade gathered the corn in her rebozo. She thanked the Mountain Spirit. She thanked the

hummingbird for guiding her. And she thanked the ants for sharing their corn.

Then she carefully made her way down the mountain with her prize. Her parents had returned from the market. Jade entered her home and spilled the corn on the floor.

"What is this?" her father asked.

172

"Corn!" Jade cried. "The Mountain Spirit gave it to me. Here, taste it!"

Her father chewed a few dry kernels, and the corn softened with each bite. It was sweet and tasty.

"Good," said her father. "But hard to chew."

"I will boil the corn in a clay pot," said her mother. "It will make pozol."

When the *pozol* was ready, Jade's father tasted it.

"Wonderful!" he exclaimed. "We must thank the Mountain Spirit for this food."

173

Student Edition pp. 172–173

Higher-Order Thinking Skills

Synthesis What conclusion can you draw from Jade's father's actions after the family eats the corn? (Since his first act is to thank the Mountain Spirit, he must believe in honoring and thanking the spirit for its gifts.)

Connect to Social Studies

New World Crops Anthropologists believe that people living in Central Mexico developed corn at least 7000 years ago from a wild grass. When explorers returned from the New World, they took corn back with them to Europe.

Team Talk Have children discuss the importance of corn. Encourage them to name foods that contain corn, and point out that corn is also used in fuel.

Skills and Strategies, continued

Skills

DAY 2

🔊 **Plot and Theme** What is the theme of this legend? (The theme is that people must remember to honor and thank those that give them gifts.)

If... children have difficulty identifying the theme,

then... remind them that the theme is a story's "big idea," and ask them to describe how and why the villagers' behavior towards the Mountain Spirit changes from the beginning to the end of the story.

They scattered kernels of corn in their garden and said a prayer of thanks.

That <u>afternoon</u> clouds gathered on the mountain peak. <u>Soon</u> a gentle rain fell. Later in the season corn plants pushed through the earth.

The corn tassels blossomed. <u>Soon</u> tender ears of corn appeared on the stalks.

"*Elotes*," Jade said as she picked the corn. That evening they ate corn, beans, and squash flavored with red chile.

When the corn was dry Jade placed some kernels in a *metate* and crushed them with a *mano*. She sprinkled water on the cornmeal.

174

The gruel was thick, like dough.

"*Masa*," Jade said. She patted the masa back and forth in her palms until it was flat and round. Then she placed it on a hot stone near the fire.

While they were eating they smelled the masa cooking on the hot stone.

"What is that sweet aroma?" asked her father.

"The masa!" Jade cried.

There on the hot stone lay the freshly baked bread. She picked it up and offered it to her parents.

Her father ate a piece. "Hum, very good!"

"Delicious!" her mother exclaimed. "What shall we call this bread?"

Jade thought a while. "I'll call it a *tortilla*."

"I am proud of you," her father said.

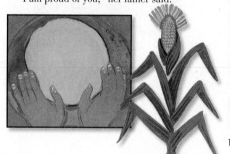

175

Student Edition pp. 174–175

Think Critically, continued

DAY 3

Higher-Order Thinking Skills
Synthesis In what way is Jade's cooking a tortilla like a scientist making a chance discovery? (Jade isn't sure what will happen when she combines corn and water to make a dough. She accidentally bakes it into bread by leaving it on a hot stone near the fire.)

Higher-Order Thinking Skills
Evaluation Are Jade and her parents good neighbors? Explain why you think as you do.

Strategies

⊙ **Monitor and Clarify** Suppose you'd mixed the tortilla dough, but you couldn't remember what to do before rolling it out. What would you do? (Possible response: I would ask myself what part of the recipe gives this information. Then I would reread that part to learn that I should knead the dough until it forms a ball and then cover it and let it sit for two minutes.)

Strategy Self-Check

Have children talk about problems they encountered as they read and what they did to solve them. Then have them explain how they monitored their comprehension of the recipe by generating a question and then rereading that portion of the recipe containing the answer.

Continue to DAY **2**

Comprehension Check p. 177a

"We must share this with our neighbors," her mother added.

In the following days Jade went from home to home, teaching the women how to make tortillas.

The corn plants grew. Corn tortillas became the favorite food of the people. Now the villagers did not have to leave their home.

During the harvest fiesta the people held a ceremony to thank the Mountain Spirit for giving them corn. They also thanked Jade, the girl who had baked the first tortilla.

176

Corn Tortilla Recipe

Tortillas are the bread of Mexico. They are used for classic Tex-Mex dishes like tacos and tostados. Have an adult help you try this tasty recipe at home.

Ingredients
- 2 cups masa harina (a traditional corn flour)
- 1 tsp sea salt
- ¼ tsp baking soda
- 2 cups very warm water
- 1 tsp oil

In a large bowl, mix corn flour, salt, baking soda, warm water, and oil.
Stir until dough stays together and does not break apart.
Knead until dough forms a large ball. It should be soft and not sticky. Cover and let stand for two minutes.
Pull off balls of dough, and roll each one into a flat, thin circle.
Have an adult heat a heavy iron pan.
Have an adult cook the tortillas until both sides are golden brown.
Eat with meat filling, shredded cheese, or plain.
Makes about 12 tortillas.

Glossary

jade	a precious stone in ancient Mexico
rebozo	a shawl worn by Mexican women
pozol	or posole, a corn and meat stew
elote	*elotl*, an ancient Mexican word for ear of corn
metate	concave rock where corn is ground
mano	smooth rock with which to grind corn
masa	dough
tortilla	traditional Mexican bread

177

Student Edition pp. 176–177

Higher-Order Thinking Skills

Evaluation A legend is often told to pass on the values of a community. What values are contained in this legend? Do you think these values are ones that should be upheld in a community?

Higher-Order Thinking Skills

Synthesis How are *The Night the Moon Fell* and *The First Tortilla* similar and different? (Both tell stories that have been passed down. They differ because *The Night the Moon Fell* explains a natural event, while *The First Tortilla* explains how corn was brought to ancient people.)

Continue to DAY **3**

Think Critically pp. 178–179

Objectives
- Use the foreshadowing in an illustration to confirm predictions.
- Identify a moral lesson as the theme of a legend.
- Identify and use adverbs that tell about manner in reading, writing, and speaking.

Comprehension Check

Have children discuss each question with a partner and share responses.

✓ **Legend** What brave deeds are celebrated in this legend? (How Jade climbs a dangerous volcano to visit a frightening Mountain Spirit, and how she brings corn to her people and bakes the first tortilla.)

✓ **Confirm predictions** How did the title page illustration help you predict the hero of this legend? Was your prediction correct? (The illustration shows Jade holding a tortilla; this foreshadows that she would make the first tortilla and be the hero.)

✓ **Connect text to world** Why do you think different cultures around the world pass down legends like *The First Tortilla* that describe a hero's bravery and accomplishments? (Possible response: Retelling these legends through the years explains how something important in the culture came to be.)

Literary Text
Moral Lessons as Themes

Identify moral lessons as themes

Use *The First Tortilla* to review the use of moral lessons as themes.

- You know that the theme is the "big idea" of a story that an author wants to communicate. Myths, fables, folktales, and legends like *The First Tortilla* have themes that teach a moral lesson.

- A moral lesson teaches the difference between right and wrong or teaches an important value or behavior. Sometimes this moral lesson is stated directly, but usually, good readers must analyze plot events to figure out it out. What is the moral lesson in *The First Tortilla*? (Remember to be thankful for what you have.)

Guide practice

Together, recall other folktales, fables, and myths that children have read. Use a T-chart to summarize the moral lesson of the story. For example:

Title of Selection	Moral Lesson of the Selection
• *The First Tortilla*	• Remember to be thankful for what you have.
• *The Night the Moon Fell*	• Friends can help us deal with difficult change.
• *The Strongest One*	• We all have our own strengths.

Graphic Organizer 25

Have small groups work together to discuss these moral lessons and compare them to that of *The First Tortilla*.

Conventions
Adverbs That Tell How

Model adverbs that tell how

Write *Anna danced merrily across the stage.* Point to each word as you read it. Ask children to identify the adverb in the sentence. *(merrily)* Then ask them to name the verb it tells about. *(danced)* Adverbs tell about verbs. Some adverbs tell how the action is done. How do these adverbs often end? (with *-ly*)

Guide practice

Write the following sentences on the board. Have children read the sentences and identify the adverb in each sentence.

> 1. **A turtle moves slowly. (slowly)**
>
> 2. **The student worked carefully. (carefully)**
>
> 3. **The stars twinkled beautifully in the sky. (beautifully)**
>
> 4. **We watched the juggler closely. (closely)**

Connect to oral language

Have the class complete these sentence frames orally using adverbs that tell how, such as *beautifully, slowly, suddenly,* and *carefully.*

> 1. The girls danced _____.
>
> 2. A whale swims _____.
>
> 3. The storm started _____.
>
> 4. The dentist worked _____.

On their own

Use *Reader's and Writer's Notebook* p. 343.

Reader's and Writer's Notebook p. 343

Differentiated Instruction

(**SI**) Strategic Intervention

Practice Adverbs About Manner If children provide adverbs that tell when or where in their oral sentences, then model the sentences with an adverb that tells how, and have children repeat them.

Daily Fix-It

3. we walk two the park.
   <u>We</u> walk <u>to</u> the park.

4. Did tom drink his juice.
   Did <u>Tom</u> drink his juice<u>?</u>

Discuss the Daily Fix-It corrections with children. Review sentence capitalization and punctuation, the capitalization of proper nouns, and the homophones *to* and *two.*

ELL

English Language Learners

Support Conventions Write familiar adjectives such as *tired, happy, loud, soft, slow,* and *quick* on the board and review them with children. Then model how adverbs can be formed by adding *-ly* to each adjective and have children read them with you. Have children follow directions that incorporate each adverb; for example, *walk quickly, yawn tiredly, smile happily, clap loudly.*

Objectives

- Generate ideas for a thank-you note.
- Recognize features of a thank-you note.

Writing—Thank-You Note
Writing Trait: Focus/Ideas

Introduce the prompt

Review with children the key features of a thank-you note. Point out that *The First Tortilla* is a legend. Remind them that the people in the story thanked the Mountain Spirit for rain and the corn that grew. Now they will write a thank-you note to someone who has prepared food for them. Explain that today children will plan their own thank-you note. Read aloud the writing prompt.

Writing Prompt

> Think about how thankful people are for food during any season. Write a thank-you note to someone who has prepared food for you.

Help children generate thank-you note ideas

Sharing the Writing

 Think Aloud To plan your thank-you note, think about someone who has prepared food for you. That will be the focus of your note. I'll start with *Mother prepares breakfast for me.*

Guide children in telling about times when someone has prepared food for them. Possible ideas are shown.

> **Mother prepares breakfast for me.**
>
> **Grandma cooks Thanksgiving dinner.**
>
> **Sister makes a picnic lunch.**
>
> **Dad cooks hamburgers for a cookout.**
>
> **Grandpa makes pizza.**

Record the responses and keep the chart displayed so that children can refer to it as they plan and draft their thank-you notes.

Have each child think about and decide who they would like to thank for preparing food for them. Circulate to guide them.

Important Ideas

INTERACT with TEXT

- **Introduce** Use *Reader's and Writer's Notebook* p. 344 to model planning a thank-you note. To plan my thank-you note, I will use a web to focus my ideas.

- **Model** First, in the circle, I will write the name of the person I am thanking and the reason I am thanking that person. I want to thank *Grandma for cooking Thanksgiving dinner*. I will write *Grandma, Thank you for cooking Thanksgiving dinner*. At the end of each spoke I will write an idea about what I'd like to include in my thank-you note. I do not have to write complete sentences on this web. These are just notes to help me plan my thank-you note. Now, I will write one idea at the end of each spoke: *fun to watch you; learned a lot; stuffed the turkey; showed me how to make a salad; made stuffing; baked pumpkin pie*. Have children include at least four ideas and explain that they do not have to write an idea for every spoke. Tell them that they can think about the order of their ideas before they write tomorrow.

Circulate to guide and assist children.

Reader's and Writer's Notebook p. 344

ROUTINE Quick Write for Fluency   Team Talk

1. **Talk** Have children take two minutes to tell a partner about who they are thanking and why they are thanking that person.

2. **Write** Each child briefly writes ideas at the ends of the spokes.

3. **Share** Each child reads their plan to their partner.

Routines Flip Chart

ELL

English Language Learners
Support Prewriting
Beginning To help children focus their thoughts, have them draw a food they like to eat. Next, make a list of the names of the foods. Then ask them who prepares the foods. Write names on the board.

Intermediate Discuss ingredients in foods they like to eat. Ask them what preparations have to be done to the food before eating, such as chopping, boiling, baking, etc. Then have them tell who does the preparing.

Advanced/Advanced-High Lead a small-group discussion to focus on holiday meals. Discuss foods they eat on these special days and who prepares the food.

Objectives
- Write legible letters of proper size.
- Understand how to use available sources to locate information.
- Apply knowledge of using sources to inquiry project.

Handwriting
Cursive Letters *n, m, x*/Letter Size

Model letter formation

Display lower-case letters: *n, m,* and *x*. Use the stroke instructions pictured below to model proper letter formation. Have children write each letter several times and circle their best ones.

D'Nealian Cursive™

Model letter size

Explain that when we write words, the letters should be the proper size. Write the phrase *the metal ax* sizing the letters correctly. When I write, I am careful to size the letters correctly. My small letters are always half the size of my tall letters. Write the phrase *the metal ax* again, using a smaller letter size but keeping the letters in correct proportion to each other. I have changed the letter size to make them smaller, but notice that my small letters are still half the size of my tall letters. Write *the metal ax* a third time, with the letters out of proportion to each other. In this example, the letter sizes differ—not all my small letters are half the size of my tall letters. By sizing my letters properly, I make it easier for others to read what I have written. Ask children which writing example is easiest to read and have them explain why.

Guide practice

Write the following phrase, using different letter sizes: *men meet at the exit*.

Team Talk Have children work in pairs to discuss what is wrong with the size of the letters in this phrase and how they would fix them. Have them write the phrase correctly. During their discussion, have children use their fingers to indicate which letters are sized too big, too small, and just right.

Research and Inquiry
Research Skill: Natural and Personal Sources

Teach

Remind children that a **source** is someone or something that can give them information. A source used outside of the classroom is a personal source. A source normally used in the classroom is a natural source.

Model

Think Aloud

Display Research Transparency 20. Here are some questions about choosing appropriate sources. We will be choosing the answer that makes the most sense. Read aloud the first question and possible answers. The *librarian* would be the best person to help me find weather forecasts.

Guide practice

Continue reading each question and answer. Have children tell what they learn from each answer. Then have children think about good sources they can use both inside and outside school to give them information about how weather changes affect us. Ask children to use their sources outside school to help them answer the inquiry questions they are best suited to answer.

On their own

Use Reader's and Writer's Notebook p. 345.

Wrap Up Your Day

✔ **Build Concepts** Monitor children's use of oral vocabulary as they respond. In *The First Tortilla,* what was the weather condition like at the beginning of the story? (dry, no rain) How would you describe Jade's journey up the mountain, terrifying or fun? (terrifying)

right

source a person or thing that can give information

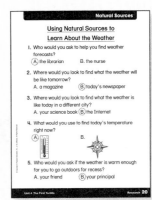

Research Transparency 20
TR DVD

Reader's and Writer's Notebook p. 345

Preview DAY 3

Tell children that tomorrow they will reread *The First Tortilla.*

Objectives
- Build oral vocabulary.
- Identify details in text.
- Share information and ideas about the concept.

Today at a Glance

Oral Vocabulary
sparkle

Phonics and Spelling
◉ Vowel Digraphs *oo, ue, ew, ui*

Fluency
Expression and Intonation

Lesson Vocabulary
awaken, cliffs, mountain, prize, rainbow, suffer, volcano

Vocabulary
Prefixes

Comprehension
Main Idea and Details

Conventions
Adverbs That Tell How

Writing
Thank-You Note

Research and Inquiry
Gather and Record Information

Concept Talk

Question of the Week

 How do changes in the weather affect us?

Build concepts

To reinforce concepts and to focus children's attention, have children sing "Changing Conditions" from the *Sing with Me* Big Book. What evidence does the song offer to show that weather is very difficult to predict? (It states that even forecasters whose job it is to predict weather get tricked by it.)

💿 *Sing with Me* Big Book Audio

Monitor listening comprehension

As children listen to "Happy Birthday, Old Man Winter!" have them think about how Tessa responds when her mom tells her that today is Old Man Winter's birthday. Then read the story aloud.

Read Aloud Anthology "Happy Birthday, Old Man Winter!"

- How do you know that Tessa has a good imagination? (Possible response: Tessa comes up with the idea of having a party to celebrate Old Man Winter's birthday.)

- Tessa suggests to her friends that they make a snow cake for Old Man Winter's party. What does this tell you about Tessa? (Possible response: Tessa is a creative person who comes up with the idea of using snow and natural objects to make and decorate a cake for the party.)

ⒺⓁⓁ **Expand Vocabulary** Use the Day 3 instruction on ELL Poster 20 to expand children's use of English vocabulary to communicate about lesson concepts.

ⒺⓁⓁ Poster 20

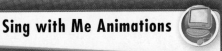
Oral Vocabulary
Amazing Words

Teach Amazing Words

Amazing Words — Oral Vocabulary Routine

(1) Introduce the Word Relate the word *sparkle* to the story. The snowflakes *sparkle* as they float down from a cloud. Supply a child-friendly definition. If things *sparkle,* they shine or glitter in the light. Have children say the word.

(2) Demonstrate Provide examples to show meaning. A diamond will *sparkle* in the sunlight. The waves *sparkle* in the moonlight. Grandpa's eyes *sparkle* whenever Grandma walks into the room.

(3) Apply Have children demonstrate their understanding. Name a word that means the opposite of *sparkle;* name a word that means almost the same thing as *sparkle.*

Routines Flip Chart

Anchored Talk

Add to the concept map

Discuss how changes in the weather affect us as you add to the concept map.

- How would you describe the weather at the beginning of *The First Tortilla?* (The weather is hot and dry.) How does the weather affect Jade and the people in her village? (Without rain, crops die.) Let's add this information under the heading *Weather affects what we grow.*

- Jade's mother talks about people having to leave home in search of food. What would this mean for the villagers? (It would mean a change in their way of life.) Yes, weather can cause changes in where people live and their way of life. Let's add this information.

- How and why does the weather change at the end of the story? (Possible response: The Mountain Spirit sends rain in response to Jade's offering.) How does this change in weather affect the villagers? (Rain makes crops grow and increases the food supply.) Let's add *Rain makes crops grow* to our map.

Amazing Words

condition	whip
predict	sparkle
terrifying	funnel
breeze	swirl

Differentiated Instruction

 Advanced

Amazing Words Pair children and have them draw a line with the ends labeled *Dark* and *Light.* Then have them place the word *sparkle* as well as its synonyms and antonyms along this continuum to compare and contrast word meanings. Encourage students to add to their list of words by checking a thesaurus and then using a dictionary to help them determine subtle differences in meanings.

English Language Learners
Vocabulary Give children small classroom objects that do and do not sparkle in the sun, for example, a square of foil, a shiny pair of scissors, a pinch of glitter, a pencil, a block, and a sheet of construction paper. Have children compare and contrast the objects by whether they sparkle. Then have them hold up each object, name it, and use it in the following sentence frame,

_____ *sparkles in the sun, but* _____ *does not.*

Objectives
• Blend and read words with vowel digraphs *oo, ue, ew,* and *ui.*
• Decode words in context and independent of context.

Phonics
Sort Words

Model word sorting

Write *book* and *moon* as heads in a two-column chart. We are going to sort words with the vowel sounds /ů/ spelled *oo* and *u* and /ü/ spelled *oo, ue, ew,* and *ui.* Write *bush.* I can blend this word, /b/ /ů/ /sh/, *bush.* I can hear that this word has the same vowel sound as in the word *book.* I will place the word *bush* on the chart under the word *book.*

Guide practice

Write the remaining words from the first chart below in random order. Have children read each word and tell you if the vowel sound in the word is /ů/ as in *book* or /ü/ as in *moon.* Complete the chart with children.

book	moon	
bush	tool	yew
foot	glue	troop
hook	blew	suit
wood	bruise	clue

Write *oo, ue, ew,* and *ui* as heads in a four-column chart. Have children duplicate the chart. Now we will sort the words with the vowel sound /ü/ as in *moon* according to each word's vowel pattern. Have children read each word with the vowel sound /ü/ as in *moon* and place it under the correct heading. Monitor children's work.

oo	*ue*	*ew*	*ui*
tool	glue	yew	suit
troop	clue	blew	bruise

Corrective feedback

For corrective feedback, have children say each word as you point to it. Provide correct pronunciation as needed.

Fluent Word Reading

Model

Write *cartoon*. I know the sounds for *c*, *ar*, *t*, *oo*, and *n*. I blend them together to read the word *cartoon*.

Guide practice

Write the words below. Say the sounds in your head for each spelling you see. When I point to the word, we'll read it together. Allow one second per sound previewing time for the first reading.

droop	due	crew	bruise	teaspoon	grew	glue

On their own

Have children read the list above three or four times, until they can read one word per second.

Blend and Read

Decode words independent of context

Have children turn to page 81 in Decodable Practice Readers 2.2 and find the first list of words. Each word in this list has the sound /ü/ spelled *oo*, *ue*, *ew*, or *ui*. Let's blend and read these words. Be sure that children identify the correct vowel sound in each word.

Next, have children read the high-frequency words.

Decodable Practice
Readers 2.2, pp. 81–82

Decode words in context

Chorally read the story along with children. Have children identify words in the story that have the /ü/ sound spelled *oo*, *ue*, *ew*, or *ui*.

Team Talk Pair children and have them take turns reading the story aloud to each other. Monitor children as they read to check for proper pronunciation and appropriate pacing.

Differentiated Instruction

 Strategic Intervention

Continue Sorting Words Add these words to the sorting activity: *zoo*, *threw*, *boot*, *due*, *cruise*, *news*, *blue*, *fruit*, *proof*, *juicy*, *stew*, *Sue*. Have children write them in the correct column for added practice.

A **Advanced**

Write Questions If children can easily blend and read this week's words, challenge them to write questions using the words.

Academic Vocabulary

vowel digraph two vowels together that stand for a single sound, as *oa* in *boat* or *ea* in *leaf*

ELL

English Language Learners
Vowel Digraphs oo, ue, ew, ui Reread the story with children. Stop periodically to ask questions that require answers using words with vowel digraphs. Assist in pronunciations and meanings.

Objectives
- Spell words with the vowel digraphs *oo, ue, ew,* and *ui.*
- Read aloud fluently with expression and intonation.

Spelling
Vowel Digraphs *oo, ue, ew, ui*

Spell high-frequency words

Write *know* and *won't*. Have children say and spell the words with you and then without you.

Dictation

Have children write these sentences. Say each sentence. Then repeat it slowly, one word at a time.

> 1. I know his new suit is blue.
>
> 2. I won't have the fruit juice. It is too sweet.
>
> 3. Did the clue fool you?

Proofread and correct

Write each sentence, spelling words one at a time. Have children circle and rewrite any misspelled words.

On their own

Use *Reader's and Writer's Notebook,* p. 346.

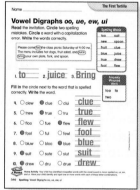

Reader's and Writer's
Notebook p. 346

Small Group Time

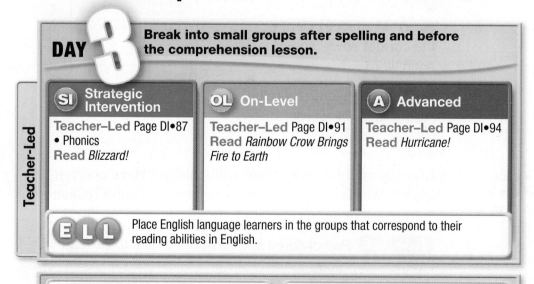

DAY 3 Break into small groups after spelling and before the comprehension lesson.

SI Strategic Intervention	**OL** On-Level	**A** Advanced
Teacher–Led Page DI•87 • Phonics **Read** *Blizzard!*	Teacher–Led Page DI•91 **Read** *Rainbow Crow Brings Fire to Earth*	Teacher–Led Page DI•94 **Read** *Hurricane!*

ELL Place English language learners in the groups that correspond to their reading abilities in English.

Practice Stations	**Independent Activities**
• Read for Meaning • Let's Write	• Read independently/Reading Log on *Reader's and Writer's Notebook,* p. RR4 • Audio Text of Main Selection

Model Fluency
Expression and Intonation

Model fluent reading
Have children turn to Student Edition p. 165. Follow along as I read this page. When I reach Jade's prayer to the Mountain Spirit, I know I need to read these words with a respectful and pleading tone because Jade is begging the Mountain Spirit for help.

Guide practice
Have children read the page with you. Then have them reread the page as a group without you until they read with expression and intonation. Continue in the same way with pages 166–167.

Corrective feedback
If... children have difficulty reading with expression and intonation, then... prompt:

- Are you reading sentences that the characters speak with expression?
- Are you letting your voice rise and fall as you read?

Reread for Fluency

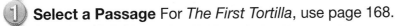

ROUTINE Choral Reading

1. **Select a Passage** For *The First Tortilla*, use page 168.
2. **Model** First, have children track the print as you read.
3. **Guide Practice** Then have children read along with you.
4. **Corrective Feedback** Have the class read aloud without you. Monitor progress and provide feedback. For optimal fluency, children should reread three to four times.

Routines Flip Chart

Check comprehension
Why might Jade be so hesitant to visit the Mountain Spirit? (She knows the way is dangerous; her father tells her that a girl cannot safely climb the steep mountain without falling.)

Differentiated Instruction

 Strategic Intervention
Fluency Point out that authors often use words like *whispered, murmured, shouted,* and *exclaimed* to signal what type of expression a reader should use when reading dialogue. Have children scan the text for these clue words.

 Advanced
Fluency Remind children that intonation is a rising and falling of the voice. Have them vary their intonation while reading page 168 to explore how it can affect meaning.

Spelling Words
Vowel Digraphs *oo, ue, ew, ui*

1. too	7. suit
2. new	8. spoon
3. fruit	9. clue
4. blue	10. juice
5. true	11. drew
6. fool	12. flew

High-Frequency Words
13. know 14. won't

Options for Oral Rereading
Use *The First Tortilla* or the Day 1 Decodable Practice Reader.

Objectives

- Review lesson vocabulary.
- Review words with prefixes.
- Establish purpose for reading text.
- Review key features of a legend.

Vocabulary
Lesson Vocabulary

Review
Lesson vocabulary

Display and review the lesson vocabulary words *awaken, volcano, mountain, cliffs, suffer, rainbow,* and *prize.* Have children read the words aloud.

Team Talk Have children work in pairs using the lesson vocabulary words to make small crossword puzzles with one word across and one word down on graph paper. One of their puzzles will need to have three words. Tell them to write the meanings for each word as clues. Then they can exchange their puzzles with other pairs of children to solve.

Prefixes

Review
Prefixes

Remind children that when they come to a word they don't know, they can look for word parts, such as prefixes. They can use prefixes to determine the meaning of words. A *prefix* is a word part that is added to the beginning of a word. One prefix is *dis-.* It means "not or do the opposite of." Remember we read the word *dislike* in "Hector and the Scarecrow" on page 161. What does *dislike* mean? (not like) Another prefix is *re-.* It can mean "again," such as in *repay.* Point out that the word *uncovered* from page 171 of *The First Tortilla* has the prefix *un-.* The prefix *un-* has been added to the word *covered.* The prefix *un-* means "not or the opposite of." The new word, *uncovered,* means "took the cover off."

Guide practice

Write *refill* and read it aloud. What is the base word in *refill?* (fill) What is the prefix in *refill?* (re-) What does *refill* mean? (to fill again)

Write the following words and have children identify the base word and prefix in each. Remind children that they can use prefixes to determine the meaning of words. Discuss the meanings. Have children use the words in sentences.

unlike (not like)	reread (read again)	untrue (not true)
replant (plant again)	distrust (not trust)	

On their own

Team Talk Have children work in pairs to identify the prefix and base word in these words: *retie, unwise, disallow, unpack, disconnect,* and *remake.* Have them discuss the meanings.

Main Selection—Second Read
The First Tortilla

Review
Main Idea and Details

Recall this week's main selection, *The First Tortilla.* Tell children that today they will read the legend again. Remind children a **main idea** is the big idea that tells what a paragraph or a story is mainly about and **details** are small pieces of information that support the main idea. Identifying the main idea can help us better understand the important idea of a text. What can you ask yourself to help you identify the main idea of a passage or a story? For more practice with main idea and details, see Let's Practice It! p. 218 on the *Teacher Resource DVD-ROM.*

Let's Practice It!
TR DVD • 218

Review
Genre: legend

Let's Read Remind children that a legend is a story that was told long ago and passed on orally. It has a hero who does brave deeds to help others, and it often teaches a lesson. Have children recall the hero in *The First Tortilla* and the lesson in this legend.

Set a purpose

Remind children that good readers read for a purpose. Guide children to set a new purpose for reading *The First Tortilla* today, perhaps to analyze how and why the villagers' lives changed thanks to Jade's courageous visit to the Mountain Spirit.

Extend thinking

Tell children they will now read *The First Tortilla* for the second time. Use the Day 3 Extend Thinking notes to encourage children to use higher-order thinking skills to go beyond the details of the story.

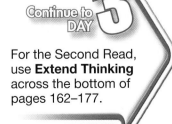

Continue to DAY **3**

For the Second Read, use **Extend Thinking** across the bottom of pages 162–177.

Second Read

Differentiated Instruction

 **Strategic Intervention**

Vocabulary Use the lesson vocabulary words in questions for children to answer. For example, *What do you often find on top of a <u>mountain</u> in winter? What <u>prize</u> might the winner of a race receive? What would a painting look like if it had a <u>rainbow</u> of colors?*

Lesson Vocabulary

awaken cause to stop sleeping

cliffs steep rock faces, like those at the edge of the sea

mountain a high, steep hill that is often rocky

prize something given to someone as a reward

rainbow a display of many colors

suffer to experience something bad or unpleasant

volcano a cone-shaped mountain with a hole in the top that sends out melted rock and gases

Academic Vocabulary

main idea the big idea that tells what a paragraph or a selection is mainly about; the most important idea of a text

details small pieces of information that support the main idea

ELL

English Language Learners
Words in Context Provide support by supplying a word bank for children during the sentence frames review activity on p. 178g.

Objectives

- Retell a narrative.
- ◎ Identify the theme of a legend.
- ◎ Ask and answer questions to monitor comprehension.
- Write clear, coherent sentences.

Check Retelling

SUCCESS PREDICTOR

Objectives
• Ask questions, clear up anything you don't understand, look for facts and details in the stories you read, and support your answers with evidence. • Identify themes in well-known fables, legends, myths, or stories.

Envision It! | Retell

READING STREET ONLINE
STORY SORT
www.ReadingStreet.com

178

Think Critically

1. Tortillas became the favorite food of the villagers. What are your favorite foods? Text to Self

2. Why does the author tell a legend about how the first tortilla was made from corn? What lesson does the author want to teach? Think Like an Author

3. What do the villagers learn by the end of the story? ◎ Plot and Theme

4. Reread the tortilla recipe on page 177. What steps does an adult need to do? Why is that important? ◎ Monitor and Clarify

5. **Look Back and Write** Look back at page 169. Do you think Jade is brave? Provide evidence to support your answer.
TEST PRACTICE Extended Response

Meet the Author and the Illustrator

Rudolfo Anaya

Rudolfo Anaya leads an active life, wanting "to do more." He has visited many places. He has fished and climbed mountains. He has been a college professor and is an author of books for children and adults.

Amy Córdova

Amy Córdova lives in the mountains of New Mexico. She has illustrated several children's books and also writes stories. She says, "When I draw, my pictures tell stories. Through my writing, I make pictures."

Read more books written by Rudolfo Anaya or illustrated by Amy Córdova.

Roadrunner's Dance

DREAM CARVER

Dream Carver

Use the Reader's and Writer's Notebook to record your independent reading.

179

Student Edition pp. 178–179

Retelling

Envision It! Have children work in pairs, retelling the story to one another. Remind children that their partners should include the characters, setting, and events from the beginning, middle, and end of the story. Children should use the retelling strip in the Student Edition. Monitor children's retelling.

Scoring rubric

Top-Score Response A top-score response makes connections beyond the text, elaborates on the author's purpose, and describes in detail the characters, setting, and plot.

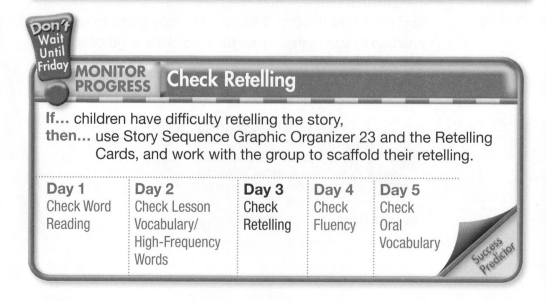

Don't Wait Until Friday

MONITOR PROGRESS Check Retelling

If... children have difficulty retelling the story,
then... use Story Sequence Graphic Organizer 23 and the Retelling Cards, and work with the group to scaffold their retelling.

Day 1	Day 2	Day 3	Day 4	Day 5
Check Word Reading	Check Lesson Vocabulary/ High-Frequency Words	Check Retelling	Check Fluency	Check Oral Vocabulary

Success Predictor

Think Critically

Text to Self

1. Encourage children to include healthful foods in their list of favorite foods.

Think Like an Author

2. Possible response: The author tells this legend to teach us that corn is an ancient and important food for many people.

 **Plot and Theme**

3. The villagers learn that they should remember to thank and honor the Mountain Spirit for his gifts.

Monitor and Clarify

4. Possible response: An adult needs to heat a heavy iron pan and cook the tortillas. It is important that an adult cook the tortillas, so that children stay safe in the kitchen.

Writing on Demand

5. **Look Back and Write** For writing fluency, assign a five-minute time limit. As children finish, encourage them to reread their response and proofread for errors.

Scoring rubric

> **Top-Score Response** A top-score response uses details from the text to support their opinion about whether Jade is brave. For example:
>
> I think that Jade is brave. I think this because she is willing to climb the steep mountain to speak to the Mountain Spirit. She doesn't turn back even when boulders fall.

Meet the author and illustrator

Read aloud page 179 as children follow along. Ask children what an author and an illustrator do.

On their own

Use p. 347 in the *Reader's and Writer's Notebook* for additional practice with plot and theme.

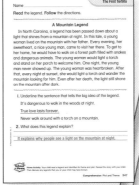

Reader's and Writer's Notebook p. 347

Differentiated Instruction

A Advanced

Look Back and Write Ask children who show proficiency with the writing prompt to describe how the villagers might honor and thank the Mountain Spirit for his gifts of rain and corn.

 INTERACT with TEXT

Strategy Response Log

Monitor and Clarify Have children revisit p. RR26 in their *Reader's and Writer's Notebook* where they described ways to monitor and clarify their understanding. After reading the story, have them add examples of fix-up strategies they used.

Plan to Assess Retelling

- ☐ Week 2: Strategic Intervention
- ☐ Week 2: Advanced
- ☐ Week 3: Strategic Intervention
- ☐ Week 4: On-Level
- ☑ Week 5: This week assess Strategic Intervention children.
- ☐ Week 6: Assess any children you have not yet checked during this unit.

Objectives

- Understand and use adverbs about manner in writing and speaking.
- Write a draft of a thank-you note.

Conventions
Adverbs That Tell How

Review
Adverbs that tell how

Remind children that adverbs that tell how provide more information about a verb: *The moon shone beautifully*.

Guide practice

Write this sentence on the board, have children read it aloud, and identify the adverb that tells how. (quickly)

> **We walk quickly during a fire drill.**

What other adverbs could we use in place of *quickly*?

Team Talk Have children write the sentences using their adverbs.

Connect to oral language

Have children complete these sentence frames orally using adverbs that tell how.

> **1. The class listened _____ to the directions.**
>
> **2. The soft breeze blew _____ through the trees.**
>
> **3. The children skipped _____ down the sidewalk.**

On their own

Use Let's Practice It! p. 221 on the *Teacher Resource DVD-ROM*.

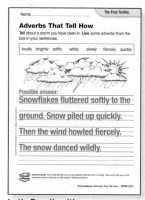

Let's Practice It!
TR DVD • 221

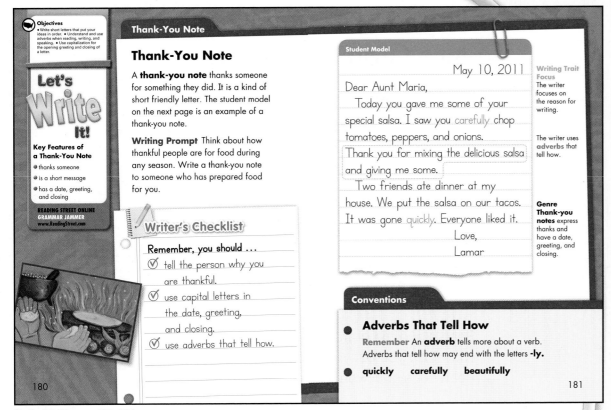

Student Edition pp. 180–181

5. Sam is marys nephew.
Sam is <u>M</u>ary<u>'</u>s nephew.

6. A fact can be prove
A fact can be prove<u>d.</u>

Discuss the Daily Fix-It corrections with children. Review names that must begin with capital letters and possessives. Also review adding -ed to words and ending punctuation.

Let's Write It!

Teach

Use pp. 180–181 in the Student Edition. Read aloud the Key Features of a Thank-You Note and the definition of a thank-you note. Help children better understand the Writing Prompt by reading it aloud and discussing the Writer's Checklist with children.

Review the student model

Then read the thank-you note on page 181 to children. Point out the date, the greeting, the body, the closing, and the signature. Talk about how the sequence of the body is both logical and chronological. Read aloud and briefly discuss the side notes about Genre, the Writing Trait, and Adverbs That Tell How.

Scoring rubric

Top-Score Response Help children understand that a top-score response is a short message that follows a logical and chronological sequence. It contains the date, a greeting, the body, a closing, and a signature. For a complete rubric see Writing Rubric 20 from the *Teacher Resource DVD-ROM.*

Connect to conventions

Read to children the Conventions note about Adverbs That Tell How. Point out the adverbs *quickly, carefully* and *beautifully*.

Objectives
- Write a draft of a thank-you note.
- Use sequence and appropriate conventions.
- Gather information.

Writing—Thank-You Note
Writer's Craft: Sequence

MINI-LESSON

Sequence

■ **Introduce** Use your web from yesterday and Writing Transparency 20A to model how writers use chronological and logical sequence. When I wrote my thank-you note, I used my web to help me decide the order in which I wanted to present my ideas.

Read aloud the draft on the Transparency to show how you put your ideas into a sequence. Point out signal words *first, then,* and *next.*

November 25 2011

Dear grandma
    Thank you for cooking thanksgiving dinner this year for all of us. It was fun to watch you happily prepare all the food. I learned so much!
    First, you baked the sweet, creamy pumkin pie so that it would have time to cool. Then you gently combined the bread cubes and broth in a bowl for a tasty stuffing that I liked a lot. Next, you stuffed the turkey and put it in the oven. as it cooked, the turky smelled awesome! Just befor dinner, you showed me how to tear the lettuce and make a delicious salad? The food disappeared quickly. You can cook for me any day of the year!

love,
Julie

Unit 4 The First Tortilla   Writing: Model **20A**

Writing Transparency 20A
TR DVD

■ Explain how children can use the web they made yesterday to draft their thank-you note. Tell them to think about the order in which they want to present their ideas and number the ideas on the web. Then they can follow the sequence as they write. Discuss these points.
- Tell why you are grateful to the person.
- Include a date, greeting, and closing.
- Write your idea in time order, or in an order that makes sense.

Today's goal is to write the thank-you note but not to rewrite each word perfectly. They can edit later to correct the words.

Guide thank-you note writing

Now it is time to write your thank-you note to someone who has prepared food for you. Have children use their web. Help them determine the sequence of their ideas. Guide children as they draft the thank-you notes.

ROUTINE **Quick Write for Fluency** **Team Talk**

1) **Talk** Have partners take one minute to talk about how they can use signal words to show the order of events.

2) **Write** Each child writes one sentence that includes a signal word.

3) **Share** Partners point out how the sentence could be improved by using a different signal word, if needed.

Routines Flip Chart

Research and Inquiry
Gather and Record Information

Teach

Tell children that today they will answer the questions from Day 1 about weather. Their goal is to learn how changes in weather affect us. Review using sources both inside and outside school. Then model how to use sources to answer inquiry questions.

Model

Think Aloud Display the questions that the class created on Day 1. I started with my sources outside school and asked this question: *What do we do when the weather is nice?* I could ask a source at school, for example the principal, who might tell me that we have recess on nice days. Record the answers next to the question.

Guide Practice

Have children use sources inside school to answer inquiry questions that weren't answered by their sources outside school. Compile the answers from all the sources. Explain that tomorrow they will review their topic and make sure all of their questions have been answered.

Make It Real Discuss with children what they do and the kinds of clothing they wear in good weather. Then ask them how these things change when there is a rain storm, a snow storm, or a heat wave.

Topic: How Weather Changes Affect Us	
Question	**Answer**
What do we do when the weather is nice?	play outside, wear light clothes, can work outside, go places, have recess

Wrap Up Your Day

✔ **Plot and Theme** What is the "big idea" of *The First Tortilla?* (A change in the weather can affect many things in life.) *Plot* is what happens in the beginning, middle, and end of the story. At the end of the story, what did Jade do? (She made the first tortilla.)

✔ **Monitor and Clarify** Remind children that good readers know that reading has to make sense. Sometimes they need to ask questions and go back and reread text.

Preview DAY 4

Tell children that tomorrow they will learn about something that is all around them but that they cannot see.

Objectives

• Discuss the concept to develop oral language.
• Build oral vocabulary.
• Identify details in text.

Today at a Glance

Oral Vocabulary
funnel, swirl

High-Frequency Words
Review

Phonics and Spelling
◎ Vowel Digraphs *oo, ue, ew, ui*

Comprehension
◎ Monitor and Clarify

Fluency
Expression and Intonation

Conventions
Adverbs That Tell How

Writing
Thank-You Note: Revise

Listening and Speaking
Give an Oral Summary

Research and Inquiry
Review and Revise Topic

Concept Talk

 Question of the Week

How do changes in the weather affect us?

Build concepts

To reinforce concepts and to focus children's attention, have children sing "Changing Conditions" from the *Sing with Me* Big Book. Why is it that some days everyone is wrong when it comes to predicting the weather? (It is impossible to accurately predict the weather all of the time because weather conditions are constantly changing.)

🔘 *Sing with Me* Big Book Audio

Review Genre: expository text

Discuss the key features of expository text: it provides facts about a topic and information about the real world. Explain that today children will hear about a special kind of terrifying and powerful wind storm in "Twisters!" by Kate Hayden. Explain that the word *twister* is often used in place of the word *tornado* in describing these storms.

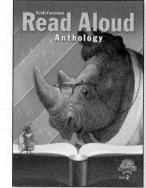

Read Aloud Anthology "Twisters!"

Monitor listening comprehension

Recall how hot, dry weather caused serious problems for Jade, her family, and the other villagers. Have children listen to "Twisters" to find out what can happen to people and property in an area where twisters occur. Read the story.

ELL **Produce Oral Language** Use the Day 4 instruction on ELL Poster 20 to extend and enrich language.

ELL Poster 20

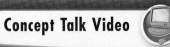

F

S

Read words independent of context

Di
wo

Ha
at

Corrective feedback

W

If..
the
wo
If..
pe
the

Read words in context

Dis
Th
the
are

Corrective feedback

Se

If..
fre
the
ecl
If..
abl
the

Oral Vocabulary
Amazing Words

Teach Amazing Words

Amazing Words **Oral Vocabulary Routine**

1. **Introduce the Word** Relate the word *funnel* to the selection. A twister is shaped like a *funnel.* Supply a child-friendly definition. A *funnel* is an object with a wide top and a tube at the bottom that is used to pour substances into a container. Have children say the word.

2. **Demonstrate** Provide examples to show meaning. Dad used a *funnel* to pour gas into the lawnmower. The cloud became a *funnel* shape and touched the ground. I used a *funnel* to pour cat food from a big bag into a smaller container.

3. **Apply** Have children demonstrate their understanding. Tell how you might use a *funnel* to help prepare materials for a painting activity.

See p. OV•2 to teach *swirl.*

Routines Flip Chart

Anchored Talk

Add to the concept map

Discuss how twisters can affect us.

• What kind of weather condition is described in "Twisters!"? (a deadly windstorm called a twister or tornado)

• What are some effects of twisters on property? (Twisters destroy buildings and fields. Twisters carry things from place to place.) Let's add this information to our chart.

• How do twisters affect what people do? (People listen for forecasters' warnings. They hide in underground shelters.) Where shall we add this information on our concept map? (We can add it under the heading *Weather affects what we do.*)

Amazing Words

condition	whip
predict	sparkle
terrifying	funnel
breeze	swirl

English Language Learners
Frontload Comprehension
Display pictures of twisters and the damage they can cause. To help children understand why some people call tornados twisters, demonstrate what it means to twist one's body and explain that this twisting or swirling movement is what air does inside a twister. Model how to draw a twister by drawing a column of overlapping ovals that narrows towards the bottom. Have children use this technique to draw and label a twister destroying property.

Objectives

- Read and identify w
  syllable patterns VC
  and VCV (*ti-ger*) an
  labic words with vo
  and diphthongs.
- Read words fluently
  and independent of

Objectives

- Apply knowledge of sound-spellings to decode unknown words when reading.
- Decode and read words in context and independent of context.
- Practice fluency with oral rereading.

Decodable Practice Reader 20C
🔊 Vowel Digraphs *oo, ue, ew, ui*

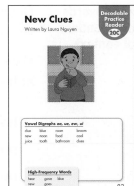

Decodable Practice Reader 20C

Decode words independent of context	Have children turn to the first page and decode each word.
Read high-frequency words	Have children identify and read the high-frequency words *hear, gave, blue, new,* and *goes* on the first page.
Preview	Have children identify and read the title and preview the story. Tell them they will decode words with vowel digraphs *oo, ue, ew,* and *ui.*
Decode words in context	Pair children for reading and listen as they decode. One child begins. Children read the entire story, switching readers after each page. Partners reread the story. This time the other child begins.

I hear it go tick. I hear it go tock.
Mom gave me a clue
to find her blue timer.
It said, "Go to the room
with the big broom."
84

The room with the broom
had this new clue in place.
It said, "Go to the room
where you sit at noon."
85

At the table, this new clue waited.
"Find that place
that keeps food cool."
86

That freezer is cold!
That food and juice are frozen.
I took that clue out!
It told me to find that place
where each tooth is brushed!
87

That clue in the bathroom
asked me to find
the room with blue rugs.
Which room has blue rugs?
88

That's my room!
The timer goes
"tick, tock."
But I can't find it!
89

The timer went "ding!"
No new clues can be found.
Mom, show me where
the timer is now!
90

Corrective feedback

If... children have difficulty decoding a word,
then... refer them to the Sound-Spelling Cards to identify the sounds in the word. Then prompt them to blend the word.

- What is the new word?
- Is the new word a word you know?
- Does it make sense in the story?

Check decoding and comprehension

Have children retell the story to include characters, setting, and events. Then have children find words with vowel digraphs *oo, ue, ew,* and *ui* in the story. Children should supply *clue, blue, room, broom, new, noon, food, cool, juice, tooth, bathroom, clues.*

Reread for Fluency

Have children reread Decodable Practice Reader 20C to develop automaticity decoding words with vowel digraphs *oo, ue, ew,* and *ui.*

ROUTINE Oral Rereading

1. **Read** Have children read the entire book orally.
2. **Reread** To achieve optimal fluency, children should reread the text three or four times.
3. **Corrective Feedback** Listen as children read. Provide corrective feedback regarding their fluency and decoding.

Routines Flip Chart

E L L

English Language Learners
Decodable Reader
Beginning Before children read, preview *New Clues,* using the illustrations to aid with understanding. Point out words in the story with vowel digraphs *oo, ue, ew,* and *ui* and have children repeat them after you.

Intermediate Give each child a word in the story containing the vowel digraph *oo, ue, ew,* or *ui.* Tell the page number and have the child point to the word on the page. Have each child make up a new sentence using the word.

Advanced/Advanced-High Pair children and have them sort the words in the list on the first page of the Decodable Practice Reader according to the vowel digraph *oo, ue, ew,* and *ui.* Have partners read the words to each other.

Objectives
- Spell words with vowel digraphs *oo, ue, ew, ui.*
- Spell high-frequency words.
- Identify facts and details in expository text.
- Relate prior knowledge to new text.
- Set purpose for reading.

Spelling
Vowel Digraphs *oo, ue, ew, ui*

Partner Review

Supply pairs of children with index cards on which the spelling words have been written. Have one child read a word while the other writes it. Then have children switch roles. Have them use the cards to check their spelling and correct any misspelled words.

On their own

Use Let's Practice It! p. 220 on the *Teacher Resource DVD-ROM.*

Let's Practice It!
TR DVD•220

Small Group Time

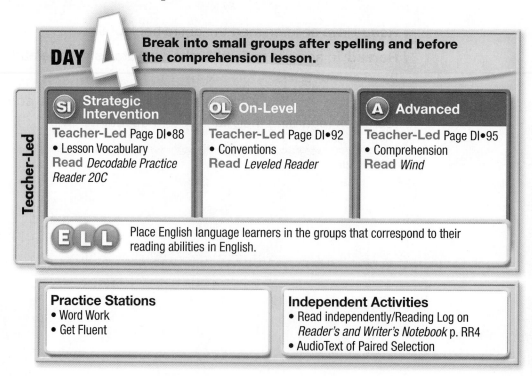

DAY 4 Break into small groups after spelling and before the comprehension lesson.

Teacher-Led

SI Strategic Intervention	OL On-Level	A Advanced
Teacher-Led Page DI•88 • Lesson Vocabulary **Read** *Decodable Practice Reader 20C*	**Teacher-Led** Page DI•92 • Conventions **Read** *Leveled Reader*	**Teacher-Led** Page DI•95 • Comprehension **Read** *Wind*

ELL Place English language learners in the groups that correspond to their reading abilities in English.

Practice Stations	**Independent Activities**
• Word Work • Get Fluent	• Read independently/Reading Log on *Reader's and Writer's Notebook* p. RR4 • AudioText of Paired Selection

Science in Reading

Academic Vocabulary

fact piece of information that can be proved to be true

details small pieces of information

expository text text that contains facts and information

Identify facts and details

Remind children that some selections contain many facts and details that support the important ideas of the selection. Good readers look for these facts and details to help them understand what they read.

Preview and predict

Read the title and the first paragraph of the selection on pages 182–185. Have children look through the selection studying the diagrams and illustrations and predict what they might learn. (Possible response: They might learn what wind is and how wind is important to things on Earth.) Ask them what clues helped them make that prediction. (Possible response: the diagrams show how air rises and falls; the illustrations show how birds, plants, and people use wind; the captions identify different kinds of winds.)

Let's Think About Genre

Expository Text Review the key features of **expository text:** It uses facts and details to explain things about a person, animal, place, object, or idea. Expository text often contains graphic features such as diagrams, illustrations, photographs, and captions. These visuals help to explain information in the text.

Activate prior knowledge

Ask children to describe what wind feels like. Then have them talk about times they have seen the wind move something. Explain that in this selection, they will learn more about what causes wind and how wind can be helpful and harmful.

Set a purpose

As children read "Wind," use Let's Think About in the Student Edition to help them focus on the features of expository text.

Objectives

- Locate facts and details in expository text.
- Support answers with facts and details.
- ◎ Monitor and clarify comprehension by generating questions and rereading to find answers or locate clues.
- Adjust reading rate to monitor and clarify.

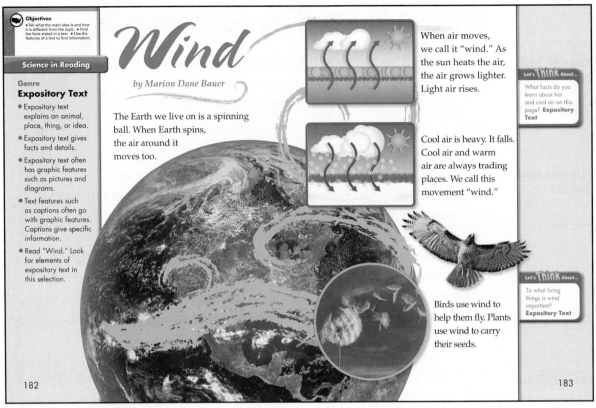

Student Edition pp. 182–183

Guide Comprehension

 ### Monitor and Clarify

Guide practice

Think Aloud As I read, I monitor and clarify my comprehension by asking questions and rereading to find answers. I also adjust my reading rate to suit the text. As I read *Corn Tortilla Recipe,* I asked myself how much flour I would need. To answer this question, I slowly and carefully reread the ingredient list to find this detail. **Have children use these strategies as they read "Wind."**

Facts and details

Think Aloud As I think about the title "Wind," I wonder what wind is. On page 183, I read the fact that when air moves, we call it wind. I will keep this fact in mind as I read more about why air moves.

Let's Think About Expository Text

Possible response: Hot air rises and cool air falls. Cool and hot air constantly trade places. This air movement is "wind."

Let's Think About Expository Text

Possible response: Birds use wind to fly. Plants use wind to carry their seeds.

We use wind to fly kites, to sail boats, and to turn windmills.

Let's Think About...

What are some different ways that people use wind? **Expository Text**

Wind moves clouds. Wind makes waves. It even makes trees bend. When the hot air is very light and the cold air is very heavy, wind can blow up a storm!

Sometimes wind spins like a puppy chasing its tail. A small spin makes a dust devil or a water spout. A strong spin makes a tornado or a hurricane.

dust devil

view of hurricane from space

tornado

Wind can be scary. Or it can sing a gentle song. Wind is all around us, but we cannot see it. We can only see what wind does.

Let's Think About...

Reading Across Texts What wind characteristics did the Mountain Spirit from *The First Tortilla* have?

Writing Across Texts Write a paragraph explaining your answer.

184

185

Student Edition pp. 184–185

Science Vocabulary

air mixture of gases around the Earth

cloud a large white or gray object in the sky made up of very small droplets of water or tiny pieces of ice

dust devil circular column of moving air containing sand and tiny particles of soil

hurricane a powerful storm with very strong winds and heavy rains

tornado a violent whirlwind that has an air column shaped like a funnel

water spout circular column of moving air that sucks up water

wind moving air

Guide Comprehension, continued

Facts and Details What conditions are necessary for wind to cause a storm? (The hot air must be very light, and the cold air must be very heavy.)

◉ **Monitor and Clarify** What would you do if you did not understand the difference between a tornado and a dust devil? (I would slowly reread the text and study the photographs looking for differences.)

Let's Think About Expository Text

Possible response: People use wind to fly kites, sail boats, and turn windmills.

Reading Across Texts Like wind, the Mountain Spirit could be both powerful and gentle and both helpful and harmful to people and other living things on Earth.

Writing Across Texts Children's paragraphs should contain facts and details describing similar characteristics that the wind and the Mountain Spirit share. It should also contain specific examples of how these characteristics could be both harmful and helpful.

Objectives
- Read aloud fluently with expression and intonation.
- Understand and use adverbs that tell how.

Check Fluency WCPM
SUCCESS PREDICTOR

Guide practice

Fluency
Read with Expression and Intonation

- Have children turn to pages 170–171 in *The First Tortilla.*
- Have children follow along as you read the pages with expression and intonation.
- Have the class read the pages with you and then reread the pages as a group until they read with expression and intonation. To provide additional fluency practice, pair nonfluent readers with fluent readers.

ROUTINE **Paired Reading**

1. **Select a Passage** For *The First Tortilla,* use pages 172–173.
2. **Model** First, have children track the print as you read.
3. **Guide Practice** Then have children read along with you.
4. **On Their Own** For optimal fluency, have partners reread three or four times.

Routines Flip Chart

Don't Wait Until Friday

MONITOR PROGRESS **Check Fluency WCPM**

As children reread, monitor their progress toward their individual fluency goals. Current Goal: 62–72 words correct per minute. End-of-Year-Goal: 90 words correct per minute.

If... children cannot read fluently at a rate of 62–72 words correct per minute,

then... have children practice with text at their independent level.

Day 1	Day 2	Day 3	Day 4	Day 5
Check Word Reading	Check Lesson Vocabulary/ High-Frequency Words	Check Retelling	Check Fluency	Check Oral Vocabulary

Success Predictor

Conventions
Adverbs That Tell How

Test practice Use *Reader's and Writer's Notebook* p. 348 to help children understand how to identify adverbs in test items. Model identifying adverbs by writing this sentence on the board, reading it aloud, and underlining the adverb.

> We waited <u>nervously</u> for the game to begin.

Then read the *Reader's and Writer's Notebook* p. 348 directions. Guide children as they mark the answer for number 1.

On their own Use *Reader's and Writer's Notebook* p. 348.

Connect to oral language After children mark the answers to numbers 1–6, review the correct choices aloud, and have children read each sentence aloud, emphasizing the adverb.

Reader's and Writer's Notebook p. 348

Differentiated Instruction

 A **Advanced**

WCPM If children already read at 90 words correct per minute, allow them to read independently.

Fluency Assessment Plan

Do a formal fluency assessment with 8 to 10 children every week. Assess 4 to 5 children on Day 4, and 4 to 5 children on Day 5. Use the fluency passage, Teacher's Edition, p. 187f.

Options for Oral Rereading

Use *The First Tortilla* or one of the week's Decodable Practice Readers.

Daily Fix-It

7. The wind blue down a tree?
The wind <u>blew</u> down a tree<u>.</u>

8. Did pam go home today
Did <u>Pam</u> go home today<u>?</u>

Discuss the Daily Fix-It corrections with children. Review the capitalization of proper nouns, sentence punctuation, and the homophones *blue* and *blew*.

Fluency WCPM

Success Predictor

Objectives

- Revise a draft by deleting phrases.

Writing—Thank-You Note
Revising Strategy

MINI-LESSON

Revising Strategy: Deleting Phrases

- Yesterday we wrote a thank-you note to someone who prepared food for us. Today we will revise. We can delete phrases that detract, or take away, from the focus of the thank-you note.

Revising Marks			
Take Out	~~	Move	↷
Add	^	Period	⊙

November 25 2011

Dear grandma

Thank you for cooking thanksgiving dinner this year ~~for all of us~~. It was fun to watch you happyly prepare all the food. I learned so much!

First, you baked the sweet, creamy pumkin pie ~~so that it would have time to cool~~. Then, you gently combined the bread cubes and broth in a bowl for a tasty stuffing ~~that I liked a lot~~. Next, you stuffed the turkey and put it in the oven. as it cooked, the turky smelled awesome! Just befor dinner, you showed me how to tear the lettuce and make a delicious salad? The food disappeared quickly. You can cook for me any day of the year!

love,
Julie

Unit 4 The First Tortilla — Writing: Revise 20B

Writing Transparency 20B
TR DVD

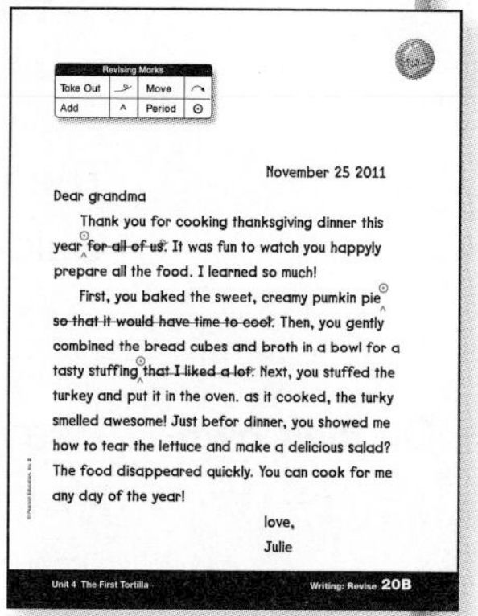

- Display the Revising Tips. To write a good thank-you note, you may need to delete, or take away a **phrase,** which is a group of words in a sentence. Sometimes phrases we don't need take the focus away from our message. So it's best to delete those phrases. Tomorrow children will proofread to correct format errors, misspellings, missing capital letters, or wrong or missing punctuation.

Revising Tips

☐ Make sure the ideas in your thank-you are in time order.

☐ Delete phrases that are unnecessary in your thank-you note.

- Use Writing Transparency 20B to model ways to delete unnecessary phrases. As I read my thank-you note, I see a few phrases that are not needed. In the first sentence, I don't need the phrase *for all of us,* so I will delete that. (Delete *for all of us.*) Proceed in the same way and delete the following phrases: *so that it would have time to cool* and *that I liked a lot*. Tell children to delete phrases they think detract from the focus of their note.

Peer conferencing

Peer Revision Pair up children and tell them switch thank-you notes with their partner. Have children read the notes and check for time-order sequence of ideas in the notes. Have them also suggest phrases that detract from the focus of the note and could be deleted.

Guide practice

Have children revise their thank-you notes. For those not sure how to revise, have children refer to the Revising Tips or the Key Features of a Thank-You Note.

Corrective feedback

Circulate to monitor and conference with children as they write. Remind them that they will have time to proofread and edit tomorrow. Today they can delete phrases that detract from the focus of their notes.

Help them understand the benefits of deleting phrases. Tell them that sometimes using phrases you don't need draws attention away from the important ideas. They should make sure that the focus of their ideas is always clear and that they don't use words that are unnecessary.

ROUTINE Quick Write for Fluency   Team Talk

1. **Talk** Read the sentences. Have children choose the one that best shows an idea without extra words.
   - The creamy pumpkin pie tasted sweet.
   - The creamy pumpkin pie tasted sweet after sampling it.
2. **Write** Write this sentence on the board: *Before dinner, I set the table.* Have children delete a phrase that isn't necessary to the idea. (before dinner)
3. **Share** Partners can read the sentences to one another and discuss why they deleted the phrase they did.

Routines Flip Chart

Differentiated Instruction

 Strategic Intervention

Finding Phrases If children have difficulty deciding if they need to delete some phrases in their thank-you notes, make a copy of their note. Then highlight some phrases. Tell them to reread the sentences first with the phrases and then without the phrases. Ask them to decide which sentences sound best, that is, which do not detract from their focus.

Academic Vocabulary

phrase a group of words in a sentence

Objectives

- Give an oral summary.
- Share information and ideas on a topic under discussion.
- Review answers to inquiry questions.
- Revise a topic based on answers to research questions.

Listening and Speaking
Give an Oral Summary

Teach oral summary

Remind children that when they give an oral summary, they tell the most important information in a logical sequence or order that makes sense. Point out that when they give an oral summary, they also should demonstrate the traits of a good speaker.

- Good speakers speak in complete sentences when summarizing.
- They include descriptive words in their summaries to help listeners paint a picture in their minds.
- Good speakers are expressive when presenting their summaries. They show emotions, build suspense, or emphasize key points.
- They focus on the topic of the summary. They present the big ideas that they want listeners to remember.
- They speak clearly and try not to repeat words or use vocal pauses like *um, mmm,* or *uh* that will distract from their presentation.

Model

Model the traits of a good speaker by sharing an oral summary of *The First Tortilla.*

 Think Aloud *The First Tortilla* is a legend that recounts the brave deeds of Jade, a young Mexican girl. In Jade's village, the people are dying of hunger due to a long drought. When a blue hummingbird tells Jade she can end the drought by visiting the Mountain Spirit to ask for rain, she agrees to go on this dangerous journey. Falling rocks and steep cliffs block her path, but she continues on. The Mountain Spirit is pleased by Jade's bravery and her gifts. He promises to send rain and gives her the gift of corn. When Jade returns to her village, she bakes the first corn tortilla and teaches this skill to others. Soon corn tortillas become the favorite food of the people.

Guide practice

As a class, give an oral summary of "Hector and the Scarecrow" or "Wind." Have children take turns adding sentences that express important ideas to the summary. As they do so, remind them to demonstrate the traits of a good speaker.

On their own

Divide the class into small groups. Have them select one other story or selection from Unit 4, with each member of the group contributing to the summary. Remind them that they should speak in complete sentences that focus on the selection topic. Then have them share their summaries with the class, and remind them to speak clearly at an appropriate pace.

Research and Inquiry
Review and Revise Topic

Teach

Tell children that the next step in their inquiry project is to review the topic to see if they have the information they set out to find. Or, did our answers lead to a different topic?

Model

We planned to find out how weather changes affect us. Display the list of inquiry questions and the answers recorded. First, I asked, "What do we do when the weather is nice?" Some answers are that we play outside, wear light clothes, can work outside, go places, and have recess. That begins to answer how the weather affects us. So we have answered our original topic, and it does not need to change.

Guide Practice

Read the other inquiry question and answers. After each answer is read, have children turn to a partner to discuss whether or not the answer gives information about how weather changes affect us. Note any new questions the children have and revise the original topic if necessary. Finally, tell children that tomorrow they will organize all the information in order to share it with others.

Wrap Up Your Day

✔ **Phonics** Write these words: *scoop, true, stew,* and *fruit.* Ask children to read the words and identify the vowel sound of /ü/ and the letters that spell that sound.

✔ **Fluency** Display *Sue wore a pretty new suit and blue boots to school.* Have children read the sentence three or four times until they can do so fluently.

Differentiated Instruction

 Strategic Intervention

More Specific Questions Some children may need to write more specific questions to focus their thinking. Work with them to name different kinds of weather in your area. Then give examples of questions for the topic, such as *What do you wear outside when the weather is warm? What do you wear when it rains? What are some things you cannot do outside when it rains?*

 Advanced

Evaluate Sources Have children discuss which sources—inside school or outside school—they thought worked best for each of the inquiry questions.

Preview DAY 5

Tell children that tomorrow they will hear more about changes that occur in the natural world.

Objectives

- Review the concept: effects of changing weather.
- Build oral vocabulary.
- Identify details in text.

Today at a Glance

Oral Vocabulary
Review

Phonics
◉ Review Vowel Digraphs *oo, ue, ew, ui*

Comprehension
◉ Plot and Theme

Lesson Vocabulary
Review

Conventions
Adverbs That Tell How

Writing
Thank-You Note

Research and Inquiry
Communicate

Check Oral Vocabulary
SUCCESS PREDICTOR

Concept Wrap Up

Question of the Week
How do changes in the weather affect us?

Review
Concept

This week we have read and listened to selections that explore how changes in weather affect us. Today you will find out why life in Tornado Alley is not as dangerous as it used to be. **Read the selection.**

- Why is life in Tornado Alley safer today? (Possible response: Today, scientists and trackers are able to give more accurate information to weather reporters who can warn viewers to take shelter.)

Review
Amazing Words

Review the meaning of this week's Amazing Words. Then display this week's concept map. Have children use Amazing Words such as *condition, predict, terrifying, funnel,* and *swirl,* as well as the chart, to answer the question, "How do changes in the weather affect us?"

Read Aloud Anthology "Twisters!"

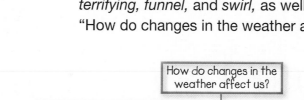

How do changes in the weather affect us?

Weather affects what we wear.	Weather affects what we do.	Weather affects property.	Weather affects what we grow.
We wear heavy clothes to keep warm in cold weather.	We can build things in the snow.	Weather changes where people live.	Without rain, crops die.
	We listen for forecasters' warnings.	Twisters destroy buildings and fields.	Rain makes crops grow.
	We hide from twisters in shelters.	Twisters carry things from place to place.	

ELL **Check Concepts and Language** Use the Day 5 instruction on ELL Poster 20 to monitor children's understanding of the lesson concept.

ELL Poster 20

Oral Vocabulary
Amazing Ideas

Connect to the Big Question

Team Talk Pair children and have them discuss how the Question of the Week connects to this unit's Big Question, "How do things change? How do they stay the same?" Tell children to use the concept map and what they've learned from this week's Anchored Talks and reading selections to form an Amazing Idea—a realization or "big idea" about **change.** Then ask each pair to share their Amazing Idea with the class.

Amazing Ideas might include these key concepts:

• The wind can change from a breeze to a twister depending on weather conditions.

• Despite progress made by scientists and weather forecasters, it can be difficult to accurately predict the weather.

It's Friday

MONITOR PROGRESS | **Check Oral Vocabulary**

Call on individuals to use this week's Amazing Words to talk about how weather affects us in positive and negative ways. Prompt discussion with the questions below. Monitor children's ability to use the Amazing Words and note which words children are unable to use.

• **What weather *conditions* might be *terrifying* to you?**

• **Why do we need forecasters to *predict* where and when a *funnel*-shaped cloud will appear?**

• **Could a strong *breeze* cause a flag to *whip* and leaves to *swirl*?**

• **What weather *conditions* would make snow *sparkle*?**

If... children have difficulty using the Amazing Words,

then... reteach the unknown words using the Oral Vocabulary Routines, pp. 155a, 160b, 178bb, 182b.

Day 1	Day 2	Day 3	Day 4	Day 5
Check Word Reading	Check Lesson Vocabulary/High-Frequency Words	Check Retelling	Check Fluency	**Check Oral Vocabulary**

Success Predictor

condition	whip
predict	sparkle
terrifying	funnel
breeze	swirl

ELL

English Language Learners

Extend Language Pair children and give them props such as an umbrella, a mitten, a sandal, and a kite. Have them work together to identify what type of weather they associate with each object. Then have them describe how each type of weather would affect what they would wear and how they would play.

Oral Vocabulary **Success Predictor**

Objectives

◎ Review words with the vowel sound /ü/ spelled *oo, ue, ew,* and *ui.*

Assess

• Spell words with the vowel sound /ü/ spelled *oo, ue, ew,* and *ui.*

• Spell high-frequency words.

Phonics

Vowel Digraphs *oo, ue, ew, ui*

Review
Target phonics skill

Write the following sentences on the board. Have children read each one, first quietly to themselves and then aloud as you track the print.

> 1. It is untrue that he grew the fruit for his juice.
>
> 2. Did the owl hoot when the storm began brewing?
>
> 3. My new bruise was black and blue.
>
> 4. The goose flew over the zoo in the moonlight.

Team Talk Have children discuss with a partner which words have /ü/ spelled *oo, ue, ew,* and *ui.* Then call on individuals to share with the class.

Spelling Test
Vowel Digraphs *oo, ue, ew, ui*

Dictate spelling words

Say each word, read the sentence, repeat the word, and allow time for children to write the word.

1. **too** — We will go to Jack's house **too**.
2. **new** — Did you read that **new** book yet?
3. **fruit** — We have two **fruit** trees in our yard.
4. **blue** — Mike has **blue** eyes.
5. **true** — Is it **true** that your uncle lives in Alaska?
6. **fool** — My sister hides my books to **fool** me.
7. **suit** — Dad bought a **suit** and shoes.
8. **spoon** — Please stir the soup with a wooden **spoon**.
9. **clue** — The clouds are a **clue** that it will rain soon.
10. **juice** — Did you taste the grape **juice?**
11. **drew** — I **drew** a ticket from the box.
12. **flew** — We **flew** to Colorado last summer.

High-Frequency Words

13. **won't** — I **won't** be able to visit you today.
14. **know** — I **know** the names of all the state capitals.

Differentiated Instruction

 Strategic Intervention

Check Spelling Give children only the letter tiles that spell one word. Have them arrange the tiles to spell the word correctly. Continue in the same way for each spelling word.

A Advanced

Extend Spelling Have children who have demonstrated proficiency in spelling the words write a rhyming poem using as many spelling words as possible.

Small Group Time

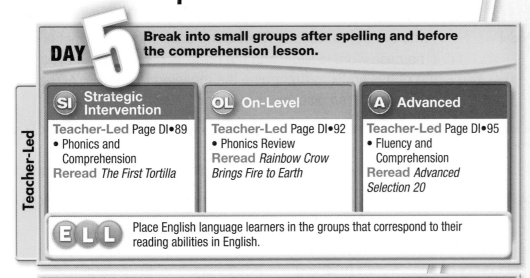

DAY 5 Break into small groups after spelling and before the comprehension lesson.

Teacher-Led

SI Strategic Intervention
Teacher-Led Page DI•89
• Phonics and Comprehension
Reread *The First Tortilla*

OL On-Level
Teacher-Led Page DI•92
• Phonics Review
Reread *Rainbow Crow Brings Fire to Earth*

A Advanced
Teacher-Led Page DI•95
• Fluency and Comprehension
Reread *Advanced Selection 20*

ELL Place English language learners in the groups that correspond to their reading abilities in English.

Practice Stations
• Words to Know
• Let's Write

Independent Activities
• Read independently/Reading Log on *Reader's and Writer's Notebook* p. RR4
• Concept Talk Video

Objectives

- Identify prefixes and use them to determine word meaning.
- Read aloud fluently with expression and intonation.
- Give an oral summary.
- Speak clearly at an appropriate rate.

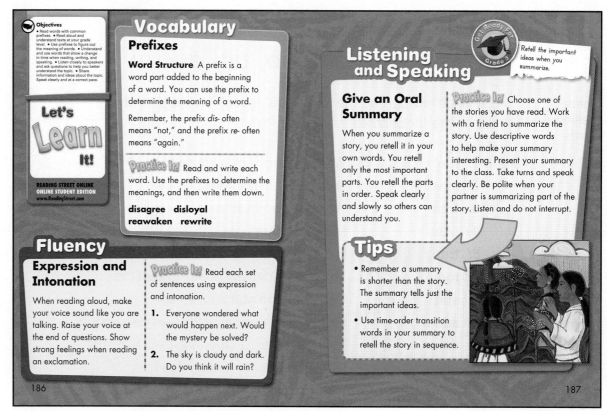

Objectives
• Read words with common prefixes. • Read aloud and understand texts at your grade level. • Use prefixes to figure out the meaning of words. • Understand and use words that show a change in time when reading, writing, and speaking. • Listen closely to speakers and ask questions to help you better understand the topic. • Share information and ideas about the topic. Speak clearly and at a correct pace.

Let's Learn It!

READING STREET ONLINE
ONLINE STUDENT EDITION
www.ReadingStreet.com

Vocabulary
Prefixes

Word Structure A prefix is a word part added to the beginning of a word. You can use the prefix to determine the meaning of a word.

Remember, the prefix *dis-* often means "not," and the prefix *re-* often means "again."

Practice It! Read and write each word. Use the prefixes to determine the meanings, and then write them down.

disagree   disloyal
reawaken   rewrite

Fluency
Expression and Intonation

When reading aloud, make your voice sound like you are talking. Raise your voice at the end of questions. Show strong feelings when reading an exclamation.

Practice It! Read each set of sentences using expression and intonation.

1. Everyone wondered what would happen next. Would the mystery be solved?

2. The sky is cloudy and dark. Do you think it will rain?

Listening and Speaking

Get Ready For Grade 3

Retell the important ideas when you summarize.

Give an Oral Summary

When you summarize a story, you retell it in your own words. You retell only the most important parts. You retell the parts in order. Speak clearly and slowly so others can understand you.

Practice It! Choose one of the stories you have read. Work with a friend to summarize the story. Use descriptive words to help make your summary interesting. Present your summary to the class. Take turns and speak clearly. Be polite when your partner is summarizing part of the story. Listen and do not interrupt.

Tips

- Remember a summary is shorter than the story. The summary tells just the important ideas.
- Use time-order transition words in your summary to retell the story in sequence.

186   187

Student Edition pp. 186–187

Vocabulary
Prefixes

Teach

Have children turn to page 186 of the Student Edition. Read and discuss the Vocabulary lesson together. Use the model to explain that prefixes are word parts added to the beginning of a word. Point out that thinking about the meaning of a prefix may help readers determine a word's meaning.

Model

Write the word *disallow*. What is the base word and what is the prefix? (The base word is *allow* and the prefix is *dis-*.) How can you use the meaning of this prefix to determine the meaning of *disallow*? (The prefix *dis-* means "not," so *disallow* means "not allow.")

Guide practice

Read the instructions for the Vocabulary Practice It! activity. Read the first word. I will use the prefix meaning to determine the meaning of *disagree*. Since *dis-* means "not," I will write that *disagree* means "not agree."

On their own

Have pairs continue reading each word and using the prefix to help them write the meaning of each word.

Corrective feedback

Circulate around the room and listen as children use a prefix to determine each word's meaning. Provide assistance as needed.

Fluency
Expression and Intonation

Teach Read and discuss the Fluency instructions.

Read words in context Give children a moment to look at the sentences. Then have them read each sentence three or four times until they can read each sentence with expression and intonation.

Listening and Speaking
Give an Oral Summary

Teach Read and discuss the Listening and Speaking lesson on page 187 of the Student Edition. Remind children that to summarize a story, they must retell the important parts in order in their own words. Point out that to make their summaries more interesting, they may use adverbs that tell how.

Model Model a summary of *The Night the Moon Fell*. This story is a myth that tells what happens when Luna the moon falls into the sea. She is sad because the fall breaks her into a million pieces. But her new friends the little fish help put her together. At the end of the story, both Luna and the fish go up into the sky together.

Introduce prompt Read the Speaking and Listening Practice It! prompt. Pair children and have them work together to choose a story and summarize it. Remind them to include adjectives and adverbs in their summaries.

Team Talk Have each pair present their summary to the class. Tell children that good speakers speak clearly and slowly so listeners can understand. Remind them that good listeners listen carefully when others are summarizing and wait their turn to speak.

Differentiated Instruction

 SI Strategic Intervention

Summarize Have children refer to the retelling strip found in the Student Edition for the story they select. Have them come up with one sentence for each picture in the strip and then combine these sentences to create a story summary.

Give an Oral Summary

In addition to using their own words to summarize the important events in a story, children at Grade 3 should also be able to use a variety of sentence patterns and appropriate vocabulary in their summaries.

ELL

English Language Learners

Prefixes Provide this sentence frame to help children analyze how a word's meaning changes when the prefix *dis-* is added: When you add the prefix *dis-* to the base word _____, the new word means "not _____."

Objectives
◎ Identify the plot and theme of a story.
• Review lesson vocabulary.
• Analyze the author's craft.

Comprehension

Plot and Theme

Review
Plot and theme

Remember that stories have a plot and a theme. A plot is the events in the beginning, middle, and end of a story. The plot helps readers figure out the story's "big idea" or the author's message. What is this big idea called? (the theme)

Read aloud the following story and have children answer the questions.

> Four-year old Noah loved spending the weekend at Grandpa's farm. One morning he decided to surprise Grandpa out in the barn. Noah looked and looked around the barn—was Grandpa playing hide-and-seek? Just then he heard a groan coming from the hayloft. He climbed the ladder and saw Grandpa lying under a bale of hay. Noah remembered what he'd learned about emergencies at preschool. He knew the bale was too heavy for him to lift, but he could call 911 on Grandpa's cell phone. A short time later, an ambulance arrived. As it pulled away, the driver called Noah a genuine hero.

1. What is the story plot? (Noah's grandpa has an accident in the barn; Noah finds his grandpa, and he calls 911 for help.)

2. What is the story theme? (Even young children can help in an emergency if they stay calm and remember what to do.)

3. What did the driver mean when he called Noah a hero? (He meant that Noah had acted bravely in a dangerous situation.)

Vocabulary
Lesson Vocabulary

Review
Lesson vocabulary

Review this week's lesson vocabulary words: *awaken, cliffs, mountain, prize, rainbow, suffer,* and *volcano.* Provide an example of two related words, having the class supply the missing word, such as *lava, erupt,* _____. (*volcano*)

Team Talk Pair children and have them take turns orally giving category clues for the remaining six words.

Corrective feedback

If... children cannot use the words in a meaningful way,
then... review the definitions on page 160f.

Literary Text
Author's Craft

Review
Literary devices

Review with children that authors often use literary devices such as foreshadowing, metaphors, and personification in the stories they write.

Teach

When authors use **foreshadowing,** they provide hints and clues about what will happen later in the story. Both text and illustrations can foreshadow. Authors also use language in a figurative way to create word pictures. Metaphors are one form of figurative language. A **metaphor** compares different things without using the words *as* or *like.* Personification is another form of figurative language. In **personification,** an idea, object, or animal is given the characteristics of a person.

Model

 The legend *The First Tortilla* contains examples of foreshadowing, metaphors, and personification. For example, in previewing and predicting what this legend would be about, we discovered that the illustration on the title page foreshadowed that Jade would be the hero of this legend.

Guide practice

Ask the following questions to guide children in identifying other examples of foreshadowing, metaphors, and personification.

- What else does the title page illustration foreshadow? (It foreshadows that Jade bakes the first tortilla, and a blue hummingbird is her friend.)

- What happens when Jade is born that foreshadows her future? (A blue hummingbird flies over her crib.)

- What is being compared in this metaphor: "butterflies danced among a rainbow of flowers." (Flowers are being compared to a rainbow.) What picture does this metaphor create in your mind? (Possible response: I see a field of colorful flowers.)

- How does the author personify the blue hummingbird? (The author describes the blue hummingbird as a messenger from the Mountain Spirit. The hummingbird talks and acts as a guide.)

On their own

Have children work with a partner. Have them find other examples of foreshadowing, metaphors, and personification in *The First Tortilla.* Have them share these examples with the class.

Differentiated Instruction

 Strategic Intervention

Author's Craft To assist children in understanding metaphors and personification, present these additional examples and have children explain the comparison or the personification: *A gentle wind kissed the flowers. Time marches on. The cave was a refrigerator. My garden is a dustbowl.*

Academic Vocabulary

foreshadowing the use of hints or clues about what will happen later in a story

metaphor a comparison that does not use *like* or *as,* such as *a heart of stone*

personification a figure of speech in which human traits are given to animals or inanimate objects, as in *The sunbeam danced on the waves.*

English Language Learners
Personification As part of the discussion of figurative language in *The First Tortilla,* have children turn to the illustration on page 169. Point out that the text on page 170 says that the *butterflies danced.* Tell children that *people* dance; butterflies fly. The author used personification to describe the movement of the butterflies.

Assess

◉ Words with Vowel Digraphs *oo, ue, ew,* and *ui*
  • Fluency: WCPM
◉ Plot and Theme

Fluency Goals

Set individual fluency goals for children to enable them to reach the end-of-the-year goal.
  • **Current Goal:** 62–72 WCPM
  • **End-of-Year Goal:** 90 WCPM

Assessment
Monitor Progress

For a written assessment of vowel digraphs *oo, ue, ew,* and *ui* and plot and theme, use Weekly Test 20, pp. 115–120.

Assess words in context

Sentence reading Use the following reproducible page to assess children's ability to read words in context. Call on children to read two sentences aloud. Start over with sentence one if necessary.

MONITOR PROGRESS	Sentence Reading

If... children have trouble reading vowel digraphs *oo, ue, ew,* and *ui*,

then... use the Reteach Lesson in *First Stop.*

Success Predictor

Assess

Fluency Take a one-minute sample of children's oral reading. Have children read the fluency passage on p. 187f.

Comprehension Have the child read the entire passage. (If the child had difficulty with the passage, you may read it aloud.) Then have the child identify the theme of the passage.

MONITOR PROGRESS	Fluency and Comprehension

If... a child does not achieve the fluency goal on the timed reading,

then... copy the passage and send it home with the child for additional fluency practice, or have the child practice with a fluent reader.

If... a child cannot identify the theme,

then... use the Reteach Lesson in *First Stop.*

Success Predictor

Monitor accuracy

Record scores Have children monitor their accuracy by recording their scores using the Sentence Reading Chart and by recording the number of words read correctly per minute on their Fluency Progress Chart in *First Stop.*

Read the Sentences

1. A few baby raccoons scooted down our road.

2. Some papers came unglued and stuck to his new suit.

3. Her scout troop is due home soon.

4. This apple is too juicy to eat without drooling.

5. Bright blue flowers grew next to the swimming pool.

6. Is it true that a screwy goose got loose?

Reproducible Page. See also Assessment Handbook. © Pearson Education, Inc.

Read the Story

Sue and the Blue Moon

My friend Sue moved far away, so I only get to see   12
her once in awhile. When Sue visited last week, we   22
talked about things we were learning in school. I told   32
her about the moon.   36

"When there is a full moon, we can see the whole   47
side of the moon. Do you know what a blue moon is?"   59
She had never heard of it.   65

I told her, "The moon is never really blue. When   75
there are two full moons in one month, the second   85
one is called a blue moon. If there is a blue moon,   97
you will not see one again for another two years.   107
That's what 'once in a blue moon' means. It is   117
something that happens only once in a while."   125

Sue said, "I guess you could call us 'blue moon   135
friends.' We only see each other once in a while." So   146
now I call Sue my "blue moon friend."   154

Reproducible Page. See also Assessment Handbook. © Pearson Education, Inc.

MONITOR PROGRESS
• Check Fluency
• Plot and Theme

Objectives
- Identify adverbs.
- Understand and use adverbs about manner in writing and speaking.

Conventions
Adverbs That Tell How

Review

Remind children that adverbs are words that tell more about a verb. Many adverbs tell how something happens. Often these adverbs end in *-ly*. Have children give examples of adverbs that tell how.

Guide practice

Write the following sentences. Have children write an adverb that tells how in the blank.

> 1. **The puppy barked _____.**
>
> 2. **During the speech, the children sat _____.**
>
> 3. **Jan ran _____ around the track.**

Connect to oral language

List the following verbs on the board. Have children work in pairs to name adverbs that end in *-ly* to tell how each action might be done. Then have them use these verbs and adverbs in oral sentences to share with the class.

> **talk   eat   sing   learn   walk   laugh**

On their own

Use Let's Practice It! p. 222 on the *Teacher Resource DVD-ROM*.

Let's Practice It!
TR DVD • 222

Daily Fix-It

9. Who spill grape jooce on the rug?
   Who <u>spilled</u> grape <u>juice</u> on the rug?

10. Jed filled to bottle with water.
    Jed filled <u>two</u> <u>bottles</u> with water.

Discuss the Daily Fix-It corrections with children. Review verb tense, the homophones *to* and *two*, formation of plurals, and the vowel digraph *ui*.

Objectives
- Edit a draft for format, spelling, punctuation, and capitalization.
- Create a final draft and present.

Writing—Thank-You Note
Writer's Craft: Adverbs

Review Revising

Remind children that yesterday they revised their thank-you notes. They may have deleted phrases. Today they will proofread their thank-you notes.

MINI-LESSON

Proofread for Adverbs and Format

■ **Teach** When we proofread, we check to make sure the adverbs and other words are spelled correctly. I can use a dictionary to check them. When we proofread a thank-you note, we check that our note has the correct format. We also check for capital letters and punctuation. It's a good idea to check for just one thing at a time.

■ **Model** Let us look at my thank-you note. Display Writing Transparency 20C. Explain that you will look at the correct spelling for adverbs. I see that *happily* is misspelled. Are all the other words spelled correctly? I see that *pumpkin* and *turkey* are misspelled. Show how you would change *happyly* to *happily, pumkin* to *pumpkin,* and *turky* to *turkey.* Next, I'm going to check for capital letters and punctuation. Model how you would change a letter at the beginning a word if it were not capitalized. Capitalize the *g* in *grandma,* the *t* in *thanksgiving,* the *a* in *as,* and the *l* in *love.* Model how you would add or change an ending punctuation mark, and change the question mark after *salad* to a period. Now I'm going to check that my thank-you note format is correct. I have the date, the greeting, the body, the closing, and the signature. But I notice that I forgot to add commas in the date and after the greeting. Add a comma between the day and the year in the date and add a comma after *Grandma.*

Writing Transparency 20C
TR DVD

Proofread

Display the Proofreading Tips. Have children proof-read their thank-you notes to correct any format errors, misspellings, missing capital letters, or errors with end punctuation. Remind children that when they write thank-you notes, they must follow the proper format. Circulate to assist children.

Proofreading Tips

☑ **Are my adverbs and other words spelled correctly? Check a dictionary.**

☑ **Did I use capital letters and punctuation correctly?**

☑ **Did I follow the correct format for a thank-you note?**

Present

Have children make a final draft of their thank-you note, with their revisions and proofreading corrections. Help as appropriate. Choose an option for children to present their thank-you notes.

Show children samples of store-bought thank-you notes. Then let them make their own thank-you notes with a design or picture on the front and their message inside.	Have children use a computer program to generate their own thank-you note. They may like to use clip-art to decorate their notes.

When they have finished, help them complete a Self-Evaluation form.

ROUTINE Quick Write for Fluency **Team Talk**

1 Talk Have children talk about other things for which they might write a thank-you note, for example, a birthday present or help they received on a project.

2 Write Each child writes a short thank-you note to that person. Encourage children to use adverbs that tell how.

3 Share Partners trade thank-you notes and read them aloud.

Routines Flip Chart

Teacher Note

Self-Evaluation Make copies of the Self-Evaluation form from the *Teacher Resource DVD-ROM,* and hand them out to children.

English Language Learners
Support Editing
Proofread the thank-you notes together. Discuss any spelling errors. Let children use a yellow highlighter to mark their errors. Then tell them to make a clean, correct copy of their thank-you notes.

Objectives
- Review concepts: how changes in the weather affect us.
- Organize information.
- Create a visual display.
- Present results of an inquiry project.

Research and Inquiry
Communicate

Teach

Tell children that today they will organize the information from the questions and answers about how changes in the weather affect us. They will use the answers to make lists.

Model

Think Aloud Display the list of inquiry questions and the answers recorded. I will review the questions and answers and circle the information I would like to include. For instance, my first question was "What do we do when the weather is nice?" One of the answers is play outside. I will include that example in a list of how nice weather affects us. Then I'll look for information for a list of how a change to stormy weather affects us.

Guide practice

Review the questions and answers with children, and have them prompt you to circle what they could use in lists.

On their own

Have children choose weather conditions and changes that come with them. Tell them to fold a piece of writing paper in half to form two columns. Direct children to write each weather condition as a column heading. When they are finished, have them share their lists with the class. Remind them how to be good speakers and listeners:

- Good speakers talk clearly at a pace that's not too fast or too slow as they share their ideas.

- Good listeners give their attention to the speaker. They wait until the speaker is finished before raising their hand to ask a question.

Topic: How Weather Changes Affect Us	
Question	**Answer—Does it address the topic?**
What do we do when the weather is nice?	play outside, wear light clothes, can work outside, go places—**YES**

Amazing Words

You've learned 0 0 8 words this week!

You've learned 1 6 1 words this year!

Wrap Up Your Week!

? Question of the Week

How do changes in the weather affect us?

Think Aloud This week we discovered how changes in the weather affect us. In the story, *The First Tortilla*, we read about how a change in the weather enabled Jade, her family, and the villagers to grow a new crop so they could stay in their village and maintain their way of life. In the selection "Wind," we read about what causes wind and how wind can be useful to plants and animals. **Have children recall their Amazing Ideas about change. Then have children use these ideas to help them demonstrate their understanding of the Question of the Week.**

Preview NEXT WEEK

Tell children that next week they will review this unit's skills and the Big Question: How do things change? How do they stay the same?

Weekly Assessment

Use pp. 115–120 of *Weekly Tests* to check:

✔ **Phonics** Vowel Digraphs *oo, ue, ew, ui*

✔  **Comprehension Skill** Plot and Theme

✔ **Lesson Vocabulary**

awaken	rainbow
cliffs	suffer
mountain	volcano
prize	

Weekly Tests

A
Advanced

OL
On-Level

SI
Strategic
Intervention

Differentiated Assessment

Use pp. 115–120 of *Fresh Reads for Fluency and Comprehension* to check:

✔ **Comprehension Skill** Plot and Theme

✔ Review **Comprehension Skill** Main Idea and Details

✔ **Fluency** Words Correct Per Minute

Fresh Reads for Fluency and Comprehension

Managing Assessment

Use *Assessment Handbook* for:

✔ **Weekly Assessment Blackline Masters for Monitoring Progress**

✔ **Observation Checklists**

✔ **Record-Keeping Forms**

✔ **Portfolio Assessment**

Assessment Handbook

Melting Too Soon

Did you know that a polar bear uses a big chunk of loose ice to cruise on the sea in much the same way you might cruise out to sea on a raft? In winter, the bear may cruise more than 100 miles from solid land. Traveling on a loose ice chunk is the bear's only way to get far enough out to hunt seals. The bear must locate food before the ice melts.

The cool, blue waters of the Arctic Ocean turn to ice every autumn. Then in winter, polar bears cruise on the chunks of ice. What if ice melts too soon and pools of water form on the chunks? If the bears choose to swim, they may drown because land is too far away to reach. If they choose to stay, the ice will melt. Will only a few polar bears soon be left, or will they learn new ways to find food? No one knows.

Scientists do know that bears today have less time to hunt in winter than in the past. Pollution may be causing this problem. For example, some pollution makes the ice melt faster. Scientists are looking for clues that will help solve the problem. People everywhere hope to learn new ways to help the polar bears.

Reproducible Page. © Pearson Education, Inc.

Advanced Selection 20 **Vocabulary:** scientists, pollution

Small Group Time

5 Day Plan

DAY 1	• Phonics • Decodable Reader
DAY 2	• Lesson Vocabulary • Leveled Reader
DAY 3	• Phonics • Leveled Reader
DAY 4	• Lesson Vocabulary • Decodable Reader
DAY 5	• Phonics Review • Comprehension Review

3 or 4 Day Plan

DAY 1	• Phonics • Decodable Reader
DAY 2	• Lesson Vocabulary • Leveled Reader
DAY 3	• Phonics • Leveled Reader
DAY 4	• Lesson Vocabulary • Decodable Reader

3 Day Plan: Eliminate the shaded box

SI Strategic Intervention   **DAY 1**

Phonics

■ **Vowel Digraphs *oo, ue, ew, ui*** Reteach p. 156a of the Teacher's Edition. Then have children spell *pool* using letter tiles. Monitor their work.

• Change the *p* in *pool* to *t*. What is the new word?

Then have children spell *glue* using letter tiles.

• Change the *g* in *glue* to *c*. What is the new word?

Have children spell *drew* using letter tiles.

• Change the *dr* in *drew* to *fl*. What is the new word?

Have children spell *suit* using letter tiles.

• Change the *s* in *suit* to *fr*. What is the new word?

Decodable Practice Reader 20A

■ **Review** Review words with vowel digraphs *oo, ue, ew, ui* and the high-frequency words *eyes, moon, another, picture, single, only,* and *thought*. Then have children blend and read these words from the story: *near, learn, closed,* and *leaping*.

> **If...** children have difficulty with any of these words, **then...** reteach the word by modeling. Have children practice the words, with feedback from you, until they can read them independently.

Have children reread the text orally. To achieve optimal fluency, children should reread the text three or four times.

Decodable Practice Reader 20A

Objectives

• Decode multisyllabic words in context by applying common letter-sound correspondences including vowel digraphs.
• Decode multisyllabic words independent of context by applying common letter-sound correspondences including vowel digraphs.

 DAY **2**

Lesson Vocabulary

■ **Review** Using Tested Vocabulary Cards, have the group practice reading *awaken, volcano, mountain, cliffs, suffer, rainbow,* and *prize.* Then read "Hector and the Scarecrow" on Student Edition p. 161 and discuss the meanings of the words.

For a complete literacy instructional plan and additional practice with this week's target skills and strategies, see the **Leveled Reader Teaching Guide.**

Concept Literacy Leveled Reader

■ **Preview and Predict** Read the title and the author's name. Have children look at the cover and ask them to describe what they see. Help children activate their prior knowledge by asking them to look through the selection and to use the photos to predict things that might take place.

Concept Literacy

■ **Set a Purpose** Remind children that setting a purpose for reading can help them better understand what they read. Guide children to pay attention to how changes in the weather affect us.

■ **Read** Provide corrective feedback as children read the selection orally. During reading, ask them if they were able to confirm any of the predictions they made prior to reading.

> **If...** children have difficulty reading the story individually,
> **then...** read a sentence aloud as children point to each word. Then have the group reread the sentences as they continue pointing. Continue reading in this way until children read individually.

■ **Retell** Have children take turns retelling the selection. Help them identify what the children do in different kinds of weather. Go through the book page-by-page and ask questions like these: What do the children like to do when the weather is cool? What do you like to do when the weather is cool? Continue in the same way asking what the children in the book like to do and what they like to do when the weather is cold, warm, hot, wet, and dry.

More Reading

Use Leveled Readers or other text at children's instructional level.

Objectives
• Use context to determine the relevant meaning of unfamiliar words.

Small Group Time

SI *Strategic Intervention*

DAY 3

Phonics

■ 🔊 **Vowel Digraphs** *oo, ue, ew, ui* Reteach p. 178d of the Teacher's Edition. Have children blend and read these additional words to help them practice the target phonics skill.

due	food	suit	new	broom	blue
stew	juice	scoop	true	chew	fruit

For a complete literacy instructional plan and additional practice with this week's target skills and strategies, see the **Leveled Reader Teaching Guide.**

Below-Level Leveled Reader

■ **Preview and Predict** Read the title, the author's name, and the illustrator's name. Have children look at the cover and ask them to describe what they see. Help children activate their prior knowledge by asking them to look through the story and to use the illustrations to predict things that might take place.

■ **Set a Purpose** Remind children that setting a purpose for reading can help them better understand what they read. Guide children to pay attention to what happens in the beginning, in the middle, and at end of the story and what they think the message, or big idea, of the story is.

■ **Read** Provide corrective feedback as children read the story orally. During reading, ask them if they were able to confirm any of the predictions they made prior to the story.

If... children have difficulty reading the story individually,
then... read a sentence aloud as children point to each word. Then have the group reread the sentences as they continue pointing.

Below-Level

■ 🔊 **Monitor and Clarify** Ask children if they had to stop and try to make sense of something as they read the story. Did you ask yourself a question? Did you reread? Lead children to see how asking questions and rereading text to find clues to answer their questions can help them to better understand a story.

Objectives
• Use ideas to make predictions.
• Establish purpose for reading selected texts.

 DAY **4**

Lesson Vocabulary

- **Review** Use pp.160e–160f in the Teacher's Edition to review the vocabulary words. Ask questions such as the following to check for understanding:

What do you think would be difficult about climbing a <u>mountain</u>?

Where do you see a <u>rainbow</u>? What colors are in a <u>rainbow</u>?

What time do you usually <u>awaken</u> in the morning?

Did you ever win a <u>prize</u>? What was the <u>prize</u>?

Which two words best describe <u>cliffs</u>—steep, rolling, rocky?

In the hot summer, which might you <u>suffer</u> from—frostbite or sunburn?

What comes out of an active <u>volcano</u>—water and ice or smoke and lava?

More Reading
Use Leveled Readers or other text at children's instructional level.

Decodable Practice Reader 20C

- **Review** Use the word lists to review vowel digraphs *oo, ue, ew, ui.* Be sure children understand that there are different spellings for the /ü/ sound. Have children blend and read the words. Then have children reread the text orally.

    If... children have difficulty reading the story individually, **then...** read a sentence aloud as children point to each word. Then have the group reread the sentences as they continue pointing. Continue reading in this way until children read individually.

Check comprehension by having children retell the story including the character, plot, and setting. Have children locate words in the story that have vowel digraphs *oo, ue, ew, ui.* List the words children identify. Then have children sort the words in a chart with columns labeled *oo, ue, ew,* and *ui.*

Decodable Practice Reader 20C

oo	ue	ew	ui
room, broom, noon, food, cool, tooth, bathroom	clue, blue, clues	new	juice

Objectives
- Decode multisyllabic words in context by applying common letter-sound correspondences including vowel digraphs.

DAY 5

SI Strategic Intervention

Phonics Review

■ **Vowel Digraphs *oo, ue, ew, ui*** Write these sentences on the board. Have children read them aloud as you track the print. Then call on individuals to blend and read the underlined words.

> <u>Sue</u> had on a <u>blue</u> <u>suit</u>.
>
> The owl gave a <u>hoot</u> and then <u>flew</u> away.
>
> I like to drink <u>cool</u> <u>fruit</u> <u>juice</u>.
>
> Mom gave me a big <u>scoop</u> of <u>stew</u>.

Comprehension Review

■ **Plot and Theme** Review that the plot of a story is what happens in the beginning, middle, and end. The theme is the message, or the big idea, of the story. Recall the plot and theme for the comprehension passage on Student Edition p. 159.

The First Tortilla

■ **Read** Have children reread this week's main selection, *The First Tortilla.*

• As you read, think about what happens in each part of the story—the beginning, the middle, and the end.

• Look for the message, or the big idea.

After reading, have children recap what happened at the beginning, in the middle, and at the end of the story. Then ask them what the message, or big idea, of the story is.

Objectives
• Decode multisyllabic words in context by applying common letter-sound correspondences including vowel digraphs.
• Analyze theme.

OL On-Level **DAY 1**

Phonics • Spelling

■  **Vowel Digraphs *oo, ue, ew, ui*** Write the following words on the board and have children practice reading words with vowel digraphs *oo, ue, ew, ui.*

spool	glue	chew	juicy

Then have children identify the letters that spell the vowel sound of /ü/.

■ **Vowel Digraphs *oo, ue, ew, ui*** Remind children that the vowel sound of /ü/ can be spelled with *oo, ui, ew,* and *ui.* Clarify the pronunciation and meaning of each word. For example, say: Yesterday I wore my new blue shirt. Have children identify the letters that spell the vowel sound of /ü/ in *too, fruit, true,* and *suit.*

Objectives
- Decode multisyllabic words independent of context by applying common letter-sound correspondences including vowel digraphs.
- Spell correctly.

OL On-Level **DAY 2**

Lesson Vocabulary

■ **Review Word Meaning** Hold up the Tested Vocabulary Cards for *awaken, volcano, mountain, cliffs, suffer, rainbow,* and *prize* and review meanings and pronunciation. Continue holding the cards and have children chorally read each word. To help children demonstrate their understanding of the words, provide them with oral sentence frames such as:

After the storm, we saw a ___ in the sky. (rainbow)

High-Frequency/
Tested Word Cards
for Grade 2
Reading PEARSON
High-Frequency/Tested Word Cards

Objectives
- Use context to determine the relevant meaning of unfamiliar words.

Pacing Small Group Instruction

20–30 min.

5 Day Plan

DAY 1	• Phonics • Spelling • Decodable Reader
DAY 2	• Lesson Vocabulary • Decodable Reader
DAY 3	• Leveled Reader
DAY 4	• Conventions • Leveled Reader
DAY 5	• Phonics Review • Leveled Reader

3 or 4 Day Plan

DAY 1	• Phonics • Spelling • Decodable Reader
DAY 2	• Lesson Vocabulary • Decodable Reader
DAY 3	• Leveled Reader
DAY 4	• Conventions • Leveled Reader

3 Day Plan: Eliminate the shaded box

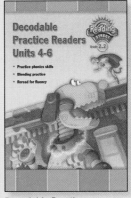

Decodable
Practice Readers
Units 4-6
• Practice phonics skills
• Blending practice
• Reread for fluency

Decodable Practice Readers

Small Group Time

For a complete literacy instructional plan and additional practice with this week's target skills and strategies, see the **Leveled Reader Teaching Guide.**

On-Level Leveled Reader

On-Level

■ **Preview and Predict** Read the title, the author's name, and the illustrator's name. Have children look at the cover, and ask them to describe in detail what they see. Help children preview the story by asking them to look through the story and to use the pictures to predict things that might take place.

■ ◉ **Plot and Theme** Before reading, remind children that setting a purpose for reading can help them better understand what they read. Guide children to pay attention to what happens at the beginning, in the middle, and at the end of the story. Tell them to be alert to the message, or big idea, of the story.

■ **Read** During reading, monitor children's comprehension by providing higher-order thinking questions. Ask:

• Is the problem at the beginning of the story a serious one? Why?

• Do you think giving fire to the crow was a better solution than stopping the snow? Why?

• The great spirit gave crow a reward for helping his friends. What does that tell you about the great spirit? What do you think of the reward?

To help children gain a better understanding of the text, build upon their responses with a group discussion.

■ ◉ **Monitor and Clarify** Remind children that good readers need to be aware when the text doesn't make sense. When the text doesn't make sense or they read something that they don't understand, readers can ask questions and reread the part of the text to find answers. Ask:

• Is there a part of the story that didn't make sense to you when you first read it? What was difficult to understand?

• What did you do to better understand what you were reading?

■ **Text to Text** Help children make connections to other stories they've read. Ask:

• How is this story similar to and different from *The First Tortilla?*

Objectives
• Seek clarification about stories.
• Analyze theme.

OL On-Level   **DAY 4**

Conventions

■ **Adverbs That Tell How** Remind children that adverbs are words that tell about verbs. Tell them that adverbs can tell how something happens. This type of adverb often ends in *-ly*.

- The word *carefully* is an adverb that tells how. Write *carefully* and use it in an oral sentence. The class listened *carefully* to the directions.

- The word *swiftly* is an adverb that tells how. Write *swiftly* and use it in an oral sentence. The deer ran *swiftly* across the field.

Continue modeling in the same way with other adverbs that tell how, such as *softly, suddenly, beautifully.* Ask children to think of sentences using these or other adverbs that tell how: *quickly, happily, loudly.*

Objectives
• Understand and use adverbs about manner in the context of reading, writing, and speaking.

More Reading

Use Leveled Readers or other text at children's instructional level.

OL On-Level **DAY 5**

Phonics Review

■ 🔊 **Vowel Digraphs *oo, ue, ew, ui*** Have children practice blending and reading words that contain this week's target phonics skills. Write the following words on the board, and read each word with the children.

stew	broom	clue	fruit	balloon
bruise	chewy	suitcase	threw	due

Then have children sort the words according to vowel digraphs.

Objectives
• Decode multisyllabic words independent of context by applying common letter-sound correspondences including vowel digraphs.

Small Group Time

Pacing Small Group Instruction

20-30 min.

5 Day Plan

DAY 1	• Phonics
	• Comprehension
DAY 2	• Comprehension
	• Main Selection
DAY 3	• Leveled Reader
DAY 4	• Comprehension
	• Paired Selection
DAY 5	• Fluency
	• Comprehension

3 or 4 Day Plan

DAY 1	• Phonics
	• Comprehension
DAY 2	• Comprehension
	• Main Selection
DAY 3	• Leveled Reader
DAY 4	• Comprehension
	• Paired Selection

3 Day Plan: Eliminate the shaded box

A Advanced DAY 1

Phonics • Comprehension

- **Vowel Digraphs *oo, ue, ew, ui*** Have children practice with longer words containing vowel digraphs *oo, ue, ew, ui.* Have them choose several words to use in sentences.

| fruitcake | fewer | schoolyard | recruiting | bedroom |
| clueless | raccoon | newspaper | untrue | pursuit |

- **Advanced Selection 20** Before reading, have children identify these words from the selection: *scientists* and *pollution.* If they do not know the words, provide oral sentences with the words in context. After reading, have children recall the two most important ideas of the selection.

Advanced Selection 20

Objectives
- Decode multisyllabic words independent of context by applying common letter-sound correspondences including vowel digraphs.

A Advanced DAY 2

Comprehension

- **Comprehension** Have children silently read this week's main selection, *The First Tortilla.* Discuss the plot—what happened in the beginning, the middle, and the end. Ask what the message, or big idea, of the story is. (Sometimes it takes courage to do something important.) Talk about what makes *The First Tortilla* a legend. (It is a story from the past about the deeds of a hero.)

- **Text to Text** Have children discuss whether they have read any other stories about a character doing something courageous to help others.

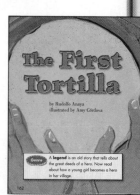

The First Tortilla

Objectives
- Analyze theme.

Advanced

DAY **3**

For a complete literacy instructional plan and additional practice with this week's target skills and strategies, see the **Leveled Reader Teaching Guide.**

Advanced Leveled Reader

Advanced Leveled Reader

- **Activate Prior Knowledge** Read the title, the author's name, and the illustrator's name. Have children look at the cover and ask them to describe in detail what they see. Then activate children's prior knowledge by asking them to identify and describe any experiences they have had with a hurricane or other storm.

- **Plot and Theme** Before reading, remind children that setting a purpose for reading can help them better understand what they read. Guide children to pay attention to the plot of the story—what happens at the beginning, in the middle, and at the end.

- **Read** During reading, monitor children's comprehension by providing higher-order thinking questions. Ask:

  - Why did Sam let Reggie out even though he knew a hurricane was coming?

  - Why do you think Reggie left the yard and didn't come right back?

  - Was staying at home and not running out to find Reggie the best decision? Why or why not?

  Build on children's answers to help them gain a better understanding of the text.

- **Monitor and Clarify** Remind children that good readers need to be aware if the text doesn't make sense or there is something they don't understand. One thing a reader can do is to ask questions and reread the part of the text to find answers or clues to answers. Ask:

  - Was there a part of the story that didn't make sense to you when you first read it? What was difficult to understand?

  - What did you do to better understand what you were reading?

- **Text to World** Help children make connections to the story. Ask:

  - What have you learned about hurricanes by watching news reports?

More Reading
Use Leveled Readers or other text at children's instructional level.

Objectives
- Seek clarification about stories.
- Analyze theme.

Small Group Time

More Reading
Use Leveled Readers or other text at children's instructional level.

A Advanced   DAY **4**

Comprehension

- **Comprehension** Have children silently read this week's paired selection, *Wind*. Discuss what facts they learned about wind in the selection. Ask children what details supported the facts. Then have children ask a question about something they didn't quite understand about the selection to monitor and clarify understanding.

  Talk about what makes *Wind* expository text. (It contains facts and information.)

- **Text to Text** Have children identify other selections they have read that are expository text.

Wind

Objectives
• Locate facts that are clearly stated in a text.

A Advanced   DAY **5**

Fluency • Comprehension

- **Fluency** Using the first few sentences of Advanced Selection 20, model reading with expression and intonation. Then have children read the selection to a partner as you listen to their reading. Provide corrective feedback.

- **Comprehension** After they have finished reading the selection, have children tell what happens at the beginning, in the middle, and at the end of the story. Then, on the back of the selection page, have them write a question they asked themselves as they read to help them monitor and clarify their understanding of the selection.

Advanced Selection 20

Objectives
• Read aloud grade-level appropriate text with fluency.

Support for English Language Learners

The ELL lessons are organized by strands. Use them to scaffold the weekly curriculum of lessons or during small group time instruction.

Academic Language

Children will hear or read the following academic language in this week's core instruction. As children encounter the vocabulary, provide a simple definition or concrete example. Then ask children to suggest an example or synonym of the word and identify available cognates.

Skill Words	theme *(tema)*	vowel *(vocal)*
	plot *(complot)*	consonant *(consonante)*
	prefix *(prefijo)*	expression *(expresion)*
Concept Words	weather	birthday
	winter	change

*Spanish cognates in parentheses

Concept Development

 How do changes in the weather affect us?

■ **Preteach Concept**

• **Prior Knowledge** Have children turn to pp. 154–155 in the Student Edition. Call attention to the pictures of the rain boots and use children's prior knowledge of rain boots. Do you recognize these kinds of boots? In what kind of weather do people wear them?

• **Discuss Concept** Elicit children's knowledge and experience of how changes in the weather affect us. How does the weather affect what we wear? Do you know what that big swirling cloud is in the picture? What could happen if something like that hit our town? Supply background information as needed.

• **Poster Talk-Through** Read the Poster Talk-Through on ELL Poster 20 aloud and work through the Day 1 activities.

■ **Daily Concept and Vocabulary Development** Use the daily activities on ELL Poster 20 to build concept and vocabulary knowledge.

Objectives
• Use prior knowledge and experiences to understand meanings in English.
• Internalize new basic and academic language by using and reusing it in meaningful ways in speaking and writing activities that build concept and language attainment.
• Use accessible language and learn new and essential language in the process.

Content Objectives
• Use concept vocabulary related to weather.

Language Objectives
• Express ideas in response to art and discussion.
• Use prior knowledge to understand meanings in English.

Daily Planner

DAY 1	• **Frontload** Concepts • **Preteach** Comprehension Skill, Vocabulary, Phonics/Spelling, Conventions • **Writing**
DAY 2	• **Review** Concepts, Vocabulary, Comprehension Skill • **Frontload Main Selection** • **Practice** Phonics/Spelling, Conventions/Writing
DAY 3	• **Review** Concepts, Comprehension Skill, Vocabulary, Conventions/Writing • **Reread Main Selection** • **Practice** Phonics/Spelling
DAY 4	• **Review Concepts** • **Read ELL/ELD Readers** • **Practice** Phonics/Spelling Conventions/Writing
DAY 5	• **Review** Concepts, Vocabulary, Comprehension Skill, Phonics/Spelling, Conventions • **Reread ELL/ELD Readers** • **Writing**

*See the ELL Handbook *for ELL Workshops with targeted instruction.*

Concept Talk Video

Use Concept Talk Video Routine (*ELL Handbook*, p. 464) to build background knowledge about the weather. For listening practice, see *Use Classroom Resources* (*ELL Handbook*, pp. 404–405).

Support for English Language Learners

Language Objectives

• Understand and use basic vocabulary.

• Learn meanings of grade-level vocabulary.

• Internalize new basic language through speaking.

English Opportunity

Use Weather Words Use the pictures on pp. 154–155 of the Student Edition as a prompt for discussion. Have children use words such as *rain, boots, tornado,* and *clear* to describe the pictures. Extend the activity by discussing other types of weather and the clothing children would wear.

Basic Vocabulary

■ **High-Frequency Words** Use the ELL Vocabulary Routines on p. 456 of the *ELL Handbook* to systematically teach the high-frequency words from this week's core lesson. The *ELL Handbook* (p. 491) contains a bank of strategies that you can use to ensure children's mastery of the high-frequency words.

Lesson Vocabulary

■ **Preteach** Use this routine to introduce the Lesson Vocabulary:

1. Distribute copies of this week's Word Cards (*ELL Handbook*, p. 143).

2. Display ELL Poster 20 and reread the Poster Talk-Through.

3. Using the poster illustrations, model how a word's meaning can be expressed with other similar words: The *mountain*, or tall land mass, has a snowy top.

4. Use these sentences to reveal the meaning of the other words.

   • What time did you *awaken* this morning? (wake up)

   • There is a big *volcano* overlooking the village. (a mountain from which lava can erupt)

   • There is a big *cliff* along the path. (a vertical rock mass)

   • I do not like to *suffer* through headaches. (experience pain)

   • The *rainbow* shone brightly after the storm. (an arc of colored light in the sky)

   • She won a *prize*. (something given for winning)

Objectives

• Internalize new basic and academic language by using and reusing it in meaningful ways in speaking and writing activities that build concept and language attainment.

• Learn new language structures, expressions, and basic and academic vocabulary heard during classroom instruction and interactions.

 English Language Learners

■ **Reteach** Give each pair one or more of the Word Cards. Provide clues for each vocabulary word's meaning. For example, hold your hands to your head and say, My head hurts. I do not like having headaches. What word means to put up with pain? Have children hold up the correct card as you present each clue.

Leveled Support

Beginning Model the correct pronunciation of each word. Have children say the vocabulary word as you present each clue. Then have them practice writing the Lesson Vocabulary words.

Intermediate Have children read and repeat the words aloud. Have each pair create a sentence using one or two words.

Advanced/Advanced-High Monitor children as they take turns reading each word to a partner. Then have children say each word aloud in a sentence.

■ **Writing** Distribute Word Cards. Write the following sentences on the board: The ___ looks like it is ready to erupt. I won the grand ___ at the raffle. Have children hold up the correct Word Card to fill in each sentence. Then have pairs make up their own sentences with the rest of the Lesson Vocabulary. Have pairs use support from peers to enhance their understanding by trading sentences with another pair. Partners should hold up the correct Word Card to fill in the sentences.

 Leveled Support

Beginning/Intermediate Write sentences for children. Read them aloud, pausing at each blank. When you pause, have children hold up the correct Word Card. Then have them write the word.

Advanced/Advanced-High Have children work in pairs to complete this writing activity independently.

Language Objectives

• Produce phrases or short sentences to show understanding of vocabulary.

• Speak using a variety of grammatical structures.

• Use peer support to enhance understanding.

ELL Teacher Tip

Teach children how to use a picture dictionary or a children's dictionary. Encourage them to use it often to find the words they need. Invite children to start their own word banks by listing frequently used vocabulary in a notebook.

ELL Workshop

Provide opportunities for children to give directions using newly acquired abstract and content-based vocabulary. *Give Directions (ELL Handbook, pp. 394–395)* supports children in this task.

Objectives

• Speak using a variety of grammatical structures, sentence lengths, sentence types, and connecting words with increasing accuracy and ease as more English is acquired.

• Use visual and contextual support from peers and teachers to read grade-appropriate content area text, enhance and confirm understanding, and develop vocabulary, grasp of language structures, and background knowledge needed to comprehend increasingly challenging language.

Support for English Language Learners

Content Objectives

- Monitor and adjust oral comprehension.

Language Objectives

- Discuss oral passages.
- Use a graphic organizer to take notes.
- Speak using grade-level vocabulary.

Graphic Organizer

Characters	
Setting	
Events	

ELL Workshop

As you give directions for using the graphic organizer, you might use *Follow Directions* (*ELL Handbook*, pp. 396–397) to support children in comprehending increasingly complex spoken directions.

ELL English Language Learners

Listening Comprehension

Old Man Winter

Tessa woke to the sound of snowplows. "Snow!" Tessa squealed. Everything outside was white. She ran downstairs and looked at the calendar. It was December 21. "Today is the first day of winter, Mom. And it snowed!" Tessa yelled.

"Yes it did," replied Mom. "Snow on Old Man Winter's birthday."

"I'm going to have a birthday party for Old Man Winter," said Tessa. Tessa called her friends Sarah and Andrew. She told them to meet her at the playground.

At the playground, Tessa asked Sarah and Andrew what special day it was. Sarah and Andrew were confused. They thought it was just an ordinary day. Then Tessa exclaimed, "Today is Old Man Winter's birthday. And we are going to have a party for him."

Tessa, Sarah, and Andrew made a cake of snow. They decorated it with pine cones, red holly berries, and sticks.

Tessa looked at the sky and whispered, "Happy Birthday, Old Man Winter." Just as she finished saying it, a single snowflake landed on her nose.

Prepare for the Read Aloud The modified Read Aloud above prepares children for listening to the oral reading "Happy Birthday, Old Man Winter!" on p. 103 of the Read Aloud Anthology.

- **First Listening: Listen to Understand** Write the title of the Read Aloud on the board. This is a story about a girl who wants to celebrate Old Man Winter's birthday. Listen to find out who Old Man Winter is. Who is Old Man Winter? What do they do to celebrate his birthday? Afterward, ask the questions again and have children share their answers.

- **Second Listening: Listen to Check Understanding** Using Story Map B (*ELL Handbook*, p. 471), work with children to record the characters, setting, and events of the story. Reread the story. Have children double-check what they have recorded in their story map.

Objectives

- Speak using grade-level content area vocabulary in context to internalize new English words and build academic language proficiency.
- Use visual and contextual support from peers and teachers to read grade-appropriate content area text, enhance and confirm understanding, and develop vocabulary, grasp of language structures, and background knowledge needed to comprehend increasingly challenging language.

Phonics and Spelling

- **Vowel Digraphs *oo, ue, ew, ui*** Use Sound Spelling Cards 68, 90, 102, and 103 to teach the sounds, pronunciations, and spellings of *oo, ue, ew,* and *ui.*

- Display card 90 to teach *oo.* This is *moon.* The middle sound is /ü/ Say it with me. Point to the letters *oo.* The sound /ü/ in *moon* is spelled *oo.* Have children say /ü/ several times as you point to *oo.* What is the sound of these two letters in *moon*?

- Display card 102 to teach *ue.* This is *glue.* The end sound is /ü/. Say it with me. Point to the letters *ue.* The sound /ü/ in *glue* is spelled *ue.* Have children say /ü/ several times as you point to *ue.* What sound does *ue* make in *glue*? Is it the same sound that *oo* makes in *moon*? That's right, *oo* and *ue* can make the same sound.

- Follow the routine above to teach *ew* (Card 68) and *ui* (card 103).

  For more practice pronouncing these sounds, use the Modeled Pronunciation Audio CD Routine (*ELL Handbook*, p. 465).

Vocabulary Skill: Prefixes

- **Teach/Model** Write *awaken* and *reawaken* on the board. Read the words aloud to the children. Point out the prefix *re-* in *reawaken.* This syllable, *re-,* is a prefix. A prefix is a word part that is added to the beginning of a word. Adding a prefix changes the meaning of a word. *Awaken* means "to wake up." The prefix *re-* means "again." *Reawaken* means "to wake up again."

- **Practice** Write these words on the board: *rewrite, redo, reread.* Have children define these words.

  Beginning/Intermediate Have children underline the prefix *re-* in each word. Have them work with partners to define the words. Remind the children that they should use the word *again* in their definition.

  Advanced/Advanced-High Challenge children to write a definition for each of the words. Then have them write a sentence using one of the words.

Content Objectives
- Identify and define the prefix *re-*.
- Identify the vowel digraph /ü/ in words.
- Review the vowel digraph /ü/ spelled *oo, ue, ew,* and *ui*.

Language Objectives
- Apply phonics and decoding skills to vocabulary.
- Discuss the meaning of the prefix *re-*.

Transfer Skills
Prefixes Some English prefixes have equivalent forms in the Romance languages. Students who are literate in these languages may be able to transfer their understanding of prefixes by using parallel examples in their home language and in English.

ELL Teaching Routine
For more practice with vowel digraphs, use the Whole-Word Blending Routine (*ELL Handbook,* p. 457).

Objectives
- Practice producing sounds of newly acquired vocabulary such as long and short vowels, silent letters, and consonant clusters to pronounce English words in a manner that is increasingly comprehensible.
- Learn relationships between sounds and letters of the English language and decode (sound out) words using a combination of skills such as recognizing sound-letter relationships and identifying cognates, affixes, roots and base words.

Support for English Language Learners

Content Objectives

- Identify the plot and theme of a text.

Language Objectives

- Write the plot and theme of a text as you identify them.

ELL Workshop

Encourage children to ask questions to monitor their understanding of instruction of comprehension skills. Use *Ask Clarifying Questions* (*ELL Handbook*, pp. 402–403) for practice.

ELL English Language Learners

Comprehension
Plot and Theme

■ **Preteach** The plot of a story is what happens. Plot must have a clear beginning, middle, and end. Plot also has a problem that needs to be solved. The theme of a story is the main, or big, idea. Have children turn to Envision It! on p. E•14 in the Student Edition. Read the text aloud together. Have children talk about the literary elements that are drawn on the page. Ask them to point out the plot and theme. Ask them what the problem and solution are.

■ **Reteach** Distribute copies of the Picture It! (*ELL Handbook*, p. 144). Have children look at the image. What is Helen doing? Could she always read? Ask them to think about what Helen's problem was and how she solved it. Then have the children read the paragraph with a partner. What was Helen's problem in the story? How did she solve it? What lesson can you learn from this story? (**Answers** Helen couldn't hear or see, so she couldn't communicate. A teacher taught her sign language. There are solutions to many problems.)

Beginning/Intermediate Make a T-chart on the board, labeled *problem* and *solution*. Have the children choral read the paragraph with you. Help them identify the problem and solution and record it in on the chart.

Advanced/Advanced-High Make a T-chart on the board labeled *problem* and *solution*. Have children choral read the passage with you. Then have them work with a partner to complete the chart.

MINI-LESSON

Academic Language

Tell children that it is very important for them to understand plot and theme. Write this paragraph on the board:

Camping with my family is great. We pitch the tent in a clear area. Then we build a fire. In the evening we sit around the campfire, roast marshmallows, and tell stories. I am always sad to go home.

Have children identify the plot and theme of the paragraph. Provide the following sentence frames: *In the beginning ___. In the middle ___. In the end ___. The big idea is ___.*

Objectives

- Understand the general meaning, main points, and important details of spoken language ranging from situations in which topics, language, and contexts are familiar to unfamiliar.

Student Edition pp. 162–163

Reading Comprehension
The First Tortilla

■ **Frontloading** Have children look through *The First Tortilla* on pp. 162–177 of the Student Edition and tell what they think makes it look like fiction, a kind of writing that has been made up. Why do you think this selection is fiction? Distribute copies of the English summary of *The First Tortilla* (*ELL Handbook*, p. 145). Have children read the summary aloud with you. Encourage them to ask questions about any ideas or unfamiliar words. If you have sent copies of the summary home, have children read it again with family members. Preview the selection by having children look at the pictures. Have them work to fill in the Story Map graphic organizer as they read.

Sheltered Reading Ask questions such as the following to guide children's comprehension:

• p. 165: What did Jade ask the Mountain Spirit for? (rain so that her garden would grow)

• p. 166: Why did Jade feel that she should listen to the hummingbird? (Her dad told her that small birds bring messages from the Mountain Spirit.)

• p. 168: When did the hummingbird speak to her again? (after her parents left for the market)

• p. 171: What gift did the Mountain Spirit give to Jade? (corn)

■ **Fluency: Expression and Intonation** Remind children that reading with expression means to read the words like you are speaking to a friend. *Intonation* is the rise and fall of your voice to signal punctuation and feeling. Read the first paragraph on p. 169, modeling expression and appropriate intonation. Have pairs choose a paragraph on p. 172. Have children read with expression and intonation as their partner listens and offers feedback. For more practice, use the Fluency: Oral Rereading Routine (*ELL Handbook*, p. 461).

After Reading Help children recall parts of the story using the Retelling Cards. Have pairs or small groups sequence the cards to show how Jade discovered how to make tortillas.

Content Objectives
• Monitor and adjust comprehension.
• Make and adjust predictions.

Language Objectives
• Read grade-level text with expression and intonation.
• Summarize text using visual support.

Graphic Organizer

What might happen?	What clues do I have?	What did happen?

Audio Support
Prepare children for reading *The First Tortilla* by using the eSelection or the AudioText CD. See the AudioText CD Routine (*ELL Handbook*, p. 464) for suggestions on using these learning tools.

ELL Teaching Routine
For more practice summarizing, use the Retelling/Summarizing Narrative Routine (*ELL Handbook*, p. 462).

ELL Workshop
Children can work cooperatively to share information about the selection. Support children with *Discuss with Classmates* (*ELL Handbook*, pp. 116–117).

Objectives
• Demonstrate listening comprehension of increasingly complex spoken English by following directions, retelling or summarizing spoken messages, responding to questions and requests, collaborating with peers, and taking notes commensurate with content and grade-level.

Support for English Language Learners

English Language Learners

For additional leveled instruction, see the **ELL/ELD Reader Teaching Guide.**

Comprehension:
How is the Weather?

■ **Before Reading** Distribute copies of the ELL and ELD Readers, *How is the Weather?*, to children at their reading level.

• **Preview** Read the title aloud with children. How important do you think it is to know what the weather is like before you leave in the morning? Invite children to look through the pictures and name what they see. Have them predict what will happen in the story based on the picture clues.

• **Set a Purpose for Reading** Let's read to find out how the weather can affect a person's day.

■ **During Reading** Follow the Reading Routine for both reading groups.

1. Read the entire Reader aloud slowly.

2. Read pages 1–5, pausing to build background knowledge or model comprehension.

3. Have children take turns reading pp. 1–5 orally in a round robin.

4. Repeat steps 2–3 above for pp. 6–8 of the Reader.

■ **After Reading** Use the exercises on the inside back cover of each Reader and invite children to share their writing.

ELD Reader   Beginning/Intermediate

■ **pp. 4–5:** Why is the man wearing a jacket? (*It is cool outside.*) Read the sentence that gives you the answer aloud.

■ **pp. 6–7:** Why is it a good day to go up in a hot-air balloon? (*It is a clear day.*) Read the sentences that give you the answer aloud.

Writing Find a sentence in the story that shows one example of the weather affecting a person's plans. Copy the sentence.

Directionality Assist beginning students who have difficulty with directionality of English text, especially students whose home language entails reading with a different directionality.

ELL Reader   Advanced/Advanced-High

■ **pp. 2–3** Why do you think some people in the picture do not have umbrellas?

■ **p. 8:** Where can you go on warm days? (*the pool*) Read the sentence that gives you the answer aloud.

Study Guide Distribute copies of the ELL Reader Study Guide (*ELL Handbook*, p. 148). Scaffold comprehension by helping children identify the beginning, middle, and end of the story. Have them write what they think the theme of the story is. (**Answers** See *ELL Handbook*, pp. 209–212.)

Objectives

• Understand the general meaning, main points, and important details of spoken language ranging from situations in which topics, language, and contexts are familiar to unfamiliar. Recognize directionality of English reading such as left to right and top to bottom.

 ELL English Language Learners

Conventions
Adverbs that Tell *How*

■ **Preteach** Explain that an *adverb* is a word that can tell *how something happens.* Whisper this question to the class: How am I speaking? (softly, quietly) Then raise your voice: How am I speaking now? (loudly) Write *softly* and *loudly* on the board. *Loudly* and *softly* are adverbs. They tell how someone does something. How are *softly* and *loudly* alike? (They both end in *-ly*.) Tell children that many adverbs end in *-ly*.

■ **Practice** Ask children to think of ways that people can walk. Elicit and write adverbs such as *slowly, quickly (or fast), noisily, quietly, sadly, happily, sleepily,* and *carefully*. Have children act out walking each way.

 Beginning/Intermediate Have children act out the adverbs as you say each one aloud.

Advanced/Advanced-High Have children write each adverb on a separate card. Working in pairs, children should take turns drawing a card to act out while their partner guesses the adverb.

■ **Reteach** Write these sentences on the board: *Jenna slowly walked down the street. The wind blew gently.* Which word tells how Jenna walked? (*slowly*) Which word tells how the wind blew? (*gently*) What is the same about these words? (*They both end in -ly.*) What do we call words that tell how something happens? (*adverbs*)

■ **Practice** Have children copy these sentences and underline the adverbs:

The storm came suddenly.   *The branches swayed wildly.*
Sara clung tightly to the tree.   *She fearfully waited for help.*

 Beginning/Intermediate Have children work in pairs to use one of the adverbs in a sentence. Monitor spelling and pronunciation.

Advanced/Advanced-High Have children write sentences with adverbs that tell *how*. Invite children to share their sentences with the class.

For more practice with adverbs that tell how, see *ELL Handbook* p. 377.

Content Objectives
• Decode and use adverbs that tell how.

Language Objectives
• Speak using adverbs that tell how.

• Write phrases or sentences using adverbs that tell how.

 Transfer Skills

Many languages do not strongly distinguish adjectives from adverbs, so children may use adjectives as adverbs. **For example:** *I walk quiet. I smile happy.* Help children remember to add *-ly* when they describe how they do an action.

Grammar Jammer

For more practice with adverbs use the Grammar Jammer for this target skill. See the Grammar Jammer Routine (*ELL Handbook,* p. 465) for suggestions on using this learning tool.

Objectives
• Develop and expand repertoire of learning strategies such as reasoning inductively or deductively, looking for patterns in language, and analyzing sayings and expressions commensurate with grade-level learning expectations.

Content Objectives

- Identify words that show the author's purpose.

Language Objectives

- Write a paragraph, showing the purpose that you (as the author) have for writing.
- Share feedback for editing and revising.

ELL Teaching Routine

For practice spelling words related to the weather, use the Spelling Routine (*ELL Handbook*, p. 463).

English Opportunity

Purpose for Writing Read aloud pp. 180–181 of the Student Edition. Ask children why someone might want to write a thank-you note. Ask children to think of other times when they might want to write a letter. Prompt by giving examples such as writing a letter to a friend in the summer, writing a letter to a newspaper, sending a get-well note to someone who is sick, or writing to the author of a book you liked. Have pairs work together to think of a reason for writing a letter. Then have them write or dictate their letter and share it with the class. Monitor children's work to provide feedback and support.

ELL English Language Learners

Expressing the Writer's Purpose

■ **Introduce** Display the paragraph model below and read it aloud. Review that an author writes for a purpose. Why is the author writing this? (*to teach the reader*) What is the author teaching? (*how to make tortillas*)

> **Writing Model**
> Mix two cups corn flour, one teaspoon sea salt, one-quarter teaspoon baking soda, two cups warm water, and one teaspoon cooking oil in a bowl. Mix the ingredients together until a dough forms. Then, knead the dough until it feels soft. Pull off a small piece and roll that into a little ball. Flatten the ball and cook the disk in an iron pan until both sides are golden brown. Enjoy your warm tortilla!

■ **Practice** Write the incomplete paragraph below on the board. Work together to complete the paragraph. (Possible answers: *peanut butter; jelly; together*)

It is easy to make a peanut butter and jelly sandwich. You need two pieces of bread, jelly, peanut butter, and a butter knife. First spread the ___ on one piece of bread. Then, spread ___ on the other slice of bread. Put the two pieces of bread ___ and eat your yummy sandwich!

■ **Write** Have children write a paragraph that shows how to do something. For ideas, they should think about things they can do easily by themselves. When finished writing, have pairs exchange papers and provide feedback for revising and editing.

Beginning Have children write their topic at the top of their paper. Then have them draw the steps for completing their task and dictate to you one sentence for each drawing. Write out their sentences and have children copy them.

Intermediate Supply children with the following sentence frame: *It is easy to ___.* Have them fill in their topic. Have them use this as their topic sentence. They can use it to get a start on their paragraph.

Advanced/Advanced-High Have children develop their paragraph independently.

Objectives

- Express opinions, ideas, and feelings ranging from communicating single words and short phrases to participating in extended discussions on a variety of social and grade-appropriate academic topics.
- Write using a variety of newly-acquired basic vocabulary and content-based grade-level vocabulary.

Interactive
Review Week

☑ Choose skills and strategies to **review** based on progress-monitoring.

☑ Focus on **target skills** or use the **flexible plan** to adjust instruction.

☑ Provide opportunities for interacting with texts—underlining, highlighting, and circling **model text** in the *Reader's and Writer's Notebook*.

☑ Develop students' understanding of genre and text structure using the **Strategy Response Log** in the *Reader's and Writer's Notebook*.

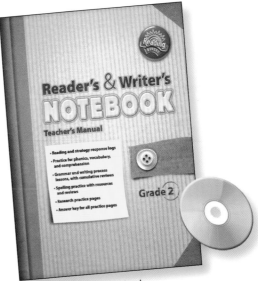

Reader's & Writer's Notebook

This Unit's Interactive Writing Review

Daily Quick Writes for Fluency

	Talk		Write	Share
Day 1	Have pairs discuss what they learned about how familiar things can help us adjust to changes.		Have children write a few sentences to summarize the discussion.	Partners can read their summaries to one another.
Day 2	Have pairs discuss what they learned about how plants change over time.		Have children write a few sentences to summarize the discussion.	Partners can read their summaries to one another.
Day 3	Have pairs discuss what they learned about changes that occur under the ground.		Have children write a few sentences to summarize the discussion.	Partners can read their summaries to one another.
Day 4	Have pairs discuss what they learned about why some changes are difficult.		Have children write a few sentences to summarize the discussion.	Partners can read their summaries to one another.
Day 5	Have pairs discuss what they learned about how changes in the weather affect people.		Have children write a few sentences to summarize the discussion.	Partners can read their summaries to one another.

Resources for Interactive Writing Review

Reader's and Writer's Notebook

Writing Rubrics and Anchor Papers

 Digital Resources
- Grammar Jammer
- Online Journal

Teacher Resources DVD-ROM

For 21st Century Writing practice, see the **E-Newsletter** Project in Unit 4, Volume 1.

For Process Writing practice, see the **Description** Lesson in Unit 4, Volume 2.

Review on Reading Street!

Our Changing World

 Big Question

How do things change?
How do they stay the same?

Daily Plan

Review

- Concept Talk
- Oral Vocabulary
- Phonics
- Spelling
- Lesson Vocabulary
- Comprehension
- Fluency
- Conventions

Day 1	Day 2	Day 3	Day 4	Day 5
How can familiar things help us with changes?	How do plants change over time?	What changes occur under the ground?	Why are some changes difficult?	How do changes in the weather affect us?

Customize Literacy
More support for a Balanced Literacy approach, see pp. CL•1– CL•45.

Customize Writing
More support for a customized writing approach, see pp. CW•11– CW•20.

Assessment
- Unit 4 Benchmark Test
- Assessment Handbook

Review this Unit's Reading Selections

A Froggy Fable
Genre: **Fable**

Life Cycle of a Pumpkin
Genre: **Expository Text**

Soil
Genre: **Expository Text**

The Night the Moon Fell
Genre: **Myth**

The First Tortilla
Genre: **Legend**

You Are Here! Unit 4 Week 6

Resources on Reading Street!

	Build Concepts		Phonics and Spelling		Vocabulary
Day 1 **Review Week 1**  How can familiar things help us with changes?	 Student Edition pp. 28–41	 Sing with Me	 Reader's and Writer's Notebook	 Sound-Spelling Cards	 Reader's and Writer's Notebook
Day 2 **Review Week 2**  How do plants change over time?	 Student Edition pp. 62–75	 Sing with Me	 Reader's and Writer's Notebook	 Sound-Spelling Cards	 Reader's and Writer's Notebook
Day 3 **Review Week 3** What changes occur under the ground?	 Student Edition pp. 92–109	 Sing with Me	 Reader's and Writer's Notebook	 Sound-Spelling Cards	 Reader's and Writer's Notebook
Day 4 **Review Week 4** Why are some changes difficult?	 Student Edition pp. 128–143	 Sing with Me	 Reader's and Writer's Notebook	 Sound-Spelling Cards	 Reader's and Writer's Notebook
Day 5 **Review Week 5** How do changes in the weather affect us?	 Student Edition pp. 162–177	 Sing with Me	 Reader's and Writer's Notebook	 Sound-Spelling Cards	 Reader's and Writer's Notebook

 Go Digital

- Big Question Video
- Concept Talk Video

- Interactive Sound-Spelling Cards

- Sing with Me Animations
- Vocabulary Activities

Big Question
How do things change? How do they stay the same?

Comprehension	Fluency	Conventions and Writing
Reader's and Writer's Notebook	Reader's and Writer's Notebook	Reader's and Writer's Notebook
Reader's and Writer's Notebook	Reader's and Writer's Notebook	Reader's and Writer's Notebook
Reader's and Writer's Notebook	Reader's and Writer's Notebook	Reader's and Writer's Notebook
Reader's and Writer's Notebook	Reader's and Writer's Notebook	Reader's and Writer's Notebook
Reader's and Writer's Notebook	Reader's and Writer's Notebook	Reader's and Writer's Notebook
• Envision It! Animations	• Leveled eReaders	• Grammar Jammer

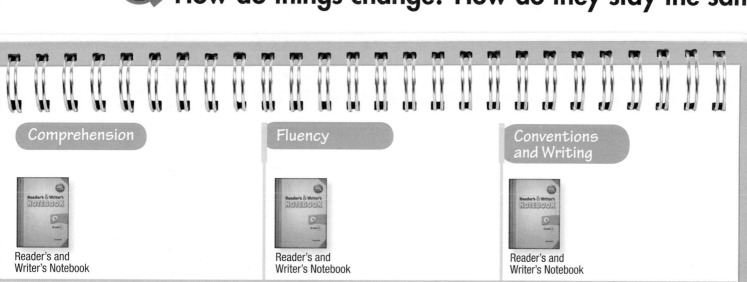

 You Are Here! Unit 4 Week 6

Week 6

My 5-Day Planner for Reading Street!

	Review Week 1 **Day 1** pages IR8–IR17	**Review Week 2** **Day 2** pages IR18–IR27
Get Ready to Read	**Concept Talk,** IR8 ❓ How can familiar things help us with changes? **Oral Vocabulary,** IR9 *preserve, represent, valuable, tough, concentration, frown, homeland, patient* **Phonics,** IR10 ◎ Final Syllable -*le* **Spelling,** IR11 Final Syllable -*le*	**Concept Talk,** IR18 ❓ How do plants change over time? **Oral Vocabulary,** IR19 *adapt, annual, nutrients, blazing, drought, ancient, massive, sprout* **Phonics,** IR20 ◎ Vowel Patterns *oo, u* **Spelling,** IR21 Vowel Patterns *oo, u*
Read and Comprehend	**Lesson Vocabulary,** IR12 *clearing, crashed, perfect, pond, spilling, splashing, traveled* **Vocabulary Skill,** IR12 ◎ Multiple-Meaning Words **Comprehension,** IR13–IR15 ◎ Skill: Draw Conclusions ◎ Strategy: Background Knowledge **Fluency,** IR15 Read with Accuracy and Appropriate Rate	**Lesson Vocabulary,** IR22 *bumpy, fruit, harvest, root, smooth, soil, vine* **Vocabulary Skill,** IR22 ◎ Antonyms **Comprehension,** IR23–IR25 ◎ Skill: Sequence ◎ Strategy: Important Ideas **Fluency,** IR25 Read with Accuracy
Language Arts	**Conventions,** IR16 Adjectives and Our Senses **Handwriting,** IR16 Cursive *l, h, e*: Letter Formation **Wrap Up Your Day,** IR17	**Conventions,** IR26 Adjectives for Number, Size, and Shape **Handwriting,** IR26 Cursive *t, i, u*: Letter Slant **Wrap Up Your Day,** IR27

You Are Here!
Unit 4
Week 6

How do things change? How do they stay the same?

Review Week 3	Review Week 4	Review Week 5
Day 3 pages IR28–IR37	**Day 4** pages IR38–IR47	**Day 5** pages IR48–IR57
Concept Talk, IR28 ❓ What changes occur under the ground? **Oral Vocabulary,** IR29 *discovery, transform, underneath, blizzard, fine, incredible, landscape, molten* **Phonics,** IR30 ◉ Diphthongs o*u, ow, oi, oy* **Spelling,** IR31 Diphthongs o*u, ow, oi, oy*	**Concept Talk,** IR38 ❓ Why are some changes difficult? **Oral Vocabulary,** IR39 *adjust, landmark, unexpected, quiver, tease, foreign, accent, forlorn* **Phonics,** IR40 ◉ Syllable Patterns **Spelling,** IR41 Syllable Patterns	**Concept Talk,** IR48 ❓ How do changes in the weather affect us? **Oral Vocabulary,** IR49 *condition, predict, terrifying, breeze, whip, sparkle, funnel, swirl* **Phonics,** IR50 ◉ Vowel Digraphs *oo, ue, ew, ui* **Spelling,** IR51 Vowel Digraphs *oo, ue, ew, ui*
Lesson Vocabulary, IR32 *grains, materials, particles, seeps, substances, texture* **Vocabulary Skill,** IR32 ◉ Suffixes **Comprehension,** IR33–IR35 ◉ Skill: Fact and Opinion ◉ Strategy: Questioning **Fluency,** IR35 Read with Appropriate Phrasing	**Lesson Vocabulary,** IR42 *balance, canyons, coral, rattle, slivers, sway, whisper* **Vocabulary Skill,** IR42 ◉ Multiple-Meaning Words **Comprehension,** IR43–IR45 ◉ Skill: Plot and Theme ◉ Strategy: Visualize **Fluency,** IR45 Read with Expression	**Lesson Vocabulary,** IR52 *awaken, cliffs, mountain, prize, rainbow, suffer, volcano* **Vocabulary Skill,** IR52 ◉ Prefixes **Comprehension,** IR53–IR55 ◉ Skill: Plot and Theme ◉ Strategy: Monitor and Clarify **Fluency,** IR55 Read with Expression and Intonation
Conventions, IR36 Comparative and Superlative Adjectives **Handwriting,** IR36 Cursive *k, j, p:* Letter Spacing **Wrap Up Your Day,** IR37	**Conventions,** IR46 Adverbs That Tell When and Where **Handwriting,** IR46 Cursive *a, d, c:* Word Spacing **Wrap Up Your Day,** IR47	**Conventions,** IR56 Adverbs That Tell How **Handwriting,** IR56 Cursive *n, m, x:* Letter Size **Wrap Up Your Day,** IR57

Week 6

Turn the page for grouping suggestions to differentiate instructions.

Differentiate Instruction on Reading Street!

	Review Week 1 **Day 1** pages IR8–IR17	**Review Week 2** **Day 2** pages IR18–IR27
SI Strategic Intervention	**Reteach and Review** • Concept Talk • Oral Vocabulary • Final Syllable -le • Spelling • Lesson Vocabulary • Multiple-Meaning Words • Draw Conclusions • Background Knowledge • Read with Accuracy and Appropriate Rate • Adjectives and Our Senses • Cursive l, h, e/Letter Formation	**Reteach and Review** • Concept Talk • Oral Vocabulary • Vowel Patterns oo, u • Spelling • Lesson Vocabulary • Antonyms • Sequence • Important Ideas • Read with Accuracy • Adjectives for Number, Size, and Shape • Cursive t, i, u/Letter Slant
OL On-Level	**Review** • Final Syllable -le • Spelling • Multiple-Meaning Words • Draw Conclusions • Background Knowledge • Adjectives and Our Senses	**Review** • Vowel Patterns oo, u • Spelling • Antonyms • Sequence • Important Ideas • Adjectives for Number, Size, and Shape
A Advanced	**Extend** • Final Syllable -le • Draw Conclusions • Background Knowledge	**Extend** • Vowel Patterns oo, u • Sequence • Important Ideas
ELL English Language Learners	**Reteach and Review** • Concept Talk • Oral Vocabulary • Final Syllable -le • Lesson Vocabulary • Multiple-Meaning Words • Draw Conclusions • Background Knowledge • Read with Accuracy and Appropriate Rate • Adjectives and Our Senses	**Reteach and Review** • Concept Talk • Oral Vocabulary • Vowel Patterns oo, u • Lesson Vocabulary • Antonyms • Sequence • Important Ideas • Read with Accuracy • Adjectives for Number, Size, and Shape

You Are Here!
Unit 4
Week 6

Big Question
How do things change? How do they stay the same?

Review Week 3	Review Week 4	Review Week 5
Day 3 pages IR28–IR37	**Day 4** pages IR38–IR47	**Day 5** pages IR48–IR57

Reteach and Review
- Concept Talk
- Oral Vocabulary
- Diphthongs *ou, ow, oi, oy*
- Spelling
- Lesson Vocabulary
- Suffixes
- Fact and Opinion
- Questioning
- Read with Appropriate Phrasing
- Comparative and Superlative Adjectives
- Cursive *k, j, p*/Letter Spacing

Review
- Diphthongs *ou, ow, oi, oy*
- Spelling
- Suffixes
- Fact and Opinion
- Questioning
- Comparative and Superlative Adjectives

Extend
- Diphthongs *ou, ow, oi, oy*
- Fact and Opinion
- Questioning

Reteach and Review
- Concept Talk
- Oral Vocabulary
- Diphthongs *ou, ow, oi, oy*
- Lesson Vocabulary
- Suffixes
- Fact and Opinion
- Questioning
- Read with Appropriate Phrasing
- Comparative and Superlative Adjectives

Reteach and Review
- Concept Talk
- Oral Vocabulary
- Syllable Patterns
- Spelling
- Lesson Vocabulary
- Multiple-Meaning Words
- Plot and Theme
- Visualize
- Read with Expression
- Adverbs That Tell When and Where
- Cursive *a, d, c*/Word Spacing

Review
- Syllable Patterns
- Spelling
- Multiple-Meaning Words
- Plot and Theme
- Visualize
- Adverbs That Tell When and Where

Extend
- Syllable Patterns
- Plot and Theme
- Visualize

Reteach and Review
- Concept Talk
- Oral Vocabulary
- Syllable Patterns
- Lesson Vocabulary
- Multiple-Meaning Words
- Plot and Theme
- Visualize
- Read with Expression
- Adverbs That Tell When and Where

Reteach and Review
- Concept Talk
- Oral Vocabulary
- Vowel Digraphs *oo, ue, ew, ui*
- Spelling
- Lesson Vocabulary
- Prefixes
- Plot and Theme
- Monitor and Clarify
- Read with Expression and Intonation
- Adverbs That Tell How
- Cursive *n, m, x*/Letter Size

Review
- Vowel Digraphs *oo, ue, ew, ui*
- Spelling
- Prefixes
- Plot and Theme
- Monitor and Clarify
- Adverbs That Tell How

Extend
- Vowel Digraphs *oo, ue, ew, ui*
- Plot and Theme
- Monitor and Clarify

Reteach and Review
- Concept Talk
- Oral Vocabulary
- Vowel Digraphs *oo, ue, ew, ui*
- Lesson Vocabulary
- Prefixes
- Plot and Theme
- Monitor and Clarify
- Read with Expression and Intonation
- Adverbs That Tell How

Week 6

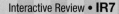

Objectives
• Review Week 1 concepts.
• Share information and ideas about the concept.
• Review Week 1 oral vocabulary.

Today at a Glance

Oral Vocabulary
preserve, represent, valuable, tough, concentration, frown, homeland, patient

Phonics and Spelling
◉ Review Final Syllable -*le*

Lesson Vocabulary
clearing, crashed, perfect, pond, spilling, splashing, traveled

Vocabulary
Skill: Multiple-Meaning Words

Comprehension
◉ Review Skill: Draw Conclusions
◉ Review Strategy: Background Knowledge

Fluency
Skill: Accuracy and Appropriate Rate

Conventions
Adjectives and Our Senses

Handwriting
Cursive Letters/Letter Formation

Writing
Quick Write for Fluency

Concept Talk

Question of the Week
How can familiar things help us with changes?

Review Week 1 selection

Today children will explore how the Question of the Week connects to *A Froggy Fable*. Read the Question of the Week above. Remind children that *A Froggy Fable* is a fable about a frog who didn't like the changes that were happening around him.

ROUTINE   Activate Prior Knowledge   Team Talk

1. **Think** Have children think about a time when a familiar thing helped them through a time of change.

2. **Pair** Have pairs of children discuss how the Question of the Week applies to the frog in *A Froggy Fable*.

3. **Share** Call on a few children to share their ideas with the group. Guide discussion and encourage elaboration with prompts such as:
   What change happened to the frog that he did not like?
   What familiar thing helped the frog?

Routines Flip Chart

Connect to the Big Question

Use these questions to connect the Week 1 question and selection to the Unit 4 Big Question, **How do things change? How do they stay the same?**

• What did the frog like about his home? What didn't he like?

• What experiences did the frog have when he was lost?

• After the frog found his way back, how did he feel about the changes around his home?

ELL Reteach Concepts and Vocabulary
Use the instruction on ELL Poster 16 to assess knowledge and concepts.

ELL Poster 16

Oral Vocabulary
Amazing Words

Amazing Words

preserve	concentration
represent	frown
valuable	homeland
tough	patient

Review
Week 1 Amazing Words

Remind children that they have learned some Amazing Words that they can use to answer the question *How can familiar things help us with changes?* Display "Favorite, Old Things" on page 16 of the *Sing with Me* Big Book. Sing the song.

Sing with Me Big Book

 Sing with Me Big Book Audio

Go over all the Amazing Words from Week 1. Ask children to listen as you say them: *preserve, represent, valuable, tough, concentration, frown, homeland, patient.* Then say them again, and have children say each word after you.

- How would you describe an expensive necklace—*valuable* or *tough?* (valuable)
- Raise your hand when I say something you might want to *preserve*—photographs, a sandwich, a wedding dress, a television. (photographs, wedding dress)
- Show me what a *frown* looks like.

Apply Amazing Words

Have children demonstrate their understanding of Amazing Words by completing these sentences orally.

> The _____ was **tough**.
>
> Sarah's _____ is **valuable**, so she wants to **preserve** it.
>
> Her dad's **frown** told her his answer was _____ .
>
> _____ is my **homeland**.
>
> The color _____ often **represents** the word *stop*.
>
> Nate used all his **concentration** on the _____ .
>
> It is difficult to be **patient** while _____ .

Differentiated Instruction

 Strategic Intervention

Supporting Word Understanding Ask children these questions to support their understanding of some of the Amazing Words. Tell them to use the word in their answer.

- What is something you would like to *preserve?*
- What do flags *represent?*
- What is *valuable* to you?
- When do you *concentrate?*
- When are times you have to be *patient?*

Writing on Demand

Develop Writing Fluency Ask children to write about a time when a familiar thing helped them deal with change. Have them write for two to three minutes. Children should write as much as they can. Tell them to try to do their best writing. You may want to discuss what children wrote during writing conferences.

Objectives
- Read words with final syllable -*le*.
- Read multisyllabic words.
- Spell words with final syllable -*le*.

Phonics

Final Syllable -*le*

Review
Phonics skill

Review the final syllable -*le* using Sound-Spelling Card 134.

Decode words independent of context

Use *Reader's and Writer's Notebook* page 349. Point out that children know how to decode these words. Then tell children they will all read the words in the row together. Allow several seconds previewing time for the first reading.

Reader's and Writer's
Notebook p. 349

Corrective feedback

If... children cannot decode all the words in the row consecutively without an error,
then... return to the first word in the row, and have children reread all the words. Repeat until children can read the words fluently.

Sound-Spelling
Card 134

Decode words in context

Use the passage on *Reader's and Writer's Notebook* page 349. Point out that there are many words with final syllable -*le* in the passage that children already know how to decode. Have children read the passage together.

Corrective feedback

If... children have difficulty decoding words with final syllable -*le*,
then... guide them in chunking the multisyllabic words and using sound-by-sound blending. Have children read each sentence. Repeat until children can read the sentences fluently.

On their own

Use *Let's Practice It!* p. 227 on the *Teacher Resource DVD-ROM*.

Let's Practice It!
TR DVD•227

Spelling
Final Syllable *-le*

Review
Week 1 spelling words

Write *cable, bundle,* and *sparkle.* Point out that these words have final syllable *-le.* Remind children that they learned how to spell words with this pattern. Use Sound-Spelling Card 134 to review how to spell words with final syllable *-le.* Review the Week 1 spelling words.

Team Talk Have children review the spelling words using index cards on which the words are written. Tell them to sort the words into the ones they know and the ones they need more practice with. Partners can quiz each other on the words in the second pile.

On their own Use *Reader's and Writer's Notebook,* p. 350.

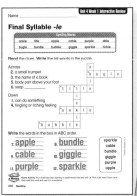

Reader's and Writer's Notebook p. 350

Unit 4 Week 1 Spelling Words

Final Syllable *-le*

1. ankle	7. bugle
2. title	8. bundle
3. apple	9. bubble
4. cable	10. giggle
5. purple	11. sparkle
6. able	12. tickle

English Language Learners

Final Syllable *-le* Remind children of the sound made by final syllable *-le.*

Beginning Write these words: *basket, bubble, gladly, giggle, spilled, ankle.* Ask children to circle the words that have the final syllable *-le* and read the words.

Intermediate Write these first syllables in one list: *ca-, pur-, ti-, spar-,* and these last syllables in another list: *-kle, -tle, -ple, -ble.* Ask children to match first and last syllables to write words: *cable, purple, title, sparkle*

Advanced/Advanced-High Write these words: *apple, bugle, giggle, cable, title, bundle, able,* and *bubble.* Have children read the words and then sort them into two groups—those with a long vowel sound in the first syllable and those with a short vowel sound in the first syllable.

Objectives
- Read lesson vocabulary words.
- Review multiple-meaning words.
- Review key features of a fable.
- Preview and predict.
- Establish purpose for reading text.

Lesson Vocabulary

Read words independent of context

Display the lesson vocabulary words. Have children read the words aloud with you. Review the definitions.

clearing—piece of land that has no trees

crashed—fell with a loud smashing noise

perfect—as good as is possible

pond—water with land all around it; a small lake

spilling—scattering everywhere

splashing—making water scatter and fall in drops

traveled—went from one place to another

Guide practice

Then have children use each word in a sentence.

Corrective feedback

If... children do not use a word correctly,
then... correct the sentence, model a sentence, and have them try again.

On their own

Use *Reader's and Writer's Notebook*, page 351.

Reader's and Writer's Notebook p. 351

Vocabulary Skill
Multiple-Meaning Words

Review **Multiple-meaning words**

Review that some words have two or more meanings. They are called multiple-meaning words. Ask what the word *block* means in each of the following sentences.

- My friend lives on the next block. (city street)
- The toddler likes to stack one block on top of another. (a toy cube)

Have children give two meanings and sentences for the words *well* and *cold*.

Guide practice

Team Talk Have children work together to come up with two different meanings and two sentences for the words *bat* and *fall*. They may use a dictionary, if needed.

Comprehension
Skills and Strategies

Review Skill

 Draw Conclusions Review what it means to draw conclusions. When you read a story or article, you use what you have read and what you know about real life to figure out more about the characters and what happens. Remind children that they know how to draw conclusions. Recall that they were able to draw conclusions about the frog and what happened in the story when they read *A Froggy Fable.*

Review Strategy

Background Knowledge Remind children that good readers use background knowledge as they read. Before, during, and after you read, you can use your background knowledge to help you understand a story or article. You think about what you already know and what you have experienced. Then you use that knowledge to help you understand what you are reading.

Review Genre

Fable Remind children that a fable is a story, usually with animal characters, that is written to teach a moral, or lesson. A fable is a story that usually has animal characters that often talk and act like humans. The author writes the story to teach a lesson.

Preview and predict

Have children read the title of the selection on p. 352 of *Reader's and Writer's Notebook.* Have children look through the selection and use the title to predict events that might happen in the selection. Tell them this selection is a fable.

Set a purpose

After we read "Greedy Groundhog," we will draw conclusions about the characters and what happens in the fable. Have children set a purpose for reading "Greedy Groundhog."

Differentiated Instruction

(A) Advanced

Extend Draw Conclusions Have children think of stories they have read recently. Ask them what conclusions they drew as they read the story. Have them tell what led them to draw those conclusions. Ask how they combined what they already knew with clues in the story.

Academic Vocabulary

fable a story, usually with animal characters, that is written to teach a moral, or lesson

Objectives
- Review skill: draw conclusions.
- Review strategy: background knowledge.
- Read aloud fluently with accuracy and appropriate rate.

Name _____

Read the fable. **Answer** the questions.

Greedy Groundhog

The forest animals were very quiet. All the animals were resting in the shade of an old barn. The summer sun was hot like a fire even though it was early in the morning. For a long time, there had been no rain. The soil was dried and cracked. Plants had died because they couldn't grow without water.

The animals that ate plants were very hungry. Those who nibbled on trees were hungry, too. They had eaten the last of the leaves, twigs, and bark.

Then one of the deer, Miss White Tail, stood up in her graceful way. "Wake up, my dear friends," she said. "We can't wait for the rain to come. We shall have to leave this place and look for food in another place."

"Good idea," Mr. Porcupine replied.

"My family is ready!" Mrs. Long Ears exclaimed.

All the animals agreed it was a good plan. So when all were gathered together, they hopped, bounced, and trotted after Miss White Tail. Soon they came to a magnificent garden! They couldn't believe their eyes. Big, bright vegetables and tall, green grass filled the garden. There were even trees in the garden with crisp leaves and bushes with juicy berries.

But the garden had a metal fence all around it. And sitting at the gate of the garden was a big, fat groundhog. "Go away!" he shouted. "I found the garden, and this is my food." He growled and scared the animals. They all ran away as fast as they could.

 Home Activity Your child used text to draw conclusions and make inferences about a fable. Read aloud a portion of a story your child has not read. Work with your child to draw conclusions and make inferences about a character or event. Pause often to ask *why, what,* and *how* questions.

352 Comprehension

Name _____

When the animals were safely away from the groundhog, Miss White Tail said, "Let's go back tomorrow. I have an idea."

Early the next morning, Miss White Tail went to the garden, carrying several large bags. "Run, Groundhog!" she yelled. "A fierce rainstorm is coming. I'm going to cover the animals with these bags to keep them from being soaked to death."

"Give me a bag!" the groundhog demanded.

"Well, OK," she said calmly. "If you really want one, let me help you put it on." Miss White Tail carefully put the bag over the groundhog. Then oh so quickly, she tied a rope around and around the groundhog's body so he couldn't move.

All the animals came running to help tie the groundhog to the fence. After that, Miss White Tail opened the garden gate, and all the hungry animals ate a delicious meal. **Moral: It is not right to be selfish.**

1. Why were the animals quiet?

___The animals were hot and hungry.___

2. Why do you think the animals decided not to wait for rain?

___Possible answer: It might not rain for a long time, and they needed food right away.___

3. How was Miss White Tail able to get into the garden?

___She tricked the groundhog to get him away from the gate and then tied him up.___

4. What words do you think describe Miss White Tail?

___Possible answer: clever, smart, calm, kind, and unselfish.___

Unit 4 Interactive Review   Comprehension   353

Reader's and Writer's Notebook pp. 352–353

Guide Comprehension
Review Draw Conclusions

Have children read the story and respond to the questions.

Corrective feedback

If... children have difficulty responding to the questions,
then... use the following to guide their responses.

1. Why were the animals hungry? What happened to their food? Help children draw conclusions about why the animals didn't have food.

2. What might have happened if the animals stayed and waited for the rain? Help children draw the conclusion that the animals may have starved if it continued not to rain and there was no food.

3. Why did Miss White Tail trick the groundhog? Help children draw the conclusion that the groundhog was selfish and wouldn't share his food with the other animals.

Comprehension
 Background Knowledge

**Review
Strategy**

Discuss strategies that children used as they read "Greedy Groundhog."

Did you use what you know about fables to help you understand this fable and the lesson it teaches? Did you use your own experiences? Have children identify how their own knowledge and experiences helped them understand the fable.

Fluency
Accuracy and Appropriate Rate

**Model fluent
reading**

Remind children that when they read, it is important to pay attention to each word, read with no mistakes, and read at an appropriate rate. Model reading the first two paragraphs of "Greedy Groundhog" on *Reader's and Writer's Notebook* page 352 with accuracy and at an appropriate rate. Have children track the print as you read.

**Guide
practice**

To provide additional fluency practice, pair children and have them read "Greedy Groundhog."

ROUTINE Paired Reading Team Talk

1. **Reader 1 Begins** Children read the story, switching readers at the end of each paragraph.

2. **Reader 2 Begins** Have partners reread; this time the other partner begins.

3. **Reread** For optimal fluency, children should reread three or four times.

4. **Corrective Feedback** Listen to children read and provide corrective feedback regarding their oral reading and their use of the blending strategy.

Routines Flip Chart

Differentiated Instruction

SI Strategic Intervention

Comprehension and Fluency
Have children reread "Greedy Groundhog" first silently and then aloud. As they read, have them think about how the characters act and speak. After children have read the story, have them tell how the animals may have felt when they got food from the garden.

Options for Oral Rereading

Use *A Froggy Fable* or one of the Week 1 Leveled Readers.

Objectives

- Identify adjectives.
- Form and join cursive letters correctly using correct letter formation.
- Write for fluency.
- Review concepts.

Conventions
Adjectives and Our Senses

Review
Adjectives

An adjective is a word that describes a person, place, or thing. Adjectives can describe how something looks, sounds, smells, feels, or tastes.

Guide practice

Read the following sentences and have children identify the adjective and the noun to which it refers in each sentence.

> Devon ate a **sour apple** at lunch.
>
> Michaela heard a **shrill whistle** outside.
>
> Last week Mother brought home a **soft, furry kitten**.
>
> What is that **horrible smell?**

Team Talk Pair children and have them choose nouns and adjectives that describe the way things look, sound, smell, feel, or taste. Then have them use their choices in sentences to share with the class.

On their own *Use Reader's and Writer's Notebook*, page 354.

Reader's and Writer's
Notebook p. 354

Handwriting
Cursive Letters *l, h, e*/Letter Formation

Review
Cursive letters

Review the proper formation of letters *l, h,* and *e*. Write each letter. Have children write the letters several times and circle their best one.

Review
Letter formation

Review that in cursive writing, letters must be formed correctly. The letters in a word must also be connected, or joined, smoothly.

Guide practice

Write the following words. Have children copy them using good letter formation. Monitor children's letter formation as they write.

he	**eel**	**heel**	**lee**

On their own Use the Day 1 section on *Reader's and Writer's Notebook,* pages 355–356.

Reader's and Writer's Notebook
pp. 355–356

ROUTINE

Quick Write for Fluency

1. **Talk** Have pairs discuss what they learned about how familiar things can help us adjust to changes.

2. **Write** Have children write a few sentences to summarize the discussion.

3. **Share** Partners can read their summaries to one another.

Routines Flip Chart

Wrap Up Your Day

Question of the Week
How can familiar things help us with changes?

Review
Concept and Amazing Words

Use these questions to wrap up this review of the Week 1 concept and to provide another opportunity for children to use the week's Amazing Words. Pair or group children to answer the questions. Have children share their responses with the class.

☑ How can being **patient** help you adjust to changes?

☑ Why might a person **frown** if an object of theirs gets lost?

☑ What kind of changes might be **tough** to deal with?

☑ What new things that you learn cause you to use a lot of **concentration?**

☑ What changes have happened in your **homeland**?

☑ What is the most **valuable** advice you can give someone who is going through major changes?

☑ How could you **preserve** a special object?

☑ What does the color red **represent** to you?

Writing Workshop

Use the writing process lesson on pages CW•11–CW•20 for this week's writing instruction.

English Language Learners
Extend Vocabulary
Beginning/Intermediate Have children frown. Tell them to give examples in complete sentences of things that might make them frown.

Advanced/Advanced-High
Read these two sentences: *He was patient as he waited in line. The doctor spoke to her patient.* Discuss the meanings of *patient.*

Homework Send home this week's Family Times Newsletter from Let's Practice It! pp. 225–226 on the *Teacher Resource DVD-ROM.*

Let's Practice It!
TR DVD•225–226

Preview DAY 2

Tell children that tomorrow they will review more skills and read "A Class Mural."

Objectives
- Review Week 2 concepts.
- Share information and ideas about the concept.
- Review Week 2 oral vocabulary.

Today at a Glance

Oral Vocabulary
adapt, annual, nutrients, blazing, drought, ancient, massive, sprout

Phonics and Spelling
◎ Review Vowel Patterns *oo, u*

Lesson Vocabulary
bumpy, fruit, harvest, root, smooth, soil, vine

Vocabulary
Skill: Antonyms

Comprehension
◎ Review Skill: Sequence
◎ Review Strategy: Important Ideas

Fluency
Skill: Read with Accuracy

Conventions
Adjectives for Number, Size, and Shape; Articles *a, an, the*

Handwriting
Cursive Letters/Letter Slant

Writing
Quick Write for Fluency

Concept Talk

Question of the Week

? How do plants change over time?

Review Week 2 selection

Today children will explore how the Question of the Week connects to *Life Cycle of a Pumpkin.* Read the Question of the Week above. Remind children that *Life Cycle of a Pumpkin* is a nonfiction article about how a pumpkin plant grows and changes from a seed to a vine with pumpkins.

ROUTINE **Activate Prior Knowledge** **Team Talk**

1 Think Have children think about how they have seen plants change over time.

2 Pair Have pairs of children discuss how the Question of the Week applies to the pumpkin plants in *Life Cycle of a Pumpkin.*

3 Share Call on a few children to share their ideas with the group. Guide discussion and encourage elaboration with prompts such as:
What do pumpkin plants start out as?
What things do pumpkin plants need to grow?

Routines Flip Chart

Connect to the Big Question

Use these questions to connect the Week 2 question and selection to the Unit 4 Big Question, **How do things change? How do they stay the same?**

- How does a pumpkin plant change as it grows?
- What changes have you seen in plants as they grow from seeds?
- How would you help a seed grow into a plant?

ELL **Reteach Concepts and Vocabulary** Use the instruction on ELL Poster 17 to assess knowledge and concepts.

ELL Poster 17

Oral Vocabulary
Amazing Words

Amazing Words

adapt	drought
annual	ancient
nutrients	massive
blazing	sprout

 Review
Week 2 Amazing Words

Remind children that they have learned some Amazing Words that they can use to answer the question *How do plants change over time?* Display "An Annual Event" on page 17 of the *Sing with Me* Big Book. Sing the song.

 Sing with Me Big Book Audio

Sing with Me Big Book

Go over all the Amazing Words from Week 2. Ask children to listen as you say them: *adapt, annual, nutrients, blazing, drought, ancient, massive, sprout.* Then say them again, and have children say each word after you.

- If something happens on an *annual* basis, how often does it happen? (every year)

- How might you describe the heat of the sun—*massive* or *blazing*? (blazing)

- What is another word for *ancient*? (very old, antique)

Apply Amazing Words

Have children demonstrate their understanding of Amazing Words by completing these sentences orally.

> The **blazing** _____ caused the **drought.**
>
> **Nutrients** help a **sprout** to _____.
>
> The crowd stared at the **massive** _____.
>
> The _____ is an **annual** event.
>
> The museum has an **ancient** _____ on display.
>
> Marco was able to **adapt** to his new _____.

Differentiated Instruction

SI Strategic Intervention

Related Words Say an Amazing Word. Ask children to say other words that come to mind when they hear the word. For example, when you say *massive,* they might think of an elephant or a tall building; when you say *nutrients,* they might think of vitamins or vegetables.

 Writing on Demand

Develop Writing Fluency Ask children to write about one or more plants they have watched change over time and the changes they have seen in the plants. Have them write for two to three minutes. Children should write as much as they can. Tell them to try to do their best writing. You may want to discuss what children wrote during writing conferences.

Objectives
• Read words with vowel patterns *oo, u*.
• Read multisyllabic words.
• Spell words with vowel patterns *oo, u*.

Phonics

 Vowel Patterns *oo, u*

Review **Phonics skill**	Review the vowel patterns *oo* and *u* using Sound-Spelling Cards 89 and 101.

Sound-Spelling
Card 89

Sound-Spelling
Card 101

Decode words independent of context	Use *Reader's and Writer's Notebook* page 357. Point out that children know how to decode these words. Then tell children they will all read the words in the row together. Allow several seconds previewing time for the first reading.

Corrective feedback

If... children cannot decode all the words in the row consecutively without an error,
then... return to the first word in the row, and have children reread all the words. Repeat until children can read the words fluently.

Reader's and Writer's
Notebook p. 357

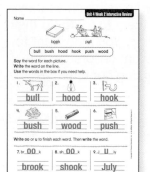

Corrective feedback

Decode words in context	Use the passage on *Reader's and Writer's Notebook* page 357. Point out that there are many words with vowel patterns *oo* and *u* in the passage that children already know how to decode. Have children read the passage together.

Corrective feedback

If... children have difficulty decoding words with vowel patterns *oo* and *u*,
then... guide them in chunking multisyllabic words and using sound-by-sound blending. Have children read each sentence. Repeat until children can read the sentences fluently.

Let's Practice It!
TR DVD•228

On their own Use Let's Practice It! p. 228 on the *Teacher Resource DVD-ROM*.

Spelling
Vowel Patterns *oo, u*

Review Week 2 spelling words

Write *cook, stood, put,* and *full.* Point out that these words have the /ù/ sound spelled with *oo* and *u.* Remind children that they learned how to spell words with this pattern. Use Sound-Spelling Cards 89 and 101 to review how to spell words with the /ù/ sound. Review the Week 2 spelling words.

Team Talk Have children review the spelling words using index cards on which the words are written. Tell them to sort the words into the ones they know and the ones they need more practice with. Partners can quiz each other on the words in the second pile.

On their own   Use *Reader's and Writer's Notebook,* p. 358.

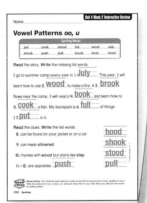

Reader's and Writer's
Notebook p. 358

Unit 4 Week 2 Spelling Words

Vowel Patterns *oo, u*

1. put	7. shook
2. cook	8. push
3. stood	9. pull
4. full	10. brook
5. wood	11. book
6. July	12. hood

English Language Learners

Vowel Patterns *oo, u* Remind children of the sound made by the vowel patterns *oo* and *u.*

Beginning Have children sort the spelling words into those with /ù/ spelled *oo* and those spelled *u.* Read the words and spell them aloud together.

Intermediate Have children find words that rhyme. (full/pull, cook/shook/brook/book, stood/wood/hood). Supply these words and have children decide which list rhymes with each new word: *hook, good, bull.*

Advanced/Advanced-High Have children make up sentences using the spelling words. Write their sentences on the board. Have children identify the spelling word and circle the *oo* or *u* that spells the /ù/ sound.

Objectives
- Read lesson vocabulary words.
- Review antonyms.
- Review key features of expository text.
- Preview and predict.
- Establish purpose for reading text.

Lesson Vocabulary

Read words independent of context

Display the lesson vocabulary words. Have children read the words aloud with you. Review the definitions.

bumpy—covered with high spots or lumps

fruit—part of a plant that contains seeds

harvest—season when crops are gathered

root—part of plant that takes in water and holds the plant in place

soil—top layer of Earth's surface

smooth—flat or even

vine—thin stem of some plants that creep along the ground or climb

Guide practice

Have children use each word in a sentence.

Corrective feedback

If... children do not use a word correctly,
then... correct the sentence, model a sentence, and have them try again.

On their own

Use *Reader's and Writer's Notebook*, page 359.

Reader's and Writer's Notebook p. 359

Vocabulary Skill
Antonyms

Review Antonyms

Review that an antonym is a word that is the opposite of another word, such as *up* and *down*.

- Which selection vocabulary word is an antonym for smooth? (bumpy)
- What does *bumpy* mean? (covered with lumps)

Have children think of other antonym pairs. Write the pairs on the board.

Guide practice

Team Talk Have children work together to give the meaning of each of the following words and then name an antonym: *tiny, empty, push, heavy.*

Comprehension
Skills and Strategies

Review
Skill

 Sequence Review what *sequence* means. Sometimes a selection tells about how something happens. You read about the things that happen and the order in which they happen. Remind children that they know how to describe the order of events in a selection. Recall that they were able to discuss the sequence of how a pumpkin goes from a seed to a pie when they read *Life Cycle of a Pumpkin.*

Review
Strategy

Important Ideas Remind children that good readers look for important ideas as they read. As you read, you can look for important facts and details. This information will help you understand a selection. These facts and details can be found in the text and in photographs, illustrations, and other graphic sources like charts and time lines. Remind children of the time line at the bottom of the pages in *Life Cycle of a Pumpkin* and discuss how it showed important ideas.

Review
Genre

Expository Text Remind children that expository text contains facts and information. Expository text is nonfiction writing that gives facts and details. It can describe real people, places, events, or things. Expository text often includes photos, drawings, or other illustrations that give more information about a topic.

Preview and predict

Have children read the title of the selection on p. 360 of *Reader's and Writer's Notebook.* Have children look through the selection and use the title to predict the sequence of events that might happen in the selection. Tell them this selection is expository text.

Set a purpose

After we read "A Class Mural," we will describe the sequence of events in making a mural. Have children set a purpose for reading "A Class Mural."

Differentiated Instruction

SI Strategic Intervention

Sequence On a small card write each event that happens as a pumpkin goes from a seed to a pie. Review the selection *Life Cycle of a Pumpkin.* Then have children work together to put the events in the correct sequence.

Academic Vocabulary

expository text text that contains facts and information; also called *informational text*

Objectives

- Review skill: sequence.
- Review strategy: important ideas.
- Read aloud fluently with accuracy.

Name _____

Read the story. **Follow** the directions and **answer** the questions.

A Class Mural

My class was learning about cities. Our teacher, Mr. Mendez, asked if we thought we could make a mural to show what city life was like. We told him we could make a great mural. Mr. Mendez said we could hang the mural in the hall when it was finished. Our mural would let other children in the school see what a city looks like.

Mr. Mendez put us in groups and gave each group one part of the mural to work on. He had put up a long sheet of mural paper on one wall. We were to use pencils, crayons, drawing paper, scissors, and paste.

The class decided to show a city street. The (first) thing we did was make a plan for the mural. We made a list of things to include. Our city street would be a busy place with a lot of people and traffic. There would be cars, taxis, trucks, and buses on the street. There would be people walking on the sidewalk and going into different kinds of buildings.

(Next) each group went to the mural paper and used pencils to draw the buildings along the street. My classmates and I drew many kinds of buildings. The buildings included tall office buildings, big stores, and small shops. We drew a bank, a movie theater, and a museum. (Then) we colored the buildings with crayons.

(After that) we drew people on sheets of colored paper. Some of us drew adults, and others drew children. We drew tall people and

School + Home **Home Activity** Your child identified the sequence of events in a story. Ask your child to tell you about an art or science project he or she did in school. Encourage your child to use order words such as *first*, *next*, *then*, and *last* to show the sequence of events.

360 **Comprehension** Sequence

Name _____

short people. We drew people dressed for shopping and people dressed for work. I drew a worker who was fixing part of the sidewalk.

(Finally) everyone cut out his or her drawings. And (last of all) each group pasted people on the city street. Our mural was finished! We thought it was a great mural. Mr. Mendez said it was wonderful.

(The next day) Mr. Mendez hung the mural in the hall by our classroom. Our friends in other classes stopped to look at it. They said it was awesome.

1. **Circle** the words in the story that give clues to the order in which things happened.

2. What happened after the class made a plan for the mural?

   _____Each group went to the mural paper and drew buildings._____

3. What happened before the children drew people for the mural?

   _____They colored the buildings with crayons._____

4. What did the children do after they drew people for the mural?

   _____They cut out their drawings of people._____

5. What happened after the mural was finished?

   _____Mr. Mendez hung the mural in the hall._____

Unit 4 Interactive Review   **Comprehension** 361

Reader's and Writer's Notebook pp. 360–361

Guide Comprehension
⟳ Review Sequence

Have children read the selection and respond to the questions.

Corrective feedback

If... children have difficulty responding to the questions,

then... use the following to guide their responses.

1. After the class decided their mural would be of a city street, what was the first thing they did? Have children identify the word *first* in order to find the sentence that tells what the class did first.

2. What did the class draw first, people or buildings? Have children find the sequence word *next* and the sentence that tells what the clas drew first.

3. What was the last thing the class did to finish their mural? Have children identify *last of all* as key words to telling the last step. Have them find the sentence that tells what the class did before Mr. Mendez hung the mural.

Comprehension
Important Ideas

Review Strategy

Discuss strategies that children used as they read "A Class Mural" and answered questions about it.

What did you do to remember important ideas, facts, and details as you read? Have children identify how they kept track of important ideas as they read.

When you answered the questions on p. 361, did you support your answers with important ideas from the text? Have children identify the evidence in the text that supported their answers.

Fluency
Read with Accuracy

Model fluent reading

Remind children that when they read, it is important to pay attention to the words they are reading and to read without mistakes. Model reading the first two paragraphs of "A Class Mural" on *Reader's and Writer's Notebook* page 360 with accuracy. Have children track the print as you read.

Guide practice

To provide additional fluency practice, pair children and have them read "A Class Mural."

ROUTINE Paired Reading Team Talk

1. **Reader 1 Begins** Children read the selection, switching readers at the end of each paragraph.
2. **Reader 2 Begins** Have partners reread; this time the other partner begins.
3. **Reread** For optimal fluency, children should reread three or four times.
4. **Corrective Feedback** Listen to children read and provide corrective feedback regarding their oral reading and their use of the blending strategy.

Routines Flip Chart

Differentiated Instruction

SI Strategic Intervention

Comprehension and Fluency
Have children reread "A Class Mural" aloud. As they read, have them think about the sequence of events. After children have read the selection, have them describe how the class made their mural.

Options for Oral Rereading

Use *Life Cycle of a Pumpkin* or one of the Week 2 Leveled Readers.

Objectives
- Identify adjectives for number, size, and shape; and articles *a, an*, and *the*.
- Form and join cursive letters correctly using correct letter slant.
- Write for fluency.
- Review concepts.

Conventions
Adjectives for Number, Size, and Shape; Articles *a, an, the*

Review
Adjectives

An adjective is a word that describes. Adjectives can describe number, size, and shape. Words like *some, few*, and *many* are adjectives that describe number. Adjectives that tell size and shape describe what an object looks like. The words *a, an*, and *the* are adjectives called articles.

Guide practice

Read the following sentences and have children identify the adjectives and articles and the nouns to which they refer.

> I counted **twelve tulips** and **a rose** in **the small garden.**
>
> **Many rocks** splashed into **the water** below.
>
> I put **an olive** on **a square piece** of pizza.

Team Talk Have members of small groups of children take turns choosing an object in the room. Have others in the group ask questions about the object's size, shape, and number until they can guess what it is.

On their own Use *Reader's and Writer's Notebook*, page 362.

Reader's and Writer's
Notebook p. 362

Handwriting
Cursive Letters *t, i, u*/Letter Slant

Review
Cursive letters

Review the proper formation of letters *t, i*, and *u*. Write each letter. Have children write the letters several times and circle their best one.

Review
Letter slant

Review that letters must have a good slant. Remember that in cursive writing, letters are slanted. Make sure your letters are slanted correctly.

Write the following words. Have children copy them using good slant as they write. Monitor children's letter slant as they write.

Guide practice

| it | hit | hut | hill | hull | tile | lie |

On their own Use the Day 2 section on *Reader's and Writer's Notebook*, pages 355–356.

ROUTINE **Quick Write for Fluency**

1. **Talk** Have pairs discuss what they learned about how plants change over time.

2. **Write** Have children write a few sentences to summarize the discussion.

3. **Share** Partners can read their summaries to one another.

Routines Flip Chart

Wrap Up Your Day

Question of the Week
How do plants change over time?

Review Concept and Amazing Words

Use these questions to wrap up this review of the Week 2 concept and to provide another opportunity for children to use the week's Amazing Words. Pair or group children to answer the questions. Have children share their responses with the rest of the class.

☑ How can a plant **adapt** in order to gather more sunlight?

☑ Why do most plants change during a **drought?**

☑ How does an **annual** flower change over time?

☑ In what ways would a plant change if it does not get the **nutrients** it needs?

☑ If the sun is **blazing** for many days straight, and there is no rainfall, how would a plant likely change?

☑ How are today's plants similar to **ancient** plants?

☑ What are some plants that can become **massive?**

☑ What can happen after a seed **sprouts?**

Writing Workshop

Use the writing process lesson on pages CW•11–CW•20 for this week's writing instruction.

ELL

English Language Learners
Enhance Amazing Words
Beginning Show pictures or draw simple illustrations that will help children's understanding of the Amazing Words. Model sentences that tell about the pictures. For example, show a picture of an area that is in a drought. *This is a drought. There is no rain. It is dry.* Have children compose more sentences about the pictures.

Intermediate Ask questions about the Amazing Words to enhance understanding. For example, ask: *If the sun is blazing, is it cloudy? If a tree is massive, is it big or small?*

Advanced/Advanced-High After you read the questions on the page, have children orally compose their own questions to ask other children. Provide enough wait time to allow children to process their thoughts.

Preview DAY 3

Tell children that tomorrow they will review more skills and read "What Is Air?"

Objectives
• Review Week 3 concepts.
• Share information and ideas about the concept.
• Review Week 3 oral vocabulary.

Today at a Glance

Oral Vocabulary
discovery, transform, underneath, blizzard, fine, incredible, landscape, molten

Phonics and Spelling
◉ Review Diphthongs *ou, ow, oy, oi*

Lesson Vocabulary
grains, materials, particles, seeps, substances, texture

Vocabulary
Skill: Suffixes

Comprehension
◉ Review Skill: Fact and Opinion
◉ Review Strategy: Questioning

Fluency
Skill: Read with Appropriate Phrasing

Conventions
Comparative and Superlative Adjectives

Handwriting
Cursive Letters/Letter Spacing

Writing
Quick Write for Fluency

Concept Talk

Question of the Week
? What changes occur under the ground?

Review Week 3 selection

Today children will explore how the Question of the Week connects to *Soil*. Read the Question of the Week above. Remind children that *Soil* is a nonfiction article about how soil is formed, the different parts of soil, how the parts are made, and how they help plants grow.

ROUTINE **Activate Prior Knowledge** **Team Talk**

(1) **Think** Have children think about a time when they dug in the soil and the things they saw in the soil.

(2) **Pair** Have pairs of children discuss how the Question of the Week applies to the plants and animals that live under the ground in *Soil*.

(3) **Share** Call on a few children to share their ideas with the group. Guide discussion and encourage elaboration with prompts such as:
What part of plants live under the ground?
What kinds of animals live under the ground? How do worms help the soil?

Routines Flip Chart

Connect to the Big Question

Use these questions to connect the Week 3 question and selection to the Unit 4 Big Question, **How do things change? How do they stay the same?**

• How do water, ice, and wind break rocks into particles that are in soil?

• When you have looked at soil, what particles have you seen?

• How do rocks changing into soil help us?

ELL Reteach Concepts and Vocabulary Use the instruction on ELL Poster 18 to assess knowledge and concepts.

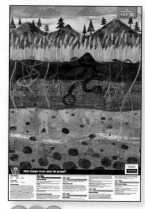
ELL Poster 18

Oral Vocabulary
Amazing Words

Review
Week 3
Amazing
Words

Remind children that they have learned some Amazing Words that they can use to answer the question *What changes occur under the ground?* Display "Underground Discovery" on page 18 of the *Sing with Me* Big Book. Sing the song.

Sing with Me Big Book

 Sing with Me Big Book Audio

Go over all the Amazing Words from Week 3. Ask children to listen as you say them: *discovery, transform, underneath, blizzard, fine, incredible, landscape, molten.* Then say them again, and have children say each word after you.

- What word means "to change"? (transform)
- How might you describe dust on a table—*molten* or *fine?* (fine)
- When is a *blizzard* more likely to happen—in winter or summer? (winter)

**Apply
Amazing
Words**

Have children demonstrate their understanding of Amazing Words by completing these sentences orally.

After the **blizzard,** our car was _____.

A seed **transforms** into a _____.

Underneath the rock, we made a(n) _____ **discovery.**

Fine _____ covered the ground.

We saw an **incredible landscape** on our _____.

Molten _____ poured from the volcano.

Amazing Words

discovery	fine
transform	incredible
underneath	landscape
blizzard	molten

Differentiated Instruction

(A) Advanced

Amazing Adventure Words
Have children visualize taking a nature walk. Tell them to think about using the Amazing Words to describe things as they walk. Say one Amazing Word at a time, and have children orally compose sentences using the word to describe something on their nature walk.

Writing on Demand

Develop Writing Fluency
Ask children to write about a time when they dug in the soil and what they found there. Have them write for two to three minutes. Children should write as much as they can. Tell them to try to do their best writing. You may want to discuss what children wrote during writing conferences.

Objectives

- Read words with diphthongs *ou, ow, oi, oy.*
- Read multisyllabic words.
- Spell words with diphthongs *ou, ow, oi, oy.*

Phonics

 Diphthongs *ou, ow, oi, oy*

Review Phonics skill

Review diphthongs *ou, ow, oi,* and *oy* using Sound-Spelling Cards 88, 94, 98, and 100.

| oi | ou | ow | oy |

Sound-Spelling Card 88   Sound-Spelling Card 94   Sound-Spelling Card 98   Sound-Spelling Card 100

Decode words independent of context

Use *Reader's and Writer's Notebook* page 363. Point out that children know how to decode these words. Then tell children they will all read the words in each row together. Allow several seconds previewing time for the first reading.

Corrective feedback

If... children cannot decode all the words in a row consecutively without an error,

then... return to the first word in the row, and have children reread all the words in the row. Repeat until children can read the words fluently.

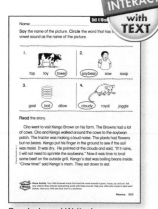

Reader's and Writer's Notebook p. 363

Decode words in context

Use the passage on *Reader's and Writer's Notebook* page 363. Point out that there are many words with diphthongs *ou, ow, oi,* and *oy* in the passage that children already know how to decode. Have children read the passage together.

Corrective feedback

If... children have difficulty decoding words with diphthongs,

then... guide them in chunking multisyllabic words and using sound-by-sound blending. Have children read each sentence. Repeat until children can read the sentences fluently.

Let's Practice It!
TR DVD•229

On their own

Use Let's Practice It! p. 229 on the *Teacher Resource DVD-ROM.*

Spelling
Spelling Diphthongs *ou, ow, oi, oy*

Review
Week 3 spelling words

Write *out, howl, coil,* and *toy.* Point out that *out* and *howl* have the /ou/ sound spelled with *ou* and *ow,* and that *coil* and *toy* have the /oi/ sound spelled with *oi* and *oy.* Remind children that they learned how to spell words with these vowel sounds, which are called diphthongs. Use Sound-Spelling Cards 88, 94, 98, and 100 to review how to spell words with the /ou/ and /oi/ sounds. Review the Week 3 spelling words.

 Have children review the spelling words using the index cards on which the words are written. Tell them to sort the words into the ones they know and the ones they need more practice with. Partners can quiz each other on the words in the second pile.

On their own   Use *Reader's and Writer's Notebook,* p. 364.

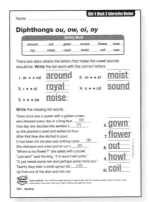

Reader's and Writer's
Notebook p. 364

Unit 4 Week 3 Spelling Words

Diphthongs *ou, ow, oi, oy*

1. around
2. out
3. gown
4. sound
5. flower
6. howl
7. toy
8. noise
9. royal
10. moist
11. coil
12. cow

ELL

English Language Learners

Diphthongs *ou, ow, oi, oy*
Remind children of the sounds spelled with *ou, ow, oi,* and *oy.*

Beginning Have children make flashcards with a spelling word on each card. Have children sort the spelling words into those with the /ou/ sound and those with the /oi/ sound. Tell them to sort again into the four spellings *ou, ow, oi,* or *oy.*

Intermediate Write the spelling words on the board leaving out the vowels *ou, ow, oi,* and *oy.* Have children take turns writing the correct diphthong in each word. Read and spell the words.

Advanced/Advanced-High Write these letters: *b, d, f, gr, l, n, r, pr, s, sh,* and *t.* Have children use the letters to add or replace letters in their spelling words to make new words with the /ou/ or /oi/ sound.

Objectives
- Read lesson vocabulary words.
- Review suffixes.
- Review key features of expository text.
- Preview and predict.
- Establish purpose for reading text.

Lesson Vocabulary

Read words independent of context

Display the lesson vocabulary words. Have children read the words aloud with you. Review the definitions.

> **grains**—tiny bits of sand, sugar, or salt
>
> **materials**—what things are made from or used for
>
> **particles**—very little pieces of something
>
> **seeps**—flows very slowly through something
>
> **substances**—materials that something is made of
>
> **texture**—the feel that things have because of the way they are made

Guide practice

Have children use each word in a sentence.

Corrective feedback

If... children do not use a word correctly,

then... correct the sentence, model a sentence, and have them try again.

On their own

Use *Reader's and Writer's Notebook*, page 365.

Reader's and Writer's Notebook p. 365

Vocabulary Skill
Suffixes

Review Suffixes

Review that a suffix is a word part that is added to the end of a base word, such as the *-ly* in *sweetly,* and the *-ful* in *playful.* Discuss their meanings.

> Write these words:
>
> | | | | |
> |---|---|---|---|
> | **nicely** | **useful** | **quickly** | **thankful** |
> | **graceful** | **bravely** | **playful** | **gladly** |

Have children identify the base word, the suffix, and the meaning of each word.

Guide practice

 Team Talk Have children work together to add a suffix *-ly* or *-ful* that makes sense to these words: *hope, soft, slow,* and *help.*

Comprehension
Skills and Strategies

Review Skill

 Fact and Opinion Review statements of fact and statements of opinion. Remember that when you read, you may find statements of fact and statements of opinion. A statement of fact is a statement that can be proved true or false. A statement of opinion is a statement of someone's judgment, belief, or way of thinking about something. Remind children that they know how to distinguish between the two. Recall that they were able to identify statements of fact and statements of opinion when they read *Soil*.

Review Strategy

Questioning Remind children that good readers ask themselves questions as they read. As you read, you can stop, think, and record questions. Then you can look for answers within the text. You can check your understanding by asking questions to clear up any confusion you may have. It's a good idea to have one or more questions in mind as you read. Then you can find the information and make notes as you read.

Review Genre

Expository Text Remind children that expository text contains facts and information. Expository text is nonfiction writing that gives facts and details. It can describe real people, places, events, or things. Expository text often includes photos, drawings, or other illustrations that give more information about a topic.

Preview and predict

Have children read the title of the selection on p. 366 of *Reader's and Writer's Notebook*. Have children look through the selection and use the title to predict any facts or opinions they think they might find. Tell them this selection is expository text.

Set a purpose

After we read "What Is Air?" we will discuss statements of fact and statements of opinion about air. Have children set a purpose for reading "What Is Air?"

Differentiated Instruction

SI Strategic Intervention

Fact and Opinion Review the definitions of fact and opinion. Have children write statements of fact and statements of opinion on small pieces of paper. Put the papers in a jar or box. Have students take turns picking a statement, identifying the type of statement it is, and telling why they think so.

Academic Vocabulary

expository text text that contains facts and information; also called *informational text*

Objectives
- Review skill: fact and opinion.
- Review strategy: questioning.
- Read aloud fluently with appropriate phrasing.

Unit 4 Week 3 Interactive Review

Name _____

Read the article.
Answer the questions.

What Is Air?

You can't see it or smell it, but you can't live without it. What is it? It's air. Most people don't think about air. What we call air is really a mix of gases. It is mostly nitrogen, but there is oxygen as well. There are very small amounts of other gases. There is also some water vapor.

Air doesn't always stay just the same. Humans breathe in air and use the oxygen in it to help run our bodies. Then we breathe out carbon dioxide. Plants use carbon dioxide and give out oxygen. The amount of water vapor changes from place to place. It also changes with the temperature.

All the air on Earth is called Earth's atmosphere. There is no definite line between our atmosphere and outer space. At about 100 kilometers (62 miles) the atmosphere becomes thinner and fades into space.

Although you can't see air itself, sometimes you can see substances that hang in the air. When the air looks like a white haze, we call it fog. Many people are afraid of fog. Fog is made up of tiny drops of water, and it can be hard to see through. Fog is like a cloud that is close to the ground.

Home Activity Your child identified facts and opinions in an article. Have your child tell his or her opinion of this article.

366 Comprehension

Unit 4 Week 3 Interactive Review

Name _____

When the air looks like a brownish yellow haze, we call it smog. Smog is made up of tiny grains of dust and particles of liquid in the air. It can be caused by air pollution from cars, factories, forest fires, volcanoes, and so on. Then it almost feels as if the air has a texture. Smog can be dangerous to human health. How? People can die from breathing the kinds of material that hang in the air. Smog also damages the leaves of plants.

1. Look at the first paragraph. Write one fact about air.

   Possible response: It is made up of mostly nitrogen.

2. Write one fact about fog.

   Possible response: Fog is made up of tiny drops of water.

3. Write one fact about smog.

   Possible response: Smog is made up of tiny grains of dust and particles of liquid in the air.

4. Underline one opinion stated in the article.
   Possible sentences are underlined.

Comprehension 367

Reader's and Writer's Notebook pp. 366–367

Guide Comprehension
⟲ Review Fact and Opinion

Have children read the selection and respond to the questions.

Corrective feedback

If... children have difficulty responding to the questions,

then... use the following to guide their responses.

1. **Which statements about fog can be proven?** Help children recognize that sentences that tell what fog looks like and what it is made of are facts because they can be proven.

2. **What does air pollution from cars, factories, and other things do to the air?** Have children find the key word *caused* and the sentence that tells about air pollution. Help children recognize that these are facts that can be proven.

3. **Which sentence in the fourth paragraph describes something that cannot be proven?** Have children find the sentence that tells how many people are afraid of the fog.

Comprehension
 Questioning

Review Strategy

Discuss strategies that children used as they read "What Is Air?"

Did you ask yourself questions as you read? Did you look for answers to the questions in the text? Have children identify the questions they asked as they read and tell whether their questions were answered in the selection.

Fluency
Read with Appropriate Phrasing

Model fluent reading

Remind children that when they read, it is important to read words that go together in a sentence in the way we normally speak. Model reading the first paragraph of "What Is Air?" on *Reader's and Writer's Notebook* page 366 with appropriate phrasing. Have children track the print as you read.

Guide practice

To provide additional fluency practice, pair children and have them read "What Is Air?"

ROUTINE Paired Reading   **Team Talk**

1. **Reader 1 Begins** Children read the selection, switching readers at the end of each paragraph.

2. **Reader 2 Begins** Have partners reread; this time the other partner begins.

3. **Reread** For optimal fluency, children should reread three or four times.

4. **Corrective Feedback** Listen to children read and provide corrective feedback regarding their oral reading and their use of the blending strategy.

Routines Flip Chart

Differentiated Instruction

SI Strategic Intervention

Comprehension and Fluency
Have children reread "What Is Air?" in a whisper-level voice. Have them think about the facts and opinions as they read, and raise their hand if they need help with a word. After they have read the selection, have children tell two facts they learned about air.

Options for Oral Rereading

Use *Soil* or one of the Week 3 Leveled Readers.

Objectives
- Identify comparative and super-lative adjectives.
- Form and join cursive letters correctly using correct letter spacing.
- Write for fluency.
- Review concepts.

Conventions
Comparative and Superlative Adjectives

Review
Comparative and superlative adjectives

Review adjectives that compare. Adjectives that compare one thing to another usually end in -er. Adjectives that compare one thing to many others usually end in -est. Some adjectives, such as *beautiful*, do not get an ending added to them to compare. Instead, the words *more* or *most* are placed before them to compare.

Guide practice

Write the following sentences. Have children identify and correct the misused adjectives.

> Kellen is the **most tall** boy in his class. (tallest)
>
> Carmen ran **fastest** than her sister Maria. (faster)
>
> Of all the flowers, the red ones are the **beautifullest**. (most beautiful)
>
> Grandma gave Austin the **goodest** gift of all. (best)

Team Talk In groups of four, have one child choose an adjective. Have the next child form the comparative form of the adjective (-er). Have the next child form the superlative form (-est). Have the last child make a sentence using the adjective in one of the comparative forms.

On their own Use *Reader's and Writer's Notebook*, page 368.

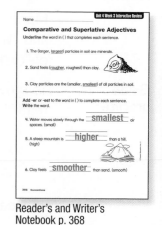

Reader's and Writer's Notebook p. 368

Handwriting
Cursive Letters *k, j, p*/Letter Spacing

Review
Cursive letters

Review the proper formation of letters *k, j,* and *p*. Write each letter. Have children write the letters several times and circle their best one.

Review
Letter spacing

Review letter spacing. Remember that in cursive writing, use good spacing between letters—not too close and not too far apart.

Guide practice

Write the following words. Have children copy them using good letter spacing. Monitor children's spacing of letters as they write.

> jet   help   jeep   kept   jut   put   kelp   pike

On their own Use the Day 3 section on *Reader's and Writer's Notebook,* pages 355–356.

ROUTINE · Quick Write for Fluency

1. **Talk** Have pairs discuss what they learned about changes that occur under the ground.

2. **Write** Have children write a few sentences to summarize the discussion.

3. **Share** Partners can read their summaries to one another.

Routines Flip Chart

Wrap Up Your Day

Question of the Week

What changes occur under the ground?

Review
Concept and Amazing Words

Use these questions to wrap up this review of the Week 3 concept and to provide another opportunity for children to use the week's Amazing Words. Pair or group children to answer the questions. Have children share their responses with the class.

☑ How can a worm help **transform** the soil?

☑ If you dig a hole, what **discovery** might you make?

☑ Does a **blizzard** occur **underneath** the ground?

☑ Through which soil particles does water flow easily— **fine** ones or large ones?

☑ What kinds of animals change the underground **landscape** by digging large burrows?

☑ There are an **incredible** number of organisms that live in soil. How do these organisms change the ground?

☑ How does **molten** magma change the land?

Writing Workshop

Use the writing process lesson on pages CW•11–CW•20 for this week's writing instruction.

ELL

English Language Learners

Extend Amazing Words
Beginning Review the meaning of *incredible*: "hard to believe." Have children use the word *incredible* to describe things. For example, *The dog runs so fast, it is incredible.*

Intermediate Have children think of things they could discover *underneath* the ground. Have them compose sentences orally using the word *underneath* to describe what can be found. Examples: *You can find worms* underneath *the ground. You can find minerals* underneath *the ground.*

Advanced/Advanced-High Discuss the meaning of the word *landscape*. Have children think of different landscapes they have actually seen or seen in pictures. Have them identify a landscape and describe it. Ask questions to encourage more detailed descriptions.

Preview DAY 4

Tell children that tomorrow they will review more skills and read "The Monster in the Maze."

Objectives
- Review Week 4 concepts.
- Share information and ideas about the concept.
- Review Week 4 oral vocabulary.

Today at a Glance

Oral Vocabulary
adjust, landmark, unexpected, quiver, tease, foreign, accent, forlorn

Phonics and Spelling
◉ Review Syllable Patterns

Lesson Vocabulary
balance, canyons, coral, rattle, slivers, sway, whisper

Vocabulary
Skill: Multiple-Meaning Words

Comprehension
◉ Review Skill: Plot and Theme
◉ Review Strategy: Visualize

Fluency
Skill: Read with Expression
(Characterization)

Conventions
Adverbs That Tell When and Where

Handwriting
Cursive Letters/Word Spacing

Writing
Quick Write for Fluency

Concept Talk

Question of the Week

Why are some changes difficult?

Review Week 4 selection

Today children will explore how the Question of the Week connects to *The Night the Moon Fell*. Read the Question of the Week above. Remind children that *The Night the Moon Fell* is a myth about the moon and the stars and how the moon fell from the sky to the bottom of the ocean.

ROUTINE **Activate Prior Knowledge** **Team Talk**

1. **Think** Have children think about a difficult change they have experienced.

2. **Pair** Have pairs of children discuss how the Question of the Week applies to Luna, the moon, in *The Night the Moon Fell*.

3. **Share** Call on a few children to share their ideas with the group. Guide discussion and encourage elaboration with prompts such as:
   What happened to Luna when she fell?
   Who helped Luna during her difficult change?

Routines Flip Chart

Connect to the Big Question

Use these questions to connect the Week 4 question and selection to the Unit 4 Big Question, **How do things change? How do they stay the same?**

- What big change happened to Luna when she fell from the sky?
- What did Luna have to do to make things change?
- Who did Luna learn she had to depend on to make a difficult change in her situation?

ELL **Reteach Concepts and Vocabulary** Use the instruction on ELL Poster 19 to assess knowledge and concepts.

ELL Poster 19

Oral Vocabulary
Amazing Words

Amazing Words

Review
Week 4
Amazing
Words

Remind children that they have learned some Amazing Words that they can use to answer the question *Why are some changes difficult?* Display "We Are Moving" on page 19 of the *Sing with Me* Big Book. Sing the song.

 Sing with Me Big Book Audio

Go over all the Amazing Words from Week 4. Ask children to listen as you say them: *adjust, landmark, unexpected, quiver, tease, foreign, accent, forlorn.* Then say them again, and have children say each word after you.

• Who might look *forlorn* — a girl who's lost her puppy or a boy who's won the spelling bee? (a girl who's lost her puppy)

• Name a famous *landmark*. (Answers will vary.)

• Show me what it looks like to *quiver*.

Apply
Amazing
Words

Have children demonstrate their understanding of Amazing Words by completing these sentences orally.

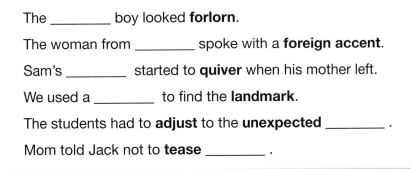

The _____ boy looked **forlorn**.

The woman from _____ spoke with a **foreign accent**.

Sam's _____ started to **quiver** when his mother left.

We used a _____ to find the **landmark**.

The students had to **adjust** to the **unexpected** _____ .

Mom told Jack not to **tease** _____ .

Amazing Words

adjust	tease
landmark	foreign
unexpected	accent
quiver	forlorn

Differentiated Instruction

SI Strategic Intervention

Ask and Answer Ask students to respond to the following questions or statements to improve their understanding of the Amazing Words:

• *What are things you can adjust?*

• *Is a flower a landmark? Is a lighthouse a landmark?*

• *What would you call visitors that you did not know were coming to your house?*

• *If a puppy quivers, what is it doing?*

• *If you tease someone, does it make them feel good?*

• *Name a foreign country.*

• *What accents have you heard?*

• *Can a computer be forlorn? Can a child be forlorn?*

Writing on Demand

Develop Writing Fluency
Ask children to write about a time when they experienced a difficult change and who helped them through the change. Have them write for two to three minutes. Children should write as much as they can. Tell them to try to do their best writing. You may want to discuss what children wrote during writing conferences.

Objectives

- Read multisyllabic words with closed syllable patterns (CVC), and open syllable patterns (CV), including compound words containing diphthongs and vowel digraphs.

- Spell multisyllabic words with closed syllable patterns (CVC), and open syllable patterns (CV), including compound words containing diphthongs and vowel digraphs.

Phonics

Syllable Patterns

Review Phonics skill

Review syllable patterns using Sound-Spelling Cards 108, 117, 147, and 149.

compound word
Sound-Spelling Card 108

digraphs and diphthongs
Sound-Spelling Card 117

VC/CV bas/ket
Sound-Spelling Card 147

V/CV ti/ger
Sound-Spelling Card 149

Decode words independent of context

Use *Reader's and Writer's Notebook* page 369. Point out that children know how to read these words. Then tell children they will all read the words in each row together. Allow several seconds previewing time for the first reading.

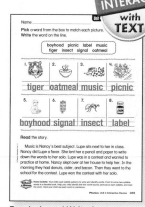

INTERACT with TEXT

Reader's and Writer's Notebook p. 369

Corrective feedback

If... children cannot decode all the words in a row consecutively without an error,
then... return to the first word in the row, and have children reread all the words in the row. Repeat until children can read the words fluently.

Decode words in context

Use the passage on *Reader's and Writer's Notebook* page 369. Point out that there are many words with syllable patterns in the passage that children already know how to decode. Have children read the passage together.

Corrective feedback

If... children have difficulty decoding words with syllable patterns,
then... guide them in chunking multisyllabic words and using sound-by-sound blending. Have children read each sentence. Repeat until children can read the sentences fluently.

Let's Practice It!
TR DVD•230

On their own   Use Let's Practice It! p. 230 on the *Teacher Resource DVD-ROM*.

Spelling
Syllable Patterns

Review
Week 4 spelling words

Write *railroad, cowboy, and soybean*. Point out that these words are compound words that have vowel digraphs and diphthongs. Remind children that they learned how to spell words with these vowel patterns. Use Sound-Spelling Cards 108 and 117 to review how to spell words with these syllable patterns. Review the Week 4 spelling words.

Team Talk Have children review the spelling words using index cards on which the words are written. Tell them to sort the words into the ones they know and the ones they need more practice with. Partners can quiz each other on the words in the second pile.

On their own Use *Reader's and Writer's Notebook,* p. 370.

Reader's and Writer's
Notebook p. 370

Unit 4 Week 4 Spelling Words
Syllable Patterns

1. downstairs
2. football
3. cowboy
4. houseboat
5. railroad
6. rainbow
7. boyhood
8. oatmeal
9. soybean
10. roadway
11. outplay
12. daydream

ELL

English Language Learners
Syllable Patterns
Beginning Have children draw pictures of the following: *foot, ball, cow, boy, house, boat, rain, bow*. Have them put the pictures together to form compound words. Write the words.

Intermediate Write the spelling words. Have children draw a line between the two words that make up each compound word. Then have them identify the diphthongs or vowel digraphs in the words.

Advanced/Advanced-High Have children combine small words to form new compound words. Write these words in one column: *down, sea, cow, bed, rain, sail, down, play*. Write these words in another column: *room, spout, girl, load, ground, coat, coast, boat. (downspout, seacoast, cowgirl, bedroom, raincoat, sailboat, download, playground)*

Objectives
- Read lesson vocabulary words.
- Review multiple-meaning words.
- Review key features of a myth.
- Preview and predict.
- Establish purpose for reading text.

Lesson Vocabulary

Read words independent of context

Display the lesson vocabulary words. Have children read the words aloud with you. Review the definitions.

> **balance**—footing; even placement of weight that lets someone stand upright
>
> **canyons**—deep valleys with steep sides
>
> **coral**—an underwater stony substance made by marine life
>
> **rattle**—make sharp knocking sounds as a result of being shaken
>
> **slivers**—small thin pieces of something that have been split off
>
> **sway**—move back and forth or side to side
>
> **whisper**—make a soft sound

Guide practice

Have children use each word in a sentence.

Corrective feedback

If… children do not use a word correctly, **then…** correct the sentence, model a sentence, and have them try again.

On their own

Use *Reader's and Writer's Notebook*, page 371.

Reader's and Writer's Notebook p. 371

Vocabulary Skill
Multiple-Meaning Words

Review
Multiple-meaning words

Review that some words have two or more different meanings. They are called multiple-meaning words. Ask what the word *well* means in each of the following sentences.

- After being sick for two days, I am now feeling *well*. (satisfactory)
- People on a farm may get water from a *well*. (hole dug for water)

Have children give two meanings and sentences for the words *bark* and *fly*.

Guide practice

Team Talk Have children work together to come up with two different meanings and two sentences for the words *pound* and *left*. They may use a dictionary, if needed.

Comprehension
Skills and Strategies

Review
Skill

 Plot and Theme Review plot and theme with children. Remember that the plot of a story is what happens in the beginning, middle, and end. The theme is the message or the big idea of the story. Remind children that they can figure out a story's theme by thinking about the events that make up the plot. Recall that they discussed plot and theme when they read *The Night the Moon Fell.*

Review
Strategy

 Visualize Remind children that good readers visualize as they read. As you read, you can visualize something, or picture it in your mind. Paying attention to how something is described can help you imagine it and understand what you read. You can picture what a character or setting looks like or what is happening in a story.

Review
Genre

Myth Remind children that a myth is a story that attempts to explain something in nature. Myths are stories that have been handed down by word of mouth from one generation to the next in many cultures. The stories sometimes explain how things came to be.

Preview and predict

Have children read the title of the selection on p. 372 of *Reader's and Writer's Notebook.* Have children look through the selection and use the title to predict what the plot and theme may be. Tell them this selection is a myth.

Set a purpose

After we read "The Monster in the Maze," we will discuss the plot and theme of change. Have children set a purpose for reading "The Monster in the Maze."

Differentiated Instruction

A **Advanced**

Plot and Theme Have children recall other stories they have read on their own. Tell them to share the plot and theme of the story with the group.

Academic Vocabulary

myth a story that attempts to explain something in nature

Objectives
- Review skill: plot and theme.
- Review strategy: visualize.
- Read aloud fluently with expression.

Unit 4 Week 4 Interactive Review

Name _____

Read the text. **Follow** the directions and **answer** the questions.

The Monster in the Maze
An Ancient Greek Myth

There once was a king who was mean to the people he ruled. All the people in the kingdom were afraid of the king. And they were afraid of something else, too. The king had a terrible monster. The people thought they had to obey the king, or he would send the monster after them.

The monster was VERY SCARY! It had a huge head with horns like a bull and a strong body like a man's body. This creature was called a minotaur, and the king kept it trapped in the middle of a maze.

One day, a Greek hero named Theseus came to help the people of this kingdom. He declared he would go into the maze and fight the minotaur. The king's daughter, a kind young maiden, heard this news. She called Theseus to meet with her. When Theseus came, she gave him a ball of string.

"You will get lost in the maze," she said. "Take this ball of string and unwind it behind you. Then you can follow the string to find your way out."

Theseus thanked the king's daughter and accepted the ball of string. Then brave Theseus headed for the maze. He entered the maze, unafraid of what might happen. He was determined to set the people free from the mean king.

Inside the maze, Theseus walked up one path and down another. But no path led him to the minotaur. Each path he took

Home Activity Your child identified the plot and theme—the big idea—of a story. Read a short fiction story with your child. Discuss the theme of the story and the events that happened.

372 **Comprehension**

Name _____

ended at a wall. Theseus twisted his way through the maze for a long time, unwinding the ball of string behind him as he went.

Suddenly, Theseus heard stomping and a tremendous roar. He had found his way to the middle of the maze. And now he was face-to-face with the frightening minotaur!

1. Underline the sentence that tells the big idea of the story.

   A king can be mean to people.
   A hero helps people in trouble.
   Monsters are scary creatures.

2. How did the king make sure the people would obey him?

   The king kept a monster that the people were afraid of.

3. What happened when Theseus went to see the king's daughter?

   She gave him a ball of string to help him find his way out of the maze.

4. Why did it take a long time for Theseus to find the minotaur?

   For a long time, Theseus kept taking paths that led to walls.

5. What do you think happened at the end of the story?

   Possible answers: Theseus killed the minotaur. The people cheered Theseus.

Comprehension 373

Reader's and Writer's Notebook pp. 372–373

Guide Comprehension
Review Plot and Theme

Have children read the myth and respond to the questions.

Corrective feedback

If... children have difficulty responding to the questions,

then... use the following to guide their responses.

1. Why did Theseus declare he would fight the minotaur? Have children find the sentence that tells Theseus's reason for fighting the minotaur.

2. Why did the king's daughter give Theseus a ball of string? How would that help him? Help children find the sentence that tells the daughter's reason.

3. What happened when Theseus entered the maze? Did Theseus find the minotaur right away? Explain. Have children find the sentences that tell that Theseus kept taking paths that led to walls.

Comprehension
 Visualize

Review **Strategy**

Discuss strategies that children used as they read "The Monster in the Maze."

Did you try to picture the story events in your mind as you read? How did forming pictures in your mind help you understand the story? Have children describe the sensory images they formed in their minds. Discuss how these images helped them understand the plot.

Fluency
Read with Expression

Model fluent reading

Remind children that when they read, it is important to read the words a character says in the way that character would say them. Explain that when we read with expression, the character and the story come alive. Model reading the third paragraph of "The Monster in the Maze" on *Reader's and Writer's Notebook* page 372 with expression. Have children track the print as you read.

Guide practice

To provide additional fluency practice, pair children and have them read "The Monster in the Maze."

ROUTINE **Paired Reading** [Team Talk]

1. **Reader 1 Begins** Children read the story, switching readers at the end of each paragraph.

2. **Reader 2 Begins** Have partners reread; this time the other partner begins.

3. **Reread** For optimal fluency, children should reread three or four times.

4. **Corrective Feedback** Listen to children read and provide corrective feedback regarding their oral reading and their use of the blending strategy.

Routines Flip Chart

Differentiated Instruction

SI Strategic Intervention

Comprehension and Fluency
Have children reread "The Monster in the Maze" aloud with expression. Have them think about what Theseus is like as they read what he does. After children have read the story, have them tell what happened in the beginning, in the middle, and at the end of the story.

Options for Oral Rereading

Use *The Night the Moon Fell* or one of the Week 4 Leveled Readers.

Objectives

- Identify adverbs that tell when and where.
- Form and join cursive letters correctly using correct word spacing.
- Write for fluency.
- Review concepts.

Conventions
Adverbs That Tell When and Where

Review
Adverbs that tell when and where

Review adverbs that tell when and where. An adverb tells more about a verb. Some adverbs tell where an action happened. Some tell when. An adverb that tells when must match the form of the verb. For example, you wouldn't say *I went to the store tomorrow.* You would say *I went to the store yesterday* or *I will go to the store tomorrow.*

Guide practice

Write the following sentences. Have children identify the adverb and the verb to which it refers.

> Carlos and Deontay **arrived late** to school.
>
> We will **leave** to go shopping **soon**.
>
> Sabrina **ate** her lunch **outside**.
>
> **First**, I **ate** toast. **Then**, I **drank** my milk.

Team Talk In pairs, have one child choose an adverb and the other child make a sentence using the adverb correctly. Then they can reverse roles.

On their own

Use *Reader's and Writer's Notebook*, page 374.

Reader's and Writer's Notebook p. 374

Handwriting
Cursive Letters *a, d, c*/ Word Spacing

Review
Cursive letters

Review the proper formation of letters *a*, *d*, and *c*. Write each letter. Have children write the letters several times and circle their best one.

Review
Word spacing

Review word spacing. Remember in cursive writing to put the proper space between words.

Guide practice

Write the following phrases. Have children copy them using good word spacing. Monitor children's spacing of words as they write.

> **chip dip**   **take a hike**   **pet duck**   **pack the cake**   **aid the cat**

On their own

Use the Day 4 section on *Reader's and Writer's Notebook*, pages 355–356.

ROUTINE Quick Write for Fluency

1. **Talk** Have pairs discuss what they learned about why some changes are difficult.

2. **Write** Have children write a few sentences to summarize the discussion.

3. **Share** Partners can read their summaries to one another.

Routines Flip Chart

Wrap Up Your Day

Question of the Week
Why are some changes difficult?

Review
Concept and Amazing Words

Use these questions to wrap up this review of the Week 4 concept and to provide another opportunity for children to use the week's Amazing Words. Pair or group children to answer the questions. Have children share their responses with the rest of the class.

☑ What are some things you can do to **adjust** to changes in your life?

☑ How would you feel if you moved to a new school and the students there began to **tease** you?

☑ Why might it be difficult to see a **landmark** building damaged by a tornado?

☑ What is an **unexpected** event that might be difficult to deal with?

☑ What is a change that might make someone **quiver** with fear?

☑ Why might a boy who speaks with a **foreign accent** have a difficult time when he first moves to the United States?

☑ What kind of changes might make a person feel **forlorn**?

Writing Workshop

Use the writing process lesson on pages CW•11–CW•20 for this week's writing instruction.

English Language Learners

Extend Amazing Words
Beginning Review the meaning of *unexpected.* Have children give examples of unexpected events. Give children support by asking questions like these: *What might be unexpected about the weather? What might be unexpected at school? What might be unexpected on a trip?*

Intermediate Pair English learners with native English speakers. Have the English speakers say one of the Amazing Words and use it in a sentence. Then have the English learner repeat the word and the sentence for practice.

Advanced/Advanced-High Ask children to expand on their understanding of a few of the Amazing Words. Give two or three children one word at a time. Have them discuss the word and use it in sentences or ask others questions using the word.

Preview DAY 5

Tell children that tomorrow they will review more skills and read "A Tale of Tails."

Objectives
• Review Week 5 concepts.
• Share information and ideas about the concept.
• Review Week 5 oral vocabulary.

Today at a Glance

Oral Vocabulary
condition, predict, terrifying, breeze, whip, sparkle, funnel, swirl

Phonics and Spelling
◉ Review Vowel Digraphs *oo, ue, ew, ui*

Lesson Vocabulary
awaken, cliffs, mountain, prize, rainbow, suffer, volcano

Vocabulary
Skill: Prefixes

Comprehension
◉ Review Skill: Plot and Theme
◉ Review Strategy: Monitor and Clarify

Fluency
Skill: Read with Expression and Intonation

Conventions
Adverbs That Tell How

Handwriting
Cursive Letters/Letter Size

Writing
Quick Write for Fluency

Concept Talk

Question of the Week
How do changes in the weather affect us?

Review Week 5 selection

Today children will explore how the Question of the Week connects to *The First Tortilla.* Read the Question of the Week above. Remind children that *The First Tortilla* is a legend about the first tortilla ever made.

ROUTINE   Activate Prior Knowledge   Team Talk

1. **Think** Have children think about how changes in the weather affect what they wear and what they do.

2. **Pair** Have pairs of children discuss how the Question of the Week applies to Jade and her people in *The First Tortilla.*

3. **Share** Call on a few children to share their ideas with the group. Guide discussion and encourage elaboration with prompts such as:
   How did the dry weather change the squash and bean plants?
   When the weather changed and rain came, how did that affect the squash, beans, and corn?

Routines Flip Chart

Connect to the Big Question

Use these questions to connect the Week 5 question and selection to the Unit 4 Big Question, **How do things change? How do they stay the same?**

• How did Jade use the gift of corn from the Mountain Spirit?

• After the rain came, how did it help the village to stay the same?

• When has changes in the weather affected your life and what did you do?

ELL **Reteach Concepts and Vocabulary** Use the instruction on ELL Poster 20 to assess knowledge and concepts.

ELL Poster 20

Oral Vocabulary
Amazing Words

Review
Week 5
Amazing
Words

Remind children that they have learned some Amazing Words that they can use to answer the question *How do changes in the weather affect us?* Display "Changing Conditions" on page 20 of the *Sing with Me Big* Book. Sing the song.

 Sing with Me Big Book Audio

Changing Conditions

Weather here is so strange.
Every new day brings a change.
Yesterday we had
A terrifying storm.
Now today it's nice and warm.

Weather's hard to predict.
Even forecasters get tricked.
No condition ever
Stays the same for long.
Some days everyone is wrong.

Sing with Me Big Book

Go over all the Amazing Words from Week 5. Ask children to listen as you say them: *condition, predict, terrifying, breeze, whip, sparkle, funnel, swirl.* Then say them again, and have children say each word after you.

- How would you describe the wind of a tornado—a *swirl or a breeze?* (a swirl)

- Name some things that *sparkle.* (stars, glitter, diamonds, sun on water.)

- What word means "really, really scary"? (terrifying)

Apply
Amazing
Words

Have children demonstrate their understanding of Amazing Words by completing these sentences orally.

> The _____ was **terrifying.**
>
> The **funnel** _____ was headed for the small town.
>
> _____ try to predict the **weather conditions** each day.
>
> Rosa thought the **breeze** felt _____ .
>
> Paul likes to **swirl** _____ together.
>
> The wind was so strong it could **whip** up a _____.
>
> The **sparkle** from her _____ caught my eye.

Amazing Words

condition	whip
predict	sparkle
terrifying	funnel
breeze	swirl

Differentiated Instruction

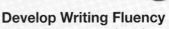 **SI** **Strategic Intervention**

Expand Meanings Expand the meanings of some of the Amazing Words. Show children a *funnel* used for pouring liquids into a jar. Discuss how this tool is similar to the *funnel* cloud of a tornado. Talk about things you can *swirl*: ice cream, paint, and frosting on a cupcake. Discuss how the word *breeze* can mean a soft wind, or it can mean something that was easy: *The math test was a breeze.*

Writing on Demand

Develop Writing Fluency
Ask children to write about a time when the weather affected their lives. Have them write for two to three minutes. Children should write as much as they can. Tell them to try to do their best writing. You may want to discuss what children wrote during writing conferences.

Objectives
- Read multisyllabic words with vowel digraphs *oo, ue, ew,* and *ui.*
- Spell multisyllabic words with vowel digraphs *oo, ue, ew,* and *ui.*

Phonics
Vowel Digraphs *oo, ue, ew, ui*

Review
Phonics skill

Review vowel digraphs *oo, ue, ew,* and *ui* using Sound-Spelling Cards 68, 90, 102, and 103.

Sound-Spelling
Card 68

Sound-Spelling
Card 90

Sound-Spelling
Card 102

Sound-Spelling
Card 103

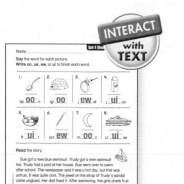

Reader's and Writer's
Notebook p. 375

Decode words independent of context

Have children complete the top half of *Reader's and Writer's Notebook* page 375 and review the answers as a group. Point out that children know how to decode these words. Then tell children they will all read the words in each row together. Allow several seconds previewing time for the first reading.

Corrective feedback

If... children cannot decode all the words in a row consecutively without an error,
then... return to the first word in the row, and have children reread all the words in the row. Repeat until children can read the words fluently.

Decode words in context

Use the passage on *Reader's and Writer's Notebook* page 375. Point out that there are many words with vowel digraphs *oo, ue, ew,* and *ui* in the passage that children already know how to decode. Have children read the passage together.

Corrective feedback

If... children have difficulty decoding words with vowel digraphs *oo, ue, ew,* and *ui,*
then... guide them in chunking multisyllabic words and using sound-by-sound blending. Have children read each sentence. Repeat until children can read the sentences fluently.

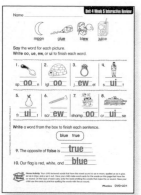

Let's Practice It!
TR DVD•231

On their own

Use Let's Practice It! p. 231 on the *Teacher Resource DVD-ROM.*

Spelling
Vowel Digraphs *oo, ue, ew, ui*

Review
Week 5 spelling words

Write *foot, clue, drew,* and *suit.* Point out that these words all have a vowel digraph spelled with *oo, ue, ew,* and *ui* and have the /ü/ sound. Remind children that they learned how to spell words with these vowel patterns. Use Sound-Spelling Cards 68, 90, 102, and 103 to review how to spell words with the /ü/ sound. Review the Week 5 spelling words.

Team Talk Have children review the spelling words using index cards on which the words are written. Tell them to sort the words into the ones they know and the ones they need more practice with. Partners can quiz each other on the words in the second pile.

On their own Use *Reader's and Writer's Notebook,* p. 376.

Reader's and Writer's
Notebook p. 376

Unit 4 Week 5 Spelling Words

Vowel Digraphs *oo, ue, ew, ui*

1. too	7. suit
2. new	8. spoon
3. fruit	9. clue
4. blue	10. juice
5. true	11. drew
6. fool	12. flew

English Language Learners
Review Vowel Digraphs *oo, ue, ew,* and *ui* Remind children the /ü/ sound can be spelled with *oo, ue, ew,* and *ui*.

Beginning Write the spelling words on the board. Have children circle the vowel digraph in each word, read the word, and then spell the word.

Intermediate Have children sort the words according to the letters that make the vowel digraph. Have pairs of children compare lists with a partner and read the words to each other.

Advanced/Advanced-High Have children find other words with the vowel digraphs *oo, ue, ew,* and *ui* that make the /ü/ sound. Have them write each word on a card. Partners can read their words to each other and then quiz each other on the spelling of the words.

Objectives
- Read lesson vocabulary words.
- Review prefixes.
- Review key features of a legend.
- Preview and predict.
- Establish purpose for reading text.

Lesson Vocabulary

Read words independent of context

Display the lesson vocabulary words. Have children read the words aloud with you. Review the definitions.

> **awaken**—cause to stop sleeping
>
> **cliffs**—steep rock faces, like those at the edge of the sea
>
> **mountain**—a high, steep hill that is often rocky
>
> **prize**—something given to someone as a reward
>
> **rainbow**—a display of many colors
>
> **suffer**—to experience something bad or unpleasant
>
> **volcano**—a cone-shaped mountain with a hole in the top that sends out melted rock and gases

Guide practice

Have children use each word in a sentence.

Corrective feedback

If... children do not use a word correctly, **then...** correct the sentence, model a sentence, and have them try again.

On their own

Use *Reader's and Writer's Notebook*, page 377.

Reader's and Writer's Notebook p. 377

Vocabulary Skill
Prefixes

Review
Prefixes

Review that a prefix is a word part that is added to the beginning of a base word, such as *un-* in *untie, re-* in *replay,* and *dis-* in *dislike.* Discuss the meanings of the prefixes and the words. Write these words:

reprint	**unlock**	**disallow**	**rename**
unfold	**disloyal**	**recount**	**unwise**

Have children identify the base word, prefix, and meaning of each word.

Guide practice

Team Talk Have children work together to add a prefix *un-, re-,* or *dis-* that makes sense to these words: *plug, trust, join, broken,* and *fill.* Tell them to discuss the meanings of the words with the prefixes.

Comprehension
Skills and Strategies

Review Skill

 Plot and Theme Review plot and theme with children. Remember that the plot of a story is what happens in the beginning, middle, and end. The theme is the message or the big idea of the story. Remind children that they can figure out a story's theme by thinking about the events that make up the plot. Recall that they discussed plot and theme when they read *The First Tortilla*.

Review Strategy

Monitor and Clarify Remind children that good readers know that reading has to make sense. You need to be aware if the text doesn't make sense and there is something you do not understand. First, decide what to do that will help you better understand what you read. One thing you can do is to ask some questions. Then you can reread the part of the text to find the answers and identify clues to answer the questions.

Review Genre

Legend Remind children that a legend is a story coming down from the past about the great deeds of a hero. Although a legend may be based on a real person and events, it is not thought of as true.

Preview and predict

Have children read the title of the selection on p. 378 of *Reader's and Writer's Notebook.* Have children look through the selection and use the title to predict what the plot and theme may be. Tell them this selection is a legend.

Set a purpose

After we read "A Tale of Tails," we will discuss the plot and theme of the legend. Have children set a purpose for reading "A Tale of Tails."

Differentiated Instruction

SI Strategic Intervention

Plot and Theme Go through the story *The First Tortilla* and ask questions about the plot: *What happened first? What happened in the middle of the story? What happened at the end?* Then ask about theme: *What is the big idea of this story?* Give students choices of themes: *Plants die if they don't have rain. Talking to the Mountain Spirit is scary. Corn is good to plant. Sometimes you need to do something brave to make a change.* Discuss why the last choice is the big idea, or theme.

Academic Vocabulary

legend a story coming down from the past about the great deeds of a hero. Although a legend may be based on historical people and events, it is not regarded as historically true.

Objectives

- Review skill: plot and theme.
- Review strategy: monitor and clarify.
- Read aloud fluently with expression and intonation.

Name _____

Unit 4 Week 5 Interactive Review

Read the legend. **Follow** the directions and **answer** the questions.

A Tale of Tails
A Native American Legend

Opossum had always thought Raccoon had a very fine tail. Although she had a furry tail like Raccoon's tail, she admired the beautiful black rings around Raccoon's tail. Opossum wanted a tail just like it.

One night when Opossum was searching for food, she spied Raccoon by a brook, having a meal of nuts, fruit, and plants. Although she was usually a shy animal, Opossum went right up to Raccoon.

"Hello, Raccoon," she said. "Nice night, isn't it?"

"Yes, it is," Raccoon replied. "I'm having good luck finding delicious things to eat."

Opossum went on to say, "I think you have a magnificent tail, Raccoon. How did you get such lovely black rings around it?"

Raccoon smiled and answered, "Well, I'd be happy to tell you, Opossum. I went looking for some long, narrow strips of bark. After I found ones that were just the right size, I wrapped them around my tail."

"Now I know," Opossum exclaimed. "The bark left black marks in rings around your tail, didn't it?"

"You didn't let me finish," Raccoon said. "The next thing I did was make a fire. Then I stuck my tail right into that fire. Soon all the fur between the strips of bark burned and turned black. I peeled off the bark and the black fur had become black rings."

Home Activity Your child read a story and identified the plot and theme of the story. Read a short fiction story with your child. After reading, have your child tell you what happened at the beginning, in the middle, and at the end of the story.

378 **Comprehension** Plot and Theme

Name _____

Unit 4 Week 5 Interactive Review

"That's what I'll do, too." Opossum thought to herself.

Opossum thanked Raccoon for the information and scurried off to gather some long, narrow strips of bark. Opossum carried the bark home and then carefully wrapped the strips around her furry tail.

Opossum made a fire and then stuck her tail into the flames. But she had made the fire too hot! The fire burned every inch of fur off her tail! For days and days, she waited and waited and waited for the fur to grow back. The fur never grew back.

1. **Underline** the sentence that tells the theme of the story.

<u>Why the opossum has a tail without fur.</u>
Why the raccoon has a furry tail.
How fire can hurt animals.

2. **Write** the sentence from the story that gives a clue to the story's theme.

The fur never grew back.

3. What does Opossum do at the beginning of the story?

Opossum asks Raccoon how to get rings on her tail.

4. What happens after Opossum and Raccoon talk to each other?

Opossum wraps her tail with bark and puts it into a fire.

5. What event takes place at the end of the story?

The fire burns all the fur off Opossum's tail.

Comprehension 379

Reader's and Writer's Notebook pp. 378–379

Guide Comprehension
 Review Plot and Theme

Have children read the story and respond to the questions.

Corrective feedback

If... children have difficulty responding to the questions,

then... use the following to guide their responses.

1. What did Opossum's tail look like in the beginning of the legend? Help children find the sentence that tells about Opossum's tail in the beginning of the legend.

2. Why did Opossum approach Raccoon? What did Opossum want to ask Raccoon? Help children find the sentences that tell about Opossum's admiration for Raccoon's tail.

3. What did Raccoon tell Opossum? Have children find the dialogue between Raccoon and Opossum and how Raccoon responds to Opossum.

4. What moral or big idea do you think the author was trying to teach? Possible response: You should be thankful for what you have and not be jealous of others.

 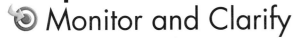
Comprehension
Monitor and Clarify

Review Strategy

Discuss strategies that children used as they read "A Tale of Tails."

Did you ask yourself questions as you read? Did you find the answers to your questions in the story? Have children tell what questions they asked as they read, and whether their questions were answered in the story.

Fluency
Read with Expression and Intonation

Model fluent reading

Remind children that when they read, it is important to read with expression and intonation. Explain that reading with expression is using their voice to express feeling, and that they should match the tone of their voice to the mood of the selection. Model reading the first paragraph of "A Tale of Tails" on *Reader's and Writer's Notebook* page 378 with expression and proper intonation. Have children track the print as you read.

Guide practice

To provide additional fluency practice, pair children and have them read "A Tale of Tails."

ROUTINE **Paired Reading** **Team Talk**

1. **Reader 1 Begins** Children read the story, switching readers at the end of each paragraph.
2. **Reader 2 Begins** Have partners reread; this time the other partner begins.
3. **Reread** For optimal fluency, children should reread three or four times.
4. **Corrective Feedback** Listen to children read and provide corrective feedback regarding their oral reading and their use of the blending strategy.

Routines Flip Chart

Differentiated Instruction

SI Strategic Intervention

Comprehension and Fluency Have children reread "A Tale of Tails" aloud with expression and intonation. Have them think about the story events as they read. After they have read the story, have them tell which part is their favorite.

Options for Oral Rereading

Use *The First Tortilla* or one of the Week 5 Leveled Readers.

DAY 5 UNIT 4 • WEEK 5 — **Interactive Review** 30–35 min.

Objectives
- Identify adverbs that tell how.
- Form and join cursive letters correctly using letter size.
- Write for fluency.

Conventions
Adverbs That Tell How

Review
Adverbs that tell how

Review adverbs that tell how. Adverbs can tell when and where something happened. Adverbs can also tell how something happened. These kinds of adverbs often end in -ly.

Guide practice

Write the following sentences. Ask children to supply adverbs that tell how to fill in each blank.

> Hope walked _____ on the rocky shore.
>
> Sam rode his bike _____ down the street.
>
> Mr. Whatley talked _____ to us.
>
> The bird sang _____ from its perch.

Team Talk Divide the class into small groups. Provide each group with a picture from a children's magazine. Have children work together to make sentences with adverbs about the picture. Have groups share their sentences with the class.

On their own Use *Reader's and Writer's Notebook*, page 380.

Reader's and Writer's Notebook p. 380

Handwriting
Cursive Letters *n, m, x*/Letter Size

Review
Cursive letters

Review the proper formation of letters *n, m,* and *x*. Write each letter. Have children write the letters several times and circle their best one.

Review
Letter size

Review letter size. Remember that in cursive writing, letters are different sizes. Make sure to use the correct letter size as you write.

Guide practice

Write the following phrases. Have children copy them using proper letter size. Monitor children's letter size as they write.

> **cake mix**   **next time**   **in the den**   **plum jam**   **ax handle**

On their own Use the Day 5 section on *Reader's and Writer's Notebook,* pages 355–356.

ROUTINE **Quick Write for Fluency**

1) **Talk** Have pairs discuss what they learned about how changes in the weather affect people.

2) **Write** Have children write a few sentences to summarize the discussion.

3) **Share** Partners can read their summaries to one another.

Routines Flip Chart

Wrap Up Your Day

Question of the Week

 ## How do changes in the weather affect us?

Review
Concept and Amazing Words

Use these questions to wrap up this review of the Week 5 concept and to provide another opportunity for children to use the week's Amazing Words. Pair or group children to answer the questions. Have children share their responses with the class.

☑ What is a **terrifying** weather **condition** that is dangerous to both people and animals?

☑ If the sun seemed to **sparkle** on the water and there was no wind, what might you want to do outdoors?

☑ What weather event might you **predict** if clouds begin to **swirl** quickly?

☑ How might a light **breeze** affect you if you are playing outside on a hot day?

☑ What do people who are outside usually do when the wind begins to **whip?**

☑ What are some things you should do if you see a **funnel** cloud?

Writing Workshop

Use the writing process lesson on pages CW•11–CW•20 for this week's writing instruction.

English Language Learners
Visual Learning: Poster Preview Prepare children for next week by using Unit 5 Week 1, ELL Poster 21. Read the Poster Talk-Through to introduce the concept and vocabulary. Ask children to identify and describe objects and actions in the art.

Selection Summary Send home the summary of *Fire Fighter!* in English and the child's home language if available. Children can read the summary with family members.

Preview NEXT WEEK

Tell children that next week they will explore the concept of Responsibility and read about firefighters.

Unit Wrap-Up

The Big Question

How do things change? How do they stay the same?

Understanding By Design

Grant Wiggins, Ed.D
Reading Street Author

"Good questions elicit interesting and alternative views and suggest the need to focus on the reasoning we use in arriving at and defending an answer . . . They cause us to rethink what we thought we understood and to transfer an idea from one setting to others."

WEEK 1

Question of the Week
 How can familiar things help us with changes?

Concept Knowledge

Children will understand that change:

• can be difficult

• can be a bit scary

• can be comforting

WEEK 2

Question of the Week
How do plants change over time?

Concept Knowledge

Children will understand that plants:

• have a growth cycle

• need sun, rain, and nutrients

• provide food and beauty

Discuss the Big Question

Help children relate the concept question for this unit to the selections and their own experiences. Write the question and prompt discussion with questions such as the following.

How do the selections show how things change or stay the same?

• *A Froggy Fable* A frog faces change, even though he wants things to stay the same.

• *Life Cycle of a Pumpkin* A pumpkin goes through great changes from seed to plant and fruit.

• *Soil* Many changes occur in the soil and particles under the ground.

• *The Night the Moon Fell* The moon faces great change when it falls into the sea.

• *The First Tortilla* Rain leads to an abundance of corn and the first tortilla.

 Question of the Week
What changes occur under the ground?

 Question of the Week
Why are some changes difficult?

 Question of the Week
How do changes in the weather affect us?

Concept Knowledge

Children will understand:

- the different kinds of soil

- how kinds of soil are formed

- the interrelationship of plants, animals, people, and soil

Concept Knowledge

Children will understand that change can:

- take us to places we have never been

- make us look at ourselves in new ways

- open us to new opportunities

Concept Knowledge

Children will understand that:

- changes in weather affect our lives

- weather changes can be unexpected

- we need rain for plants to grow

Do you think change is good? Why or why not?
Possible answer:

- Yes, because we need to change to grow up. Change is part of life.

What is the biggest change you have faced in your life?

- Responses will vary.

Unit Assessment

Use Unit 4 *Benchmark Test* to check:

✔ **Passage Comprehension**

✔ **Writing Conventions**

✔ **Phonics**

✔ **Vocabulary**

✔ **Writing**

✔ **Fluency**

Unit and End-of-Year Benchmark Tests

Managing Assessment

Use *Assessment Handbook* for:

✔ **Weekly Assessment Blackline Masters for Monitoring Progress**

✔ **Observation Checklists**

✔ **Record-Keeping Forms**

✔ **Portfolio Assessment**

Assessment Handbook

Customize Your Writing

Weekly Writing Focus
Writing Forms and Patterns

- Instruction focuses on a different **product** each week.
- Mini-lessons and models help children learn key features and **organizational patterns**.

Grade 2 Products biography, personal narrative, realistic fiction, journal, expository nonfiction, thank-you note, and so on

Grade 2 Organization Patterns cause and effect, beginning, middle, and end, main idea and details, letter, and so on

Daily Writing Focus
Quick Writes for Fluency

- **Writing on Demand** Use the Quick Write routine for **writing on demand**.
- The Quick Write **prompt and routine** extend skills and strategies from daily writing lessons.

Unit Writing Focus
Writing Process ①②③④⑤

- Six **writing process** lessons provide structure to move children through the steps of the writing process.
- One-week and two-week pacing allows lessons to be used in **Writing Workshop**.

Steps of the Writing Process Plan and Prewrite, Draft, Revise, Edit, Publish and Present

Grade 2 Writing Process Products personal narrative, directions, compare and contrast essay, description, persuasive letter, research report

Writing on Reading STREET

MINI-LESSON

- Daily 10-minute mini-lessons focus instruction on the **traits** and **craft** of good writing.
- Instruction focuses on one writing trait and one writer's craft skill every week.

Traits focus/ideas, organization, voice, word choice, sentences, conventions

Craft drafting strategies, revising strategies, editing strategies

Read Like a Writer

- Use **mentor text** every week as a model to exemplify the traits of good writing.
- **Interact with text** every week to learn the key features of good writing.

Mentor Text Examine literature in the Student Edition.

INTERACT with TEXT Underline, circle, and highlight model text in the *Reader's and Writer's Notebook*.

Write Guy
Jeff Anderson

Need Writing Advice?

Writing instruction is all about creating effective writers. We don't want to crush the inner writer in a child by over-correcting and over-editing. What makes effective writing instruction? Children need to write, write, write! But is that enough? Probably not. All kinds of instruction and guidance go into making an effective writer.

The Write Guy offers advice on teacher and peer conferencing, focusing on writing traits, revising strategies, editing strategies, and much, much more.

Customize Your Writing

Sometimes you want to spend more time on writing—perhaps you do a **Writing Workshop**. This one- or two-week plan for the unit level writing projects can help.

1 Week Plan	Day 1	Day 2	Day 3	Day 4	Day 5
① **Plan and Prewrite**	■	■			
② **Draft**			■		
③ **Revise**				■	
④ **Edit**					■
⑤ **Publish**					■

2 Week Plan	Day 1	Day 2	Day 3	Day 4	Day 5	Day 6	Day 7	Day 8	Day 9	Day 10
① **Plan and Prewrite**	■	■	■	■						
② **Draft**					■	■	■			
③ **Revise**								■		
④ **Edit**									■	
⑤ **Publish**										■

Grade 2 Unit Writing Projects

Internet Guy
Don Leu

Unit Writing Project 1–21st Century Project

Unit 1 Poetry Book

Unit 2 Pen Pal E-mail

Unit 3 Story Exchange

Unit 4 E-Newsletter

Unit 5 Interview

Unit 6 Blog

Unit Writing Project 2–Writing Process

Unit 1 Personal Narrative

Unit 2 Directions

Unit 3 Compare and Contrast Essay

Unit 4 Description

Unit 5 Persuasive Letter

Unit 6 Research Report

Description

Writing Prompt

Write about something in nature that changes. Describe the thing and tell how it changes.

Purpose Describe

Audience A nature lover

Introduce genre and prompt

Tell children that in this lesson they will learn more about a kind of writing called a description. A description creates a picture of a person, place, or thing. When you write a description, you use details that help readers see, hear, smell, taste, or feel what you are describing.

Introduce key features

Key Features of a Description

- creates a clear picture of a person, place, or thing
- uses words that appeal to readers' senses
- uses strong adjectives and vivid details
- introduces the topic in the title and the opening sentence

Academic Vocabulary

Description A good description helps readers visualize, or picture in their minds, what the writer is describing.

English Language Learners

Introduce Genre Point out that a description tells about how something looks, sounds, smells, tastes, and/or feels. Explain that a good description helps readers "see" what the writer is describing. Discuss with children the key features of a description that appear on this page.

Objectives
- Understand and identify the key features of a description.
- Generate ideas for writing by drawing, listing key ideas, and sharing ideas.
- Select a topic.

1 PREWRITE Plan and Prewrite

MINI-LESSON

Read Like a Writer

■ **Examine Model Text** Let's look at an example of a description. Display and read aloud to children "The Maple Tree" on Writing Transparency WP19. Ask children where the writer tells what she will describe. (in the title and opening sentence) Point out the strong adjectives the writer uses, such as *tiny, pale green, hot, bright red,* and *bare.* Explain that the writer uses details that help readers see, hear, and feel the tree. Read aloud examples of these details.

> **The Maple Tree**
>
> The maple tree in my backyard grows tiny pale green leaves in spring. In summer its leaves get bigger and greener. The tree's shade feels good when the sun is hot.
>
> In fall the tree's leaves turn bright red. They are beautiful when the sun shines on them. Then the leaves begin to fall. They cover the ground and crunch when you walk on them.
>
> Soon the tree is bare. It stays that way through winter. Snow lies on its branches. The tree looks dead, but it's not. When spring comes, the tree will grow tiny leaves again.
>
> Unit 4 Description • PLAN and PREWRITE   Writing Process **19**

Writing Transparency WP19
TR DVD

■ **Evaluate Model Text** Display "Traits of a Good Description" on Writing Transparency WP20. Discuss each trait with children. First read the name of the trait and remind them what it means. Then read aloud the statement, explaining any unfamiliar words. Finally, help children understand how the statement applies to the model description.

> **Traits of a Good Description**
>
> | | |
> |---|---|
> | Focus/Ideas | Description sticks to topic and gives details. |
> | Organization | Writer introduces topic in title and opening sentence. Description provides details in an order that is clear. |
> | Voice | Description is lively and interesting. Writer likes the topic. |
> | Word Choice | Writer uses good adjectives that help readers imagine the details and vivid verbs to create a picture in the reader's mind. |
> | Sentences | Sentences are complete and sound smooth. Writer uses short and long sentences. |
> | Conventions | Writer uses good grammar, capitalization, and spelling. |
>
> Unit 4 Description • PLAN and PREWRITE   Writing Process **20**

Writing Transparency WP20
TR DVD

Generate ideas for writing

Reread the writing prompt (on page CW•11) to children. The writing prompt asks you to describe something in nature that changes and tell how it changes. Encourage children to generate ideas for their descriptions using these strategies:

✔ Draw pictures of things in nature they know well. Discuss whether or not these things change and if so, how.

✔ Look through books and magazines to find things in nature that change.

✔ Make a list of as many ideas as they can. Circle their best ideas.

Corrective feedback

If... children have difficulty choosing a topic,
then... have them share their ideas with a partner and get feedback on which ideas sound most interesting to another person.

Narrow topic

Have children ask themselves questions about the ideas on their list. They might ask: *What do I know about this topic? Do I know enough details to write a good description of it? Is it too big a topic? Too small?* Model how to narrow the choices on a list to one topic using the example list shown.

Think Aloud I thought of three ideas. Now I will choose one. I don't think I know enough about the desert. I couldn't describe it very well. Seasons is a large topic to describe in a few paragraphs. I would need to narrow it down more. I do know about our dog Rex. I can think of many details about how he has changed.

Topic Ideas

the desert

seasons

our dog Rex

Write Guy
Jeff Anderson

Use Mentor Text

Have children look back at the unit selection *Life Cycle of a Pumpkin* in this unit. This expository text describes each stage of a pumpkin's growth using strong adjectives. Discuss why strong adjectives are important in the description. Tell children that they will write a description of something in nature that changes, using strong adjectives to paint a picture.

Differentiated Instruction

 Strategic Intervention

Alternative Writing Prompt
Think about a place outside that you like. Draw a picture of what the place looks like in summer. Draw a picture of what it looks like in winter. Write a paragraph that describes the place in each season. Tell how it changes.

 Advanced

Alternative Writing Prompt
Write your description as dialogue, or conversation, between you and another person. Have the person ask you questions that you answer by giving descriptive details. Then with a partner read your dialogue aloud.

UNIT 4 Writing Process

Objectives
- Understand the criteria for an effective description.
- Plan a description by organizing ideas.
- Sequence ideas in sentences to prepare and write a first draft.

 1 PREWRITE Plan and Prewrite

MINI-LESSON

Planning a First Draft

■ **Use a Details Web** Display Writing Transparency WP21 and read it aloud to children.

Think Aloud I write my topic, our dog Rex, in the center of the web. Around the center, I write details about how Rex looks and acts. Now I can start writing a first draft of my description by introducing my topic in the opening sentence and using my details to write sentences that create a picture for my readers.

Writing Transparency WP21
TR DVD

■ Have children use the Details Web graphic organizer on *Reader's and Writer's Notebook* page 381 to help them record ideas for their description. Before you begin writing, decide what details will best help your readers see, hear, smell, taste, or feel what you are describing. Write sentences with these details in an order that makes sense.

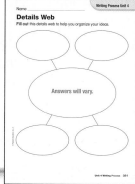

Reader's and Writer's Notebook, p. 381

 Draft

Display rubric

Display Scoring Rubric WP4 from the *Teacher Resource DVD-ROM*. Read aloud and discuss with children the traits and criteria that you choose. Encourage children to think about these criteria as they develop drafts of their descriptions. Tell them that rubrics such as this one are often used to evaluate and score writing.

Scoring Rubric: *Description*

	4	3	2	1
Focus/Ideas	Reader can understand the description	Reader can understand part of the description	Reader cannot understand the description very well	Reader cannot understand the description
Organization	Topic clearly stated at beginning followed by many strong details	Topic stated at beginning; some strong details follow	Topic not stated at beginning; few strong details	No stated topic or strong details
Voice	Clearly shows how you feel about the topic	Shows a little how you feel about the topic	Does not show very well how you feel about the topic	Does not show how you feel about the topic
Word Choice	Has words that help readers "see"	Some words help readers "see"	Words do not help readers "see"	Words are hard to read
Sentences	Sentences are complete and not all alike	Sentences are complete	Some sentences are not complete	Sentences not complete or clear
Conventions	Uses good punctuation and grammar	Uses fair punctuation and grammar	Uses poor punctuation and grammar	Uses very poor punctuation and grammar

Prepare to draft

Have children look at the details webs they worked on earlier. Ask them to make sure that their details webs are complete. If they are not, have children finish them now. Use your details web as you write the draft of your description. You will have a chance to revise your draft later.

Corrective feedback

If... children do not understand how the Scoring Rubric can be used to evaluate writing,
then... show them how you can use the Scoring Rubric to evaluate and score one or more traits of the model description on Writing Transparency WP19.

Differentiated Instruction

 Strategic Intervention

Plan a First Draft Let children dictate to you the details they want to use in their descriptions. Record their details and note whether these appeal to people's senses. Ask children questions that prompt them to add details.

ELL

English Language Learners

Prepare to Draft Invite children to talk with you about what they plan to write. Record key words and ideas that they mention and help them generate language for other key words and ideas. See the *ELL Handbook* for additional strategies that support the writing process.

UNIT 4 Writing Process

Objectives

• Choose strong adjectives to use in descriptive details.
• Write a first draft of a description.
• Revise a draft of a description.

② Draft

MINI-LESSON

Writing Trait: Word Choice

◼ **Use Strong Adjectives** List the strong adjectives below on the board. Explain that these adjectives can be used in place of a weak adjective such as *nice.* Point out that strong adjectives help create a more descriptive picture for readers. Say this sentence: I have a nice pet. Then say the sentence replacing *nice* with each strong adjective. Ask children how they picture the pet when they hear each sentence.

Strong Adjectives

large

cuddly

fluffy

noisy

lively

◼ Have children use *Reader's and Writer's Notebook* page 382 to practice using strong adjectives.

Reader's and Writer's
Notebook, p. 382

Develop draft Remind children that when they write their first drafts, they want to get their ideas down on paper. Suggest that they try these drafting strategies:

✔ Write *See, Hear, Smell, Taste,* and *Feel* as headings. Write as many details about their topic as they can under the headings.

✔ Think about their topic and write a list of the strong adjectives that come to mind.

✔ Choose the best details and strongest adjectives to use in their description.

③ Revise

Writer's Craft: Deleting Words, Phrases, or Sentences

■ Remind children that good writers delete, or take out, words, phrases, or sentences when they don't tell about the topic or they aren't needed. Deleting unnecessary words helps avoid wordiness. Discuss with children why the writer deleted the phrase: *It seems like* the tulips bloomed quickly.

The tulips bloomed quickly.

■ Have children use *Reader's and Writer's Notebook* page 383 to practice deleting words, phrases, and sentences.

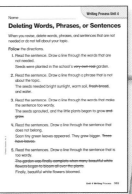

Reader's and Writer's Notebook, p. 383

Write Guy
Jeff Anderson

The Sunny Side

I like to look for what's *right* in children's writing rather than looking for things I can fix. Most children don't write flawlessly, but they will learn what they are doing well if we point it out—and chances are they will do it again the next time they write!

Revise model Use Writing Transparency WP22 to model how to revise a description.

Think Aloud I deleted the second sentence because it was not about the topic, our dog Rex. In the third sentence, I changed the adjective *big* to *huge* because his paws looked so large! However, I added the adjective *wet* twice because it helps give a better picture of Rex's tongue, both earlier and now.

Writing Transparency WP22, TR DVD

E L L

English Language Learners
Revise for Word Choice To help children add strong adjectives to their writing, work with them to develop word webs with a weak adjective in the center and around it strong adjectives that can replace it. Encourage children to use a children's dictionary, if available, to find strong adjectives.

3 Revise

Objectives
- Revise a draft of a description.
- Edit a revised draft of a description to correct errors in grammar, punctuation, capitalization, and spelling.

Revise draft

We have written first drafts of our descriptions. Now we will revise our drafts. When we revise, we try to make our writing clearer and more interesting to read.

Peer conferencing

Peer Revision Write the questions that you choose from the Revising Checklist on the board. If you elect to use peer revision, help pairs of children exchange and read each other's drafts. Read aloud the checklist, one question at a time. Ask children to answer each question about their own draft or their partner's draft. Remind them to think about where words, phrases, or sentences could be deleted to make the writing clearer or less wordy.

Help children revise their descriptions using their own ideas or their partner's comments as well as what they have learned about descriptions to guide them.

Revising Checklist

✔ Does the description stay focused on the topic?

✔ Is the topic clearly stated in the title or the opening sentence?

✔ Are the details arranged in an order that makes sense?

✔ Is the writer interested in the topic?

✔ Does the writer use strong adjectives and words that appeal to the senses to make a picture in readers' minds?

✔ Are there words, phrases, or sentences the writer could delete to make the description clearer or less wordy?

4 Edit

Editing Strategy: Read Your Work Aloud

■ Explain this editing strategy to children: Read your work aloud to help you find errors. Sometimes it is easier to find errors when you hear them. Model this strategy using Writing Transparency WP23. If you elect to teach proofreading marks, explain what they mean and how they are used as you discuss the errors on the transparency.

 Think Aloud I listen for errors as I read my work aloud. In the first paragraph, *He trips* doesn't sound right. It should be *tripped* because the other verb in the sentence is *ran,* and both verbs should tell about the past. In the second paragraph, I can hear that I used the wrong article. *An* should be *a* because *grown* begins with a consonant sound. I also added a comma in the third sentence because *head* is an item in a series. I corrected the word *gigle* to *giggle* in two places.

Writing Transparency WP23
TR DVD

■ Have children edit the paragraph on *Reader's and Writer's Notebook* page 384. Help them use proofreading marks.

Help children edit their own drafts. Provide a simple rubric to help them check their spelling, grammar, punctuation, and capitalization.

Reader's and Writer's
Notebook, p. 384

Technology Tips

Children who type their descriptions on computers may find these tips useful as they edit:

✔ Set margins, line lengths, borders, shading, paragraph indents, and other features using the Format menu.

✔ Ask a friend or use the Help menu when they have questions about how to do something on the computer.

Differentiated Instruction

A Advanced

Apply Editing Skills As they edit their work, children can consider these ways to improve it.

- Make sure every sentence tells a detail about the topic.
- Look for places to substitute strong adjectives for weak ones or to add vivid details.

Editing Tip

Using the Correct Articles Explain that the words *a, an,* and *the* are called articles. *The* can be used with singular and plural nouns (*the dog, the dogs*); *a* and *an* are used only with singular nouns (*a tree, an apple*). *A* is used before a word that begins with a consonant sound (*a tan rock*); *an* is used before a word that begins with a vowel sound (*an odd rock*). As they edit, children should make sure they have used the correct articles.

ELL

English Language Learners
Support Editing When reviewing a child's draft, focus on ideas more than errors. If you find consistent grammatical errors, choose one or two skills for attention during editing. Use the appropriate lessons in the *ELL Handbook* to explicitly teach the English conventions.

Objectives
- Write and present a final draft of a description.
- Evaluate one's own writing.

 Publish and Present

Present

Remind children of the writing process steps they read about on *Reader's and Writer's Notebook* page 384. After they have revised and edited their description, have children write a final draft. Explain that it is a time for them to share their writing with others. Offer children two ways to present their work:

Read aloud their descriptions in small groups. Ask questions about the descriptions.	Draw or find pictures to go with their descriptions. Post both on a bulletin board.

MINI-LESSON

Evaluating Writing

■ Prepare children to evaluate their description. Display and read aloud Writing Transparency WP24. Model the self-evaluation process.

Think Aloud My description is focused on one topic, our dog Rex. I introduce my topic in my title and opening sentence. I organized my details to tell first about Rex as a puppy and then about Rex as a grown dog. Strong adjectives and vivid details appeal to readers' senses and create a picture of Rex. I show clearly how I feel about Rex. I used a variety of sentences. My punctuation and grammar are good.

Rex

Rex was a puppy when we first got him. His body was small, but he had a big head, huge paws, and long ears. He tripped on his ears when he ran. He was so funny to watch. Rex would climb into my lap and lick my face with his wet tongue. That made me giggle.

Now Rex is a grown dog. His head and paws aren't too big anymore. When he runs, he doesn't trip on his ears. Rex can't climb into my lap now, but he still licks my face with his wet tongue. That still makes me giggle.

Unit 4 Description • PUBLISH   Writing Process **24**

Writing Transparency WP24
TR DVD

■ Help children use the Scoring Rubric to evaluate their descriptions. They can save their work in a portfolio to help them monitor their development as writers. Encourage them to build on their skills and to note areas to improve.

Customize Literacy in Your Classroom

Table of Contents
for Customize Literacy

Customize Literacy is organized into different sections, each one designed to help you organize and carry out an effective literacy program. Each section contains strategies and support for teaching comprehension skills and strategies. *Customize Literacy* also shows how to use weekly text sets of readers in your literacy program.

Weekly Text Sets
to Customize Literacy

The following readers can be used to enhance your literacy instruction.

	Decodable Readers	Concept Literacy Reader	Below-Level Reader	On-Level Reader	Advanced Reader	ELD Reader	ELL Reader
Unit 4 WEEK 4	Boyhood Dreams; Jack's Daydreams; Joy's Raincoat	New Faces and Places	Snakeskin Canyon	Too Many Frogs!	A Quiet Place	Adam's New Soccer Team	Adam's New Soccer Team
Unit 4 WEEK 5	Is It True?; Sally's New Puppy; New Clues	All Kinds of Weather	Blizzard!	Rainbow Crow Brings Fire to Earth	Hurricane!	How Is the Weather?	How Is the Weather?

Customize Literacy in Your Classroom

Instruction in comprehension skills and strategies provides readers with avenues to understanding a text. Through teacher modeling and guided, collaborative, and independent practice, students become independent thinkers who employ a variety of skills and strategies to help them make meaning as they read.

Mini-Lessons for Comprehension Skills and Strategies

Envision It!
A Comprehension Handbook

Unit 1	Character, Main Idea, Setting, Main Idea, Facts and Details, Monitor and Clarify, Important Ideas
Unit 2	Cause and Effect, Author's Purpose, Facts and Details, Compare and Contrast, Summarize, Story Structure
Unit 3	Author's Purpose, Draw Conclusions, Compare and Contrast, Sequence, Fact and Opinion, Questioning, Predict and Set Purpose
Unit 4	Draw Conclusions, Sequence, Fact and Opinion, Plot, Theme, Background Knowledge, Visualize
Unit 5	Fact and Opinion, Cause and Effect, Literary Elements, Main Idea, Text Structure, Inferring
Unit 6	Compare and Contrast, Author's Purpose, Draw Conclusions, Sequence, Facts and Details, Monitor and Clarify, Summarize

Envision It! | Visual Skills Handbook
Author's Purpose
Categorize and Classify
Cause and Effect
Compare and Contrast
Draw Conclusions
Fact and Opinion
Generalize
Graphic Sources
Literary Elements
Main Idea and Details
Sequence

Envision It! | Visual Strategies Handbook
Background Knowledge
Important Ideas
Inferring
Monitor and Clarify
Predict and Set Purpose
Questioning
Story Structure
Summarize
Text Structure
Visualize

Anchor Chart Anchor charts are provided with each strategy lesson. These charts incorporate the language of strategic thinkers. They help students make their thinking visible and permanent and provide students with a means to clarify their thinking about how and when to use each strategy. As students gain more experience with a strategy, the chart may undergo revision.

See pages 109–136 in the *First Stop on Reading Street* Teacher's Edition for additional support as you customize literacy in your classroom.

Good Readers DRA2 users will find additional resources in the *First Stop on Reading Street* Teacher's Edition on pages 112–114.

Contents

Pacing Guide

This chart shows the instructional sequence from *Scott Foresman Reading Street* for Grade 2. You can use this pacing guide as is to ensure you are following a comprehensive scope and sequence. Or, you can adjust the sequence to match your calendar, curriculum map, or testing schedule.

Grade 2

READING	UNIT 1 Week 1	Week 2	Week 3	Week 4	Week 5 (REVIEW WEEK)	UNIT 2 Week 1	Week 2
Phonics	Short Vowels	Long Vowels CVC*e*	Consonant Blends	Inflected Endings	Consonant Digraphs	*r*-Controlled *ar, or, ore, oar*	Contractions
High-Frequency Words	*someone, somewhere, friend, country, beautiful, front*	*everywhere, live, work, woman, machines, move, world*	*couldn't, love, build, mother, bear, father, straight*	*water, eyes, early, animals, full, warm*	*together, very, learn, often, though, gone, pieces*	*family, once, pull, listen, heard, break*	*laugh, great, you're, either, certainly, second, worst*
Comprehension Skill	Character and Setting	Main Idea and Details	Character and Setting	Main Idea and Details	Facts and Details	Cause and Effect	Author's Purpose
Comprehension Strategy	Monitor and Clarify	Text Structure	Story Structure	Important Ideas	Predict and Set Purpose	Summarize	Text Structures
Fluency	Appropriate Rate	Read with Accuracy	Accuracy and Appropriate Rate	Attend to Punctuation	Read with Expression/Intonation	Accuracy and Appropriate Rate	Read with Expression/Intonation

	UNIT 4 Week 1	Week 2	Week 3	Week 4	Week 5 (REVIEW WEEK)	UNIT 5 Week 1	Week 2
Phonics	Syllables C + *le*	Vowels *oo, u* (as in *book*)	Diphthongs *ou, ow/ou/*	Syllables CV,CVC	Vowels *oo, ue, ew, ui* (as in *moon*)	Suffixes *-ly, -ful, -er, -ish, -or*	Prefixes *un-, re-, pre-, dis-*
Comprehension Skill	Draw Conclusions	Sequence	Fact and Opinion	Plot and Theme	Plot and Theme	Fact and Opinion	Cause and Effect
Comprehension Strategy	Background Knowledge	Important Ideas	Questioning	Visualize	Monitor and Clarify	Important Ideas	Visualize
Vocabulary Strategy/Skill	Context Clues/Multiple-Meaning Words	Context Clues/Antonyms	Word Structure/Suffixes	Context Clues/Multiple-Meaning Words	Word Structure/Prefixes	Word Structure/Suffixes	Dictionary/Unfamiliar Words
Fluency	Accuracy and Appropriate Rate	Read with Accuracy	Appropriate Phrasing	Characterization	Read with Expression/Intonation	Read with Accuracy	Accuracy and Appropriate Rate

> Are you the adventurous type? Want to use some of your own ideas and materials in your teaching? But you worry you might be leaving out some critical instruction children need? **Customize Literacy** can help.

REVIEW WEEK

UNIT 3

REVIEW WEEK

Week 3	Week 4	Week 5	Week 1	Week 2	Week 3	Week 4	Week 5
r-Controlled *er, ir, ur*	Plurals	Long *a: a, ai, ay*	Long *e: e, ee, ea, y*	Long *o: o, oa, ow*	Compound Words	Long *i: i, ie, igh, y*	Comparative Endings
enough, toward, above, ago, word, whole	*people, sign, shall, bought, probably, pleasant, scared*	*door, behind, brought, minute, promise, sorry, everybody*	*science, shoe, won, guess, village, pretty, watch*	*picture, school, answer, wash, parents, company, faraway*	*today, whatever, caught, believe, been, finally, tomorrow*	*their, many, alone, buy, half, youngest, daughters*	*only, question, clothes, money, hours, neighbor, taught*
Facts and Details	Cause and Effect	Compare and Contrast	Author's Purpose	Draw Conclusions	Compare and Contrast	Sequence	Fact and Opinion
Background Knowledge	Story Structure	Inferring	Questioning	Visualize	Summarize	Predict and Set Purpose	Inferring
Read with Appropriate Phrasing	Express Characterization	Accuracy	Read with Appropriate Rate	Accuracy and Appropriate Rate	Express Characterization	Attend to Punctuation	Read with Expression and Intonation

REVIEW WEEK

UNIT 6

REVIEW WEEK

Week 3	Week 4	Week 5	Week 1	Week 2	Week 3	Week 4	Week 5
Silent Consonants	*ph, gh/f/, ck, ng*	Vowels *aw, au, augh, al*	Inflected Endings	Abbreviations	Syllables *-tion, -ture, -ion*	Suffixes *-ness, -less, -able, -ible*	Prefixes *mis-, mid-, micro-, non-*
Plot and Theme	Character and Setting	Main Idea and Details	Compare and Contrast	Author's Purpose	Draw Conclusions	Sequence	Facts and Details
Background Knowledge	Story Structure	Inferring	Monitor and Clarify	Summarize	Questioning	Text Structure	Predict and Set Purpose
Dictionary/ Classify and Categorize	Word Structure/ Compound Words	Word Structure/ Suffixes	Context Clues/ Homophones	Context Clues/ Multiple-Meaning Words	Context Clues/ words from other languages	Context Clues/ Unfamiliar Words	Dictionary/ Multiple-Meaning Words
Read with Expression/ Intonation	Express Characterization	Appropriate Phrasing	Accuracy and Appropriate Rate	Read with Accuracy	Appropriate Phrasing	Accuracy and Appropriate Rate	Appropriate Phrasing

Pacing Guide

Grade 2

UNIT 1

LANGUAGE ARTS	Week 1	Week 2	Week 3	Week 4	Week 5
Speaking, Listening, and Viewing	Why We Speak/ Why We Listen	Be a Good Speaker/Listen Attentively	Recognize Purposes of Media	Narrate in Sequence	Dramatize
Research and Study Skills	Media Center/ Library	Reference Sources	Personal Sources	Parts of a Book	Maps
Grammar	Sentences	Subjects	Predicates	Statements and Questions	Commands and Exclamations
Weekly Writing; Trait of the Week	Personal Narrative/ Conventions	Expository Paragraph/ Sentences	Realistic Story/ Organization	Brief Report/ Word Choice	Play Scene/ Conventions
Writing	Keyboarding/Personal Narrative				

REVIEW WEEK

UNIT 2

	Week 1	Week 2
Speaking, Listening, and Viewing	Give and Follow Directions	Explain Purposes of Media
Research and Study Skills	Notes	Time Line
Grammar	Nouns	Proper Nouns
Weekly Writing; Trait of the Week	Narrative Nonfiction/ Voice	Biography/ Focus/Ideas

UNIT 4

	Week 1	Week 2	Week 3	Week 4	Week 5
Speaking, Listening, and Viewing	Media Techniques	Make an Announcement	Speak Well	Media Techniques	Give an Oral Summary
Research and Study Skills	Thesaurus	Personal Sources	Diagram	E-mail	Natural and Personal Sources
Grammar	Adjectives and Our Senses	Adjectives for Number, Size, and Shape	Adjectives That Compare	Adverbs That Tell When and Where	Adverbs That Tell How
Weekly Writing; Trait of the Week	Friendly Letter/ Organization	Expository Nonfiction/ Word Choice	Short Expository Report/ Sentences	Narrative Poem/ Voice	Thank-You Note/ Focus/Ideas
Writing	E-Newsletter/Description				

REVIEW WEEK

UNIT 5

	Week 1	Week 2
Speaking, Listening, and Viewing	Identify Cultural Characteristics in Media	Give a Demonstration
Research and Study Skills	Online Directory	Bar Graph
Grammar	Pronouns	Singular and Plural Pronouns
Weekly Writing; Trait of the Week	Narrative Nonfiction/ Word Choice	Realistic Story/ Organization

REVIEW WEEK

UNIT 3

Week 3	Week 4	Week 5
Ask and Answer Questions	Explain Purposes of Media	Give and Follow Directions
Chapter Headings	Encyclopedia	Read a Web Page
Singular and Plural Nouns	Plural Nouns That Change Spelling	Possessive Nouns
Expository Nonfiction/ Word Choice	Fairy Tale/ Organization	Folk Tale/ Sentences

Electronic Pen Pal/Directions

REVIEW WEEK

Week 1	Week 2	Week 3	Week 4	Week 5
Make Introductions	Solve Problems	Summarize Information	Give a Description	Describe Media Technique
Picture-Graph	Newspaper and Periodicals	Interview	Alphabetized Index	Search Internet
Verbs	Verbs with Singular and Plural Nouns	Verbs for Past, Present, and Future	More About Verbs	Verbs: *Am, Is, Are, Was,* and *Were*
Animal Fantasy/Voice	Friendly Letter/ Focus/Idea	Narrative Poem/ Conventions	Realistic Story/ Word Choice	Review/ Organization

Story Starters/Compare and Contrast Essay

REVIEW WEEK

UNIT 6

Week 3	Week 4	Week 5
Listen for Facts and Opinions	Maintain Focus in a Narrative Presentation	Speak to Your Audience
Online Reference Sources	Tables	Evaluate Online Sources
Using *I* and *Me*	Different Kinds of Pronouns	Contractions
Journal Entry/ Voice	Animal Fantasy/ Conventions	Humorous Story/ Sentences

Community Interview/Persuasive Letter

REVIEW WEEK

Week 1	Week 2	Week 3	Week 4	Week 5
Use Vocabulary to Express Ideas	Evaluate Ads	Listen to a Description	Identify Conventions	Listen for Speaker's Purpose
Globe	Chart	Interview a Natural Source	Schedules	Interview a Natural Source
Capital Letters	Quotation Marks	Prepositions	Commas	Commas in Compound Sentences
Realistic Story/ Organization	Descriptive Poem or Song/ Voice	Invitation or Letter/ Sentences	Compare-Contrast Text/ Focus/Ideas	Persuasive Statement/ Word Choice

Blogging/Research Report

Teaching Record Chart

This chart shows the critical comprehension skills and strategies you need to cover. Check off each one as you provide instruction.

Reading/Comprehension	DATES OF INSTRUCTION		
Use ideas (e.g., illustrations, titles, topic sentences, key words, and foreshadowing) to make and confirm predictions.			
Ask relevant questions, seek clarification, and locate facts and details about stories and other texts and support answers with evidence from text.			
Establish purpose for reading selected texts and monitor comprehension, making corrections and adjustments when that understanding breaks down (e.g., identifying clues, using background knowledge, generating questions, re-reading a portion aloud).			
Identify moral lessons as themes in well-known fables, legends, myths, or stories.			
Compare different versions of the same story in traditional and contemporary folktales with respect to their characters, settings, and plot.			
Describe how rhyme, rhythm, and repetition interact to create images in poetry.			
Identify the elements of dialogue and use them in informal plays.			
Describe similarities and differences in the plots and settings of several works by the same author.			
Describe main characters in works of fiction, including their traits, motivations, and feelings.			
Distinguish between fiction and nonfiction.			
Recognize that some words and phrases have literal and non-literal meanings (e.g., take steps).			

Tired of using slips of paper or stickies to make sure you teach everything you need to? Need an easier way to keep track of what you have taught, and what you still need to cover? **Customize Literacy** can help. **99**

Reading/Comprehension	DATES OF INSTRUCTION		
Read independently for a sustained period of time and paraphrase what the reading was about, maintaining meaning.			
Identify the topic and explain the author's purpose in writing the text.			
Identify the main idea in a text and distinguish it from the topic.			
Locate the facts that are clearly stated in a text.			
Describe the order of events or ideas in a text.			
Use text features (e.g., table of contents, index, headings) to locate specific information in text.			
Follow written multi-step directions.			
Use common graphic features to assist in the interpretation of text (e.g., captions, illustrations).			
Establish purposes for reading selected texts based upon content to enhance comprehension.			
Ask literal questions of text.			
Monitor and adjust comprehension (e.g., using background knowledge, creating sensory images, re-reading a portion aloud, generating questions).			
Make inferences about text using textual evidence to support understanding.			
Retell important events in stories in logical order.			
Make connections to own experiences, to ideas in other texts, and to the larger community and discuss textual evidence.			

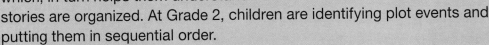

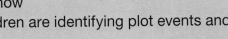

Student Edition pp. EI•14–EI•15

Objectives

- Children understand that a story is made up of events that happen in sequential order.
- Children identify a problem and a solution in a story.
- Children identify a story's beginning, middle, and end.
- Children can take plot events and put them in story order.

Plot

What is it?   **Plot** refers to the events in a story. Plot, along with characters, setting, and theme, make up literary elements in stories. Identifying plot requires readers to recognize the important events in a story, which, in turn helps them understand how stories are organized. At Grade 2, children are identifying plot events and putting them in sequential order.

How Good Readers Use the Skill   Understanding plot means readers have a sense of the important events in a story. This means they understand that in a story a character has a problem and the story unfolds as the character tries solve it. Good readers are alert to the relationship of characters to plot. They ask questions and make and confirm predictions as they read to understand how the story will play out.

Texts for Teaching

Student Edition
- *The Night the Moon Fell*, 2.2, pages 128–143
- *The First Tortilla*, 2.2, pages 162–177
- *Bad Dog, Dodger*, 2.2, pages 264–277

Leveled Readers
- See pages 22–27 for a list of Leveled Readers.

Teach the Skill

Use the **Envision It!** lesson on pages EI•14–EI•15 to visually review plot.

Remind children that:

- the **plot** is the pattern of important events in a story that lead to a character fulfilling a goal or solving a problem.
- every story has a beginning, middle, and end.

Practice

Model telling the plot of a familiar story.

The story of Peter Rabbit is all about a mischievous rabbit who sneaks into the farmer's garden to get some vegetables. Peter then gets trapped and must find a way to escape. He runs really fast when the farmer's back is turned and gets back home.

Talk with children about what parts of the story you included. Ask: Did I tell everything that happens in the story? What parts did I leave out? Help children understand that you told only what happened in the beginning, the middle, and the end. Have volunteers retell a story in the same way.

If... children have difficulty retelling,

then... ask them to only tell what happens at the beginning, middle, and end.

Apply

As children read stories, have them retell what happens in the beginning, middle, and end.

Writing

Children can list their favorite stories and choose one to retell.

Mini-Lesson 2

Teach the Skill
Use the **Envision It!** lesson on pages EI•14–EI•15 to visually review plot.

Remind children that:
- the **plot** is the pattern of important events in a story that lead to a character fulfilling a goal or solving a problem.
- in a story, a character has a problem which he or she works to solve.
- events in a story happen in a logical order.

Practice
Supply children with a familiar story. Have volunteers retell the story. Then distribute cards (or groups of cards) with main events from the story. Ask children to read their cards and arrange themselves in order. Have each group retell the story using their cards. Talk about how the events in a story happen in a specific order. Where do we learn what the character's problem is? How does the character solve the problem? Could the character solve his or her problem in a different order? Would that be the same or a different story?

If... children have difficulty identifying parts of the plot,
then... have children work with three events: beginning, middle, end.

Apply
As children read, have them think about the order of events. Can they tell what happens at the beginning, in the middle, and at the end?

Writing
Children can write sentences that summarize a favorite story.

Mini-Lesson 3

Teach the Skill
Use the **Envision It!** lesson on pages EI•14–EI•15 to visually review plot.

Remind children that:
- the **plot** is the pattern of important events in a story that lead to a character fulfilling a goal or solving a problem.
- in a story, a character has a problem which he or she works to solve.
- events in a story happen in a logical order.

Practice
Begin a discussion about favorite stories. Explain that children are now reading stories that are sometimes complicated. They can keep track of events in a story using a story map. Model how to complete a story map. (You might have several events in the middle.) Then have groups choose a story they have read and complete a map for it.

| **Beginning Character's Problem:** |
| ↓ |
| **Middle** |
| ↓ |
| **End How the Problem Was Solved:** |

If... children have difficulty identifying parts of the plot,
then... have children work with three events: beginning, middle, end.

Apply
As children read, have them think about the order of events. Can they tell what happens at the beginning, in the middle, and at the end?

Writing
Children can write sentences that summarize the plot of a favorite television show.

Theme

Student Edition pp. EI•14–EI•15

Objectives

- Children answer questions to identify the big idea, or theme, in a story.
- Children talk about things that the characters learn in the story that are related to the big idea.
- Children relate big ideas to themselves.

What is it? The **theme** of a story, or the big idea, is why an author writes a story. The theme, along with characters, setting, and plot, make up literary elements in stories. Identifying the theme requires readers to look for the author's reasons for writing. It allows them to take away ideas that last beyond the story. At Grade 2, children are identifying the big idea of stories.

How Good Readers Use the Skill Understanding the theme of a story requires higher level thinking. Readers ask questions, such as *What does the author want me to know or learn from this story? Does the big idea relate to things I have experienced in my life?* Children learn to use the literary elements and language in a story to think about theme. Older readers connect themes within stories and make connections between stories that share similar themes.

Texts for Teaching

Student Edition
- *The Night the Moon Fell,* 2.2, pages 128–143
- *The First Tortilla,* 2.2, pages 162–177
- *Bad Dog, Dodger*, 2.2, pages 264–277

Leveled Readers
- See pages 22–27 for a list of Leveled Readers.

Teach the Skill

Use the **Envision It!** lesson on pages EI•14–EI•15 to visually review theme.

Remind children that:
- **theme** is the big idea in a story.
- the theme in some stories is stated.

Practice

Remind children that an author often writes a story to teach a reader something or to support a big idea. Explain that some authors include a lesson or a moral as part of the story. Read or retell an Aesop fable, such as "The Tortoise and the Hare." Read the moral ("Slow and steady win the race" or "A person who is slow and steady will win over a person who is fast but doesn't finish.") Talk with children about this big idea. Ask: Is this big idea only about races or tortoises and hares? Why or why not? **If...** children have difficulty identifying big ideas, **then...** ask them to think about what lesson a character learns.

Apply

As children read other stories, have them think about what the author might want them to learn by reading the story.

Writing

Children can write a fable-like moral for a favorite story.

Customize Literacy

Teach the Skill

Use the Envision It! **lesson on pages EI•14–EI•15 to visually review theme.**

Remind children that:
- the **theme** is the big idea of a story. You can use information about characters, setting, and plot from the story to understand this big idea.
- the **theme** of a story is the *why* of a story, the point the author is trying to make. The theme may be a lesson, such as, "Honesty is the best policy."

Practice
Talk about some of the stories you have read, asking: What do you think the big idea of the story is? Is the big idea of *Cinderella* that she gets married? Help children understand that one big idea in that story is that being kind is rewarded and being mean is not. Begin a chart and list some big ideas of stories you have read. Encourage children to think what the author might want us to learn.

Story	Big Idea	Why We Think So
"The Lion and the Mouse"	Big isn't always best.	A small mouse saves a big lion.

If... children have difficulty choosing a theme,
then... provide one or two choices and have children select one and tell why it is a good choice.

Apply
As children read the assigned text, have them ask "What is the meaning or lesson of this story?"

Writing
Children can write a story and think about its message.

Teach the Skill

Use the Envision It! **lesson on pages EI•14–EI•15 to visually review theme.**

Remind children that:
- **theme** is the big idea in a story.
- many stories may have the same theme.

Practice
Begin a list of children's favorite stories. Talk about the list. Ask: How could we group some of the stories? (by topic, setting, genre, and so on) Point out that many authors write books that have the same theme. Suggest the following themes and have the class list favorite stories. Ask: What do we like about our favorite books? What do we remember most? Help children understand that we may not always remember specific events, but that we may remember big ideas. Children may have other big ideas they wish to put on the chart.

Friends Help Each Other	Families Are Important	Nothing Stays the Same
Frog and Toad *Charlotte's Web*	*Little House on the Prairie* *Dear Juno*	*A Froggy Fable* *Ramona Quimby*

If... children have difficulty identifying themes,
then... talk about what they remember about their favorite books.

Apply
As children read, have them think about the big ideas and ask: *What does the author want me to learn?*

Writing
Children can choose a favorite book and write what a big idea might be.

Visualize

Mini-Lesson

Student Edition p. EI•27

Objectives

- Children use their own experiences and details from the text to visualize.
- Children create mental images to gain information and better comprehend what they read.

Texts for Teaching

Student Edition

- *Dear Juno,* 2.1, pages 388–405
- *The Night the Moon Fell,* 2.2, pages 128–143
- *Carl the Complainer,* 2.2, pages 230–247

Leveled Readers

- See pages 22–27 for a list of Leveled Readers.

Understand the Strategy

Visualizing means creating pictures in the mind. These pictures are created by combining what readers already know with descriptive words in a text. Visualizing involves all the senses, not just sight.

Teach

Use the **Envision It!** lesson on page EI•27 to review visualizing.

Remind children that authors use descriptive language to help us "place" events in a story, to understand characters, to picture events, and so on. We call this visualizing and it means to see pictures in your mind. Use a piece of text that describes an event to model making pictures in your mind. Think aloud as you do. The chart below has some examples based on a passage about children in Iceland who rescue baby pufflings.

Details from Text	What I Visualize
• Thousands of puffins nest on rocky coasts of Iceland.	• I hear a lot of squawking. I think the ground is slippery with bird droppings.
• The baby birds need to get to the sea, but city lights confuse them. Some die.	• I feel the dampness of the sea. I can feel the rocky ground.
• Students come out at night to help the pufflings get to the water.	• I see little birds running crazily. • I see shadows made by moonlight.

Practice

Supply children with a text and have them work in pairs to visualize. Then bring the groups together and talk about the pictures they made in their minds as they read. Make sure children identify details from text that helped them visualize.

If... children have difficulty visualizing,

then... model, describing the pictures you form as you read.

Apply

Remind children to make pictures as they read, using what they already know and the details the author puts in the text.

Anchor Chart

Anchor charts help children make their thinking visible and permanent. With an anchor chart, the group can clarify their thinking about how to use a strategy. Display anchor charts so readers can use them as they read. Here is a sample chart for visualizing.

Visualizing

1. Preview. Look at the pictures. Is this a story? Is it informational?

2. Read a little to see what it is all about.

3. Read to see how the author tells about places and people.

4. Close your eyes and make pictures in your mind.

5. Look for details. How do things smell? taste? feel? sound? look?

6. Make a chart or a web to write down details that help you visualize.

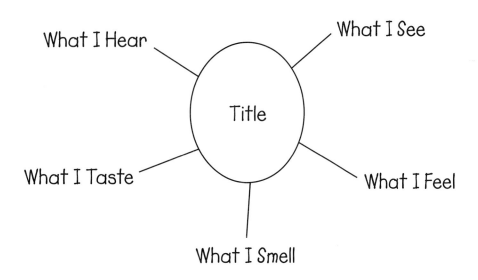

What I Hear

What I See

Title

What I Taste

What I Feel

What I Smell

Anchor Chart

Using Multiple Strategies

Good readers use multiple strategies as they read. You can encourage children to read strategically through good classroom questioning. Use questions such as these to help children apply strategies during reading.

Questioning

- Who or what is this question about?
- Where can you look to find the answer to this question?
- What do you want to know about _____?
- What questions to do you have about the _____ in this selection? Use the words *who, what, when, where, why,* and *how* to ask your questions.
- Do you have any questions after reading?

Graphic Organizers

- What kind of graphic organizer could you use to help you keep track of the information in this selection?

Monitor and Clarify

- Does the story or article make sense?
- What don't you understand about what you read?
- Do you need to reread, review, read on, or check a reference source?
- Do you need to read more slowly or more quickly?
- What is a _____? Where could you look to find out?

Predict and Set Purpose

- What do you think this story or article will be about? Why do you think as you do?
- What do you think you will learn from this selection?
- Do the text features help you predict what will happen?
- Based on what has happened so far, what do you think will happen next?
- Is this what you thought would happen?
- How does _____ change what you thought would happen?

Preview

- What do the photographs, illustrations, or graphic sources tell about the selection?
- What do you want to find out? What do you want to learn?

Background Knowledge

- What do you already know about _____?
- Have you read stories or articles by this author before?
- How is this selection like others that you have read?
- What does this remind you of?
- How does your prior knowledge help you understand _____?
- Did the text match what you already knew? What new information did you learn?

Story Structure

- Who are the characters in this story?
- What is the setting?
- What is the problem in this story? How does the problem get solved?
- What is the point of this story?

Summarize

- What two or three important ideas have you read so far?
- How do the text features relate to the important ideas?
- Is there a graphic organizer that can help you organize the information before you summarize?

Text Structure

- How has the author organized the writing?
- What clues tell you that the text is structured _____?

Visualize

- When you read this, what do you picture in your mind?
- What do you hear, see, or smell?
- What do you think _____ looks like? Why do you think as you do?

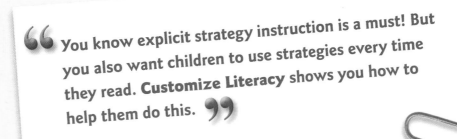

" You know explicit strategy instruction is a must! But you also want children to use strategies every time they read. **Customize Literacy** shows you how to help them do this. "

Glossary of Literacy Terms

This glossary lists academic language terms that are related to literacy.
They are provided for your information and professional use.

A

alliteration	the repetition of a consonant sound in a group of words, especially in poetry
allusion	a word or phrase that refers to something else the reader already knows from history, experience, or reading
animal fantasy	a story about animals that talk and act like people
answer questions	a reading strategy in which readers use the text and prior knowledge to answer questions about what they are reading
antonym	a word that means the opposite of another word
ask questions	a reading strategy in which readers ask themselves questions about the text to help make sense of what they read
author's point of view	the author's opinion on the subject he or she is writing about
author's purpose	the reason the author wrote the text
autobiography	the story of a real person's life written by that person

B

background knowledge	the information and experience that a reader brings to a text
biography	the story of a real person's life written by another person

C

cause	why something happens
character	a person, an animal, or a personified object in a story
chronological order	events in a selection, presented in the order in which they occurred
classify and categorize	put things, such as pictures or words, into groups
climax	the point in a story at which conflict is confronted
compare	tell how things are the same
comprehension	understanding of text being read—the ultimate goal of reading
comprehension strategy	a conscious plan used by a reader to gain understanding of text. Comprehension strategies may be used before, during, or after reading.
conclusion	a decision or opinion arrived at after thinking about facts and details and using prior knowledge
conflict	the problem or struggle in a story
context clue	the words, phrases, or sentences near an unknown word that give the reader clues to the word's meaning
contrast	tell how things are different

Instruction

details	small pieces of information
dialect	form of a language spoken in a certain region or by a certain group of people that differs from the standard form of that language
dialogue	written conversation
diary	a day-to-day record of one's activities and thoughts
draw conclusions	arrive at decisions or opinions after thinking about facts and details and using prior knowledge

D

effect	what happens as the result of a cause
etymology	an explanation of the origin and history of a word and its meaning
exaggeration	a statement that makes something seem larger or greater than it actually is
expository text	text that contains facts and information. Also called *informational text.*

E

fable	a story, usually with animal characters, that is written to teach a moral, or lesson
fact	piece of information that can be proved to be true
fairy tale	a folk story with magical characters and events
fantasy	a story that could not really happen
fiction	writing that tells about imaginary people, things, and events
figurative language	the use of language that gives words a meaning beyond their usual definitions in order to add beauty or force
flashback	an interruption in the sequence of events of a narrative to include an event that happened earlier
folk tale	a story that has been passed down by word of mouth
foreshadowing	the use of hints or clues about what will happen later in a story

F

generalize	make a broad statement or rule after examining particular facts
graphic organizer	a drawing, chart, or web that illustrates concepts or shows how ideas relate to each other. Readers use graphic organizers to help them keep track of and understand important information and ideas as they read. Story maps, word webs, Venn diagrams, and KWL charts are graphic organizers.
graphic source	a chart, diagram, or map within a text that adds to readers' understanding of the text

G

H

historical fiction	realistic fiction that takes place in the past. It is an imaginary story based on historical events and characters.
humor	writing or speech that has a funny or amusing quality
hyperbole	an exaggerated statement not meant to be taken literally, such as *I'm so hungry I could eat a horse.*

I

idiom	a phrase whose meaning differs from the ordinary meaning of the words. *A stone's throw* is an idiom meaning "a short distance."
imagery	the use of language to create beautiful or forceful pictures in the reader's mind
inference	conclusion reached on the basis of evidence and reasoning
inform	give knowledge, facts, or news to someone
informational text	writing that contains facts and information. Also called *expository text*.
interview	a face-to-face conversation in which someone responds to questions
irony	a way of speaking or writing in which the ordinary meaning of the words is the opposite of what the speaker or writer is thinking; a contrast between what is expected and what actually happens

J

jargon	the language of a special group or profession

L

legend	a story coming down from the past about the great deeds of a hero. Although a legend may be based on historical people and events, it is not regarded as historically true.
literary elements	the characters, setting, plot, and theme of a narrative text

M

main idea	the big idea that tells what a paragraph or a selection is mainly about; the most important idea of a text
metacognition	an awareness of one's own thinking processes and the ability to monitor and direct them to a desired goal. Good readers use metacognition to monitor their reading and adjust their reading strategies.
metaphor	a comparison that does not use *like* or *as*, such as *a heart of stone*
meter	the pattern of beats or accents in poetry

monitor and clarify a comprehension strategy by which readers actively think about understanding their reading and know when they understand and when they do not. Readers use appropriate strategies to make sense of difficult words, ideas, or passages.

mood the atmosphere or feeling of a written work

moral the lesson or teaching of a fable or story

motive the reason a character in a narrative does or says something

mystery a story about mysterious events that are not explained until the end, so as to keep the reader in suspense

myth a story that attempts to explain something in nature

M

narrative a story, made up or true, that someone tells or narrates

narrator a character or someone outside the selection who tells the story

nonfiction writing that tells about real things, real people, and real events

N

onomatopoeia the use of words that sound like their meanings, such as *buzz* and *hum*

opinion someone's judgment, belief, or way of thinking

oral vocabulary the words needed for speaking and listening

outcome the resolution of the conflict in a story

O

paraphrase retell the meaning of a passage in one's own words

personification a figure of speech in which human traits or actions are given to animals or inanimate objects, as in *The sunbeam danced on the waves.*

persuade convince someone to do or to believe something

photo essay a collection of photographs on one theme, accompanied by text

play a story that is written to be acted out for an audience

plot a series of related events at the beginning, middle, and end of a story; the action of a story

poem an expressive, imaginative piece of writing often arranged in lines having rhythm and rhyme. In a poem, the patterns made by the sounds of the words have special importance.

pourquoi tale a type of folk story that explains why things in nature came to be. *Pourquoi* is a French word meaning "why."

P

Instruction

P

predict	tell what a selection might be about or what might happen in a text. Readers use text features and information to predict. They confirm or revise their predictions as they read.
preview	look over a text before reading it
prior knowledge	the information and experience that a reader brings to a text. Readers use prior knowledge to help them understand what they read.
prop	an item, such as an object, picture, or chart, used in a performance or presentation

R

reading vocabulary	the words we recognize or use in print
realistic fiction	a story about imaginary people and events that could happen in real life
repetition	the repeated use of some aspect of language
resolution	the point in a story where the conflict is resolved
rhyme	to end in the same sound(s)
rhythm	a pattern of strong beats in speech or writing, especially poetry
rising action	the buildup of conflicts and complications in a story

S

science fiction	a story based on science that often tells what life in the future might be like
semantic map	a graphic organizer, often a web, used to display words or concepts that are meaningfully related
sensory language	the use of words that help the reader understand how things look, sound, smell, taste, or feel
sequence	the order of events in a selection or the order of the steps in which something is completed
sequence words	clue words such as *first*, *next*, *then*, and *finally* that signal the order of events in a selection
setting	where and when a story takes place
simile	a comparison that uses *like* or *as*, as in *as busy as a bee*
speech	a public talk to a group of people made for a specific purpose
stanza	a group of lines in a poem
steps in a process	the order of the steps in which something is completed

story map	a graphic organizer used to record the literary elements and the sequence of events in a narrative text
story structure	how the characters, setting, and events of a story are organized into a plot
summarize	give the most important ideas of what was read. Readers summarize important information in the selection to keep track of what they are reading.
supporting detail	piece of information that tells about the main idea
symbolism	the use of one thing to suggest something else; often the use of something concrete to stand for an abstract idea

S

tall tale	a humorous story that uses exaggeration to describe impossible happenings
text structure	the organization of a piece of nonfiction writing. Text structures of informational text include cause/effect, chronological, compare/contrast, description, problem/solution, proposition/support, and ask/answer questions.
theme	the big idea or author's message in a story
think aloud	an instructional strategy in which a teacher verbalizes his or her thinking to model the process of comprehension or the application of a skill
tone	author's attitude toward the subject or toward the reader
topic	the subject of a discussion, conversation, or piece of text

T

visualize	picture in one's mind what is happening in the text. Visualizing helps readers imagine the things they read about.

V

Instruction

Section 3 Matching Books and Readers

Leveled Readers Skills Chart

Scott Foresman Reading Street provides more than six hundred leveled readers. Each one is designed to:

- Practice critical skills and strategies
- Build fluency
- Build vocabulary and concepts
- Develop a lifelong love of reading

Grade 2

Title	Level*	DRA Level	Genre	Comprehension Strategy
The Rescue Dogs	C	3	Narrative Nonfiction	Summarize
Country Mouse and City Mouse	D	4	Traditional Tales	Monitor and Clarify
All About Astronauts	D	4	Expository Nonfiction	Text Structure
Camping with Pup	D	4	Animal Fantasy	Story Structure
Deserts	D	4	Expository Nonfiction	Important Ideas
Too Many Rabbit Holes	D	4	Fantasy/Play	Predict and Set Purpose
A Class Play	D	4	Realistic Fiction	Text Structure
The Barn Raising	D	4	Nonfiction	Background Knowledge
Working Dogs	D	4	Expository Nonfiction	Story Structure
Where Is Fish?	D	4	Fantasy	Inferring
Our School Science Fair	D	4	Realistic Fiction	Questioning
Let's Send a Letter!	D	4	Narrative Nonfiction	Visualize
Using a Net	D	4	Expository Nonfiction	Summarize
Ana Is Shy	E	6–8	Realistic Fiction	Predict and Set Purpose
Sink or Float?	E	6–8	Narrative Nonfiction	Inferring
The Camping Trip	E	6–8	Realistic Fiction	Background Knowledge
How to Grow Tomatoes	E	6–8	How-to	Important Ideas
How a Seed Grows	E	6–8	Expository Nonfiction	Questioning
Snakeskin Canyon	E	6–8	Realistic Fiction	Visualize
Blizzard!	E	6–8	Realistic Fiction	Monitor and Clarify
The New Kid in Bali	F	10	Realistic Fiction	Monitor and Clarify
Desert Animals	F	10	Expository Nonfiction	Important Ideas
Camping at Crescent Lake	F	10	Realistic Fiction	Story Structure
An Astronaut Space Walk	F	10	Expository Nonfiction	Story Structure
Service Workers	F	10	Expository Nonfiction	Important Ideas
What Can You Do?	F	10	Narrative Nonfiction	Visualize
Sally and the Wild Puppy	F	10	Humorous Fiction	Background Knowledge
Join an Adventure Club!	F	10	Narrative Nonfiction	Story Structure
Andrew's Mistake	F	10	Realistic Fiction	Inferring
Glooskap and the First Summer: An Algonquin Tale	G	12	Folk Tale	Predict and Set Purpose

* Suggested Guided Reading Level. Use your knowledge of children's abilities to adjust levels as needed.

The chart here and on the next few pages lists titles of leveled readers appropriate for children in Grade 2. Use the chart to find titles that meet your children's interest and instructional needs. The books in this list were leveled using the criteria suggested in *Matching Books to Readers: Using Leveled Books in Guided Reading, Grades K–3* by Irene C. Fountas and Gay Su Pinnell. For more on leveling, see the *Reading Street Leveled Readers Leveling Guide.*

Target Comprehension Skill	Additional Comprehension Instruction	Vocabulary
Cause and Effect	Fact and Opinion	High-Frequency Words
Character and Setting	Fact and Opinion	High-Frequency Words
Main Idea and Details	Author's Purpose	High-Frequency Words
Character and Setting	Main Idea and Details	High-Frequency Words
Main Idea and Details	Compare and Contrast	High-Frequency Words
Facts and Details	Character and Setting	High-Frequency Words
Author's Purpose	Facts and Details	High-Frequency Words
Facts and Details	Cause and Effect	High-Frequency Words
Cause and Effect	Compare and Contrast	High-Frequency Words
Compare and Contrast	Author's Purpose	High-Frequency Words
Author's Purpose	Plot and Theme	High-Frequency Words
Draw Conclusions	Sequence	High-Frequency Words
Compare and Contrast	Draw Conclusions	High-Frequency Words
Sequence	Cause and Effect	High-Frequency Words
Fact and Opinion	Sequence	High-Frequency Words
Draw Conclusions	Character and Setting	Word Structure/Prefixes
Sequence	Fact and Opinion	Context Clues/Antonyms
Fact and Opinion	Facts and Details	Context Clues/Unfamiliar Words
Plot and Theme	Draw Conclusions	Context Clues/Multiple Meanings
Plot and Theme	Main Idea and Details	Picture Clues/Multiple Meanings
Character and Setting	Plot and Theme	High-Frequency Words
Main Idea and Details	Compare and Contrast	High-Frequency Words
Character and Setting	Main Idea and Details	High-Frequency Words
Character and Setting	Sequence	High-Frequency Words
Fact and Opinion	Author's Purpose	Word Structure/Suffixes
Cause and Effect	Facts and Details	Dictionary Skills/Unfamiliar Words
Plot and Theme	Sequence	Dictionary Skills/Unfamiliar Words
Character and Setting	Plot and Theme	Dictionary Skills/Unfamiliar Words
Main Idea and Details	Character and Setting	Word Structure/Compound Words
Facts and Details	Character and Setting	High-Frequency Words

Leveled Readers Skills Chart Continued

Grade 2

Title	Level*	DRA Level	Genre	Comprehension Strategy
Be Ready for an Emergency	G	12	Narrative Nonfiction	Summarize
Let's Work Together!	G	12	Realistic Fiction	Text Structure
Farming Families	G	12	Expository Nonfiction	Background Knowledge
Growing Up	G	12	Realistic Fiction	Story Structure
Three Great Ballplayers	G	12	Autobiography/Biography	Monitor and Clarify
America's Birthday	G	12	Expository Nonfiction	Summarize
Special Chinese Birthdays	G	12	Narrative Nonfiction	Questioning
Down on the Ranch	G	12	Historical Fiction	Story Structure
Just Like Grandpa	G	12	Realistic Fiction	Predict and Set Purpose
Showing Good Manners	H	14	Nonfiction	Inferring
Dotty's Art	H	14	Realistic Fiction	Questioning
Living in Seoul	H	14	Narrative Nonfiction	Visualize
Arachnid or Insect?	H	14	Expository Nonfiction	Summarize
The International Food Fair	H	14	Realistic Fiction	Predict and Set Purpose
Thomas Adams: Chewing Gum Inventor	I	16	Biography	Inferring
Making Travel Fun	I	16	Expository Nonfiction	Background Knowledge
How Do Plants Grow?	I	16	Expository Nonfiction	Important Ideas
A Slice of Mud Pie	I	16	Realistic Fiction	Questioning
Too Many Frogs!	I	16	Humorous Fiction	Visualize
Rainbow Crow Brings Fire to Earth	J	18	Narrative Nonfiction	Monitor and Clarify
Keeping Our Community Safe	J	18	Expository Nonfiction	Important Ideas
Annie Makes a Big Change	J	18	Realistic Fiction	Visualize
Hubert and Frankie	J	18	Animal Fantasy	Background Knowledge
Everyone Can Make a Difference!	K	20	Narrative Nonfiction	Story Structure
Freda the Signmaker	K	20	Humorous Fiction	Inferring
Women Play Baseball	K	20	Narrative Nonfiction	Monitor and Clarify
American Revolution Heroes	K	20	Biography	Summarize
Country Friends, City Friends	L	24	Realistic Fiction	Monitor and Clarify
Look at Our Galaxy	L	24	Expository Nonfiction	Text Structure
At Home in the Wilderness	L	24	Historical Fiction	Story Structure

* Suggested Guided Reading Level. Use your knowledge of children's abilities to adjust levels as needed.

You know the theory behind leveled books: they let you match books with the interest and instructional levels of your children. You can find the right reader for every child with this chart.

Target Comprehension Skill	Additional Comprehension Instruction	Vocabulary
Cause and Effect	Fact and Opinion	High-Frequency Words
Author's Purpose	Facts and Details	High-Frequency Words
Facts and Details	Cause and Effect	High-Frequency Words
Cause and Effect	Compare and Contrast	High-Frequency Words
Compare and Contrast	Draw Conclusions	Context Clues/Homophones
Author's Purpose	Fact and Opinion	Context Clues/Unfamiliar Words
Draw Conclusions	Cause and Effect	Context Clues/Synonyms
Sequence	Main Idea and Details	Word Structure/Suffixes
Facts and Details	Compare and Contrast	Word Structure/Compound Words
Compare and Contrast	Author's Purpose	High-Frequency Words
Author's Purpose	Plot and Theme	High-Frequency Words
Draw Conclusions	Sequence	High-Frequency Words
Compare and Contrast	Draw Conclusions	High-Frequency Words
Sequence	Cause and Effect	High-Frequency Words
Fact and Opinion	Sequence	High-Frequency Words
Draw Conclusions	Character and Setting	Word Structure/Prefixes
Sequence	Fact and Opinion	Context Clues/Antonyms
Fact and Opinion	Facts and Details	Context Clues/Unfamiliar Words
Plot and Theme	Draw Conclusions	Context Clues/Multiple Meanings
Plot and Theme	Main Idea and Details	Context Clues/Multiple Meanings
Fact and Opinion	Author's Purpose	Word Structure/Suffixes
Cause and Effect	Facts and Details	Dictionary Skills/Unfamiliar Words
Plot and Theme	Sequence	Dictionary Skills/Unfamiliar Words
Character and Setting	Plot and Theme	Dictionary Skills/Unfamiliar Words
Main Idea and Details	Character and Setting	Word Structure/Compound Words
Compare and Contrast	Draw Conclusions	Context Clues/Homophones
Author's Purpose	Fact and Opinion	Context Clues/Unfamiliar Words
Character and Setting	Plot and Theme	Amazing Words
Main Idea and Details	Author's Purpose	Amazing Words
Character and Setting	Main Idea and Details	Amazing Words

Matching Books & Readers

Leveled Readers Skills Chart Continued

Grade 2

Title	Level*	DRA Level	Genre	Comprehension Strategy
A World of Birthdays	L	24	Narrative Nonfiction	Questioning
A Cowboy's Life	L	24	Historical Fiction	Text Structure
Voting Day	L	24	Realistic Fiction	Predict and Set Purpose
The First People to Fly	L	24	Realistic Fiction	Predict and Set Purpose
The Hummingbird	M	28	Expository Nonfiction	Important Ideas
Special Animal Helpers	M	28	Narrative Nonfiction	Summarize
The Hoover Dam	M	28	Expository Nonfiction	Text Structure
Many Types of Energy	M	28	Expository Nonfiction	Background Knowledge
Stripes and Silver	M	28	Play	Story Structure
Saint Bernards and Other Working Dogs	N	30	Expository Nonfiction	Inferring
Maggie's New Sidekick	N	30	Fantasy	Questioning
Communicating Then and Now	N	30	Expository Nonfiction	Visualize
How Can Animals Help?	N	30	Narrative Nonfiction	Summarize
Hank's Tortilla Factory	N	30	Realistic Fiction	Predict and Set Purpose
A Few Nifty Inventions	N	30	Expository Nonfiction	Inferring
Starting a New Life	N	30	Expository Nonfiction	Background Knowledge
Plants Grow Everywhere	O	34	Expository Nonfiction	Important Ideas
Compost: Recycled Waste	O	34	Narrative Nonfiction	Questioning
A Quiet Place	O	34	Realistic Fiction	Visualize
Hurricane!	O	34	Expository Nonfiction	Monitor and Clarify
Services and Goods	O	34	Narrative Nonfiction	Important Ideas
A Vet for All Animals	O	34	Narrative Nonfiction	Visualize
Training Peanut	O	34	Realistic Fiction	Background Knowledge
Protect the Earth	P	38	Narrative Nonfiction	Story Structure
Marty's Summer Job	P	38	Realistic Fiction	Inferring
Baseball Heroes Make History	P	38	Autobiography/Biography	Monitor and Clarify
Living in a Democracy	P	38	Expository Nonfiction	Summarize
Celebrations and Family Traditions	P	38	Narrative Nonfiction	Questioning
Living on a Ranch	P	38	Realistic Fiction	Text Structure
Happy New Year!	P	38	Realistic Fiction	Predict and Set Purpose

* Suggested Guided Reading Level. Use your knowledge of children's abilities to adjust levels as needed.

You know the theory behind leveled books: they let you match books with the interest and instructional levels of your children. You can find the right reader for every child with this chart. "

Target Comprehension Skill	Additional Comprehension Instruction	Vocabulary
Draw Conclusions	Cause and Effect	Context Clues/Synonyms
Sequence	Main Idea and Details	Word Structure/Suffixes
Facts and Details	Compare and Contrast	Word Structure/Compound Words
Facts and Details	Character and Setting	Amazing Words
Main Idea and Details	Compare and Contrast	Amazing Words
Cause and Effect	Cause and Effect	Amazing Words
Author's Purpose	Facts and Details	Amazing Words
Facts and Details	Cause and Effect	Amazing Words
Cause and Effect	Compare and Contrast	Amazing Words
Compare and Contrast	Author's Purpose	Amazing Words
Author's Purpose	Plot and Theme	Amazing Words
Draw Conclusions	Sequence	Amazing Words
Compare and Contrast	Draw Conclusions	Amazing Words
Sequence	Cause and Effect	Amazing Words
Fact and Opinion	Sequence	Amazing Words
Draw Conclusions	Character and Setting	Word Structure/Prefixes
Sequence	Fact and Opinion	Context Clues/Antonyms
Fact and Opinion	Facts and Details	Context Clues/Unfamiliar Words
Plot and Theme	Draw Conclusions	Context Clues/Multiple Meanings
Plot and Theme	Main Idea and Details	Context Clues/Multiple Meanings
Fact and Opinion	Author's Purpose	Word Structure/Suffixes
Cause and Effect	Facts and Details	Dictionary Skills/Unfamiliar Words
Plot and Theme	Sequence	Dictionary Skills/Unfamiliar Words
Character and Setting	Plot and Theme	Dictionary Skills/Unfamiliar Words
Main Idea and Details	Character and Setting	Word Structure/Compound Words
Compare and Contrast	Draw Conclusions	Context Clues/Homophones
Author's Purpose	Fact and Opinion	Context Clues/Unfamiliar Words
Draw Conclusions	Cause and Effect	Context Clues/Synonyms
Sequence	Main Idea and Details	Word Structure/Suffixes
Facts and Details	Compare and Contrast	Word Structure/Compound Words

Matching Books & Readers

Section 3 Matching Books and Readers

What Good Readers Do

You can use the characteristics and behaviors of good readers to help all your children read better. But what are these characteristics and behaviors? And how can you use them to foster good reading behaviors for all your children? Here are some helpful tips.

Good Readers enjoy reading! They have favorite books, authors, and genres. Good readers often have a preference about where and when they read. They talk about books and recommend their favorites.

Develop this behavior by giving children opportunities to respond in different ways to what they read. Get them talking about what they read, and why they like or dislike it.

This behavior is important because book sharing alerts you to children who are somewhat passive about reading or have limited literacy experiences. Book sharing also helps you when you select books for the class.

Good Readers select books they can read.

Develop this behavior by providing a range of three or four texts appropriate for the child and then letting the student choose.

This behavior is important because children gain control over reading when they can choose from books they can read. This helps them become more independent in the classroom.

Good Readers read independently for longer periods of time.

Develop this behavior by taking note of the level of support children need during guided reading. Use this information to gauge independent reading time accordingly.

This behavior is important because children become better readers when they spend time reading many texts at their independent level.

Good Readers use text features to help them preview and set purposes.

Develop this behavior by having children use the title and illustrations in fiction texts or the title, contents, headings, and other graphic features in nonfiction texts to make predictions about what they will be reading.

This behavior is important because previewing actually makes reading easier! Looking at features and sampling the text enables readers to predict and set expectations for reading.

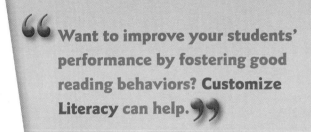

" Want to improve your students' performance by fostering good reading behaviors? **Customize Literacy** can help. "

Good Readers predict and ask questions before and while they read.

Develop this behavior by asking questions. After reading a passage, ask children what they think will happen next in a fiction text. Have them ask a question they think will be answered in a nonfiction text and read on to see if it is.

This behavior is important because when children predict and ask questions as they read, they are engaged. They have a purpose for reading and a basis for monitoring their comprehension.

Good Readers read meaningful phrases aloud with appropriate expression.

Develop this behavior by giving children lots of opportunities to read orally. As they read, note children's phrasing, intonation, and attention to punctuation and give help as needed.

This behavior is important because reading fluently in longer, meaningful phrases supports comprehension and ease in reading longer, more complex texts.

Good Readers read aloud at an appropriate reading rate with a high percent of accuracy.

Develop this behavior by timing children's oral reading to calculate their reading rates. You can also record children's miscues to determine a percent of accuracy. This will help identify problems.

This behavior is important because when children read fluently texts that are "just right," they find reading more enjoyable. A fluent reader is able to focus more on constructing meaning and is more likely to develop a positive attitude toward reading.

Matching Books & Readers

Section 3 Matching Books and Readers

Good Readers use effective strategies and sources of information to figure out unknown words.

CH-

QU-

ST-

Develop this behavior by teaching specific strategies for figuring out unknown words, such as sounding out clusters of letters, using context, reading on, and using references.

This behavior is important because when readers have a variety of strategies to use, they are more able to decode and self-correct quickly. Readers who do these things view themselves as good readers.

Good Readers construct meaning as they read and then share or demonstrate their understanding.

Develop this behavior by having children retell what they read or write a summary of what they read in their own words.

This behavior is important because the ability to retell or write a summary is essential for success in reading. It shows how well a student has constructed meaning.

Good Readers locate and use what is explicitly stated in a text.

Develop this behavior by asking questions that require children to go back into the text to find explicitly stated information.

This behavior is important because the ability to recall, locate, and use specific information stated in a text enables readers to respond to literal questions, as well as to support opinions and justify their responses.

Good Readers make connections.

Develop this behavior by asking questions to help children make connections: *What does this remind you of? Have you ever read or experienced anything like this?*

This behavior is important because making connections helps readers understand and appreciate a text. Making connections to self, the world, and other texts supports higher-level thinking.

Good Readers interpret what they read by making inferences.

Develop this behavior by asking questions to help children tell or write about what they think was implied in the text: *Why do you think that happened? What helped you come to that conclusion?*

This behavior is important because the ability to go beyond the literal meaning of a text enables readers to gain a deeper understanding. When children make inferences, they use background knowledge, their personal knowledge, and the text to grasp the meaning of what is implied by the author.

Good Readers determine importance and evaluate what they read.

Develop this behavior by always having children identify what they think is the most important message, event, or information in a text.

This behavior is important because readers must be able to sort out important from interesting information. The ability to establish and/or use criteria and provide support when making judgments is an important critical-thinking skill.

Good Readers support their responses using information from a text and/or their own background knowledge.

Develop this behavior by always asking children to give the reason(s) they identified an event, message, or ideas as most important.

This behavior is important because the ability to justify one's response is important for all learners. It enables others to know the basis for a decision and provides an opening for further discussion.

Matching Books & Readers

Conversation Starters

Asking Good Questions When children read interesting and thought-provoking books, they want to share! You can encourage children to think critically about what they read. Use questions such as the following to assess comprehension as well as evoke good class/group discussions.

Author's Purpose

- Why did the author write this piece?

- How does figuring out the author's purpose help you decide how to read the text?

Cause and Effect

- Why did these events happen? How might they have been different if the causes had been different?

- What clues helped you know what caused these events to happen?

Compare and Contrast

- What clue words show the author is comparing and/or contrasting in this article?

- How are the fictional characters and events in this story like and/or different from real people and events you know of?

Draw Conclusions

- Based on what you have read, seen, or experienced, what can you conclude about this event in the selection?

- This story seems to be a fantasy. Why might you conclude this?

- What conclusions can you draw about the characters?

Fact and Opinion

- Is this a statement of fact or a statement of opinion? How do you know?

- This seems to be a statement of opinion. Why is it really a statement of fact? (Alternately: This seems to be a statement of fact. Why is it really a statement of opinion?)

Graphic Sources

- How does the author use graphic sources (chart, maps, illustrations, time lines, and so on) to support ideas and opinions?

- This selection has many graphic sources. Which one or ones best help you understand the events or ideas in the selection? Why?

Literary Elements: Character, Setting, Plot, Theme

- Describe the main character at the beginning of the story and at the end of the story. How and why does he or she change?

- How is the setting important to the story? How might the story be different if its time or its place were different?

- What does the main character want at the beginning of the story? How does the main character go about trying to achieve this?

- In a few sentences, what is the plot of the story?

- What is the theme of the story? Use details from the story to support your statement.

Main Idea and Details

- What is the main idea of this paragraph or article? What are some details?

- The author makes this particular statement in the article. What details does the author provide to support that statement?

Sequence

- What is the sequence of events in the text?

- Is the order of events important in this story? Why or why not?

- Based on what has already happened, what will most likely happen next?

Matching Books & Readers

Connecting Science and Social Studies

Scott Foresman Reading Street Leveled Readers are perfect for covering, supporting, or enriching science and social studies content. Using these books ensures that all children can access important concepts.

Grade 2 Leveled Readers

Science

Earth and Space Science

Nonfiction Books

- *All About Astronauts*
- *An Astronaut Space Walk*
- *Desert Animals*
- *Deserts*
- *Hurricane!*
- *Look at Our Galaxy*

Fiction Books

- *Blizzard!*
- *Maggie's New Sidekick*
- *Rainbow Crow Brings Fire to Earth*
- *A Slice of Mud Pie*

Life Science

Nonfiction Books

- *Arachnid or Insect?*
- *Compost: Recycled Waste*
- *Farming Families*
- *How a Seed Grows*
- *How Can Animals Help?*
- *How Do Plants Grow?*
- *How to Grow Tomatoes*
- *Plants Grow Everywhere*
- *A Vet for All Animals*

Fiction Books

- *Annie Makes a Big Change*
- *Camping at Crescent Lake*
- *Growing Up*
- *Too Many Rabbit Holes*
- *Where Is Fish?*

Physical Science

Nonfiction Books

- *Many Types of Energy*
- *Sink or Float?*

Fiction Books

- *The Hummingbird*
- *Our School Science Fair*

Grade 2 Leveled Readers

Social Studies

Citizenship

Nonfiction Books

- *America's Birthday*
- *The Barn Raising*
- *Be Ready for an Emergency*
- *Everyone Can Make a Difference!*
- *Join an Adventure Club!*
- *Keeping Our Community Safe*
- *Protect the Earth*
- *The Rescue Dogs*
- *Service Workers*
- *Special Animal Helpers*
- *Using a Net*
- *What Can You Do?*
- *Working Dogs*

Fiction Books

- *Andrew's Mistake*
- *Camping with Pup*
- *Freda the Signmaker*
- *Hubert and Frankie*
- *Let's Work Together!*
- *Marty's Summer Job*
- *Sally and the Wild Puppy*
- *Stripes and Silver*
- *Too Many Frogs!*
- *Training Peanut*

Culture

Nonfiction Books

- *Celebrations and Family Traditions*
- *Living in Seoul*
- *Showing Good Manners*
- *Special Chinese Birthdays*
- *A World of Birthdays*

Fiction Books

- *Ana Is Shy*
- *The Camping Trip*
- *Country Friends, City Friends*
- *Dotty's Art*
- *The First People to Fly*
- *Glooskap and the First Summer: An Algonquin Tale*
- *Happy New Year!*
- *The International Food Fair*
- *Just Like Grandpa*
- *Living on a Ranch*
- *The New Kid in Bali*
- *Voting Day*

Economics

Nonfiction Books

- *Services and Goods*

Fiction Books

- *Country Mouse and City Mouse*
- *A Quiet Place*
- *Snakeskin Canyon*

History

Nonfiction Books

- *A Few Nifty Inventions*
- *The Hoover Dam*
- *Living in a Democracy*
- *Making Travel Fun*
- *Saint Bernards and Other Working Dogs*
- *Starting a New Life*
- *Women Play Baseball*

Fiction Books

- *At Home in the Wilderness*
- *A Class Play*
- *A Cowboy's Life*
- *Down on the Ranch*
- *Hank's Tortilla Factory*

Government

Nonfiction Books

- *Communicating Then and Now*
- *Let's Send a Letter!*

More Great Titles

Biography

- *American Revolution Heroes*
- *Baseball Heroes Make History*
- *Thomas Adams: Chewing Gum Inventor*
- *Three Great Ballplayers*

Connecting Science and Social Studies

Need more choices? Look back to Grade 1.

Grade 1 Leveled Readers

Science

Earth and Space Science

Nonfiction Books
- All About the Weather
- The Communication Story
- Over the Years
- Ready for Winter?
- Using the Telephone

Fiction Books
- Cody's Adventure
- Marla's Good Idea
- What a Detective Does

Life Science

Nonfiction Books
- All About Food Chains
- Animals Change and Grow
- Around the Forest
- Around the World
- Baby Animals in the Rain Forest
- Bees and Beekeepers
- The Dinosaur Detectives
- The Dinosaur Herds
- Fun in the Sun
- Honey
- In My Room
- Learn About Butterflies
- Learn About Worker Bees
- Let's Go to the Zoo
- Let's Visit a Butterfly Greenhouse
- Look at Dinosaurs
- A Mighty Oak Tree
- Monarchs Migrate South
- People Help the Forest
- The Seasons Change
- Seasons Come and Go
- What Animals Can You See?

Life Science

Fiction Books
- Bix the Dog
- Britton Finds a Kitten
- Carlos Picks a Pet
- Cary and the Wildlife Shelter
- Mac Can Do It!
- Mack and Zack
- Plans Change
- Sam
- The Sick Pets
- Time for Dinner
- What Brown Saw
- Which Animals Will We See?
- Which Fox?

Physical Science

Nonfiction Books
- The Inclined Plane
- Simple Machines at Work
- Simple Machines in Compound Machines

Grade 1 Leveled Readers

Social Studies

Citizenship

Nonfiction Books
- *A Class*
- *A Garden for All*
- *Great Scientists: Detectives at Work*
- *Here in My Neighborhood*
- *A New Library*
- *Puppy Raiser*
- *The Story of the Kids Care Club*
- *Ways to Be a Good Citizen*

Fiction Books
- *The Art Show*
- *At Your Vet*
- *Big Wishes and Her Baby*
- *Double Trouble Twins*
- *Fly Away Owl!*
- *Grasshopper and Ant*
- *Hank's Song*
- *Let's Build a Park!*
- *Look at My Neighborhood*
- *My Little Brother Drew*
- *On the Farm*
- *Paul's Bed*
- *A Play*
- *Rules at School*
- *Space Star*
- *Squirrel and Bear*
- *That Cat Needs Help!*

Culture

Nonfiction Books
- *Cascarones Are for Fun*
- *My Babysitter*
- *Special Days, Special Food*
- *We Are a Family*
- *What Makes Buildings Special?*

Fiction Books
- *Go West!*
- *Grandma's Farm*
- *Gus the Pup*
- *Jamie's Jumble of Junk*
- *A New Baby Brother*
- *A Party for Pedro*
- *A Visit to the Ranch*
- *Where They Live*

History

Nonfiction Books
- *School: Then and Now*
- *Treasures of Our Country*

Fiction Books
- *Loni's Town*

Government

Nonfiction Books
- *America's Home*
- *Our Leaders*

Fiction Books
- *Mom the Mayor*

Connecting Science and Social Studies

Need more choices? Look ahead to Grade 3.

Grade 3 Leveled Readers

Science

Earth and Space Science

Nonfiction Books
- The Frozen Continent: Antarctica
- Fun with Hobbies and Science!
- Gemstones Around the World
- Grandpa's Rock Kit
- How to Measure the Weather
- Measuring the Earth
- Meet the Stars
- Pictures in the Sky

Fiction Books
- What a Day!
- Journey Across the Arctic

Life Science

Nonfiction Books
- A Pet Bird
- All About Birds
- All About Penguins
- Animal Tracking: Learn More About It
- Animals of the Concrete Jungle
- Coral Reefs
- Desert Life
- The Field Trip
- Free in the Sea
- Growing Vegetables
- Ice Fishing in the Arctic
- Largest, Fastest, Lightest, Longest
- Life in the Arctic
- Raisins
- Rescuing Whales
- These Birds Can't Fly!
- Whales and Other Amazing Animals

Life Science

Fiction Books
- The Best Field Trip Ever!
- Bills and Beaks
- Buddy Ran Away
- Grape Season
- The Hunters and the Elk
- In the Fields
- Swimming in a School
- Swimming Like Buck
- Toby the Smart Dog

Grade 3 Leveled Readers

Social Studies

Citizenship

Nonfiction Books
- *Sweet Freedom!*
- *Symbols, Signs, and Songs of America*

Fiction Books
- *Buddy Goes to School*
- *Camping with Aunt Julie*
- *The Opposite Cousins*
- *Our Garden*
- *Puppy Problems*

Culture

Nonfiction Books
- *A Child's Life in Korea*
- *A Walk Around the City*
- *Celebrate Around the World*
- *China's Special Gifts to the World*
- *His Favorite Sweatshirt*
- *Let's Go Have Fun!*
- *Life Overseas*
- *Mixing, Kneading, and Baking*
- *New York's Chinatown*
- *The French Connection*
- *The World of Bread!*

Fiction Books
- *A Tea Party with Obâchan*
- *Bobby's New Apartment*
- *Cowboy Slim's Dude Ranch*
- *E-mail Friends*

Culture

- *Grandmother Spider Steals the Sun*
- *Iguana Takes a Ride*
- *Kapuapua's Magic Shell*
- *The Last Minute*
- *Lily's Adventure Around the World*
- *The Magic of Coyote*
- *One Forest, Different Trees*
- *The Road to New York*
- *The Three Bears and Goldilocks*
- *The Thunder and Lightning Men*

Economics

Nonfiction Books
- *It's a Fair Swap!*
- *It's a World of Time Zones*
- *Let's Make a Trade*
- *What's Money All About?*

Fiction Books
- *A Family of Collectors*
- *Joanie's House Becomes a Home*
- *Let's Surprise Mom*
- *The Market Adventure*
- *The Metal Detective*
- *Mr. Post's Project*
- *The Shopping Trip*

History

Nonfiction Books
- *Across the English Channel*
- *Celebrate Independence Day/Celebra El Día de la Independencia*
- *Changing Times: Women in the Early Twentieth Century*
- *Greek Myths*
- *The Statue of Liberty: A Gift From France*

Fiction Books
- *A Trip*
- *The Winning Point*
- *With a Twist*

More Great Titles

Biography
- *Extraordinary Athletes*
- *Great Women in U. S. History*
- *Thomas Hart Benton: Painter of Murals*

Trial Lessons

Use your colleagues' experiences to help as you think about new ways to connect content and children. Use the following plan to create a mini-lesson. It should last twenty minutes. Get the support of your colleagues as you try something new and then reflect on what happened.

Be Creative! As you develop a plan for a mini-lesson, use these four words to guide planning: *purpose, text, resources,* and *routine.*

- **Purpose:** Decide on a skill or strategy to cover. Define your purpose for teaching the lesson.

- **Text:** Develop a list of the materials you could use. Ask your colleagues for suggestions.

- **Resources:** Make a list of the available resources, and consider how to use those resources most effectively. Consider using the Leveled Readers listed on pages CL22–CL27 and CL34–CL39 of Customize Literacy.

- **Routine:** Choose an instructional routine to structure your mini-lesson. See the mini-lessons in Customize Literacy for suggestions.

Try It! Try out your lesson! Consider audio- or videotaping the lesson for later review. You may wish to invite a colleague to sit in as you teach. Make notes on how the lesson went.

How Did It Go? Use the self-evaluation checklist on page CL43 as you reflect on your trial lesson. This provides a framework for later discussion.

Discuss, Reflect, Repeat Solicit feedback from your teacher study group. Explain the lesson and share your reflections. Ask for suggestions on ways to improve the lesson. Take some time to reflect on the feedback. Modify your lesson to reflect what you have learned. Then try teaching the lesson again.

Checklist for Teacher Self-Evaluation

How Well Did I ...	Very Well	Satisfactory	Not Very Well
Plan the lesson?			
Select the appropriate level of text?			
Introduce the lesson and explain its objectives?			
Review previously taught skills?			
Directly explain the new skills being taught?			
Model the new skills?			
Break the material down into small steps?			
Integrate guided practice into the lesson?			
Monitor guided practice for student understanding?			
Provide feedback on independent practice?			
Maintain an appropriate pace?			
Assess student understanding of the material?			
Stress the importance of applying the skill as they read?			
Maintain students' interest?			
Ask questions?			
Handle student questions and responses?			
Respond to the range of abilities?			

May be reproduced for classroom use. © Pearson Education, Inc.

Building Community

Books for Teachers

Children aren't the only ones who need to read to grow. Here is a brief list of books that you may find useful to fill your reading teacher basket and learn new things.

A Professional Bibliography

Adams, M. J. "Alphabetic Anxiety and Explicit, Systematic Phonics Instruction: A Cognitive Science Perspective." *Handbook of Early Literacy Research.* The Guilford Press, 2001.

Adams, M. J. *Beginning to Read: Thinking and Learning About Print.* The MIT Press, 1990.

Afflerbach, P. "The Influence of Prior Knowledge and Text Genre on Readers' Prediction Strategies." *Journal of Reading Behavior,* vol. XXII, no. 2 (1990).

Armbruster, B. B., F. Lehr, and J. Osborn. *Put Reading First: The Research Building Blocks for Teaching Children to Read.* Partnership for Reading, Washington, D.C., 2001.

Bear, D. R., M. Invernizzi, S. Templeton, and F. Johnston. *Words Their Way.* Merrill Prentice Hall, 2004.

Beck, I., M. G. McKeown, and L. Kucan. *Bringing Words to Life: Robust Vocabulary Instruction.* The Guilford Press, 2002.

Biemiller, A. "Teaching Vocabulary in the Primary Grades: Vocabulary Instruction Needed." *Vocabulary Instruction Research to Practice.* The Guilford Press, 2004.

Blachowicz, C. and P. Fisher. "Vocabulary Instruction." *Handbook of Reading Research,* vol. III. Lawrence Erlbaum Associates, 2000.

Cunningham, P. M. and J. W. Cunningham. "What We Know About How to Teach Phonics." *What Research Says About Reading Instruction,* 3rd ed. International Reading Association, 2002.

Daniels, H. *Literature Circles.* 2nd ed. Stenhouse Publishers, 2002.

Dickson, S. V., D. C. Simmons, and E. J. Kame'enui. "Text Organization: Instructional and Curricular Basics and Implications." *What Reading Research Tells Us About Children with Diverse Learning Needs: Bases and Basics.* Lawrence Erlbaum Associates, 1998.

Diller, D. *Making the Most of Small Groups: Differentiation for All.* Stenhouse Publishers, 2007.

Duke, N. K., V. S. Bennett-Armistead, and E. M. Roberts. "Bridging the Gap Between Learning to Read and Reading to Learn." *Literacy and Young Children: Research-Based Practices.* The Guilford Press, 2003.

Duke, N. K. and C. Tower. "Nonfiction Texts for Young Readers." *The Texts in Elementary Classrooms.* Lawrence Erlbaum Associates, 2004.

Ehri, L. C. and S. R. Nunes. "The Role of Phonemic Awareness in Learning to Read." *What Research Has to Say About Reading Instruction.* 3rd ed. International Reading Association, 2002.

Fountas, I. C. and G. S. Pinnell. *Guided Reading: Good First Teaching for All Children.* Heinemann, 1996.

Fountas, I. C. and G. S. Pinnell. *Matching Books to Readers: Using Leveled Books in Guided Reading,* K-3. Heinemann, 1999.

Harvey, S. and A. Goudvis. *Strategies That Work: Teaching Comprehension to Enhance Understanding.* 2nd ed. Stenhouse Publishers, 2007.

Hiebert, E. H. and L. A. Martin. "The Texts of Beginning Reading Instruction." *Handbook of Early Literacy Research.* The Guilford Press, 2001.

Indrisano, R. and J. R. Paratore. *Learning to Write, Writing to Learn. Theory and Research in Practice.* International Reading Association, 2005.

Juel, C., G. Biancarosa, D. Coker, and R. Deffes. "Walking with Rosie: A Cautionary Tale of Early Reading Instruction." *Educational Leadership* (April 2003).

National Reading Panel. *Teaching Children to Read.* National Institute of Child Health and Human Development, 1999.

Pressley, M. *Reading Instruction That Works: The Case for Balanced Teaching,* 3rd ed. The Guilford Press, 2005.

Smith, S., D. C. Simmons, and E. J. Kame'enui. "Word Recognition: Research Bases." *What Reading Research Tells Us About Children with Diverse Learning Needs: Bases and Basics.* Lawrence Erlbaum Associates, 1998.

Snow, C., S. Burns, and P. Griffin, eds. *Preventing Reading Difficulties in Young Children.* National Academy Press, 1998.

Vaughn, S., P. G. Mathes, S. Linan-Thompson, and D. J. Francis. "Teaching English Language Learners at Risk for Reading Disabilities to Read: Putting Research into Practice." *Learning Disabilities Research & Practice,* vol. 20, issue 1 (February 2006).

Building Community

Let's Learn
Amazing Words

Definitions, examples, and **applications** to use with the Oral Vocabulary in each lesson.

The Night the Moon Fell

Amazing Words **Oral Vocabulary Routine**

DAY 1

landmark

1) **Introduce** A *landmark* is an object, such as a tree or building, that can help people find their way.

2) **Demonstrate** The windmill was a *landmark* for finding the road to the farm. The sailors did not get lost because they used the lighthouse as a *landmark*.

3) **Apply** What might people use as a *landmark* in a big city?

unexpected

1) **Introduce** When something is *unexpected*, it happens without warning or notice.

2) **Demonstrate** Today's storm was *unexpected*. I received an *unexpected* letter from my friend.

3) **Apply** How would you feel if someone gave you an *unexpected* birthday party?

DAY 2

quiver

1) **Introduce** *Quiver* means "to shake all over."

2) **Demonstrate** Some people *quiver* with excitement. The scared boy *quivered* with fear.

3) **Apply** Show me how you *quiver.*

DAY 3

Instruction for this day can be found in the Oral Vocabulary lesson.

DAY 4

accent

1) **Introduce** An *accent* is the particular way people speak English in other countries.

2) **Demonstrate** My neighbor is from France and speaks English with a French *accent.*

3) **Apply** Who have you heard speak with an *accent*? What sort of accent was it?

The First Tortilla

Let's Learn
Amazing Words

Definitions, examples, and **applications** to use with the Oral Vocabulary in each lesson.

Amazing Words Oral Vocabulary Routine

 **DAY 1**

predict

1 **Introduce** *Predict* means "to tell what will happen before it happens."

2 **Demonstrate** Mom *predicts* I will do well on my math test. I *predict* you will win the race.

3 **Apply** Would you *predict* the weather for yesterday or for tomorrow?

terrifying

1 **Introduce** Something that is *terrifying* is frightening.

2 **Demonstrate** An explosion is *terrifying*. The monsters in that movie were *terrifying*.

3 **Apply** Name a word that means about the same as *terrifying*.

 **DAY 2**

whip

1 **Introduce** *Whip* means "to move or pull something quickly."

2 **Demonstrate** The strong wind *whipped* the branches of the trees. My dog *whipped* the stick from my hand and ran off with it.

3 **Apply** What other things outside could be *whipped* by a strong wind?

 **DAY 3**

Instruction for this day can be found in the Oral Vocabulary lesson.

 **DAY 4**

swirl

1 **Introduce** Things that *swirl* move along in a twisting way.

2 **Demonstrate** I watched water in a brook *swirl* over rocks. Seed pods *swirled* in the air.

3 **Apply** Show me a *swirling* motion with your hand.

UNIT 4 — Acknowledgments

Acknowledgments

Text

Grateful acknowledgment is made to the following for copyrighted material:

Page 28: From *A Froggy Fable* by John Lechner. Copyright © 2005 by John Lechner.

Page 62: From *The Life Cycle of a Pumpkin* by Ron Fridell and Patricia Walsh. Copyright © 2001 Harcourt Education, Ltd. Used by permission.

Page 80: "How Do Seeds Know Which Way Is Up?" from *Where Fish Go in Winter and Other Great Mysteries* by Amy Goldman Koss, copyright © 1987 by Amy Goldman Koss. Used by permission of Dial Books for Young Readers, A Division of Penguin Young Readers Group, A Member of Penguin Group (USA) Inc., 345 Hudson Street, New York, NY 10014. All rights reserved.

Page 92: From *Soil* by Sally Walker. Copyright © 2007 by Sally Walker. All rights reserved. No part of this book may be reproduced or transmitted in any form or by any means, electronic or mechanical, including photocopying, recording, or by any information storage or retrieval system, without permission in writing from the publisher. Reprinted by permission of Lerner Publishing Group, Inc.

Page 128: From *The Night the Moon Fell* by Pat Mora. Text copyright © 2000 by Pat Mora. Illustrations copyright © 2000 by Domi.

Page 162: From *The First Tortilla* by Rudolfo Anaya. Text copyright © 2007 by Rudolfo Anaya. Illustrations copyright © 2007 by the University of New Mexico Press.

Page 192: Reprinted with the permission of Aladdin Paperbacks, an imprint of Simon & Schuster Children's Publishing Division from *Wind* by Marion Dane Bauer. Copyright © 2003 Marion Dane Bauer.

Page 198: *Fox Forgets!* by Angela Royston. Copyright © 1998 Dorling Kindersley Limited, London. Reprinted by permission.

Page 230: From *Carl the Complainer* by Michelle Knudsen. Text copyright © 2005 by Kane Press, Inc. Illustrations copyright © 2005 by Maryann Cocca-Leffler. All rights reserved. No part of this book may be reproduced or transmitted in any form or by any means, electronic or mechanical, including photocopying, recording, or by any information storage or retrieval system, without permission in writing from the publisher. This edition published by arrangement with Kane Press, Inc. New York, NY, represented by Lernent Publishing Group, Inc.

Page 252: "Fishermen" by Juan Bautista Grosso from *Singing Horse* by Alma Flor Ada and F. Isabel Campoy. Text copyright © 2000 Alma Flor Ada and F. Isabel Campoy. Illustrations by Claudia Legnazzi. Edition copyright © 2000 Santillana USA Publishing Company, Inc.

Page 264: Reprinted with the permission of Margaret K. McElderry Books, an imprint of Simon & Schuster's Children's Publishing Division from *Bad Dog, Dodger!* by Barbara Abercrombie. Text copyright © 2002 Barbara Abercrombie.

Page 296: From *Horace and Morris but mostly Dolores* by James Howe, illustrated by Amy Walrod. Text copyright © 1999 by James Howe, Illustrations copyright © 1999 by Amy Walrod. Reprinted with permission of Atheneum Books for Young Readers, an imprint of Simon & Schuster Children's Publishing Division. All rights reserved.

Page 332: *The Signmaker's Assistant* by Tedd Arnold. Copyright © 1992 by Tedd Arnold. Published by arrangement with Dial Books for Young Readers, A Division of Penguin Young Readers Group, A Member of Penguin Group (USA) Inc., 345 Hudson Street, New York, NY 10014. All rights reserved.

Page 352: Action Without Borders Web site, www.idealist.org/kt/youthorgs.html. Reprinted by permission.

Page 368: From *Just Like Josh Gibson* by Angela Johnson, illustrated by Beth Peck. Text copyright © 2004 by Angela Johnson, Illustrations copyright © 2004 by Beth Peck. Reprinted with permission of Simon & Schuster Books For Young Readers, an imprint of Simon & Schuster Children's Publishing Division. All rights reserved.

Page 400: *Red, White, And Blue* by John Herman, and illustrated by Shannan Stirnweis. Text Copyright © John Herman, 1998. Illustrations Copyright © Shannan Stirnweis, 1998. Published by arrangement with Grosset & Dunlap, a division of Penguin Young Readers Group, a member of Penguin Group (USA) Inc. All rights reserved.

Page 434: From *A Birthday Basket for Tía* by Pat Mora, illustrated by Cecily Lang. Text copyright © 1992 by Pat Mora, Illustrations copyright © 1992 by Cecily Lang. Reprinted with permission of Simon & Schuster Books For Young Readers, an imprint of Simon & Schuster Children's Publishing Division. All rights reserved.

Page 452: From www.kidparties.com/traditions.htm. Reprinted by permission.

Page 466: *Cowboys* by Lucille Recht Penner. Text Copyright © Lucille Recht Penner, 1996. Illustrations Copyright © Ben Carter, 1996. Published by arrangement with Grosset & Dunlap, a division of Penguin Young Readers Group, a member of Penguin Group (USA) Inc. All rights reserved.

Page 492: From *The Cowboy's Handbook* by Tod Cody, copyright © 1966 by Breslich & Foss. Used by permission of Cobblehill Books, an affiliate of Dutton Children's Books, A Division of Penguin Young Readers Group, A Member of Penguin Group (USA) Inc., 345 Hudson Street, New York, NY 10014. All rights reserved.

Page 504: From *Grace for President* by Kelly DiPucchio. Text copyright © 2008 by Kelly DiPucchio. Illustrations copyright © 2008 by LeUyen Pham.

Note: Every effort has been made to locate the copyright owner of material reproduced on this component. Omissions brought to our attention will be corrected in subsequent editions.

Illustrations

Cover: Scott Gustafson, **E11–E112** Robert Neubecker; **28–41** Wednesday Kirwan; **46–51** Ariel Pang; **216–276** Laura Ovresat; **235** Maryann Cocca-Leffler; **266–278** Diane Greeneseid; **386–389** Clint Hansen; **400–416** Shannan Stirnweis; **412** Derek Grinnell; **W2–W15** Alessia Girasole.

Photographs

Every effort has been made to secure permission and provide appropriate credit for photographic material. The publisher deeply regrets any omission and pledges to correct errors called to its attention in subsequent editions.

Unless otherwise acknowledged, all photographs are the property of Pearson Education, Inc.

Photo locators denoted as follows: Top (T), Center (C), Bottom (B), Left (L), Right (R), Background (Bkgd)

18 (C) ©Larry Mulvehill/Corbis; **20** ©Don B. Stevenson/Alamy Images; **25** (CR) Jupiter Images; **26** (T) ©Don Meyer/PhotoLibrary Group, Ltd., (C) ©Scott Speakes/Corbis, PhotoLibrary Group, Ltd., (C) ©Scott Speakes/Corbis; **27** (T) ©Wataru Yanagida/Getty Images; **54** (B) ©Helmut Meyer zur Capellen/aefa /Corbis; **59** (TR) ©Stockxpert; **60** (B) ©BUILT Images/PhotoLibrary, (C) ©Steve Belkowitz/Getty Images, (T) Corbis; **62** (TR) ©Royalty-Free/Corbis, (Bkgd) Getty Images; **64** (TC) ©Ben Klaffke, (CR) ©Royalty-Free/Corbis; **65** (TR) ©Dwight R. Kuhn, (TL) ©Royalty-Free/Corbis; **66** (TR, TL) ©Dwight R. Kuhn; **67** (CR) ©Dwight R. Kuhn, (TC) ©Simon? Thaler/Index Stock Imagery; **68** (CR) ©Ben Klaffke, (T) ©Steve Solum/Index Stock Imagery; **69** (TR, T) ©Dwight R. Kuhn; **70** (T, BR) ©Ben Klaffke; **71** (CR) ©Dwight R. Kuhn, (T) ©Reuters/Corbis; **72** (T) ©Dwight R. Kuhn, (CR) Getty Images; **73** (T) ©Barry Lewis/Corbis, (CR) ©Matthew Klein/Corbis; **74** (TR) ©Royalty-Free/Corbis, (TL) ©Tony Freeman/PhotoEdit; **75** ©Richard Hamilton Smith/Corbis; **80** (C) ©David Aubrey/Corbis; **84** (B) ©Tom McHugh/Photo Researchers, Inc.; **90** (BR) ©Blue/Alamy, (BC) ©Cn Boon/Alamy, (C) ©Garden Picture Library/PhotoLibrary Group, Ltd., (B) ©imageclng/Alamy, (BR) ©Stefan Sollfors/Alamy; **91** Getty Images; **92** (Inset, Bkgd) Getty Images; **94** ©Image Source; **95** (T) ©Michael Habicht/Animals Animals/Earth Scenes, (C) ©Peter Gould/OSF/Animals Animals/Earth Scenes; **96** (B) ©Marli Miller/Visuals Unlimited; **97** (TL) ©Paul Springett/Alamy, (TR) ©Robert & Jean Pollock/Visuals Unlimited; **98** (T) ©Douglas Peebles Photography/Alamy; **99** (CR) ©Mark A. Schneider/Visuals Unlimited, (B) Harry Taylor/©DK Images; **100** (CR) ©Dennis Kunkel/Phototake, (T) ©Peter Arnold, Inc./Alamy Images; **101** (B) ©Jacana/Photo Researchers, Inc.; **102** (Inset) ©Kenneth W. Fink/Photo Researchers, Inc.; **103** ©Michael S. Yamashita/Corbis; **105** ©Marli Miller/Visuals Unlimited; **106** (T) ©Aldo Pavan/Grand Tour/Corbis; **107** (T) ©Age Fotostock/SuperStock; **109** (Bkgd) ©Glow Images/SuperStock, ©Michael Boys/Corbis; **114** (T) ©Corbis/Jupiter Images, (BR) ©Tom McHugh/Photo Researchers, Inc.; **115** (T) ©David K. Werk/Alamy, (BR) ©Corbis/Jupiter Images; **116** (BR) ©Arthur Morris/Corbis, (T) ©W. Perry Conway/Corbis; **117** (C) ©Corbis/Jupiter Images; **120** (B) ©Ashley Cooper/Corbis; **126** (B) ©Floresco Productions/Corbis, (T) ©Momatiuk-Eastcott/Corbis, (C) ©Stuart Westmorland/Corbis; **127** (CR) ©Valueline/Punchstock; **148** ©Craig Aurness/Corbis; **154** (B) Index Open; **155** ©Digital Vision Ltd./SuperStock; **160** (C) ©Karl Weatherly/Corbis, (B) ©moodboard/Corbis, (T) ©Randy Faris/Corbis; **182** ©Kevin Anthony Horgan/Getty Images; **183** (CR) ©Geostock/Getty Images, (BL) ©Martin Barraud/Getty Images; **184** (CL) ©Alan R. Moller/Getty Images, (TR) Getty Images, (TC) ©Guy Grenier/Masterfile Corporation, (BL) ©Guy Motil/Corbis, (TL) ©Michael Melford/Getty Images; **188** (C) ©Randy Faris/Corbis; **185** (CR) Getty Images, (TR) ©Stan Osolinski/Getty Images; **188** (C) ©Jim Sugar/Corbis; **190** (B) Index Open; **194** (T) ©Mark & Audrey Gibson/PhotoLibrary Group, Ltd., (C) ©Nancy G. Fire Photography/Alamy Images, (B) Alamy Images; **198** (C) ©Tim Ross/Index Stock Imagery, (Bkgd) ©Comstock Images/Jupiter Images; **199** (B) ©Walter Bibikow/Index Stock Imagery, (Bkgd) ©Mark Barrett/Index Stock Imagery; **200** (TR) Lynton Gardiner/©DK Images, (R) ©Richard Leeney/©DK Images, (TL) ©Roberts Company, Inc., (BL) ©Royalty-Free/Corbis; **201** (R) ©DK Images, (BC) Getty Images; **202** (CR) Lynton Gardiner/©DK Images, (TR, BR) ©DK Images; **203** (TR) Lynton Gardiner/©DK Images; **204** (Bkgd) ©Jim Pickerell/Stock Connection, (C) Lynton Gardiner/©DK Images; **205** (C) Lynton Gardiner/©DK Images; **206** (C) ©James McLoughlin; **207** (BR) ©Rubberball Productions/Getty Images, (BC) Corbis; **208** (B) Getty Images; **209** (C) Lynton Gardiner/©DK Images; **210** (TL, BL) Lynton Gardiner/©DK Images, (BR) Lynton Gardiner/©DK Images; **211** (TC) Getty Images; **216** (TC) ©Roberts Company, Inc.; (Bkgd) Comstock Images/Getty Images; **217** ©Royalty-Free/Corbis; **222** (B) ©Scott Stulberg/Corbis; **228** (T) ©Holloway/Getty Images, (B) ©Image Source/Getty Images, (C) ©Nancy R. Cohen/Getty Images; **254** (T) ©Kazumasa Yanai/MIXA/Getty Images, (B) ©Shawn Frederick/Getty Images; **256** (B) ©Bob Sacha/Corbis; **262** (T) ©Index Stock Imagery/PhotoLibrary Group, Ltd., (C) ©Tim Pannell/Corbis, (B) Jupiter Images; **288** ©Jacky Chapman/Alamy Images; **293** (T) ©Stockxpert; **294** (T) ©Joel Sartore/National Geographic/Getty Images, (C) ©Phillip Lee Harvey/PhotoLibrary, (B) ©Randy Faris/Corbis; **319** (BR) ©Bob Gomel/Corbis, (TR) ©Lori Adamski Peck/Getty Images; **320** (TR) ©Tim Pannell/Corbis; **321** ©Lori Adamski Peck/Getty Images; **322** (T) Getty Images; **324** (B) ©Jerryworks/Masterfile Corporation; **330** (B) ©Chuck Eckert/Alamy, (C) ©Culture/Alamy, (C) ©Gary Blake/Alamy Images; **352** ©Tom Stewart/Corbis; **353** (TR) Getty Images, (CR) ©Jacob Taposchaner/Taxi/Getty Images; **358** (C) ©Mira/Alamy Images; **360** (R) ©Stan Liu/Icon SMI/Corbis; **366** (C) ©David R. Frazier PhotoLibrary, Inc./Alamy, (T) ©Fancy/Veer/Corbis, (B) ©Joe Belanger/Alamy; **390** (T) Getty Images; **392** (B) ©Ali Kabas/Alamy Images; **398** (C) ©Andrew Olney/OJO Images/Getty Images, (T) ©Jim Dandy/Stock Illustration Source/Getty Images, (B) Getty Images; **404** (CR) ©PoodlesRock/Corbis, (TR) ©Bettmann/Corbis, (BL) Stock Montage Inc.; **408** (T) Composite photograph of the almost 200-year-old Star Spangled Banner, the flag that inspired the national anthem. Smithsonian's National Museum of American History, ©2004; **409** (C) Corbis, (CR) Getty Images; **410** (T) The Granger Collection, NY; **412** ©Bjorn G. Bolstad/Photo Researchers, Inc.; **414** (BL) Corbis; **417** Digital Vision; **423** ©Terence Beddis/Getty Images; **426** ©Robert Landau/Corbis; **432** (T) ©D. Hurst/Alamy Images, (B) Getty Images, (C) Jupiter Images; **452** (C) ©JLP/Jose L. Pelaez/Corbis; **454** Getty Images; **458** (B) Jupiter Images; **464** (C) ©Konrad Wothe/Alamy Images, (T) ©Mark J. Barrett/Alamy Images, (B) ©Tim Graham/Alamy Images; **466** (C) ©Jean Michel Guillaud; **492** (BR) Brand X Pictures, (TR) ©C Squared Studios/Getty Images, (TR, T) Getty Images; **496** (B) ©Tim Mantoani/Masterfile Corporation; **501** (CR) ©Hisham Ibrahim/Corbis; **502** (C) ©Jeff Greenberg/Alamy Images, (B) ©David & Peter Turnley/Corbis, (T) ©Leighton Mark/Corbis; **525** (T) ©Marilyn Angel Wynn/Nativestock Pictures/Corbis, (BL) ©The Bridgeman Art Library/Getty Images; **526** (TR) Getty Images; **527** (C) Indian Sweat House, Mendocino County, CA by Carleton Watkins, 1861-1871, #H87.204 /19/ State Library of Victoria, Melbourne, Australia; **538** (B) ©Karl Weatherly/Corbis; **541** (T) ©Glyn Thomas/PhotoLibrary Group, Ltd.; **543** (C) ©BUILT Images/PhotoLibrary.

Teacher Editions

KWL Strategy: The KWL Interactive Reading Strategy was developed and is used by permission of Donna Ogle, National-Louis University, Skokie, Illinois, co-author of *Reading Today and Tomorrow*, Holt, Rinehart & Winston Publishers, 1988. (See also the *Reading Teacher*, February 1986, pp. 564–570.)

Understanding by Design quotes: Wiggins, G. & McTighe, J. (2005). *Understanding by Design*. Alexandria, VA: Association for Supervision and Curriculum Development.

Illustrations
Cover Scott Gustafson
Running Header Steven Mach

Photographs
Every effort has been made to secure permission and provide appropriate credit for photographic material. The publisher deeply regrets any omission and pledges to correct errors called to its attention in subsequent editions.

Unless otherwise acknowledged, all photographs are the property of Pearson Education, Inc.

Teacher Notes

Teacher Resources

Looking for Teacher Resources and other important information?

In the **First Stop** on Reading Street

- **Dear Second Grade Teacher**
- **Research into Practice on Reading Street**
- **Guide to Reading Street**
- **Assessment on Reading Street**
- **Customize Writing on Reading Street**
- **Differentiated Instruction on Reading Street**

- **ELL on Reading Street**
- **Customize Literacy on Reading Street**
- **Digital Products on Reading Street**
- **Teacher Resources for Grade 2**
- **Index**

Teacher Resources

Looking for Teacher Resources and other important information?

In the **First Stop** on Reading Street

- **Dear Second Grade Teacher**

- **Research into Practice on Reading Street**

- **Guide to Reading Street**

- **Assessment on Reading Street**

- **Customize Writing on Reading Street**

- **Differentiated Instruction on Reading Street**

- **ELL on Reading Street**

- **Customize Literacy on Reading Street**

- **Digital Products on Reading Street**

- **Teacher Resources for Grade 2**

- **Index**